A Dictionary of Grammatical Terms in Linguistics

This is a dictionary of grammatical terms written for students and teachers of linguistics. It covers a huge number of descriptive terms in syntax and morphology, both contemporary and traditional, as well as the most important theoretical concepts from the most influential contemporary approaches to the theory of grammar. It also includes the chief terminology from mathematical and computational linguistics. Apart from definitions and examples, the book also provides pronunciations, notational devices and symbols, earliest sources of terms and suggestions for further reading, as well as recommendations about competing and conflicting usages.

This book has few theoretical axes to grind; it devotes space to the various theoretical approaches in proportion to their recent importance, but it concentrates most heavily on non-theory-bound descriptive terminology. This makes it unlikely to date quickly, and it should remain a definitive reference source for many years to come.

A Dictionary of Grammatical Terms in Linguistics

R. L. Trask

London and New York

First published in 1993 by
Routledge
11 New Fetter Lane, London EC4P 4EE

Simultaneously published in the USA and Canada
by Routledge Inc.
29 West 35th Street, New York, NY 10001

Typeset in 10/12 pt Times, Linotronic 300 by
Florencetype Ltd, Kewstoke, Avon
Printed in Great Britain by T.J. Press (Padstow) Ltd, Padstow, Cornwall

British Library Cataloguing in Publication Data
Trask, Robert Lawrence
A Dictionary of Grammatical Terms in
Linguistics
I. Title
410.3

Library of Congress Cataloging in Publication Data
Trask, R. L. (Robert Lawrence)
A dictionary of grammatical terms in linguistics / R. L. Trask.
p. cm.
Includes bibliographical references and index.
1. Grammar, Comparative and general—Terminology.
I. Title.
P152.T7 1993
415'.014–dc20 92–24806

ISBN 0–415–08627–2
0–415–08628–0 (pbk)

For Lisa,
in gratitude, in affection, in tzatziki
and in Valley Close

Contents

Preface	viii
Acknowledgements	xi
List of abbreviations	xii
Guide to pronunciation	xiii
A Dictionary of Grammatical Terms in Linguistics	1
References	311

Preface

This dictionary is intended primarily for students and teachers of linguistics, though I hope it may also prove useful to others who sometimes want to look up unfamiliar or half-remembered grammatical terms. Unlike other dictionaries of linguistics, this one concentrates exclusively on the terminology of grammar – mainly on syntax (sentence structure), but also to some extent on morphology (word structure).

Naturally, to keep this book down to a manageable size, I have had to make a selection from the thousands of terms which make an appearance somewhere in the grammatical literature. However, the 1,500 or so terms which are defined here should include virtually every term you are likely to encounter outside of highly specialized monographs.

Aware of the typically short lifespan of the terms coined by the proponents of particular theoretical frameworks, I have chosen to devote the larger part of this dictionary to purely descriptive terms which have been and are widely used by grammarians of varying theoretical persuasions, and which seem likely to remain current for some time, such as *antipassive*, *Bach–Peters sentence*, *ergative*, *gapping*, *gender*, *inalienable possession*, *infix*, *island constraint*, *pied piping* and *subcategorization*.

With terms denoting theoretical constructs, I have been a little more selective, but terms which are used in at least two major theories of grammar are normally included: *binding*, *c-command*, *Head Feature Convention*, *LP rule*, *specifier*, *unaccusative*, *X-bar system*.

The specific terminology of particular theories of grammar is treated as follows. Given the dominant position of Government–Binding Theory, the terminology of that framework is covered in some considerable detail: *A-bar binding*, *barrier*, *Burzio's generalization*, *exceptional case marking*, *m-command*, *proper government*, *theta role*. Rather more limited coverage is provided for four other frameworks: Generalized Phrase Structure Grammar, Lexical–Functional Grammar, Relational Grammar and Role-and-Reference Grammar. The specific terminology of other frameworks is, regrettably, not covered, though every theory of grammar known to me receives an entry under its name.

There is considerable coverage of terms associated with mathematical linguistics and more limited coverage of computational linguistics: *chart parser, context-free grammar, counting grammar, Earley algorithm, indexed grammar, linear bounded automaton, Peters–Ritchie results*.

Finally, the terminology of traditional grammar, including a few rhetorical terms of grammatical relevance, is also included: *anacoluthon, bahuvrihi, common noun, conjugation, indirect object, relative clause, zeugma*.

Competing and conflicting usages are noted and described, and recommendations are often provided; examples of troublesome terms are *anaphor, aorist, intransitive, middle* and *small clause*. As far as possible, I have tried to identify the original sources of the terms, and for many of the more important terms I have suggested further reading.

The alphabetical order used is one which ignores both hyphens and spaces between words. Thus, for example, *aorist* precedes *A-over-A Constraint*, while *command domain* precedes *commander*, which precedes *command relation*.

The pronunciation given is that typical of the south of England. Speakers of other varieties of English will, I hope, find little difficulty in making any necessary adjustments, though there are admittedly a few words whose pronunciations are unpredictably different in North American English, such as *theta*.

In an enterprise of this kind, it is no doubt inevitable that there will prove to be a few errors and omissions. If you find any, I will be pleased to hear about them. You can write to me at the School of Cognitive and Computing Sciences, University of Sussex, Falmer, Brighton BN1 9QH, UK, or e-mail me at larryt@uk.ac.susx.cogs (from within the UK) or at larryt@cogs.susx.ac.uk (from elsewhere).

R. L. Trask
Brighton, England

Acknowledgements

I should like to express my particular thanks to Dick Hudson for suggesting and encouraging this work, and to Claire L'Enfant and the Routledge editorial board for their patience, encouragement and valuable advice. I am also indebted to an anonymous reader, who made a number of useful suggestions for improving the book, and to Fred Householder, who kindly assisted me in tracking down some elusive historical information. Alexis Manaster-Ramer patiently corrected a number of errors in an earlier version. Finally, I'm indebted to Jenny Potts for an outstanding job of copy-editing.

I owe an enormous debt to all my fellow linguists, past and present, whose works I have shamelessly pillaged for terms, definitions, examples, recommendations and historical information. They run into the hundreds, and it is impossible to name them all here, but a few of them must be singled out for the special attention they have devoted to questions of terminology, attention which has been of the greatest assistance to me in preparing this dictionary: Bernard Comrie, John Lyons, Peter Matthews and, above all, my former teacher Geoff Pullum; if there is any clarity and precision in these definitions, Geoff deserves a great deal of the credit. Naturally, the shortcomings are entirely my own responsibility.

Special mention is due to the linguist who, perhaps even more than Noam Chomsky, has shown a phenomenal talent for coining enduring terms which now seem as familiar as 'noun' and 'verb': John Robert Ross. Haj, your fingerprints are all over our discipline.

A different kind of debt is owed to all my students, colleagues and fellow bridge-players, who, during the past year, have patiently put up with what must at times have seemed a singular lack of concentration on the business at hand, while the dictionary was occupying the lion's share of my attention.

Finally, I would like to thank Lisa Wale for her support and for her inimitable style of encouragement during the period when this dictionary consisted largely of a blank word-processor screen and a few embarrassingly bad definitions. Lisa, this one's for you.

Abbreviations

Abstr. n.	abstract noun
adj.	adjective
CF(G)	Context-Free (Grammar)
GB	Government–Binding Theory
GPSG	Generalized Phrase Structure Grammar
HPSG	Head-Driven Phrase Structure Grammar
LFG	Lexical–Functional Grammar
n.	noun
pl.	plural
RG	Relational Grammar
RRG	Role-and-Reference Grammar
TG	Transformational Grammar
v.	verb
vi.	intransitive verb
vt.	transitive verb

Guide to pronunciation

The pronunciation represented is that of the south of England.

/p/	pop	/z/	zoos	/ɜː/	bird
/t/	tot	/ʒ/	measure	/ɛə/	bare
/k/	cook	/m/	mum	/ə/	banana
/b/	bib	/n/	nun	/æ/	bat
/d/	did	/ŋ/	sing	/ɑː/	bard
/g/	gag	/l/	lull	/ɒ/	pot
/tʃ/	church	/r/	ray	/aɪ/	bite
/dʒ/	judge	/w/	way	/aʊ/	bout
/f/	fife	/j/	you	/ɔː/	bawd
/θ/	think	/iː/	beat	/ɔɪ/	boy
/s/	sauce	/ɪ/	bit	/əʊ/	boat
/ʃ/	shush	/i/	city	/ʌ/	but
/h/	hay	/ɪə/	beard	/ʊ/	put
/v/	verve	/eɪ/	bayed	/uː/	boot
/ð/	either	/e/	bet	/ʊə/	poor

Diacritics

Raised bar	primary stress: /grəˈmætɪkl̩/
Lowered bar	secondary stress: /sə͵bɔːdɪˈneɪʃn̩/
Bar below	syllabic consonant: /kənˈdɪʃn̩/

A Dictionary of Grammatical Terms in Linguistics

A

A 1. See **adjective**. 2. See under **SAP**.

A-bar /'eɪˌbɑː/ *n.* The one-bar projection of the lexical category Adjective, posited to provide suitable structures for adjective phrases like *very proud of Lisa*, analysed as [AP[Deg*very*] [A'[A*proud*][PP*of Lisa*]]].

A-bar binding /'eɪbɑːˌbaɪndɪŋ/ *n.* (also **non-argument binding**) In GB, **binding** by a category which is not in **argument** position, such as a fronted WH-item: *Whoᵢ did you see* eᵢ? A-bar binding applies to **variables** (WH-traces); such a trace must be bound by a suitable WH-item which c-commands it. Cf. **A-binding**.

A-bar position /'eɪbɑː pəˌzɪʃn̩/ *n.* In GB, an NP-position which is not an **A-position**, particularly the Comp position.

abbreviatory convention /əˈbriːviətri kənˈvenʃn̩/ *n.* Any conventional notation which allows two or more distinct rules with elements in common to be written as a single **rule schema**. Common conventions include **parentheses**, **braces**, **vertical bars** and the **Kleene star**.

abbreviatory variable *n.* A variable whose possible values are restricted to a specified set. Cf. **essential variable**.

abessive /æbˈesɪv/ *n.* or *adj.* A case form typically expressing the meaning of 'without': Finnish *rahatta* 'without money' (*raha* 'money').

A-binding /'eɪ ˌbaɪndɪŋ/ *n.* (also **argument binding**) In GB, **binding** by a category which is in **argument** position, such as a subject or a (direct) object. A-binding applies to **anaphors** (reflexives, reciprocals and NP-traces): each of these must be bound in its governing category; that is, it must be coindexed with a c-commanding category within this domain. A category so bound is 'A-bound'; otherwise, it is 'A-free'. Cf. **A-bar binding**.

ablative /'æblətɪv/ *n.* or *adj.* A case form which typically indicates the source of a movement: Turkish *evden* 'from the house' (*ev* 'house').

Ablaut /'ɑːplaʊt/ *n.* (also **vowel alternation**) Grammatical inflection by variation in the vowel of a root, as in English *sing, sang, sung.* Cf. **Umlaut,** and see the remarks there. Grimm (1819).

absolute comparative /'æbsəluːt/ *n.* A construction involving a **comparative** form with no overt **standard**: *the younger generation; Whizzo washes whiter.*

absolute construction *n.* A constituent linked semantically and intonationally to the rest of its sentence, but lacking any overt expression of a syntactic linkage: [*The day being cloudy,*] *we decided to stay home; The two women,* [*their business completed,*] *retired to the bar.* Often the term is extended to sentence adverbs like *however.*

absolute exception *n.* In some analyses, a label applied to certain lexical items which obligatorily undergo, or fail to undergo, a process which is usually optional. Thus, for example, while passives like *She is considered to be clever* are normally related to corresponding actives like *They consider her to be clever*, the verb *say* is exceptional: it can only appear in the passive form *She is said to be clever*, the active form **They say her to be clever* being non-existent. Hence *say* is a 'positive absolute exception' to passivization. The term is also sometimes used in morphology: while verbs in *-ition* (like *prohibition*) are often derived from related verbs (like *prohibit*), *perdition* has no such corresponding verb, at least superficially, and some analysts would posit an underlying verb stem *perdit-* which is a positive absolute exception to noun formation.

absolute possessive *n.* A possessive form of a personal pronoun which functions as a pronoun, rather than as a determiner, such as English *mine* or *yours*: *Mine is bigger than yours.* NOTE: The term 'possessive pronoun' would seem more appropriate, but unfortunately that term has long been in use to label the possessive determiners like *my* and *your.*

absolute-relative tense *n.* A tense form which takes as its intrinsic point of reference a point in time other than the present moment, such as the past anterior (*I had already seen him*) or the future-in-the-past (*I was going to see him*), both of which take some past moment as their point of reference. Cf. **absolute tense, relative tense.** See Comrie (1985a) for discussion.

absolute tense *n.* A tense form which takes the present moment as its point of reference, such as the simple past, present and future tenses found in many languages. The term is traditional, but regrettable, since the so-called **absolute-relative tenses** have just as much claim to being considered 'absolute'. Cf. **relative tense**, **absolute-relative tense**. See Comrie (1985a) for discussion.

absolute transitive *n.* A construction in which an intrinsically transitive verb occurs with no overt direct object, the subject of the verb being interpreted as an agent and the construction being interpreted as active: *Janet smokes*; *Lisa is eating*. The term is also applied to the distinctive subclass with a reflexive interpretation: *Lisa undressed*; *John is shaving*. See also **unspecified object deletion**, **pseudo-intransitive**. Jespersen (1961, III: 320).

absolute universal *n.* A universal which holds for every single natural language without exception. Some linguists would argue, for example, that the **structure-dependence** of grammatical rules is just such a universal. Cf. **relative universal**.

absolutive /'æbsəluːtɪv/ *n.* or *adj.* 1. In an **ergative language**, the case form which marks both the subject of an intransitive verb and the direct object of a transitive verb, and which contrasts with the **ergative** (sense 1). For example, in the ergative language Basque the NPs *gizona* 'the man' and *mutila* 'the boy' take the absolutive case suffix zero in such examples as *Gizona heldu da* 'The man arrived', *Gizonak mutila ikusi du* 'The man saw the boy' and *Mutilak gizona ikusi du* 'The boy saw the man', while the transitive subjects bear the ergative case suffix *-k*. 2. By extension, the category consisting of intransitive subjects and transitive direct objects.

abstract /'æbstrækt/ *adj.* Denoting an analysis of a structure or phenomenon which is significantly different from its surface representation; sometimes more specifically denoting an element which is postulated as being present even though it has no overt phonetic realization. For example, some analyses of the sentence *I enjoy bridge* would postulate an abstract node called AUX or INFL in the tree which serves as a locus for tense marking but which has no overt realization in the sentence, and some analyses of *Lisa seems to be happy* would posit an abstract underlying structure along the lines of *seems* [*Lisa to be happy*]. *Abstr.* *n.* **abstractness** /æb'stræktnɪs/.

abstract noun *n.* A noun whose meaning is an abstract concept (*truth, beauty, magnitude, consequence*) or a noun denoting an event (*arrival, explosion*). Cf. **concrete noun**.

acceptability /əkseptə'bɪlɪti/ *n.* The degree to which a proposed sentence or utterance is adjudged permissible and interpretable by native speakers. A sentence which is **well-formed** according to the requirements of the grammar may be considered unacceptable because of processing difficulties or pragmatic factors: *Flounder flounder badger badger flounder*; *The book the professor the students who are doing well like recommended is good*; *Arabic is learning John*. *Adj.* **acceptable** /ək'septəbl̩/.

accessible subject /ək'sesəbl̩/ *n.* In GB, a particular structural relation which may hold between nodes in a sentence. A node A is an accessible subject for another node B if the coindexation of A and B does not violate any grammatical principles. The notion of an accessible subject is important in the definition of a **governing category**. Chomsky (1981).

accidence /'æksɪdəns/ *n.* A traditional term for what is now usually called **inflectional morphology**.

ACC-ing /æk'ɪŋ/ *n.* The construction in which a **gerund** has a subject NP in the objective (accusative) case: *I don't like him doing that*. Cf. **POSS-*ing***.

accusative /ə'kjuːzətɪv/ *n.* or *adj.* 1. A case form typically marking the direct object of a transitive verb: Latin *puellam* (from *puella* 'girl') in *Puellam vidi* 'I saw the girl'. 2. Another term for **objective**, particularly in GB, where Accusative is the conventional name of the abstract Case assigned to an NP by a governing verb or preposition.

accusative and infinitive *n.* A traditional name for a construction found in certain languages, including Latin and English, involving an infinitival VP with an overt subject in the accusative (objective) case: *I would like him to come*.

accusative language *n.* (more fully, **nominative–accusative language**) A language in which subjects of intransitive verbs and subjects of transitive verbs are usually treated identically for grammatical purposes, while direct objects of transitive verbs are treated differently. Most familiar European languages, including

English, are accusative. *Abstr. n.* **accusativity** /ə‚kjuːzəˈtɪvɪti/.
Cf. **ergative language**.

acronym /ˈækrənɪm/ *n.* A word formed by combining the initial
letters of the principal words in a phrase: *laser*, from *light amplifi-
cation by the stimulated emission of radiation*; *NATO*, from *North
Atlantic Treaty Organization*.

across-the-board /ə‚krɒs ðə ˈbɔːd/ *adj.* (**ATB**) Denoting certain
extraction phenomena in which the extracted constituent is simultaneously related to a gap in every conjunct of a coordination: *That
book you were reading* e *and Lisa wanted to buy* e *is out in
paperback*; *That's the player Janet was talking about* e *and wants* e *to
win*. In English and some other languages, ATB phenomena constitute a systematic class of exceptions to the **Coordinate Structure
Constraint**. Ross (1967); revived by Williams (1978).

active /ˈæktɪv/ *adj.* 1. (of a clause) Denoting a construction, usually
involving a transitive verb, in which the grammatical subject of the
verb typically (though not exceptionlessly) represents the agent
performing the action, and the direct object represents the patient:
Attila invaded Europe; *I've washed the car*; *Lisa wants a BMW*; *She
has beautiful eyes*. In many (not all) languages, the active construction contrasts with an overt **passive** construction, and sometimes
with additional **voices**. In the vast majority of languages, the active
construction is the unmarked construction for transitive verbs, involving the least marked form of the verb and the simplest possible
case marking on the argument NPs. 2. (of a verb) Denoting that
form of a (usually transitive) verb which occurs in active constructions (where these contrast with passives or other voices); the active
form is usually the morphologically simplest (unmarked) form of all
those participating in voice contrasts. Cf. **passive**, **middle** (sense 1),
circumstantial, **applicative**, and see **voice**. 3. An occasional synonym for **dynamic**; this usage should be avoided, because of the
obvious potential confusion with the more usual senses of 'active'.

active language *n.* (also **agentive language**) A language in which
subjects of both transitive and intransitive verbs which are semantically agents are treated identically for grammatical purposes, while
non-agent subjects and direct objects are treated differently.
Among languages exhibiting this pattern are Sumerian, Batsbi (NE
Caucasian), Crow (Siouxan) and Eastern Pomo (Hokan). The
following examples from Eastern Pomo show the use of the two
subject pronouns *há:* 'I' (agent) and *wí* 'I' (non-agent): *Há: mí:pal*

šá:ka 'I killed him'; *Há: wádu:kìya* 'I'm going'; *Wí ʔéčkiya* 'I sneezed'. The correlation is rarely perfect; usually there are a few verbs or predicates which appear to be exceptional. In some active languages lexical verbs are rigidly divided into those taking agent subjects and those taking non-agent subjects; in others some lexical verbs can take either to denote, for example, differing degrees of control over the action. See Merlan (1985) for discussion. Cf. **ergative language**, **accusative language**, and see also **split intransitive**, **fluid-intransitive**. Sapir (1917).

actor /'æktə/ *n.* 1. An extension of the semantic notion of **agent** to include certain other argument NPs which are not strictly agents but which pattern like agents for grammatical purposes. For example, the subject NP *Lisa* would usually be considered an actor in each of the following examples: *Lisa bought a skirt*; *Lisa noticed the incident*; *Lisa received a letter*; *Lisa slept soundly*. Roughly, then, an actor is that argument NP exercising the highest degree of independent action in the clause. The label is not necessarily restricted to animate NPs: Halliday (1976), for example, regards as actors the subject NPs in the examples *The sun is shining* and *His popularity declined*. This category is important in most **functional grammars** (sense 2), particularly in RRG. Cf. **undergoer**. 2. An overtly marked case form found in certain languages (notably Philippine languages) which covers approximately the semantic range just described. See Schachter (1976) for discussion.

adequacy, levels of /'ædɪkwəsi/ *n.* Any of various sets of criteria for evaluating formal grammars. The best-known criteria are those of Chomsky (1964): a grammar achieves **observational adequacy** if it correctly generates the observed data; it achieves **descriptive adequacy** if it also expresses all **linguistically significant generalizations**; it achieves **explanatory adequacy** if it provides a principled basis for choosing among competing grammars all of which achieve descriptive adequacy. An independent characterization, proposed in Chomsky (1957), is that in terms of **external** and **internal** adequacy: a grammar is **externally adequate** if it correctly accounts for the data; it is **internally adequate** if it exhibits such characteristics as generality, economy and simplicity. Yet a third set of criteria distinguishes **weak** and **strong** adequacy: a grammar is **weakly adequate** if it generates the right set of strings, and **strongly adequate** if it does this and also assigns to each string the correct structure.

adessive /æd'esɪv/ *n.* or *adj.* A case form found in certain languages, typically expressing the notion of adjacency, corresponding to English *at*, *on* or *near*: Finnish *pöydällä* 'on the table' (*pöytä* 'table'). Cf. **locative**, **inessive**.

Adj See **adjective**.

adjacency /ə'dʒeɪsn̩sɪ/ *n.* The linear relation holding between two elements in a sentence which are not separated by any other element. In frameworks utilizing **empty categories**, an empty category is often sufficient to prevent adjacency between the elements on either side of it. *Adj.* **adjacent** /ə'dʒeɪsn̩t/.

Adjacency Parameter *n.* In GB, the putative **parameter** by which a language does or does not exhibit the **Adjacency Principle**.

Adjacency Principle *n.* In GB, the requirement that a complement which can be Case-marked must occur adjacent to the head of its phrase and cannot be separated from it by other material. Thus, for example, a transitive verb in English must not be separated from its direct object, to which it assigns Case: **John saw yesterday a film*. The putative universal nature of this principle is called into question by such languages as Spanish, in which *Juan vio ayer una película*, literally 'John saw yesterday a film', represents the unmarked word order.

adjectival passive *n.* The passive participle of a (typically transitive) verb functioning as an adjective: *a newly discovered fossil*, *well-taught children*, *a ruined city*, *He is happily married*, *That island is uninhabited*; intransitive examples include *their long-departed spirits* and *Johnny is almost grown-up*. The existence of adjectival passives provides some of the strongest evidence in favour of a purely lexical analysis of passive constructions, as proposed, for example, in LFG and HPSG. See also *unpassive*.

adjective /'ædʒɪktɪv/ *n.* (**Adj** or **A**) A **lexical category**, or a lexical item belonging to this category, found in many, though not all, languages, inflectionally and distributionally distinct from the categories Noun and Verb, with which it typically shares the characteristic of being an **open class** whose members have real semantic content. Canonical adjectives typically have meanings expressing permanent or temporary attributes, such as *big*, *old*, *green*, *happy* and *dry*, and indeed in some languages adjectives constitute a **closed class** containing only a dozen or so such items (Dixon 1977a), but more typically the class contains a large number of items with meanings that may be more noun-like or verb-like, such as *stony*, *shiny*, *dead*, *astonishing* and *musical*. Among the grammatical characteristics often displayed by adjectives are attributive position (*a big house*), predicate position (*That house is big*), comparison (*bigger*, *biggest*) and inflection for gender, number and case as required by agreement with, or government by, a head noun (not in English, but consider French *un vieux livre* 'an old book', *une vieille maison* 'an old house', *des vieilles maisons* 'old houses', etc.) *Adj.* **adjectival** /ædʒɪkˈtaɪv̩/.

adjective phrase *n.* (**AdjP** or **AP**) A phrase exhibiting a distribution similar to that of a lexical adjective and semantically acting as a modifier of a noun or a noun phrase: *very big, proud of her achievements, more expensive than that one*. An adjective phrase usually has an adjective as its lexical head and in the X-bar system is regarded as the maximal projection of the lexical category Adjective, A-double-bar.

adjoined relative clause /əˈdʒɔɪnd/ *n.* A type of relative clause which is not contained within the clause in which its head is located, and which is therefore typically separated from its head. The pattern occurs in English, where it is an optional variant of the more usual pattern: *That man has arrived* [*who you've been waiting for*]. In some other languages, however, the adjoined relative is the only possibility, as in the Australian language Warlpiri. Cf. **correlative clause**. Hale (1976).

AdjP See **adjective phrase**.

adjunct /ˈædʒʌŋkt/ *n.* A category which is a modifier of a lexical head without being subcategorized for by that lexical head and which could in principle be removed without affecting well-formedness; e.g., in the sentence *I saw Lisa in the park yesterday*, the phrases *in the park* and *yesterday* are adjuncts of the verb. In some versions of the X-bar system, an adjunct is formally defined as a category which is a sister of a one-bar projection and a daughter of another one-bar projection; some definitions add the (English-specific) requirement that it follow its one-bar sister. *Adj.* **adjunctival** /ædʒʌŋkˈtaɪv̩/. Cf. **complement**, **attribute**.

adjunction /əˈdʒʌŋkʃən/ *n.* Any of various procedures for incorporating material into a tree, such as **sister-adjunction**, **daughter-adjunction**, **Chomsky-adjunction** or **tree-adjunction**. In some frameworks the term is used without qualification to label the only type of adjunction recognized, such as for Chomsky-adjunction in GB or for tree-adjunction in tree-adjoining grammars. *V.* **adjoin** /ə'dʒɔɪn/.

Adjunct-Island Condition *n.* The requirement that a WH-dependency cannot cross the boundary of an adjunct: *Who did he see the boss [before talking to* e]*?* The constraint runs into difficulties with apparent counterexamples like *Who did you go to Paris to visit* e*?*

adjutative /ə'dʒuːtətɪv/ *n.* or *adj.* An inflected form of the verb which indicates that the subject helps someone else to do something: Tigrinya *ʔaqqatäle* 'he helped to kill' (*qätäle* 'he killed'). The adjutative forms part of the **voice** system in languages in which it occurs.

adnominal /æd'nɒmɪnl̩/ *adj.* Denoting any constituent which occurs inside a noun phrase and which modifies or specifies the head noun. An adnominal constituent may be variously a determiner, an adjective, a prepositional phrase or a relative clause, all of these being illustrated by the example *the young girl in the blue dress who you were talking to*.

adposition /ædpə'zɪʃn̩/ *n.* A superordinate label including the categories **preposition** and **postposition**, required because the traditional term **preposition**, both etymologically and in practice, is restricted to adpositions which precede their objects. *Adj.* **adpositional** /ædpə'zɪʃənl̩/.

Adv 1. See **adverb**. 2. See **adverbial**.

advancement /əd'vɑːnsmənt/ *n.* In RG, the process by which the logical or canonical form of a clause is restructured so as to move some NP into a higher-ranking position on the **Relational Hierarchy**: e.g., passivization, in which an underlying object is advanced to subject. *V.* **advance** /əd'vɑːns/.

adverb /'ædvɜːb/ *n.* A **lexical category**, or a member of this category, whose members are usually grammatical adjuncts of a verb and most typically express such semantic notions as time, manner, place, instrument or circumstance: *yesterday, slowly, here*. Adverbs rarely exhibit distinctive inflectional morphology, though many languages allow manner adverbs to be compared (*slowly, more slowly, most slowly*) and to take degree modifiers (*very slowly, rather slowly*). Some languages, including English, exhibit a subclass of adverbs with rather distinctive properties, known as **sentence adverbs**. *Adj.* **adverbial**. NOTE: traditional grammar, with its paucity of lexical categories, conventionally assigns to the category Adverb the degree modifiers like *very*, the prepositional specifiers like *just* and a rather miscellaneous collection of other items of doubtful class, like *not, however, yes, please* and the first *as* of *as big as a house*; such use of the category Adverb as a grammatical dustbin can hardly be justified, but many reputable dictionaries and textbooks continue this practice.

adverbial /əd'vɜːʃbiəl/ 1. *n.* Any category with a distribution and function similar to that of a lexical adverb, such as *tomorrow night, in the garden, when she arrives* or *in order to find out*, regardless of its surface syntactic realization, which may be that of a lexical adverb, an adverb phrase, a noun phrase, a prepositional phrase, an adverbial clause or a non-finite VP. The term 'adverbial' is thus a functional one. A detailed classification of adverbials, using a somewhat idiosyncratic terminology, is given in Quirk *et al.* (1985). 2. *adj.* Pertaining to **adverbs** or to **adverbials**.

adverbial clause *n.* (also **oblique clause**) A subordinate clause which bears to its main clause any of a range of semantic relations similar to those borne by adverbs, such as time, manner, place, instrument, circumstance, concession, purpose, result, cause or condition. Adverbial clauses in English are typically marked by the presence of **subordinators** such as *after, when, whenever, while, as, although, because* and *if*. See Thompson and Longacre (1985) for discussion.

adverbial participle *n.* An **adverbial** headed by a participle: [*Arriving a little early,*] *I decided to take a stroll* and [*Encouraged by her success,*] *she persevered*. See **small clause** (sense 1).

adverb phrase *n.* (AdvP) A phrase whose lexical head is an adverb: *very quietly, right here*.

adverb preposing *n.* The construction in which an adverb that more typically occurs inside a VP occurs instead at the beginning of the sentence: *Carefully she decanted the wine*.

adversative passive /əd'vɜːsətɪv/ *n.* A distinctive construction found in certain languages, notably Japanese, which typically expresses a (usually unfavourable) effect on some person. For example, the Japanese active sentence *Jochuu ga yamemashita* 'The maid quit' has the corresponding passive *Jochuu ni yamerare-mashita*, literally 'To the maid it was quit', which means roughly

'The maid quit on me', i.e., 'The maid quit and I (or somebody) was adversely affected by it'.

AdvP See **adverb phrase**.

affective construction /əˈfektɪv/ See **dative subject construction**.

affectum /əˈfektəm/ *n*. A traditional label for a direct object NP which exists before the action denoted in its clause and is affected in some way by that action, e.g., *the table* in the example *John ruined the table*. Cf. **effectum**.

affirmative /əˈfɜːmətɪv/ *adj*. Denoting a sentence or form in which no syntactic negative element is present; negative elements which are derivationally bound within single words and which are invisible to the syntax, such as *un-* in *unhappy*, do not count.

affix /ˈæfɪks/ *n*. A bound morpheme which can only occur attached to a word or stem. Affixes may be **derivational**, like *-ness* and *pre-*, or **inflectional**, like plural *-s* and past-tense *-ed*. Affixes are divided into **prefixes**, **suffixes**, **circumfixes**, **infixes** and **superfixes**. *Adj*. **affixal** /ˈæfɪksl̩/.

affixation /æfɪkˈseɪʃn̩/ *n*. The process of attaching an **affix** to a base, as in the derivation of *unhappy* or *happiness* from *happy*.

afterthought construction /ˈɑːftəθɔːt/ See **right dislocation**.

agent /ˈeɪdʒənt/ *n*. The **semantic role** borne by an NP which is perceived as the conscious instigator of an action, such as *Lisa* in *Lisa finished her thesis*, *Lisa made me wash the car* and *This picture was painted by Lisa*. Agent is one of the **deep cases** recognized in Case Grammar, and one of the **theta roles** recognized in GB. Cf. **actor**.

agentive language /əˈdʒentɪv/ See **active language**.

agentless passive /ˈeɪdʒəntləs/ *n*. (also **short passive**) A passive construction containing no overt expression of the agent: *My wallet has been stolen*.

agent phrase *n*. In a passive construction, the oblique phrase expressing the agent, such as *by the police* in *Janet was arrested by the police*.

agglutinating language /əˈgluːtɪneɪtɪŋ/ *n*. A language whose morphology is predominantly characterized by **agglutination**. Examples are Turkish, Basque, Japanese, Swahili and Hungarian.

Cf. **isolating language**, **inflecting language**. Wilhelm von Humboldt; see Horne (1966) for discussion.

agglutination /əˌgluːtɪˈneɪʃn̩/ *n.* A type of morphological structure in which words can be readily divided into a linear sequence of distinct morphemes, each of which typically has a fairly consistent shape and a single consistent meaning or function. An example is provided by Swahili *alikuona* 'he saw you', consisting of *a-* 'he' + *-li-* Past + *-ku-* 'you' + *-on-* 'see' + *-a* Indicative; compare *atakuona* 'he will see you', *nilikuona* 'I saw you', *aliniona* 'he saw me', and so on.

AGR /ˈægə/ *n.* In some analyses, a feature or an abstract category posited as a locus of agreement features. In GPSG, for example, AGR is a feature which takes such values as [PERSON] and [NUMBER]. In GB, AGR is variously regarded as a feature or as an abstract node.

agreement /əˈgriːmənt/ *n.* (also **concord**) The grammatical phenomenon by which the appearance of one item in a sentence in a particular form requires a second item which is grammatically linked with it to appear in a particular form. Agreement takes place within the range of choices offered within one or more grammatical categories which are morphologically marked on certain classes of words, such as number, gender, case, person or tense. The English sentence *These books are expensive* illustrates agreement in number between the plural noun *books* and the determiner *this* (of which *these* is the plural) and also between the plural noun phrase *these books* and the verb *be* (of which *are* is a plural form). See Barlow and Ferguson (1988) for a discussion of agreement phenomena. NOTE: strictly speaking, 'agreement' for gender or person is not agreement, but **government**. For example, in the French phrase *une vieille maison* 'an old house', the adjective *vieille* takes its feminine form because *maison* is feminine, but *maison* has no form which is not feminine: it is the *presence* of *maison*, and not its *form*, which requires the feminine adjective. Nevertheless, it is traditional to refer to such cases as instances of agreement, though some writers use some label such as 'governmental concord' for instances of this kind.

Aktionsart (pl. **Aktionsarten**) /ækˈtjəʊnzɑːt, -n̩/ *n.* 1. A distinction of **aspect** which is expressed lexically, rather than grammatically: *eat*, *nibble*, *devour*. 2. (especially among Slavicists) A distinction of aspect which is expressed by derivational morphology: Russian *pisat'* 'write', *popisat'* 'do a bit of writing', *spisat'* 'copy', *vypisat'* 'write out, excerpt', *zapisat'* 'write down, record'.

algorithm /'ælgərɪðm̩/ *n*. Any explicit mechanical procedure consisting of a specified series of steps which, if executed in order, will guarantee a solution to any one of a specified class of problems. Efficient algorithms are essential in the construction of **parsers**. *Adj*. **algorithmic** /ælgə'rɪðmɪk/. See Harel (1987).

alienable possession /'eɪliənəbl̩/ *n*. A type of possessive construction in which the possessed item could in principle be separated from the possessor: *Janet's cigarettes*, *my car*. In some languages, alienable possession is distinguished grammatically from **inalienable possession**; see examples under that entry.

allative /'ælətɪv/ *n*. or *adj*. A case form which typically indicates the goal of motion: Basque *etxera* 'to the house' (*etxe* 'house').

allomorph /'æləmɔːf/ *n*. (also **alternant**) One of two or more surface forms which are assumed by a single morpheme in varying circumstances. The negative prefix *in-*, for example, exhibits several allomorphs in such words as *indecent*, *impossible*, *irrational* and *ignoble*. *Abstr. n*. **allomorphy** /'æləmɔːfi/. Nida (1948).

Alpha Movement /'ælfə ˌmuːvmənt/ *n*. (also **Move-alpha** or **Move-α**) The single transformational rule occurring in most versions of GB. Usually expressed as 'Move-alpha', it can be stated more fully as 'Move any category to a different position'. The massive overgeneration which this rule would produce in isolation is heavily constrained by the other components of the grammar. Chomsky (1980).

alternant /'ɔːltənənt/ See **allomorph**.

alternation /ɔːltə'neɪʃn̩/ *n*. A synonym for **allomorphy**, but one often preferred for instances in which the variation in form is systematic in nature, such as the [s]/[z]/[iz] alternation in the English plural morpheme (*cats/dogs/foxes*), or in which it is confined to a single segment, as in the [k]/[s] alternation observed in *electric/electricity*.

ambiguity /æmbɪ'gjuːɪti/ *n*. The phenomenon in which a single string of words receives two or more sharply distinct meanings. An ambiguity may be purely lexical, as in *This lovely port is mentioned in Captain Cook's diaries*, or it may be structural, as in *Young boys and girls are easily frightened*, *Visiting relatives can be a nuisance* and *Anne likes horses more than Mark*. Complex examples of ambiguity exist, such as the classic *Janet made the robot fast*, which is multiply ambiguous, involving both lexical and structural ambiguities. An ambiguous string is loosely referred to as an 'ambiguous sentence'; more precisely, such a string corresponds to two or more distinct sentences. Ambiguity is pervasive in natural languages, and its presence is commonly assumed to mean that adequate formal grammars must be **ambiguous grammars**. Ambiguity constitutes a major headache for parsers; see also **local ambiguity**, **global ambiguity**. *Adj.* **ambiguous**.

ambiguity test *n.* Any criterion proposed for distinguishing true ambiguity from instances of mere vagueness. An example is the contradiction test, by which the putatively acceptable example *That dog isn't a dog – it's a bitch* supposedly demonstrates the lexical ambiguity of *dog*. See Zwicky and Sadock (1975) for discussion.

ambiguous grammar /æm'bigjʊəs/ *n.* A formal grammar for a particular language which assigns at least two different structural descriptions (parses) to at least one string of words. It is usually assumed that natural languages are **inherently ambiguous**, and that any plausible grammar for a natural language must therefore be an ambiguous grammar, but see Pullum (1984a) for some discussion.

ambiposition /'æmbɪpə,zɪʃn̩/ *n.* 1. An **adposition** which can function either as a preposition or as a postposition, such as English *notwithstanding*: *notwithstanding this result*; *this result notwithstanding*. 2. An occasional synonym for **circumposition**. NOTE: this second usage is not recommended.

American structuralism /ə'merɪkn̩/ See **structuralism** (sense 2).

amphibious verb /æm'fɪbiəs/ See **labile verb**.

anacoluthon (pl. **anacolutha**) /ænəkə'luːθən, -θə/ *n.* An abrupt change from one grammatical construction to another in the middle of an utterance, leaving the original construction incomplete: *I think you ought to – well, do it your own way*. *Abstr. n.* **anacoluthia** /ænəkə'luːθiə/. Cf. **zeugma**, **aposiopesis**, **syntactic blend**.

analogy /ə'nælədʒi/ *n.* The process by which a grammatical form or pattern is altered so as to conform to another form or pattern existing in the language. Examples include the historical replacement of the English plural forms *ky* and *kine* by *cows*, the introduction of the verbal pattern *dive/dove* into American English on the model of *drive/drove*, and the use by children of such regularized forms as *sheeps* and *goed*. *Adj.* **analogical** /ænə'lɒdʒɪkl̩/.

analytic /ænə'lɪtɪk/ *adj.* Denoting a construction in which grammatical distinctions are expressed by the use of separate auxiliary words, rather than by variation in the forms of words: *more beautiful, will have been eaten.* Cf. **synthetic**.

analytic language *n.* A language characterized by a predominance of analytic constructions; an **isolating language**. Cf. **synthetic language**. Schlegel (1818); see Horne (1966) for discussion.

analysable /'ænəlaɪzəbl̩/ *adj.* Denoting a structure which is capable of serving as input to a transformational rule; the structure is said to be 'analysable' by the rule. *Abstr. n.* **analysability** /ˌænəlaɪzə'bɪlɪti/.

anaphor /'ænəfɔː/ *n.* 1. (also **pro-constituent, pro-form**) An item with little or no intrinsic meaning or reference which takes its interpretation from another item in the same sentence or discourse, its **antecedent**. For example, in *I asked Lisa to check the proofs, and she did it*, the items *she* and *did it* are anaphors, taking their interpretations from their antecedents *Lisa* and *check the proofs*, respectively. Pronouns (more precisely, pro-NPs) are the most familiar anaphors, but pro-N-bars, pro-VPs and pro-sentences also exist. NOTE: some traditional grammarians restrict the term 'anaphor' to an item which follows its antecedent, preferring **cataphor** for a similar item which precedes its antecedent, but the distinction seems to be without significance, and is not normally made today. 2. In GB, one of a specified subclass of anaphors in sense 1, consisting of reflexive and reciprocal items such as *herself* and *each other*, and also NP-traces, which in that framework are analysed as having different properties from the other traditional anaphors, called **pronominals**. *Adj.* **anaphoric** /ænə'fɒrɪk/; *Abstr. n.* **anaphora** /ə'næfərə/.

anaphoric binding *n.* The LFG term for the **binding** of overt **anaphors** (sense 1), as in *Lisa$_i$ acquitted herself$_i$ well* and *Lisa$_i$ asked me to help her$_i$*. Cf. **anaphoric control**.

anaphoric control *n.* In LFG, the domain of those instances of **control** which are non-obligatory (optional or arbitrary), as in *Lisa realized it was necessary to work hard*. Cf. **functional control, anaphoric binding**.

anaphoric island *n.* A category no proper constituent of which can serve as the antecedent of an **anaphor** (sense 1). Most familiarly, words serve as anaphoric islands, as illustrated by the ill-formed example *Janet has been imprisoned, and I want to visit her there*, in which the anaphor *there* is unable to refer to the noun *prison* when this is an element of the word *imprisoned*; cf. *Janet has been put into prison, and I want to visit her there.* Postal (1969).

anastrophe /ə'næstrəfi/ *n.* The use of an abnormal word order for rhetorical effect: *She walked in pastures green*; *I've travelled the world around.*

ancestor /'ænsestə/ *n.* A particular relation that may hold between two nodes in a tree. A node A is an ancestor of a distinct node B iff A **dominates** B. Cf. **mother**, **descendant**.

animacy hierarchy /'ænɪməsi/ *n.* A hierarchy, or rather a set of hierarchies, which is grammatically significant in many languages. In this hierarchy, first and second person outrank third person, pronouns outrank common nouns (with proper nouns sometimes occupying an intermediate position) and human nouns outrank non-human animate nouns, which in turn outrank inanimate nouns. (The last of these is sometimes called the **chain-of-being hierarchy**.) The animacy hierarchy is important in determining the order of NPs in some languages; in others, **split ergativity** operates in terms of it. Silverstein (1976).

animate /'ænɪmət/ *adj.* Denoting a noun or noun phrase which is perceived as referring to a conscious, volitional entity, a human or higher animal. Animate noun phrases exhibit distinctive grammatical behaviour in some languages, such as in Basque, in which animate NPs form their local cases in a different manner from inanimate NPs, or in Navaho, in which an animate subject or object must always precede an inanimate one. *Abstr. n.* **animacy** /'ænɪməsɪ/. Cf. **inanimate**.

annotated /'ænə,teɪtɪd/ *adj.* (of a tree structure) Containing information or structure beyond the node labels and the representation of domination and precedence relations, such as feature specifications on the nodes or additional arcs linking nodes. Trees containing **empty categories** are sometimes also regarded as annotated.

antecedent /ænti'si:dənt/ *n.* 1. The item from which an **anaphor** derives its meaning or reference. In the example *After she came in,*

Lisa poured herself a drink, the NP *Lisa* is the antecedent of both *she* (in the more obvious reading) and *herself*. 2. See **protasis**.

antecedent government *n*. In GB, one of the two instances of **proper government**. See under that entry.

antiaccusative /ˌæntiəˈkjuːzətɪv/ *adj*. Denoting a case-marking system, found in a minority of **accusative languages**, in which there is an overt case marking on subjects, but no overt case marking on direct objects. Jacobsen (1979).

antiergative /ˌænti'ɜːɡətɪv/ *adj*. Denoting a system in which a single case form is used to mark all subjects, and also direct objects when no overt subject is present, but in which a distinct case form marks the direct object when an overt subject is present. Finnish and Welsh are among the languages reported as exhibiting this pattern. Comrie (1975).

antipassive /ˌæntɪˈpæsɪv/ *n*. or *adj*. A superficially intransitive construction whose subject is an agent and which contains an oblique NP representing an underlying direct object, particularly one which contrasts with a canonical transitive construction. An example from Yup'ik Eskimo: *Qimugta ner'uq neq-mek* dog-Abs eat:3Sg fish-Abl 'The dog ate some fish', contrasting with the canonical transitive *Qimugte-m neraa neqa* dog-Erg eat:3Sg:3Sg fish-Abs 'The dog ate the fish'. Antipassives are frequent in **ergative languages**; often, though not necessarily, they serve to indicate a direct object which is indefinite or only partially affected. A parallel can be drawn with English contrasts like *John struck at Bill* vs. *John struck Bill*, in which the intransitive construction indicates a partially affected object. Construction, Kuryłowicz (1946); term, Silverstein (1976).

aorist /ˈeɪərɪst/ *n*. or *adj*. 1. A verb form marked for past tense but unmarked for aspect. 2. A verb form marked for both past tense and perfective aspect. 3. A verb form marked for perfective aspect. 4. A conventional label used in a highly variable manner among specialists in particular languages to denote some particular verb form or set of verb forms. For example, Lewis (1967) uses the term to label those Turkish verb forms marked for durative/habitual aspect, while the aorist of Ancient Greek represents a set of morphologically related forms exhibiting complex tense/aspect behaviour. NOTE: in view of this great terminological confusion, Comrie (1976) recommends the avoidance of the term 'aorist' in linguistic theory. *Adj*. **aoristic** /eɪəˈrɪstɪk/. Ancient Greek grammar: 'unbounded'.

A-over-A Constraint /ˌeɪəvərˈeɪ/ *n.* A proposed constraint upon the application of grammatical rules, particularly transformational rules, by which, in any case in which a category A is embedded within a larger example of the same category A, a rule which refers to the category A may only apply to the larger (higher) instance of A. The A-over-A Constraint, proposed in Chomsky (1964), represented the first attempt at combining the **island constraints** of Ross (1967) into a single more general principle; it was not successful, and, in spite of an attempt by Bresnan (1976) to rescue it with a modified form called the **Relativized A-over-A Principle**, it has generally been discarded in more recent work in favour of other approaches, notably the **Subjacency Condition**.

AP /eɪ ˈpiː/ See **adjective phrase**.

apodosis /əˈpɒdəsɪs/ *n.* (also **consequent**) In a conditional sentence, the clause which expresses the consequence of the fulfilment of the conditional clause, e.g., *I'll tell her* in the sentence *If I see Lisa, I'll tell her*. Cf. **protasis**.

apo koinou construction /ɑːpəʊ ˈkɔɪnuː/ *n.* Any construction in which a single element must apparently be simultaneously assigned to two different constituents, as in the archaic *I have an uncle is a mighty earl*.

aposiopesis /ˌæpəʊsaɪəˈpiːsɪs/ *n.* The act of leaving an utterance unfinished for rhetorical effect: *If I can't raise the money . . .*

A-position /ˈeɪpəˌzɪʃn̩/ *n.* (also **argument position**) In GB, a position occupied by an argument NP in its canonical place, specifically a subject, (direct) object or object of a preposition. Cf. **A-bar position**.

appellative /əˈpelətɪv/ See **common noun**.

Applicational Grammar /æplɪˈkeɪʃənl/ *n.* A theory of grammar developed by Sebastian Šaumjan, consisting essentially of a formalization of Case Grammar in which (possibly universal) underlying semantic structures are mapped directly onto surface syntactic structures by the application of operators. The system employs a formidable algebraic notation which is both typographically awkward and hard to read; it is presented in Šaumjan (1977).

applicative /əˈplɪkətɪv/ *n.* or *adj.* 1. A construction found in certain languages, notably Bantu languages, in which an underlying indirect or oblique object is realized as a surface direct object, the verb usually bearing a distinctive inflection expressing the semantic relation borne by the surface direct object. Some languages exhibit a range of such constructions, one for each of the semantic roles which can be realized as a direct object (Recipient, Benefactive, Instrument, etc.). Consider the following examples from Chi-Mwi:ni, the first being a canonical transitive, the second an instrumental applicative (Kisseberth and Abasheikh 1977):

> Nu:ru Ø-tilanzile: nama ka: chisu
> Nuru Subj-cut   meat with knife
> 'Nuru cut the meat with a knife.'

> Nu:ru Ø-tilangi*l*ile: nama chisu
>   Subj-cut-APPL
> 'Nuru cut the meat with a knife.'

In the second example, though not in the first, *chisu* 'knife' can be the subject of a corresponding passive, showing clearly its status as a direct object:

> Chisu sh-tilangi*l*ila: nama na Nu:ru
> knife Subj-was cut-APPL meat by Nuru
> 'The knife was used to cut the meat by Nuru.'

The applicative forms part of the voice system in such languages. Cf. **circumstantial**. 2. (also **applied verb**, **prepositional verb**) A verb form used in such a construction.

appositive /əˈpɒzɪtɪv/ *n*. A noun phrase which immediately follows another noun phrase of identical reference, the whole sequence behaving like a single noun phrase with respect to the rest of the sentence. Appositives are most typically **non-restrictive**: the reference of the first noun phrase is clear, and the appositive serves only to provide additional information. The phrases set off by commas in the following examples are appositives: *Paris, the greatest city in France, is changing its face*; *His newest book, the last one in the trilogy, concludes the saga*. Some appositives, however, are **restrictive** (required for identification of the reference of the first noun phrase), such as *Shelley* in the example *I'm writing a biography of the poet Shelley*. An appositive is said to be **in apposition to** the preceding NP.

appositive clause *n*. Another name for a **non-restrictive** relative clause.

approximative /ə'prɒksɪmətɪv/ *n.* or *adj.* A case form occurring in certain languages which typically serves to express such notions as 'as far as', 'up to' or 'until': Basque *etxeraino* 'as far as the house' (*etxe* 'house').

arc /ɑːk/ *n.* 1. In a tree diagram, any one of the lines connecting a node to its mother. 2. In RG and Arc Pair Grammar, an arrow connecting an element to the rest of its syntactic structure and labelled to show the grammatical relation that element bears at each stage of reorganization of the sentence. 3. In a transition network, any one of the lines connecting two nodes, or states. 4. A line serving a similar linking function in any of various other types of graphical representation.

Arc Pair Grammar /ɑːk 'pɛə/ *n.* A theory of grammar which views syntactic structure primarily in terms of grammatical relations and which is essentially a formalized version of **Relational Grammar**. Arc Pair Grammar represents the syntactic structure of a sentence by a kind of relational network of arcs called a 'pair network'. The framework has enjoyed little popularity, perhaps partly because its graphical representations are both typographically awkward and hard to read, and partly because of its flamboyant terminology. Arc Pair Grammar was proposed by David Johnson and Paul Postal (1980); a convenient introduction is Postal (1982).

argument /'ɑːgjʊmənt/ *n.* 1. A noun phrase bearing a specific grammatical or semantic relation to a verb and whose overt or implied presence is required for well-formedness in structures containing that verb. Arguments may be identified either in terms of grammatical relations (Subject, Direct Object, etc.) or in terms of semantic roles (Agent, Patient, etc.). Some frameworks distinguish **internal arguments** and **external arguments**: the former occur inside the verb phrase and are subcategorized for by the verb (direct objects, indirect objects), while the latter occur outside the VP (subjects). The term is borrowed from formal logic. 2. (with reference to a function) An object to which the function can be applied and for which it returns a value.

argument binding See **A-binding**.

argument position /pə'zɪʃn̩/ See **A-position**.

argument structure *n.* The specification, for a verb or predicate, of the number and types of arguments which it requires for well-formedness.

article /ˈɑːtɪkl̩/ *n*. A **determiner** which lacks independent meaning but serves to indicate the degree of definiteness or specificity of the noun phrase in which it occurs, e.g., the English 'definite article' *the* and 'indefinite article' *a*.

ascension /əˈsenʃn̩/ *n*. Another name for **raising**, preferred in RG.

ascriptive sentence /əˈskrɪptɪv/ *n*. A sentence in which some property is ascribed to the subject NP: *Lisa is a translator*; *She is very clever*. An ascriptive sentence differs from an **equational sentence** in that it cannot be reversed: **A translator is Lisa*. The term is normally confined to **copular sentences** with non-verbal predicates; hence *She is a smoker* is an ascriptive sentence, but the semantically similar *She smokes* is not. Cf. **equational sentence**.

aspect /ˈæspekt/ *n*. A grammatical category which relates to the internal temporal structure of a situation. Aspect is most commonly reflected in the form of the verb, and in many languages the expression of aspect is intimately bound up with the expression of **tense**, from which, however, aspect must be distinguished. In English, for example, the forms *I did it*, *I was doing it* and *I used to do it* are all past tense, but they express different aspects. Among the aspectual categories often expressed in languages are **perfective**, **imperfective**, **perfect**, **progressive**, **habitual**, **durative**, **punctual** and **iterative**. *Adj*. **aspectual**. See Comrie (1976) and Dahl (1985) for discussion.

Aspects **model** /ˈæspekts ˌmɒdl̩/ *n*. Another name for the **Standard Theory** of TG, used because that theory was first presented in Chomsky's 1965 book *Aspects of the Theory of Syntax*.

aspectual verb /æˈspektʃʊəl/ *n*. A lexical verb or auxiliary which primarily expresses a distinction of aspect, such as *start*, *finish*, *continue*, *last*, progressive *be* or perfect *have*.

assignment /əˈsaɪnmənt/ *n*. Any process by which some rule, principle or component of a grammar introduces some element into a representation of structure. One may speak, for example, of the assignment of accusative case to a noun phrase, or of the assignment of an asterisk to a structure which fails to meet the requirements of a component of the grammar.

associative network /əˈsəʊʃiətɪv/ See **semantic network**.

asterisk /ˈæstərɪsk/ *n*. 1. A symbol conventionally indicating that the material following it is grammatically ill-formed, e.g., **She* *smiled me*. Cf. **question mark, per cent sign, hash mark**. NOTE: this convenient and universally used notation has apparently been independently invented several times as an extension of its long-established use in historical linguistics to mark unattested forms; it was used by Sweet (1898), but its modern use dates from Hill (1958). (In contrast, the citation of ill-formed strings, without distinctive marking, goes back at least to the Greek grammarian Apollonius Dyscolus; see Householder (1973).) 2. See **Kleene star**.

asyndeton /æ'sɪndɪtn̩/ *n*. Coordination between sentences without the use of a coordinating conjunction: *It was the best of times; it was the worst of times*. *Adj*. **asyndetic** /æsɪn'detɪk/.

asyntactic /eɪsɪn'tæktɪk/ *adj*. Lacking a syntactic structure.

ATB See **across-the-board**.

atelic /eɪ'tiːlɪk/ *adj*. 1. Denoting an activity which has no recognizable goal the achievement of which would necessarily bring the activity to an end, as in the examples *Janet is sleeping* and *Lisa speaks good French*. 2. Denoting a verb or predicate which, intrinsically or in a particular instance, exhibits this semantic property, such as the verbs in the preceding examples. Cf. **telic**. See Comrie (1976) for discussion. Garey (1957).

ATN /eɪ tiː 'en/ See **augmented transition network**.

attraction /ə'trækʃən/ *n*. The phenomenon in which a verb agrees, not with its subject, but with another NP which is closer to it: *The posture of your blows are yet unknown* (Shakespeare); *I wonder whether the right kind of supplies are being sent*.

attribute /'ætrɪbjuːt/ *n*. 1. An item which occurs in **attributive** (sense 1) position. In some versions of the X-bar system, an attribute is formally defined as a category which is the sister of an N-bar and the daughter of another N-bar; some definitions add the (English-specific) requirement that it precede its N-bar sister. Cf. **adjunct**. Bloomfield (1933). 2. More generally, any constituent, regardless of its syntactic position, which serves to express a property of some entity, such as the predicate in an **ascriptive sentence**. 3. The property expressed by such a constituent. 4. In LFG, a **feature** occurring as an argument of a function in **f-structure**. An attribute may take as its value either an atomic symbol, a **semantic form** or another f-structure. See the examples under **f-structure**. *Adj*. **attributive**.

attribute grammar *n.* In computational linguistics, a type of context-free grammar augmented by properties ('attributes') assigned to its categories.

attributive /ə'trɪbjʊtɪv/ *adj.* 1. (of a word) Denoting an item which occurs inside a noun phrase and serves to qualify or restrict the meaning of the head noun of that NP. Examples include *red* in *the red book*, *in the garden* in *the people in the garden*, *Lisa's* in *Lisa's essay* and *newspaper* in *this newspaper headline*. Cf. **predicative**. NOTE: traditional accounts often apply the label 'adjective' to nouns in attributive position, such as *newspaper* in the last example; this usage should be avoided. 2. (of a sentence) A less usual synonym for **ascriptive**. NOTE: this second use of 'attributive', while reasonable in itself, leads to an unfortunate potential confusion, since ascriptive sentences are precisely those which involve items which are **predicative** (i.e., *not* 'attributive' in sense 1).

augmentative /ɔːg'mentətɪv/ *n.* or *adj.* 1. A derivational affix which can be added to a word to express a notion of large size, sometimes with additional overtones of excess, awkwardness or unpleasantness: Spanish *-ón*, *-azo*, *-ote*. 2. A word derived by the use of such an affix: Spanish *ricachón* 'stinking rich' (*rico* 'rich'), *ginebrazo* 'bloody great shot of gin' (*ginebra* 'gin'), *favorzote* 'heck of a favour' (*favor* 'favour'). Cf. **diminutive**.

augmented transition network /ɔːg'mentɪd/ *n.* (ATN) An extension of a **recursive transition network** which has been enriched by the presence of a memory and by the ability to augment arcs with actions and conditions that make reference to that memory, thus enabling it to handle dependencies such as agreement and displacement. The memory is usually represented as a set of local variables called 'registers'. ATNs were until recently widely used in natural-language processing, but they have now been largely supplanted by **chart parsers**.

Autolexical Syntax /ˌɔːtəʊ'leksɪkl̩/ *n.* A theory of grammar characterized by the presence of three autonomous modules (morphology, syntax, semantics), each having the form of a context-free phrase structure grammar, plus an additional subsystem, the 'interface', which includes the lexicon. A sentence is represented by a single tree structure in each of the three modules, the match-up among the three representations being mediated by the interface. Autolexical Syntax draws heavily upon the machinery of GPSG, but it is unusual among theories of grammar in that its structure is strongly motivated by data from languages which are very different from English, particularly by cases of morphosyntactic mismatch such as clitics and incorporation. The framework was proposed by Jerrold Sadock (1985); the most accessible presentation is Sadock (1991). See Gazdar and Pullum (1985) for some comments on the mathematical and computational properties of the framework.

automaton (pl. **automata**) /ɔː'tɒmətən, -ə/ *n.* An abstract mathematical device which is capable of performing certain computations. An automaton is essentially an implementation of a **transition network** to perform some particular task, frequently that of **recognition**. It consists of a number of states, each accompanied by a set of instructions telling it which other state to move to on encountering any one of the possible input characters. It accepts input, one character at a time, moving from state to state in response. Eventually it either accepts the input as valid and halts, rejects the input as invalid and halts or, in some cases, fails to halt and goes on computing forever. Automata can be defined which are equivalent to many classes of formal grammars. Three types which are of linguistic interest are **finite automata**, **pushdown automata** and **linear bounded automata**. The most powerful type of automaton is the **Turing machine**.

autonomy of syntax /ɔː'tɒnəmi/ *n.* The doctrine that syntax can and should be studied in isolation from other branches of linguistics and most particularly from semantics. This doctrine has been widely held for decades, in spite of the vigorous attack upon it by the proponents of **Generative Semantics**, but more recently linguists have often been willing to accept that syntactic analyses must, at least sometimes, take note of semantic facts.

AUX /ɔːks/ *n.* 1. See **auxiliary**. 2. In some theories of grammar, an abstract category which is postulated as being universally present in sentences and which serves as the locus for certain grammatical categories, notably tense. AUX was postulated by Chomsky (1957) and was found in most versions of TG; in GB, it has been replaced by the category INFL, which serves some of the same functions. 3. In certain languages, such as the Australian language Warlpiri, an overt, non-verbal constituent of the sentence which serves as the locus of tense and agreement, often regarded as a realization of AUX in sense 2.

auxiliary /ɔːg'zɪliəri/ *n.* 1. In English, one of a small set of lexical items having certain properties in common with verbs but also exhibiting a number of other distinct properties. The English auxiliaries are usually divided into the **modal auxiliaries** and the **non-modal auxiliaries**. See Palmer (1987) for a detailed account of the properties of auxiliaries. There has long been a vigorous debate on the issue of whether the English auxiliaries should be regarded as verbs or as members of a distinct lexical category; Pullum and Wilson (1977) provided the classic case for adopting the former position, one which is accepted by the majority of frameworks today, though GB clings firmly to the latter. 2. More generally, any item in a language, whether verbal or not, which serves as a locus of expression for such categories as tense, aspect, mood or agreement.

aversive /əˈvɜːsɪv/ *n.* or *adj.* An overt case form found in many Australian languages which typically expresses the meaning 'for fear of': Yidiny *bamayida* 'for fear of the people' (*bama* 'people'). Dixon (1977b).

B

Bach–Peters sentence /ˌbɑːk ˈpiːtəz/ *n.* A sentence containing two **anaphors** (sense 1), each of which has as its **antecedent** a noun phrase containing the other: [*The woman who was sitting next to him*ᵢ]ⱼ *smiled at* [*the man who offered her*ⱼ *a light*]ᵢ. Such sentences provide insuperable difficulties for theories of anaphora which derive pronouns from the reduction of full noun phrases. Bach (1970).

Bach's generalization /bɑːks/ *n.* The observation that an object NP which controls an empty subject in a complement clause must be overtly present. Hence *Lisa persuaded us to go* is well formed, but **Lisa persuaded to go* is not, because of the absence of an overt NP controlling the empty subject of *to go*. In contrast, *Lisa promised to go* is well-formed, since the verb *promise* exerts subject control. There are also more complex cases in which the empty subject binds an **anaphor** (sense 2) in the complement clause: *The evidence led one/*∅/*us to conclude for oneself that she was guilty.* Cf. *∅ To conclude for oneself that she is guilty would be rash.* Bach (1979).

back-formation /ˈbæk fɔːˌmeɪʃn̩/ *n.* 1. A word formed by the removal from another word of a morph which resembles a familiar affix, e.g., *edit* from *editor*, *sculpt* from *sculptor*, and *peddle* from *pedlar*, all by removal of a morph resembling the agent suffix *-er*, as in *writer*. 2. A word formed by the reanalysis of a compound word and the subsequent removal of an affix which was not originally an immediate constituent, such as *sky-dive* from *sky-diving* (originally [*sky*]+[*diving*], but reanalysed as [*sky-dive*]+[*-ing*], or *pied-pipe* from *pied piper*, originally [*pied*]+[*piper*], but reanalysed as [*pied-pipe*]+[*-er*]. 3. The process of forming a word in either of these ways.

backgrounding /ˈbækˌɡraʊndɪŋ/ *n.* 1. The discourse phenomenon by which some element of an utterance is marked to indicate that it is to be interpreted as part of the context in which the rest of the utterance is made. Some languages provide explicit grammatical means for this, such as the Japanese topic marker *wa*, which indicates that the preceding phrase is to be taken as a context for what follows. 2. The discourse phenomenon by which information is presented which merely carries a narrative along, without introducing new entities or events, sometimes associated with intransitive clause structure and with stative and durative aspect and non-volitional verbs. Hopper and Thompson (1980). 3. Any of various syntactic processes by which a syntactic **pivot** (most often a subject) is demoted to a non-pivot position or removed entirely from the clause. Passive and antipassive constructions are frequently used for this purpose. Backgrounding may or may not be accompanied by the **foregrounding** of some other element: the English passive construction always foregrounds another element, while **impersonal passives** typically involve backgrounding without foregrounding. Foley and Van Valin (1984). Cf. **foregrounding.**

backtracking /ˈbækˌtrækɪŋ/ *n.* The action of a parser which, on encountering an element which cannot be accommodated within the structure it has provisionally constructed, reverses its most recent steps in order to try a different analysis. The minimalization of such backtracking is a major goal in the construction of efficient parsers.

backward pronominalization /ˈbækwəd prəʊnɒmɪnəlaɪˈzeɪʃn̩/ *n.* (also **cataphora**) A construction in which a pronoun precedes its antecedent, as in *After she$_i$ came in, Janet$_i$ sat down.* See also **precede-and-command condition**.

bahuvrihi /bɑːhuːˈvriːhi/ *n.* (also **exocentric compound**) A type of compound word in which one element modifies or restricts the other and the whole denotes an entity which is a hyponym of an un-expressed semantic head: *highbrow, bluebell, hatchback, redskin, heavy-handed, pickpocket, scarecrow.* The verb+object type is rare in English, but highly productive in Romance languages: Spanish *tocadiscos* 'record player' (*toca-* 'play' + *discos* 'records'). Sanskrit grammar.

bar /bɑː/ *n.* In the **X-bar system**, the conventional name for the feature attached to a lexical category to indicate a **projection** of that category. For example, the category Noun (N) is usually assumed to have the one-bar projection N-bar (notated as $\bar{N}$, N' or N^1) and the two-bar projection N-double-bar (represented as $\bar{\bar{N}}$, N'' or N^2).

bare infinitive /bɛə/ *n.* (also **base, base form**) In English, the stem of a verb functioning as a non-finite form, such as *do* in *You must do it.* Cf. *to*-**infinitive.**

bare-NP adverbial /bɛəˆr en 'piː/ *n.* An **adverbial** which consists of a noun phrase unaccompanied by a preposition. Only a small number of English nouns can function as the heads of such adverbials, including *way*, *place*, *time* and temporal nouns like *day* and *minute*: *I did it that way/the same way/the way she did it*; *Do it this minute/the minute she arrives*; *I've seen that every place I've been*; cf. **I did it the same manner*; **I've seen that every country I've been.*

barrier /'bæriə/ *n.* In GB, a category which blocks **government** across its boundary. For example, the German verb *schreiben* 'write' can assign Accusative Case to an NP which it governs (as in *Er schreibt einen Roman* 'He is writing a novel', where *einen Roman* is Accusative), but it must not do so to an NP in a following PP (as in *Er schreibt mit einem Bleistift* 'He is writing with a pencil', where *einem Bleistift* is Dative). We say that the PP node is a barrier to government, and hence to Case assignment. Broadly speaking, maximal projections are barriers, but the facts are considerably more complicated than this. In recent work in GB, the notion of a barrier has been developed so as to subsume the notion of a **bounding node**; the idea is that one barrier blocks government, while two barriers block movement. Chomsky (1986).

base /beɪs/ *n.* 1. (also **base form**) In morphology, a morph, variously consisting of a **root**, a **stem** or a word, which serves, upon the addition of a single further morpheme, as the immediate source of some particular formation: thus, for example, *happy* is the base for the formation of both *unhappy* and *happily*, while *unhappy* is the base for the formation of both *unhappily* and *unhappiness*. This usage is recommended by Matthews (1974). 2. (also **base form**) See **stem**. 3. (also **base form**) See **bare infinitive**. 4. In some **derivational** theories of grammar, notably TG and GB, that part of a grammar which is responsible for generating underlying representations of sentences, which are then modified by other components of the grammar (notably the transformational rules) to produce surface structures. Typically the base is regarded as consisting of a set of categorial rules and the lexicon.

base-generated /'beɪs ˌdʒenəreɪtɪd/ *adj.* In a **derivational** theory of grammar, denoting a structure provided by the **base** (sense 4), before or without the subsequent application of rules from other components of the grammar, notably the transformational rules.

basic word order /ˌbeɪsɪk 'wɜːd ɔːʁə/ *n.* The normal, unmarked or most frequent order of elements in the sentences of a language, usually expressed in terms of the order of Subject, Object and Verb. Most languages have a readily recognizable basic word order, such as SVO for English, VSO for Welsh and SOV for Japanese. In some languages, however, a basic word order is difficult or impossible to discern, either because the order of elements appears to be completely free, because different word orders are used for different grammatical purposes (say, with different verbal aspects) or because subjects cannot be unambiguously identified. All six possible orderings of S, O and V are attested as basic word orders, though the frequencies vary enormously. Reliable statistics are difficult to come by, but it appears that SOV is the most frequent basic word order, followed by SVO, with VSO considerably less common, and VOS, OVS and OSV being successively rarer. At least some basic word orders correlate strongly with typological characteristics, as first pointed out by Greenberg (1963). See **VSO language** and so on; see also **object-initial language**.

benefactive /ˌbenɪ'fæktɪv/ *n.* or *adj.* 1. A case form typically indicating the individual for whose benefit something is done: Basque *gizonarentzat* 'for the man' (*gizona* 'the man'). 2. (also **beneficiary**) This semantic relation, regardless of its surface expression, particularly when regarded as a semantic or grammatical primitive. Beneficiary is one of the **deep cases** recognized in Case Grammar, though it is sometimes conflated with Recipient or with Goal or with both.

big PRO /bɪg/ See **PRO**.

binary branching /ˌbaɪnəri 'brɑːntʃɪŋ/ *n.* 1. The structure shown by a node with exactly two daughters. 2. The requirement, advocated by some linguists, that no node in a tree should ever be allowed to have more than two daughters; this requirement places an attractive constraint on possible tree structures, but certain constructions, notably ditransitive verbs and coordinate constructions like *Tom, Dick and Harry*, pose severe difficulties for such a constraint.

binding /'baɪndɪŋ/ *n.* 1. A relation between two NPs in a sentence (one of them possibly an empty category) by which the interpretation of one of them (the one which is **bound**) is determined by the interpretation of the other (the one which **binds** it); i.e., they must be **coreferential**. For example, in *Janet hates herself*, the item *herself* must be bound by *Janet*; in *Fred asked Bill to see him*, *him* cannot be bound by *Bill* but may be bound by *Fred*; in *Who did you want to see* e?, the empty category must be bound by *who*. The notion of binding is particularly associated with the GB framework, in which it is fundamental, as the name of that framework suggests. Within GB, the range of coreference phenomena analysed as instances of binding is somewhat more restricted than might have been anticipated, since certain examples involving empty categories are regarded as instances of a distinct relation called **control**. See **Binding Theory, A-binding** and **A-bar binding**. Chomsky (1980). 2. The degree of influence exercised by a main-clause agent over an agent in its complement clause, with binding types supposedly ranked as follows, from weakest to strongest: direct speech < indirect speech < verbs of belief, knowledge and doubt < emotive verbs < verbs of attempt or manipulation (including commands and requests) < causatives and successful outcome verbs like *finish* and *succeed*. Givón (1980).

Binding Theory /'baɪndɪŋ ˌθiəri/ *n.* In GB, the module which deals with most coreference phenomena among NPs, including empty categories. Both overt NPs and empty categories are divided into types by the two binary features [anaphoric] and [pronominal], as follows:

Features	*Overt*	*Empty*
[−a, −p]	R-expression	WH-trace ('variable')
[−a, +p]	Pronominal	pro
[+a, −p]	Anaphor	NP-trace
[+a, +p]	—	PRO

These classes are subject to the following Binding Principles:

1 An anaphor [+a] is bound in its governing category.
2 A pronominal [+p] is free in its governing category.
3 An R-expression is free everywhere.

Binding Theory applies only to **A-binding**; WH-traces are subject to the independent requirement of **A-bar binding**. An NP is **bound** if it is coindexed with another NP which c-commands it; otherwise it is **free**. The **governing category** of an NP is a specified local domain. The conflicting requirements of Principles 1 and 2 mean that a [+a, +p] category can only exist if it has no governing category and is hence ungoverned; an overt NP in this position would fall foul of the **Case Filter** of **Case Theory** and hence cannot exist. PRO is never bound, but is subject to the independent requirement of **control**. See Sells (1985) or Haegeman (1991) for discussion. Chomsky (1981).

binyan (pl. **binyanim**) /'bɪnjən, -ɪm/ *n*. In Semitic languages, one of the systematic set of derived forms of a verbal root typically expressing distinctions of voice or Aktionsarten. Some examples from Arabic: *katab* 'write', *kattab* 'cause to write', *kaatab* 'correspond', *ʔaktab* 'cause to write', *takaatab* 'write to each other', *nkatab* 'subscribe'. Hebrew grammar.

blend /blend/ *n*. 1. (also **portmanteau word**) A word formed by **blending**. 2. See **syntactic blend**.

blending /'blendɪŋ/ *n*. The process of word formation by the combination of arbitrary parts of existing words: *smog* (*smoke* plus *fog*), *brunch* (*breakfast* plus *lunch*), *Oxbridge* (*Oxford* plus *Cambridge*), *chunnel* (*channel* plus *tunnel*). See Bauer (1983) for discussion.

blocking /'blɒkɪŋ/ *n*. The phenomenon by which the existence of a regular derived form is apparently prevented by the prior existence of a distinct word with the identical meaning. Thus, for example, while *purchase* yields *purchaser*, *steal* does not yield *stealer, which is blocked by *thief*. Similarly, while *curious* yields *curiosity*, *furious* does not yield *furiosity, which is blocked by *fury*.

bondedness /'bɒndɪdnəs/ *n*. The putative degree to which specifiers and modifiers are bound to a head noun within a noun phrase. The behaviour of **ligatures** in Austronesian languages suggests the following hierarchy of bondedness, from tightest to loosest: article > deictic > interrogative > quantifier > adjective > relative clause. Foley (1980).

Boolean conditions on analysability /'buːliən kən'dɪʃṇz/ *n*. In a formal system, the property of having no connectives other than those equivalent to *and*, *or* and *not*. After the mathematician George Boole.

bottom–up /bɒtəm'ʌp/ *adj*. Denoting an approach to parsing sentences which begins with the individual words and combines them step-by-step into larger constituents until the whole sequence can be legitimately recognized as a sentence. Cf. **top–down**.

bound /baʊnd/ *adj*. The participle of **bind**, as in **binding**. See **Binding Theory**. NOTE: do not confuse the related terms **bind, bound, binding, Binding Theory** with the entirely distinct group of terms **bounding, bounded, boundedness, bounding node, Bounding Theory**.

bound anaphora *n.* A synonym for **anaphora**, the longer form occasionally being preferred to indicate that **exophoric** items are excluded.

boundary /ˈbaʊndri/ *n.* Either extremity of any constituent. One may speak, for example, of a 'morpheme boundary', a 'word boundary', a 'clause boundary', an 'NP-boundary', and so on. The two boundaries of a constituent are conventionally marked by brackets in a **(labelled) bracketing**.

bounded /ˈbaʊndɪd/ *adj.* (of a particular dependency or rule) Constrained to hold or apply within a specified domain; **local**. Cf. **unbounded**. *Abstr. n.* **boundedness** /ˈbaʊndɪdnəs/.

bound form *n.* Any morph which cannot stand alone as a word form, but which must be accompanied in all its occurrences by one or more additional morphs to produce a well-formed word. Bound forms are quite various in their nature; some examples are the English derivational affixes *re-* (as in *rewrite*) and *-er* (as in *writer*), the inflectional affixes plural *-s* (as in *dogs*) and *-ing* (as in *writing*), the clitics *-'ll* (as in *He'll do it*) and possessive *-'s* (as in *John's book*), the combining forms *step-* (as in *stepmother*), *eco-* (as in *ecosystem*) and *-phobia* (as in *arachnophobia*), the Latin verbal root *am-* 'love' and the present and perfect stems *ama-* and *amav-* of the same verb (as in *amat* 'he loves' and *amavi* 'I have loved'), the Turkish passive inflection *-n-* (as in *yenmek* 'to be eaten') and the Arabic verbal root *ktb* 'write' (as in *kataba* 'he wrote' and *maktu:b* 'written'). As illustrated here, it is conventional, when citing a bound form in isolation, to use one or more hyphens to indicate its bound nature.

bounding node /ˈbaʊndɪŋ/ *n.* In GB, a node which limits the distance over which some grammatical rule or process is allowed to apply. The bounding nodes usually recognized are NP and S, or NP and S-bar, the difference possibly depending on the particular language. In recent work, the notion of a bounding node has been subsumed under the notion of a **barrier**. See **Subjacency Condition**.

Bounding Theory /ˈbaʊndɪŋ ˌθɪəri/ *n.* In GB, that module which deals with constraints upon the permissible degree of separation in a structure of two elements which are both involved in the statement of a single grammatical rule. The principal such constraint is the **Subjacency Condition**.

bound morpheme *n.* A **morpheme** which can never stand alone to make a word but which must always be combined with at least one other morpheme, such as the derivational affixes *re-* and *-er* (in *rewrite* and *writer*), the inflectional affixes plural *-s* and past *-ed* (in *cats* and *lived*) and the Latin verbal roots *am-* 'love' and *scrib-* 'write' (in *amat* 'she loves' and *scribebam* 'I was writing'). Cf. **free morpheme**.

braces /'breɪsɪz/ *n.* (also **curly brackets**) 1. A notational convention used to combine in a single rule schema two or more rules which are identical except for the presence of different elements at one point; the alternative elements are listed within a pair of braces. For example, the two rules VP → V NP PP and VP → V NP AdvP could be abbreviated by the schema VP → V NP {PP, AdvP}. Braces were extensively used in the early days of generative grammar, but are rarely seen today. 2. A similar notational convention used to combine, for expository convenience, two or more examples which differ at only a single point, as illustrated by the example

$$\text{I want} \quad \left\{ \begin{array}{l} \emptyset \\ \text{her} \\ \text{*herself} \end{array} \right\} \quad \text{to do it}$$

3. A conventional notation for representing **morphemes**; for example, *cats* can be represented as {*cat*} + {Plural}, and *took* as {*take*} + {Past}.

bracketing /'brækɪtɪŋ/ *n.* A linear representation of constituent structure which conventionally employs (square) brackets to indicate constituents. An example is [[[*Your*] [[*young*] [*man*]]] [[*is*] [*here*]]]. Such a bracketing is exactly equivalent to an unlabelled tree structure. If, in addition, each bracketed constituent is labelled for its syntactic category, the result is a **labelled bracketing**. Wells (1947).

bracketing paradox /'brækɪtɪŋ ˌpærədɒks/ *n.* 1. A phenomenon in which the constituent structure required by the syntax is inconsistent with the grouping manifested by the morphology. A simple example is the English *He'll do it*, in which the sequence ['*ll do it*] is arguably a constituent, but the overlapping sequence [*he'll*] constitutes a morphological unit. More elaborate examples occur in West Greenlandic Eskimo, in which *Ammassannik marlunnik nerivunga* 'I ate two sardines', literally 'sardine-Instr two-Instr ate-I', can be optionally realized as *Marlunnik ammassattorpunga*, literally 'two-Instr sardine-ate-I', with the noun phrase being partly realized as a bound form inside the verb. 2. A similar phenomenon in which the morphological structure of a phrase is inconsistent with the grouping manifested by the phonological words of which it is composed: *transformational grammarian*, which morphologically appears to consist of *transformational grammar* plus *-ian*.

branching node /'brɑːntʃɪŋ/ *n.* 1. A node in a tree which has two or more daughters. 2. (rare) A category for which the rules in the grammar provide at least one expansion with two or more daughters.

brother-in-law agreement /'brʌðərɪnlɔː/ *n.* Agreement with a constituent which has been displaced from its normal position by a dummy; an example is *There are two people at the door*, in which the verb, instead of agreeing with the apparent surface subject *there*, agrees with the NP which has been displaced from subject position by the dummy. Perlmutter (1983a).

Burzio's generalization /'buːrtsiəʊ/ *n.* In GB, a generalization embracing passive verbs, raising verbs and unaccusative verbs, as follows: (a) a verb which lacks an external argument fails to assign Accusative Case; and (b) a verb which fails to assign Accusative Case fails to theta-mark an external argument. Its function is to force a non-subject NP into an empty subject position. Burzio (1986).

C

C In GB, a common abbreviation for **COMP** in the sense of **COMP node**.

canonical /kə'nɒnɪkl̩/ *adj*. Denoting a pattern or structure which is the most typical, most frequent or least marked among competing possibilities. For example, the canonical structure of English transitive sentences may be represented as Subject–Verb–Object–(Adjuncts), as illustrated by the example *Lisa buys her dresses in Paris*.

CAP /siː eɪ 'piː/ See **Control Agreement Principle**.

case /keɪs/ *n*. 1. A distinctive, overtly marked form which can be assumed by an NP to indicate that that NP bears some identifiable grammatical or semantic relation to the rest of the sentence. In English, overt case marking is confined to a few pronouns (*I/me*; *they/them*), but some other languages, such as German, Russian, Latin, Basque and Finnish, exhibit elaborate case systems typically involving about three to six distinct forms, but sometimes a dozen or more. Among the most frequently distinguished cases are the **nominative**, **accusative**, **absolutive**, **ergative**, **dative**, **genitive**, **instrumental**, **comitative**, **locative**, **allative** and **ablative**, but many others exist. 2. (usually capitalized) In GB, a putatively universal abstract property of noun phrases which is an extension of 'case' in sense 1. Every overt NP, in this view, must be marked by the grammar as bearing exactly one of a set of abstract 'Cases', the names and natures of which are reminiscent of some of the traditional cases in sense 1: Nominative, Accusative, Genitive, etc. When it is necessary to distinguish Case in the GB sense from case in sense 1, one speaks of 'abstract Case' and 'morphological case', respectively. See **Case Theory**. 3. See **deep case**.

Case Filter *n*. In GB, the principal requirement imposed by the module called **Case Theory**. It stipulates that every overt (non-empty) NP must be assigned exactly one (abstract) Case. Its function is to ensure that NP-Movement is obligatory in passive structures and in structures involving raising verbs and unaccusative verbs; it also guarantees that only PRO is possible as the subject of certain non-finite verbs.

Case Grammar *n.* A theory of grammar which regards **deep cases** as the grammatical primitives in terms of which sentences are constructed. Case Grammar was proposed by Charles Fillmore (1968), and was developed particularly by Wallace Chafe (1970) and John Anderson (1971). Its ideas have greatly influenced certain contemporary theories of grammar, notably GB and Lexicase.

Case Theory /ˈkeɪs ˌθɪəri/ *n.* In GB, one of the principal modules of the framework, consisting of various Case-marking conventions and the **Case Filter**. The module is responsible for ensuring that every overt NP in a sentence is marked as possessing exactly one of a set of abstract properties called 'Cases', such as Nominative, Accusative or Genitive, as required by the Case Filter. Essentially, this Case marking is a device for ensuring that every such NP occupies a position which is in certain respects well-formed; it is largely concerned with preventing NPs from appearing in arbitrary positions in which they cannot be suitably interpreted. Though there is only one set of Cases, Case Theory recognizes two types of Case assignment: 'inherent' case is assigned at D-structure, while 'structural' case is assigned at S-structure, the difference reflecting roughly the difference between cases assigned by particular lexical items and those assigned in particular syntactic configurations. Chomsky (1980).

cataphor /ˈkætəfɔː/ *n.* A traditional name for an **anaphor** (sense 1) which precedes its antecedent, now rarely used. *Adj.* **cataphoric** /ˌkætəˈfɒrɪk/; *abstr. n.* **cataphora** /kəˈtæfərə/.

Categorial Grammar /ˌkætəˈgɔːriəl/ *n.* A particular theory of grammar which is formulated in terms of a small number of basic syntactic categories, a larger number of derived categories which are defined in terms of the basic ones and a set of operations (rules) for combining these categories into syntactic structures. In the conventional notation, a derived category X is represented as a fraction whose denominator shows another category which X can combine with and whose numerator shows the category that results. Thus, if S (sentence) and N (noun) are taken as the basic categories, an intransitive verb may be represented as (S/N), meaning that it combines with a noun to produce a sentence, a transitive verb may be represented as ((S/N)/N), meaning that it combines with a noun to produce an intransitive verb, and a determiner may be repre-

sented as (N/N), meaning that it combines with a noun to produce a
noun. Most versions add a directional element, specifying whether a
category combines with another to its left or to its right. Categorial
Grammar was originally developed by logicians, notably Leśniewski
(1929) and Ajdukiewicz (1935), but it was first brought to the
attention of linguists by Bar-Hillel (1953), who coined the term
(1964). Though similar ideas had been expressed less rigorously by
Jespersen and Hjelmslev, Categorial Grammar was still largely
ignored by linguists until its use by the logician Montague (1970)
attracted the attention of Bach, whose 1979 paper brought the
framework into the linguistic mainstream, and since then it has been
the subject of vigorous research; the rather sparse machinery of
earlier Categorial Grammar has been elaborated in a number of
linguistically interesting ways, and it has been shown that the unelaborated framework is weakly equivalent to context-free grammars. See Oehrle *et al.* (1988) for a comprehensive summary of
recent work.

categorial rule *n*. A rule which expands some category into a string
of daughters: a **phrase structure rule** or an **immediate dominance
rule**.

category /'kætəgri/ *n*. 1. A labelled node in a tree. This is the sense
employed in such GB locutions as 'governing category' and 'Move
alpha, where alpha is a category'. 2. In a theory of syntactic features, any matrix of such features which is permitted by the system
and which is hence available to serve as a node in a tree. This is the
sense in which the term is used in GPSG. 3. A term of very wide and
diverse application, variously denoting any of several classes of
formal objects. Usage of the term is so varied that no general
definition is possible; in practice, a category is simply any class of
related grammatical objects which someone wants to consider.
Certain classes of categories are widely recognized and have established names, such as **syntactic category** and **grammatical category**,
but it is entirely unremarkable to encounter the term 'category'
applied to such diverse notions as 'Subject', 'clitic' 'topic' and
'transitive verb'. *Adj.* **categorial**.

category-neutral rule /ˌkætəgri 'njuːtrəl/ *n*. A **phrase structure
rule** or **immediate dominance rule** which makes no reference to
specific categories like NP and VP; an example is the rule X' → X,
YP*, which says that a one-bar category can consist of a lexical head
and any number of maximal projections. Such rules are the primary

source of constituent structure in HPSG and in recent versions of GB.

category-valued feature /'kætəgri ˌvæljuːd/ *n*. A **feature** whose value is a syntactic category. An example is the GPSG feature [SLASH], which indicates the presence of a gap, and whose value is a syntactic category representing the nature of the gap, as in the example [SLASH NP].

catenative verb /'kætɪnətɪv/ See **control verb**.

causal /'kɔːzl̩/ *adj*. Denoting an adverbial clause or phrase which expresses the notion 'because (of)': *Because of the fog, we had to land in Luton*; *I'm late because I missed my train*. Some languages have an overt case form for this purpose: Basque *-engatik*, as in *euriarengatik* 'because of the rain' (*euria* 'the rain').

causative /'kɔːzətɪv/ *n*. or *adj*. 1. A transitive construction, related to a second, simpler, transitive or intransitive construction, from which it differs by the additional presence of an agent NP perceived as the direct instigator of the action expressed in the simpler construction. Causatives in this sense are susceptible of a variety of surface syntactic expressions in English and other languages. Here are some English examples illustrating the most frequent patterns; in each case, the second sentence is the causative of the first, and the NP *Lisa* is the agent in the causative: *Tim smiles a lot*/*Lisa makes Tim smile a lot*; *I washed the car*/*Lisa made me wash the car* or *Lisa had me wash the car* or *Lisa got me to wash the car*. Sometimes, but more controversially, the label 'causative' is extended to less obvious cases such as the following: *The potatoes boiled*/*Lisa boiled the potatoes*; *He decided to go*/*Lisa persuaded him to go*; *The corkscrew got lost*/*Lisa lost the corkscrew*; *The celery fell on the floor*/*Lisa dropped the celery on the floor*. In this extended sense, the term is being used in a purely semantic way, and many linguists would prefer to restrict the use of the term to syntactically productive examples such as the earlier group. 2. A verb form, of the type found in certain languages, used to express overtly such a causative construction. Turkish, for example, has a productive causative formation, illustrated in the following examples: *Yumurta pişiyor* 'The egg is cooking'/*Ali yumurtayɨ pişiriyor* 'Ali is cooking the egg'; *Mehmet öldü* 'Mehmet died'/*Ali Mehmedi öldürdü* 'Ali killed Mehmet'/*Hasan Aliye Mehmedi öldürttü* 'Hasan made Ali kill Mehmet'. Such verb forms form part of the **voice** system in languages exhibiting them. See Shibatani (1976); Comrie (1985b)

c-command /'siːkəmɑːnd/ *n.* The most important of the **command relations**. The name has been applied to several distinct relations in the literature, but the classical formulation is 'A node A c-commands another node B iff the lowest branching node which properly dominates A also properly dominates B', and it seems best to retain this usage, resorting to different names, where necessary, to pick out slightly different relations. C-command has proved to be a fundamental notion in analysing tree structures, on a par with **mother**, **daughter** and **sister**. It is particularly important in GB, in which it is the primary source of locality and in which it plays a crucial role in defining **government**, one of the fundamental ideas of that framework. The inverse of c-command was first identified by Klima (1964) under the name 'in-construction-with'; the relation itself was first defined by Reinhart (1974), who called it 'superiority'. The name 'c-command' was reportedly suggested by G.N. Clements and was originally a shortening of 'constituent-command', a name which is not normally used. NOTE: for a few years in the 1980s, the name 'c-command' was often applied to the relation now called **m-command**, but the original usage seems now to have been restored, though one also finds the label 'strict c-command' applied to the original definition; m-command is also sometimes called 'c-command in the sense of Aoun and Sportiche'.

centrality /sen'træləti/ *n.* The requirement that the **initial symbol** of a generative grammar should be the maximal projection of a lexical category. Centrality is obeyed in GPSG, in which the initial symbol S is regarded as the maximal projection of the lexical category Verb, and in GB, in which the initial symbol S-bar (= CP) is regarded as the maximal projection of the lexical category Comp, but it is not obeyed in LFG, in which the initial symbol S is not regarded as a projection of any lexical category. Kornai and Pullum (1990).

centre-embedding /'sentər ɪmˌbedɪŋ/ *n.* A type of construction in which the material contained in one clause is interrupted by a second clause: *The book the professor recommended is good*, in which the relative clause *the professor recommended* is centre-embedded in the matrix clause *The book is good*. Multiple centre-embeddings are notoriously difficult for speakers to process: *The book the professor the students who are doing well like recommended is good*. Nevertheless, they are very common in some languages; the following example from the central Sudanic language Moru illustrates the normal and only way of expressing possession (Hagège 1976):

kokyE [toko [odrupi [ma ro] ro] ri] drate
dog wife   brother me of of of is-dead
'My brother's wife's dog is dead.'

Unlimited centre-embeddings cannot be even weakly generated by **regular grammars (finite-state grammars)**, and they form the basis of the proof that natural languages cannot be **regular languages**. *Adj.* **centre-embedded** /ɪmˈbedɪd/. Chomsky (1957).

cf. 1. In scholarly work, the conventional abbreviation for 'compare', from Latin *confer* 'bring together'. 2. By confusion, but very commonly, an abbreviation for 'see' or 'refer to', for which the conventional abbreviation is *v*. (Latin *vide* 'see'). NOTE: this second usage is simply illiterate, but it is nearly universal in the contemporary linguistic literature.

CFG See **context-free grammar**.

CFL See **context-free language**.

CF-PSG See **context-free grammar**.

CF-PS-rule See **context-free rule**.

CF-rule See **context-free rule**.

chain /tʃeɪn/ See **path** (sense 2).

chain-of-being hierarchy /ˌtːeɪnəvˈbiːɪŋ/ *n.* A hierarchy of noun phrases, ranked according to semantic features such as humanness and animacy, which is grammatically important in some languages, especially in those exhibiting **inverse person marking**. An example is the hierarchy found in Navaho, which is essentially Human > Animal > Inanimate; in a Navaho sentence, a lower-ranking NP may not precede a higher-ranking one, and the verb is inflected to indicate the grammatical relation borne by each NP; see examples under **inverse person marking**.

chart parser /tʃɑːt/ *n.* A parser that uses a particular data structure, a 'chart', to record the current state of the parse, including particularly its successful attempts at parsing subconstituents of the string it is working on. This can greatly reduce the time spent in backtracking. Chart parsers are at present the most widely employed type of parser in natural-language processing.

checking /ˈtʃekɪŋ/ *n.* Any procedure for determining whether some category is legal, in particular, for determining whether it is identical to, or at least consistent with, another category. Checking procedures are essential in frameworks employing **unification**; that used in LFG is particularly powerful, and is responsible for much of the formal and computational complexity of that framework (Berwick 1984).

Chinese box /ˌtʃaɪniːz ˈbɒks/ *n*. A rarely used graphical device for representing the constituent structure of a sentence, equivalent to an unlabelled **bracketing**. Example:

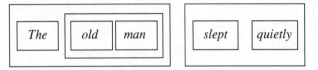

chômeur /ʃəʊˈmɜː/ *n*. In RG and Arc Pair Grammar, a noun phrase which represents an underlying subject or object but which appears on the surface as an oblique NP in a peripheral position, such as the agent phrase in a passive construction. An NP which is a chômeur is said to be **en chômage** /ɑːn ʃəʊˈmɑːʒ/ (French: 'unemployed person'). Perlmutter and Postal (unpublished work); Chung (1976).

Chomsky-adjunction /ˈtʃɒmski/ *n*. In TG, a type of movement rule in which the moving category is attached under a node which was apparently not present before the movement and which is identical to another node, previously present, which now becomes its daughter. Here is an abstract example, in which the moving node E is Chomsky-adjoined to the node C:

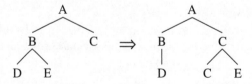

Chomsky-adjunction is the only type of adjunction recognized in GB, where it is usually called simply 'adjunction'.

Chomsky Hierarchy *n*. A hierarchy of classes of formal grammars ranked according to their **weak generative capacity** (i.e., according to the sets of strings which they can characterize). Chomsky's original formulation (Chomsky 1959) included four classes; from weakest to most powerful, these are **regular grammars**, **context-free grammars**, **context-sensitive grammars** and **unrestricted grammars**. Other classes of grammars have sometimes been defined which fall into intervening positions in this hierarchy, such as **indexed grammars**. Mathematical linguists have often been interested in determining the positions occupied in the hierarchy by well-articulated theories of grammar such as TG, GB, LFG and GPSG; see Partee *et al.* (1990) for some discussion. See also **Peters–Ritchie results**. NOTE: no comparable hierarchy is available, or even possible, for grammars considered in terms of their **strong generative capacity** (Manaster-Ramer 1987b).

Chomsky normal form /tʃɒmski nɔːməl 'fɔːm/ *n.* The form of a **context-free grammar** in which every rule is either of the form A → BC or of the form A → *a*, where A, B and C are non-terminals and *a* is a terminal. For every context-free grammar there is a weakly equivalent grammar in this form. Chomsky (1959).

Church's thesis /'tʃɜːtʃɪz ˌθiːsɪs/ *n.* (also **Church–Turing Thesis**) The conjecture that every possible **algorithm** is equivalent to some **Turing machine**. The linguistic version of this is that the class of **unrestricted grammars** is weakly equivalent to the class of Turing machines. This conjecture, proposed by the logician Alonzo Church and the mathematician Alan Turing, has never been proved, and indeed cannot be proved until a fully explicit characterization of the notion of an algorithm is obtained, but it is universally believed to be true.

circumfix /'sɜːkəmfɪks/ *n.* An affix which is realized as a combination of a prefix and a suffix, such as Tigrinya *bi-* . . . *-gize* 'at the time when' or the Chukchi 'recessive' *e-* . . . *-ke*, the latter illustrated in *e-tejkev-ke it-ek* 'not to fight'; cf. *tejkev-ek* 'to fight'.

circumposition /ˌsɜːkəmpə'zɪʃn̩/ *n.* A combination of a preposition and a postposition functioning together as a single adposition, such as Mandarin *dào* . . . *lǐ* 'into', illustrated in *Wǒ bǎ shuǐ dào dào guòn lǐ* I Acc water pour to can in 'I pour water into the can'.

circumstantial /ˌsɜːkəm'stænʃl̩/ *n.* or *adj.* 1. A construction found in certain languages in which an underlying indirect or oblique object appears as the surface subject, the verb often being overtly marked to show the underlying semantic role of its subject. Languages with circumstantials may have several different ones, one for each underlying role which can appear as surface subject. Circumstantials form part of the **voice** system in such languages; essentially, they represent an extension of the familiar passive construction, in which an underlying direct object appears as surface subject. Here is an example from the VOS language Malagasy, illustrating a canonical transitive and a corresponding circumstantial with an instrument as subject (Keenan 1976b):

> manasa lamba amin'ity savony ity Rasoa
> wash   clothes with-this soap   this Rasoa
> 'Rasoa is washing clothes with this soap.'

> anasan-dRasoa lamba ity savony ity
> wash-by-Rasoa clothes this soap   this
> 'This soap is being used to wash clothes with by Rasoa.'

2. One of the distinctively inflected verb forms used in such a construction. Cf. **passive**, **applicative**, and see **voice**.

citation form /saɪ'teɪʃn̩ fɔːm/ *n*. That particular form of a lexical item which is used to name it when talking about it as a linguistic object or when entering it in a dictionary. When a lexical item has only a single form, like English *under* or *beautiful*, or when it has one form that shows no overt inflection, like *dog*, *big* or *take*, the choice of citation form is obvious (at least to linguists and lexicographers, though native speakers may prefer an inflected form). When a lexical item exists only as a set of overtly inflected forms, however, one of these must be somewhat arbitrarily chosen as the citation form; linguists and lexicographers (and native speakers) may vary in their choices. One criterion is to choose the form which occurs most frequently or in the widest variety of constructions; another is to choose the morphologically simplest form; a third is to choose the form which is most useful for predicting the remaining forms. These criteria may conflict. Thus, for example, in citing Latin nouns, it is conventional to use the nominative singular, which is always used in subject position, even though the grammatically more specialized genitive singular is generally a better guide to the remaining forms of the noun, as illustrated by *rex* 'king', genitive singular *regis*, whose remaining forms are all constructed on the base *reg-*. Similarly, in citing verbs in Polynesian languages, it is conventional to use the morphologically simpler intransitive form, from which the transitive form is generally impossible to predict, even though from the transitive form the intransitive form can almost always be predicted; see examples under **subtraction**.

CKY algorithm /siːkeɪ'waɪ/ *n*. A standard algorithm for parsing context-free grammars, which runs in cubic time.

classical Transformational Grammar /'klæsɪkl̩/ *n.* A name sometimes given to the **Standard Theory** of Transformational Grammar proposed in Chomsky (1965) and to the work of the following few years which took this book as its basis.

classifier /'klæsɪfaɪə/ *n.* One of a set of specialized grammatical words which, in certain languages, typically or obligatorily form constituents of certain types of noun phrases, especially those containing numerals, the choice of classifier being determined by the semantic characteristics of the head noun. Most often, each lexical noun obligatorily selects a particular classifier, though in some classifier languages a single noun can appear with any of several classifiers, depending on the meaning of the whole noun phrase. Classifiers usually form a closed class with anywhere from about twenty members (as in Malay) to over a hundred (as in Vietnamese), though Tzeltal is reported to have about four hundred. In some cases classifiers can also function as ordinary nouns in the language, taking classifiers of their own when serving as heads of NPs; in other cases the classifiers are entirely specialized grammatical words. The semantic range of a classifier can be very general, like that of Malay *ekor* 'tail', used with all names of non-human animals (as in *dua ekor tikus* 'two rats', literally 'two tail rat'), or it can be highly specific, like that of Malay *kaki* (no independent meaning), reportedly used only for counting long-stemmed flowers. See **noun classification**.

clause /klɔːz/ *n.* Any constituent dominated by the initial symbol S, particularly one which forms part of a larger structure. Clauses are conventionally divided into **main clauses** and **subordinate clauses**. NOTE: in traditional grammar, a clause is regarded as excluding any subordinate clauses embedded in it; in all contemporary work, however, such embedded clauses are considered to form part of the matrix clause.

clause chaining /'tʃeɪnɪŋ/ *n.* A type of sentence structure, observed in certain languages, in which only a single clause (usually the last one) contains an ordinary finite verb, all the other clauses containing instead specialized subordinate verb forms (called 'medial' or 'dependent' forms) usually marked to indicate whether they have the same argument NPs and tense as the finite verb or different ones. Clause chaining is particularly frequent in the Papuan languages of New Guinea; here is an example from Iatmul (Foley 1986):

nkəy-ət   yɨ-kə   waalə klə-laa   yə-nt-əy-an   ntɨ nkət
house-to go-and dog get-and-then come-he-Unreal-if him him-to
vɨ-kɨyə-wɨn
see-Unreal-I
'If he comes after he has gone to the house and got the dog, I'll see
him.'

Here the last verb alone is finite; the penultimate verb is marked to
show a different subject, while the first two verbs consist of bare
stems with relational elements appended and are interpreted as
having the same subject as the immediately following verb. See
Foley (1986) for discussion.

clausemate /ˈklɔːzmeɪt/ *n.* Either of two constituents in a tree
structure related by the property that every S-node that dominates
one of them also dominates the other one. Clausemates are thus
items which appear in the same simple clause; equivalently, they are
items each of which S-commands the other. See **mate relation**.

clausemate condition /kənˈdɪʃn̩/ *n.* Any condition which requires
that two items involved in the statement of some grammatical rule
must be clausemates. In English, for example, a reflexive pronoun
and its antecedent must normally be clausemates.

clause union /ˈjuːnjən/ *n.* The apparent realization on the surface as a
single clause of what consists underlyingly of two separate clauses, one
of them a verb–complement clause. The following examples from
Spanish illustrate this phenomenon, the first showing two clauses on
the surface, the second (arguably) the union of the two clauses:

Quiero mostrártelos.
I-want show-you-them
'I want to show you them.'

Te los   quiero mostrar.
you them I-want show
'I want to show you them.'

The term is particularly associated with RG and Arc Pair Grammar,
though similar analyses have been advocated by linguists working in
other frameworks. See also **clitic climbing**. Aissen (1977).

clear-cases principle /ˈklɪəˌkeɪsɪz/ *n.* The principle that, in
cases in which the well-formedness or lack of it of certain examples
is not obvious to native speakers, the procedure should be to write
the simplest possible grammar for other, clear, cases, and to let the

resulting grammar decide on the status of the questionable examples. This principle was often seen as fundamental in the early days of generative grammar, but it has proved to be less helpful than once hoped, and it is now invoked only infrequently.

cleft sentence /kleft/ *n.* A marked structure in which a focused constituent is extracted from its logical position and often set off with some additional material, including an extra verb. The unmarked sentence *John bought a car yesterday* is related to several possible cleft sentences, such as *It was John who bought a car yesterday*, *It was a car that John bought yesterday* and *It was yesterday that John bought a car*. Cf. **pseudo-cleft sentence**. Jespersen (1937:83).

cline /klaɪn/ *n.* A one-dimensional grammatical continuum resembling a hierarchy except that, instead of consisting of a small finite number of discrete elements, it permits unlimited differentiation. For example, the category **agent** might be regarded as a cline, since some NPs are more obviously agents than others, and the dividing line between agents and non-agents is by no means obvious. The term was coined by Michael Halliday, and is particularly associated with **Systemic Grammar** and its antecedents; most other theories of grammar insist upon rigid either/or membership or non-membership of categories, which is highly convenient if not always realistic. The term **squish** expresses a similar notion.

clipping /'klɪpɪŋ/ *n.* The process by which a word is derived from a longer word of identical meaning by the arbitrary removal of some part of the longer word, illustrated by *bus* from *omnibus*, *phone* from *telephone*, *gym* from *gymnasium*, *porn* from *pornography*, *mike* from *microphone*, *mimeo* from *mimeograph* and *bi* from *bisexual*. Sometimes the term is extended to cases like *Havana* (from *Havana cigar*) and *canary* (from *canary bird*).

clitic /'klɪtɪk/ *n.* An item which exhibits behaviour intermediate between that of a word and that of an affix. Typically, a clitic has the phonological form of a separate word, but cannot be stressed and is obliged to occupy a particular position in the sentence in which it is phonologically bound to an adjoining word, its **host**. Examples of clitics include the English negative *-n't*, as in *couldn't*, the French subject pronouns *je*, *tu*, etc., which are bound to a following finite verb (as in *je vais* 'I'm going'), and Basque *be* and Turkish *de*, both meaning 'also', which are bound to the preceding word (as in *zu be*, *siz de* 'you too'). Clitics are sometimes divided into **proclitics**, which are bound to a following host (like *je*), and **enclitics**, which are bound to a preceding host (like *-n't*, *be* and *de*). Clitics may form clusters, as in French *je te vois* 'I see you', in which both the subject pronoun *je* 'I' and the object pronoun *te* 'you' are bound to the following verb. There is a widespread tendency for clitics to occur obligatorily in the second position in a sentence, known as **Wackernagel's position**; the statement that clitics tend to do this is known as **Wackernagel's Law** (after Wackernagel (1892), who first made the observation). See Sadock (1991) for an excellent brief review of the properties of clitics and of the analytical problems they give rise to. Nida (1946); Ancient Greek: 'leaning'.

clitic climbing /ˈklaɪmɪŋ/ *n*. The phenomenon in which a clitic appears overtly in a higher clause, even though it is logically a constituent of a lower clause. The use of the term 'clitic climbing' implies an analysis in which the clauses in question are regarded as remaining distinct, with one being embedded under the other. Cf. the discussion under **clause union**, and see the Spanish example there. Aissen (1977).

clitic doubling /ˈdʌblɪŋ/ *n*. The phenomenon in which a sentence contains a clitic whose reference is identical to that of a full noun phrase in the same sentence. Clitic doubling is frequent and even obligatory in some languages, such as Spanish: *Le di un anillo a María* 'I gave Maria a ring', literally 'to-her I-gave a ring to Maria'; *Eso no me lo negarás* 'You won't deny me that', literally 'that not me it you-will-deny'; *Te lo darán a ti* 'They'll give it to *you*', literally 'you it they-will-give to you'.

closed class /ˈkləʊzd klɑːs/ *n*. A **lexical category**, typically with a small membership, to which new members are added only rarely and with difficulty. In English, such categories as Preposition, Determiner, Conjunction and Degree Modifier are closed classes; in some other languages, Adjective is also a closed class (Dixon 1977a). Cf. **open class**.

closed function /ˈfʌŋkʃn̩/ *n*. In LFG, a complement or adjunct which requires no control by an NP outside it: [*With three regulars injured,*] *Surrey are underdogs*; *She announced* [*that dinner was ready*]. Cf. **open function**.

closure /ˈkləʊʒə/ *n*. A particular property which may be exhibited by a formal system with respect to some operation. The system is said to be closed under that operation if the application of the operation to any objects in the set defined by the system always results in another object in the set. See Partee *et al.* (1990) for a summary of the closure properties of classes of formal languages. See also **finite closure**.

CNPC See **Complex NP Constraint**.

cognate object /ˈkɒgneɪt/ *n.* A direct object whose semantic content is more or less identical to that of the verb which governs it. The direct objects in the following examples are cognate objects: *I dreamed a dream last night*; *She sang a song*; *I'm thinking terrible thoughts*.

cognitive grammar /ˈkɒgnɪtɪv/ *n.* Any approach to grammatical description which is based on, or purports to be based on, our understanding of cognitive processing in the human brain. The best-known such proposal is that of Langacker (1987, 1991). Langacker's approach is based upon conceptual classification and particularly upon imagery; it maintains that syntax and semantics are inseparable, and seeks an integrated theory of linguistic structure, rejecting the conventional separation of linguistic description into different components; it also rejects a good deal of the formalization typical of most other approaches. An overview of the framework is presented in Langacker (1988).

coindexing /kəʊˈɪndeksɪŋ/ *n.* 1. A notational device for indicating that two NPs have the same referent. The most usual convention is the use of identical subscripts, chosen from the set $i, j, k, \ldots$, on the NPs in question. In the example *After she$_i$ came in, Lisa$_i$ sat down*, *she* and *Lisa* are coindexed to show that they refer to the same individual. 2. In some theories of grammar, notably GB, a formal procedure for attaching such indices, which in these frameworks are regarded as part of the syntactic structure of the sentence.

collapsing /kəˈlæpsɪŋ/ *n.* The combining of two or more rules into a single **rule schema** by the use of some **abbreviatory convention**. *V.* **collapse** /kəˈlæps/.

collective noun /kəˈlektɪv/ *n.* A noun whose meaning is a group of individuals: *committee*, *government*, *class*. Collective nouns in British English are notable for their ability when singular to take either singular or plural verb agreement: *The committee has made a decision* or *The committee have made a decision*. In some other languages, collective nouns exhibit a distinctive morphology.

collocational restriction /kɒləˈkeɪʃənl rɪˌstrɪkʃn̩/ *n.* A **selectional restriction**, particularly one which is unusually idiosyncratic or language-specific: *grill* (US *broil*) collocates with *meat* but not with *bread*, while the reverse is true for *toast*. Firth (1951).

combining form /kəmˈbaɪnɪŋ fɔːm/ *n.* 1. A bound form of a lexical stem which is used in word formation; e.g., Basque *gizon* 'man' has the combining form *giza-* in such formations as *gizajo* 'poor fellow' (suffix *-jo*) and *giza–sorgin* 'sorcerer' (*sorgin* 'witch'). 2. A bound form, usually of Greek or Latin origin, which in word formation behaves as an affix in some respects but not in others: *astro-*, *bio-*, *electro-*, *-crat*, *-phile* and *-phobia*. The difficulty with regarding such forms strictly as affixes is that words can be formed consisting entirely of such combining forms, such as *biocrat* and *electrophile*; if these forms are affixes, then such words contain no root. See Bauer (1983) for discussion.

comitative /ˈkɒmɪtətɪv/ *n.* or *adj.* 1. A case form typically indicating an individual in whose company something is done: Basque *gizonarekin* 'with the man' (*gizona* 'the man'). 2. A derived form of an intrinsically intransitive verb in which an underlying comitative (sense 1) relation is added to the valency of that verb, which then functions as a transitive: Dyirbal *ninay* 'sit', *ninamal* 'sit with'.

command /kəˈmɑːnd/ *n.* 1. The original and still widely used name for **S-command**. 2. A generic term for any **command relation**. 3. One of the **sentence types** of traditional grammar, most typically expressing an order: *Put that vase down!* See **imperative**.

command domain *n.* (of a node A) The set of all the nodes in the tree to which A bears one of the **command relations**.

commander /kəˈmɑːndə/ *n.* A node which bears a **command relation** to another node.

command relation /rɪˈleɪʃn̩/ *n.* Any of various relations which may hold between two nodes in a tree. A command relation has the general form 'A node A X-commands another node B iff the lowest node of category X which properly dominates A also properly dominates B', with the different values of X determining the various command relations which can be defined; some versions add the further requirement 'and neither A nor B dominates the other', but this is rarely, if ever, crucial. The earliest command relation to be defined was **S-command**; others include **c-command**, **m-command**,

k-command and **IDC-command**. See Barker and Pullum (1990) for a detailed account of command relations. See also **f-command**.

comment /'kɒment/ *n.* (also **rheme**) In some analyses, that part of a sentence which is separate from the **topic** and which typically contains new information. The topic/comment distinction is overtly marked in some languages.

common gender /'kɒmən/ *n.* 1. In a language with **gender**, the property of a noun which can be assigned to more than one gender, with an appropriate and predictable difference of meaning. For example, the French nouns *enfant* 'child', *collègue* 'colleague', *prof* 'teacher' and *hypocrite* 'hypocrite' take the masculine gender when referring to males but the feminine gender when referring to females. Cf. **epicene**. 2. A conventional label for a gender class in certain European languages representing the merger of earlier distinct masculine and feminine genders and contrasting with the historical neuter.

common noun *n.* (also **appellative**) A noun which is not a **proper noun**: *dog*, *beauty*, *arrival*.

Comp /kɒmp/ 1. See **complementizer**. 2. See **complement**. 3. See **COMP node**. 4. See **comparative**.

comparative /kəm'pærətɪv/ *n.* or *adj.* 1. A construction in which some entity is characterized as possessing some property to a greater or lesser degree than some other entity. Examples are *Janet is taller than Lisa* and *This book is less interesting than that one*, the second example illustrating the 'comparative of inferiority'. 2. In a language exhibiting three degrees of comparison for adjectives and/or adverbs, an inflected or analytic form of one of these representing the second degree of comparison: *bigger*, *more beautiful*, *more slowly*. Cf. **positive**, **superlative**, **excessive**, **elative** (sense 2).

comparative deletion *n.* The phenomenon in which, in a comparative construction, a gap appears in a position in which a repetition of the compared item might logically have been expected: *Lisa has more teddy bears than I have* e; *Fred is taller than Bill is* e. Compare the absence of a gap in examples like *Lisa has more teddy bears than I have socks*. Cf. **subdeletion**.

comparative subdeletion See **subdeletion**.

competence /'kɒmpɪtəns/ *n.* An abstract idealization of a native speaker's knowledge of the grammar of her/his language. The term is specifically defined to exclude such factors as memory limitations, slips of the tongue, interruptions and processing difficulties resulting from multiple recursion, ambiguity, sheer length or pragmatic implausibility. The descriptions constructed by generative grammarians are usually intended as grammars of competence. Cf. **performance**, **I-language**. Chomsky (1965).

complement /ˈkɒmplɪmənt/ *n*. 1. Any constituent which forms part of the **nucleus** (sense 1) of a category with a lexical head and which is subcategorized for by that lexical head. In the example *Lisa put the book on the table*, the NP *the book* and the locative phrase *on the table* are complements of the verb *put*, and the NP *the table* is a complement of the preposition *on*. In some versions of the X-bar system, a complement is formally defined as a category which is a sister of a lexical category X and a daughter of its one-bar projection X-bar. Cf. **adjunct**, **specifier**. 2. (also **predicate complement**) A traditional label for a category occurring in a predicate which is interpreted as describing or referring to another NP in the sentence. For example, in *Lisa is a translator*, *a translator* is a complement of the subject *Lisa* (a 'subject-complement'), while in *He called me a fool*, *a fool* is a complement of the object *me* (an 'object-complement').

complement clause *n*. A finite or non-finite clause which serves as a **complement** (sense 1) to some lexical item. In the NP *the report that war has broken out*, the clause *that war has broken out* is a complement of the noun *report* (it is a 'noun-complement clause'); in *Lisa told me she would come*, the clause *she would come* is a complement of the verb *told* (it is a 'verb-complement clause'). See Noonan (1985).

complementizer /ˈkɒmplɪmənˌtaɪzə/ *n*. A grammatical formative which serves to mark a complement clause, such as English *that* and *whether* in *Lisa said that she would come* and *I don't know whether she smokes*. Rosenbaum (1967).

Complementizer–Gap Constraint *n*. The constraint, applying in English but not in some other languages, by which an overt complementizer may not immediately precede a gap, as illustrated by **Who do you think that* e *is coming?*, as contrasted with *Who do you think* e *is coming?* The phenomena covered by this constraint are also known as ***that*-trace effects**.

complexity theory /kəm'pleksɪti θɪəri/ *n.* A branch of computational mathematics which investigates the degree of difficulty of classes of problems as expressed in terms of the computational resources required to apply the most efficient algorithms available, and hence the time and space required to solve such problems on a computer. Complexity theory is important in the construction of efficient **parsers**. See Barton *et al.* (1987).

complex NP /'kɒmpleks en'piː/ *n.* A noun phrase containing both a lexical head and a clause attached to that head. The two main types are NPs containing relative clauses, such as *the man who came to dinner*, and those containing noun-complement clauses, such as *the rumour that she's about to resign*. Ross (1967).

Complex NP Constraint *n.* (**CNPC**) An **island constraint** which states that a complex NP is an island: *The guy Gina is going out with is French*, but **Who is the guy* e *is going out with French?* Ross (1967).

complex object *n.* A label occasionally applied to the combination of a direct object with a following object complement, as in *They called their son Jason* and *Lisa made me happy*. Cf. **small clause** (sense 2). Jespersen (1961, II:10).

complex preposition *n.* An item which behaves syntactically just like an ordinary preposition but which has an internal structure consisting of two or more words: *out of*, *in spite of*, *up till*.

complex sentence *n.* A traditional name for a sentence containing one or more subordinate clauses. Cf. **compound sentence**.

complex symbol /'sɪmbl̩/ *n.* A **syntactic category** which consists of a matrix of syntactic features, e.g., [NOUN][BAR 2][PERSON 3] [PLURAL −] (a third-person singular noun phrase). Virtually all contemporary theories of grammar regard syntactic categories as complex symbols, largely as a means of dealing with the phenomenon of **cross-categorization**. Cf. **monad**. Complex symbols were first used by Harman (1963), though Harris (1951) had earlier proposed the idea somewhat inexplicitly; the term was coined by Chomsky (1965).

complex verb See **compound verb**.

COMP node *n.* A node in a tree whose daughter is most usually a complementizer. The COMP node is usually regarded as the daughter of an S-bar and the sister of an S. In GB, this node is considered to have certain special properties and to play a fundamental role in syntax; it is regarded as a lexical category whose maximal projection CP is identified with the category S-bar, and it serves as a **landing site** for WH-Movement.

component /kəm'pəʊnənt/ *n.* Any one of the more-or-less autonomous subsystems postulated in various theories of grammar; a **module**.

composition /ˌkɒmpə'zɪʃn̩/ See **compounding**.

compound /'kɒmpaʊnd/ *n.* A word formed by **compounding**.

compounding /'kɒmpaʊndɪŋ/ *n.* The process of forming a word by combining two or more existing words: *newspaper*, *paper-thin*, *babysit*, *video game*. See **bahuvrihi**, **endocentric compound**.

compound sentence *n.* A traditional name for a sentence consisting of two or more main clauses, either combined in an overt coordinate construction with a conjunction, or juxtaposed asyndetically. Cf. **complex sentence**.

compound verb *n.* (also **complex verb**) A verb formed from two elements, one being a simple lexical verb and the other being another lexical item such as a noun or a preposition. Examples: English phrasal verbs like *take off*, *make up*; Latin prepositional compounds like *abire* 'go away' (*ab* 'away from' plus *ire* 'go'); Basque nominal compounds like *amets egin* 'dream' (*amets* 'dream' plus *egin* 'do'). Certain English sequences that might not appear to be constituents behave like compound verbs under passivization, such as *speak of*: *We spoke of her in admiring terms*; *She was spoken of in admiring terms*.

computational complexity /ˌkɒmpjʊ'teɪʃənl̩/ *n.* Of a problem or a class of problems, the degree of difficulty involved in obtaining a solution, as expressed in terms of demand on computational resources (time, memory space, etc.). Cf. **formal complexity**.

computational linguistics *n.* 1. (formerly, and still occasionally) A very broad label covering virtually any activity involving computers and natural language, such as machine translation of natural-language texts, computer searching of texts or the preparation of concordances for literary works by computer. Now usually called 'literary and linguistic computing'. 2. (more usually today) A synonym for **natural-language processing**.

concatenation /kən̩ˌkætə'neɪʃn̩/ *n.* In certain approaches to grammatical description in which sentences are regarded primarily as strings, the formal operation by which two strings are linked together in linear sequence to form a longer string.

conceptual distance /kən,septʃʊəl ˈdɪstəns/ *n.* A very general abstract conception of the degree of 'tightness' holding between two elements which are bound in a form or construction. For example, **inalienable possession** is held to express a smaller degree of conceptual distance than **alienable possession**, and **aspect** is often held to be conceptually closer to a verb or proposition than **tense**. See also **iconicity**. Haiman (1985).

concessive clause /kənˈsesɪv/ *n.* A type of **adverbial clause** which carries the implication that the proposition it contains might have been expected to exclude the proposition expressed in the main clause but in fact does not. Concessive clauses in English are typically introduced by such subordinators as *although, though, even though*: *Although it had been raining heavily for days, the cricket pitch was in good condition.*

conclusive /kənˈkluːsɪv/ *n.* or *adj.* (also **egressive**) An aspectual form, explicitly marked in some languages, expressing the notion 'to finish doing'. An example is the Japanese *-te shimau* construction, illustrated in *Ikeda-san wa sono hon o yonde shimatta* Ikeda-Mr Topic that book Acc read-*te shimau*-Past 'Mr Ikeda has finished reading that book'. Dahl (1985).

concord /ˈkɒŋkɔːd/ See **agreement**.

concrete noun /kɒŋˈkriːt/ *n.* A noun whose meaning is perceived as a physical entity: *dog, tree, elbow, wine, mountain*. Cf. **abstract noun**.

conditional /kənˈdɪʃənl̩/ *n.* or *adj.* A conventional name for certain verb forms occurring in some languages, notably Romance languages, which typically express some notion of remoteness, supposition, approximation or implied condition. Semantically, the conditional is really a mood, but formally it behaves more like part of the tense system. The conditional is usually formally distinct from the **subjunctive** in languages in which the label is used, though the uses of the two sets of forms may overlap. Here are some examples from Spanish, in each of which the verb form ending in *-ía* is a conditional: *Sería interesante* 'It would be interesting'; *Tendría unos treinta años* 'He must have been about thirty'; *Dijo que lo haría luego* 'He said he'd do it later'.

conditional clause *n.* A type of **adverbial clause** which expresses a condition upon whose fulfilment the proposition expressed in the main clause depends. Conditional clauses in English are usually marked by the subordinator *if*. An example is the first clause in *If it rains, we'll have to postpone the match*.

conditional sentence *n.* A sentence consisting of two clauses, one of which (the **protasis** or **antecedent**) expresses a condition whose fulfilment or non-fulfilment is relevant to the degree of reality assigned to the other (the **apodosis** or **consequent**). Conditional sentences are often divided into two types: 'open' conditionals, in which the fulfilment of the condition is seen as a realistic possibility, and 'remote' or 'counterfactual' conditionals, in which the fulfilment of the condition is seen as impossible, contrary to fact or at least unlikely. Examples of open conditionals: *If you buy the wine, I'll make dinner*; *If she caught the 8.00 train, she must have been in London before noon*. Examples of counterfactual conditionals: *If I spoke better French, I could get a job in Paris*; *If Grant had been put in command earlier, the Civil War might have ended sooner*. See Palmer (1986) for discussion.

conditioning /kən'dɪʃənɪŋ/ *n.* The phenomenon in which the variation in form of a morpheme exhibiting **allomorphy** is determined in a more or less regular manner by its environment. For example, the English plural morpheme has three regular alternants [s]/[z]/[iz], the choice being conditioned by the nature of the preceding segment: *cats* [s], *dogs* [z], *foxes* [iz]; the Spanish word for 'and' has the form *y* in most circumstances (*Miguel y Pedro*), but the form *e* if the following word begins with the vowel [i] (*Miguel e Ignacio*); the Basque first-person singular agreement marker in verbs has the form *-da* if anything follows it in the same word, but *-t* otherwise (*dakit* 'I know', *dakidan* 'which I know').

configurational language /kən,fɪgjʊ'reɪʃən̩l/ *n.* A language in which sentences typically have a **configurational structure**; such languages are usually characterized by fairly rigid word order and by the infrequency of **discontinuous constituents**. English is usually considered a paradigm case of a configurational language. Cf. **nonconfigurational language**.

configurational structure *n.* A hierarchical syntactic structure of the familiar kind, in which each constituent typically consists of some smaller constituents, and the tree structure exhibits considerable downward branching. *Abstr.* *n.* **configurationality** /kənˌfɪgjʊreɪʃə'nælɪti/. Cf. **non-configurational**.

conjoining /kən'dʒɔɪnɪŋ/ *n.* The phenomenon by which two or more constituents are combined in a **coordinate structure**. *V.* **conjoin** /kən'dʒɔɪn/. Cf. **embedding**.

conjugation /kɒndʒʊ'geɪʃn̩/ *n.* 1. The inflection of (particularly finite) verbs. 2. (of a particular lexical verb) The complete paradigm of inflected forms which the verb can assume. 3. (of a particular language) One of the several classes into which verbs may be divided by their inflectional behaviour, such as the traditional four conjugations of Latin verbs.

conjunct /'kɒndʒʌŋkt/ *n.* Any one of the constituents which are conjoined in a **coordinate structure**: in the coordinate NP *Chomsky and his students*, both *Chomsky* and *his students* are conjuncts.

conjunct doubling /'dʌblɪŋ/ *n.* The phenomenon by which one conjunct of a coordinate structure is expressed twice, once by itself and again within another conjunct. An example is Basque *Lisa ta biok joan gara* 'Lisa and I went', literally 'Lisa and both-of-us we-went'. Cf. **conjunct union**. R. L. Trask (unpublished work).

conjunction /kən'dʒʌŋkʃn̩/ *n.* 1. A closed lexical category, or a lexical item belonging to this category, whose members serve to construct coordinate structures, such as *and*, *or* and *but* in English. 2. In traditional grammar, a much larger category consisting of the modern categories Conjunction, Complementizer and Subordinator. This traditional category is no longer recognized in linguistics, but it is still used in many reputable dictionaries and textbooks. 3. See **coordinate structure**.

conjunction reduction /rɪ'dʌkʃn̩/ *n.* In some derivational theories of grammar, the putative process by which conjoined sentences which are identical apart from one constituent in each are reduced to a coordination of the two constituents which distinguish them. In such a view, an example like *Tom washed and dried the dishes* is derived from an underlying *Tom washed the dishes and Tom dried the dishes*, while *Tom washed the dishes and mopped the floor* is derived from *Tom washed the dishes and Tom mopped the floor*. This once-popular analysis cannot cope with such coordinations as *Tom and Bill are brothers*, and it enjoys little support today.

conjunct union /'juːnjən/ *n.* The phenomenon by which one conjunct of an underlying coordinate structure is suppressed on the surface, being realized only by an agreement morph. An example is Turkish *Hasanla gittik* Hasan-with we-went 'Hasan and I went'. Cf. **conjunct doubling**. Aissen (1987).

consequent /'kɒnsɪkwent/ See **apodosis**.

constant growth property /ˌkɒnstənt 'grəʊθ prɒpəti/ *n.* The property of a formal language in which, if all the sentences of the language are listed in order of increasing length, no two successive sentences differ in length by more than a constant k. Natural languages appear to have this property. Joshi (1983).

constituency test /kən'stɪtʃʊənsi/ *n.* Any of various criteria which have been proposed for identifying constituents in sentences. Among the criteria often advanced are the following: only a constituent can be a conjunct in a coordinate structure; only a constituent can be fronted; only a constituent can undergo certain types of ellipsis; only a constituent can serve as a fragment; only a constituent can serve as the antecedent of a pro-form; only a constituent can be clefted; a constituent cannot be interrupted by a parenthetical. No such test is infallible, but their combined weight often at least serves to rule out some analyses. See Radford (1988) or Trask (1991) for discussion and illustration of some of these tests.

constituent /kən'stɪtʃʊənt/ *n.* Any part of a sentence which is regarded as forming a distinct syntactic unit within the overall structure of the sentence, on the ground that it behaves as a unit with respect to certain criteria, such as displacement, coordination, ellipsis and the possibility of its serving as antecedent to a pro-form. In a tree diagram, a constituent is represented as a branch dominated by a single node. Usually only a continuous sequence can qualify as a constituent, but some approaches permit the recognition of **discontinuous constituents**. *Abstr. n.* **constituency**.

constituent structure *n.* (also **phrase structure**) A type of hierarchical structure which, in most theories of grammar, is posited for most or all sentences in most or all languages. In a constituent structure analysis, a sentence is assumed to consist of a small number of units (each a continuous sequence) called its **(immediate) constituents**, each of which also consists of a few still smaller constituents, each of which in turn also consists of even smaller constituents, and so on, until the minimal syntactic units (words or morphemes) are reached. This kind of structure is most readily displayed in a **tree** of the familiar sort. The notion of syntactic structure as constituent structure was first explicitly proposed by Bloomfield (1933); it has been one of the central ideas in American linguistics ever since, and it is arguably the principal respect in which the grammatical analyses of the American structuralists were taken over more or less intact by Chomsky and the generativists who followed him. The putative universality of constituent structure has, however, been denied in at least two important ways. First, some linguists, while accepting the reality of constituent structure in general, maintain that certain languages (the so-called **non-configurational languages** or **W-star languages**) are distinguished by the complete (or nearly complete) absence of constituent structure; some would further hold that certain constructions may be non-configurational even in languages in which configurationality (constituent structure) is the norm. Second, and more radically, certain theories of grammar, notably those characterized as **dependency grammars**, decline to recognize the existence of constituent structure at all, preferring instead to posit a quite different kind of syntactic organization. See **immediate constituent analysis**, **tree**.

constraint /kən'streɪnt/ *n.* Any formal limitation on the range of application of some grammatical rule or rules, particularly one which refers crucially to the possible inputs to such rules. Many proposed constraints are more or less overtly labelled as such, like the **island constraints** of Ross (1967) or the **Subjacency Condition** of GB, but many other grammatical principles not so obviously named are really constraints on rules as well, such as the **Head Feature Convention**. The formulation of constraints on rules has been increasingly regarded as important in recent years; within GB, it is typically seen as more important than the formulation of the rules themselves. Cf. **filter**.

construal, rule of /kən'struːəl/ *n.* In GB, any rule which relates an **anaphor** (sense 2) to its antecedent. Ken Hale (unpublished work).

construction /kən'strʌkʃn̩/ *n.* Any grammatical structure which occurs systematically in some language, or any particular instance of it. See Zwicky (1987) for a discussion of constructions in recent grammatical theory.

constructional alternation /kən'strʌkʃənl̩/ *n.* The use of two different constructions for the same grammatical purpose. An example is the use of two competing possessive constructions in

Amharic: *bet-e* 'house-my' and *yä-na bet* 'of-me house', both meaning 'my house'.

Constructional Grammar *n.* An approach to grammatical characterization proposed by Hockett (1961), essentially an elaboration of
immediate constituent analysis.

constructional   homonymity /hɒmə'nɪmɪti/   See   **structural
ambiguity**.

constructive grammar /kən'strʌktɪv/ *n.* Any grammar which can
be represented in the form of an **algorithm** capable of determining
which sentences are in the language defined by the grammar; a
generative grammar (sense 1).

construct state /'kɒnstrʌkt steɪt/ *n.* In certain languages, notably
Semitic languages, an overtly inflected form which is assumed by a
noun to indicate that it is possessed or modified by another noun or
NP which itself may exhibit no overt inflection. For example, in
Hebrew, 'the scarf' is *ha-tsaʿif* and 'the girl' is *ha-yalda*, but 'the
girl's scarf' is *tsəʾif ha-yalda*, in which *tsaʿif* 'scarf' appears in its
construct state *tsəʾif* to indicate that it is possessed. Cf. **izafet**.

construe /kən'struː/ *vt.* 1. To analyse the grammatical structure of;
to parse. 2. **to be construed with**: To form part of a grammatical
structure with. For example, in both *She turned on the light* and *She
turned the light on*, the particle *on* must be construed with the verb
turned.

consuetudinal /kɒnswɪ'tjuːdɪnl̩/ See **habitual**.

context /'kɒntekst/ *n.* 1. The immediate linguistic environment of
some item, often the immediately preceding and/or following items
in the linear order of elements within a sentence, but sometimes
including other items which are further away, when these are
regarded as being in some way linked with it. 2. The linguistic or
extralinguistic situation in which an utterance is made.

context-free grammar /kɒntekst'friː/ *n.* (**CFG**) (more fully,
context-free phrase structure grammar, or **CF-PSG**) (also **type 2
grammar**) A formal grammar in which all of the rules which directly
license local subtrees are **context-free rules**. Among current theories of grammar, GPSG represents the principal attempt at constructing context-free grammars which are adequate for the
characterization of the grammars of natural languages.

context-free language *n.* (**CFL**) 1. A formal language generated by a **context-free grammar**. If null productions are uniformly excluded or permitted, the set of context-free languages is a proper subset of the **context-sensitive languages**. 2. A natural language whose grammar can be adequately represented by such a formal grammar. At present it appears that most, but not all, natural languages are so representable, at least in terms of **weak generative capacity**, the ones which are not being those few exhibiting certain types of **cross-serial dependencies** or of **reduplication**.

context-freeness /kɒntekst'friːnəs/ *n.* The property of a natural language whose grammar can be adequately represented as a **context-free grammar**. There has long been a debate over whether natural languages exhibit context-freeness; given the difficulty of obtaining results about strong generative capacity, this debate has inevitably centred on weak generative capacity. Dismissals of CFGs in the early days of generative grammar were too hasty, a fact brought out particularly by Harman (1963). Postal (1964a) presented a famous argument that Mohawk was not CF, and the next two decades saw further arguments published; however, Pullum and Gazdar (1982) successfully demolished all arguments for non-context-freeness published up to that date, and Pullum (1984b) demolished two further arguments. Bresnan *et al.* (1982) succeeded in showing that the cross-serial dependencies in Dutch apparently precluded any linguistically satisfying CF-analysis, but the Dutch data could still be weakly generated by a CFG. Soon after, however, things changed: Huybregts (1984) converted the Dutch argument into an apparently valid form; Culy (1985) presented an apparently valid demonstration that the African language Bambara was not even weakly CF; and Shieber (1985) published his celebrated account of the cross-serial dependencies of Swiss German, which is now regarded as the definitive case of a language which cannot be even weakly generated by a CFG (Shieber's argument contains a minor flaw, noted and repaired by Manaster-Ramer (1988)). A handful of languages are now known which are not even weakly CF, but, as Gazdar and Pullum (1985) stress, the overwhelming majority of constructions in all natural languages can be elegantly and efficiently analysed in terms of CFGs. See Pullum (1986a, 1987) for an account of the history of this issue.

context-free phrase structure grammar See **context-free grammar**.

context-free rule *n.* (**CF-rule**) (more fully, **context-free phrase structure rule**, or **CF-PS-rule**) 1. A **rewrite rule** which expands exactly one category into an ordered string of zero or more categories and for the application of which no environment is specified. Examples are the rules NP → Pron, S → NP VP, VP → V NP NP and NP → *e*. 2. In the writings of Noam Chomsky and his associates, a rewrite rule which expands exactly one category into an ordered string of one or more categories and for the application of which no environment is specified. This definition differs from the previous one in excluding null productions like the rule NP → *e*. Cf. **context-sensitive rule**, **immediate-dominance rule**. NOTE: Chomsky's definition has the benefit of historical priority, but it is clear that the practice of the American structuralists which Chomsky was proposing to formalize actually requires the first definition; in any case, the first definition is now almost universally preferred by those linguists who take phrase structure rules seriously, following Bar-Hillel *et al.* (1961). See Manaster-Ramer and Kac (1990) for discussion.

context-sensitive grammar /ˌkɒntekst ˈsensɪtɪv/ *n.* (**CSG**) (more fully, **context-sensitive phrase structure grammar**, or **CS-PSG**) (also **type 1 grammar**) A formal grammar in which all of the rules which directly license local subtrees have the form of either **context-sensitive** or **context-free rules**. In some conceptions, no CSG is allowed to contain any null productions.

context-sensitive language *n.* (**CSL**) 1. A formal language generated by a **context-sensitive grammar**. 2. A natural language whose grammar can be adequately represented by such a grammar. At present it appears that the grammars of natural languages do not require anything like the full power of context-sensitive grammars, at least as far as **weak generative capacity** is concerned. However, since at least some natural languages are clearly not context-free, there is some interest in defining classes of languages which are 'mildly context-sensitive', that is, which are generated by grammars with only a small amount of context-sensitivity. Two attempts at this are represented by **indexed grammars** and **tree-adjoining grammars**.

context-sensitive rule *n.* (**CS-rule**) (more fully, **context-sensitive phrase structure rule**, or **CS-PS-rule**) A **rewrite rule** which expands exactly one category into an ordered string of one or more categories and for the application of which some environment is specified. An abstract example is the rule A → B C / _____ D, meaning that a category A which is immediately followed by the category D can be expanded into the string B C; this rule cannot be applied to instances of A not immediately followed by D. Such rules are little used in syntax, but the mechanism typically used for lexical insertion in TG and GB is equivalent to the use of CS-rules; for example, the subcategorization frame for the verb *give* in these frameworks could be represented as V → *give/* _____ NP NP, meaning that *give* can be inserted into a V node immediately followed by two NPs. The ban on null productions is relaxed in some conceptions. The interpretation of CS-rules as local subtrees requires some care; see **node admissibility condition**, and see the discussion in Partee *et al.* (1990). Cf. **context-free rule**.

continuous /kən'tɪnjʊəs/ 1. *n.* or *adj.* A synonym for **progressive** (but see the comments under that entry). 2. *adj.* Denoting a constituent or other grouping which is realized on the surface as a single uninterrupted sequence.

contraction /kən'trækʃn̩/ *n.* A single phonological word representing a sequence of two or more separate word forms: *won't* for *will not*, *she's* for *she is* or *she has* and *he'd've* for *he would have*.

control /kən'trəʊl/ *n.* 1. The phenomenon by which a VP complement with no overt subject is interpreted semantically as having some NP as subject, either another NP appearing overtly in the sentence or an arbitrary (unspecified) NP. Control phenomena are particularly important in GB, in which a separate module (**Control Theory**) is posited to deal with them, and in which the non-overt subject is conventionally represented by a distinct empty category called PRO. Examples: *John promised Mary* [PRO *to go*], in which PRO is controlled by the subject *John* ('subject-control'), *John persuaded Mary* [PRO *to go*], in which PRO is controlled by the object *Mary* ('object-control') and [PRO *Smoking*] *causes cancer*, in which PRO exhibits arbitrary control. The first two examples exhibit 'obligatory control', called **functional control** in LFG; arbitrary control and 'optional control' (as in *She thinks* [PRO *going topless*] *is fun*) are called **anaphoric control** in LFG. 2. The phenomenon by which one category in a sentence requires **agreement** on another category.

Control Agreement Principle *n.* (**CAP**) A proposed universal principle governing the distribution of agreement phenomena in sentences. The principle may be briefly and informally stated as follows: functors may agree with nominal arguments. The notion of a 'functor' required here is somewhat technical; see Gazdar *et al.*

(1985) for a formalization within the GPSG framework. Keenan (1974).

controller /kən'trəʊlə/ *n* 1. The NP which is interpreted as the subject of a non-finite verb phrase in a **control structure**. See the discussion under **control** (sense 1). 2. See **governor** (sense 3).

control structure *n*. A structure involving a non-finite VP and a **control verb**, such as *I want Lisa to do it* or *Lisa promised to come*.

Control Theory *n*. The module in GB which deals with **control** (sense 1) phenomena. At present this is the least well-articulated module in the framework.

control verb *n*. (also **Equi verb**, **catenative verb**) A verb which takes a following VP complement, such as *want*, *promise* or *persuade*. In GB, the VP complement is assumed to have a non-overt subject NP called PRO, whose interpretation is determined by the principles of **Control Theory**. Control verbs are conventionally divided into 'subject-control verbs' like *promise*, whose subject is interpreted as the subject of the following VP, and 'object-control verbs' like *persuade*, whose object is interpreted as the subject of the following VP.

conversion /kən'vɜːʒn̩/ See **zero-derivation**.

cooccurrence restriction /kəʊə'kʌrəns rɪˌstrɪkʃn̩/ *n*. A very general label for any kind of limitation on the simultaneous occurrence in a syntactic structure of two elements, with reference either to their presence or absence or to their forms. Some of the principal classes of cooccurrence restrictions are **subcategorization**, **agreement** and **government**.

coordinate structure /kəʊ'ɔːdɪnət/ *n*. (also **conjunction**) A syntactic structure in which two or more constituents are joined ('conjoined') in such a way that each of them has an equal claim to be considered a head of that structure. In a typical coordinate structure, all of the conjoined constituents (the **conjuncts**) are of the same category, and the whole structure is an instance of the same category; often a **conjunction** (such as *and* or *or*) is present as an overt expression of the coordination. Examples: *Mandela and his followers are angry* (conjoined NPs); *In rugby, you can run with the ball, kick it or pass it* (conjoined VPs); *Napoleon surrendered and the war was over* (conjoined Ss); *Lisa is very graceful and an accomplished skater* (AP exceptionally conjoined with NP).

Coordinate structures are unusual among syntactic structures in a number of respects; many theories of grammar posit special machinery to cope with them. See Payne (1985b).

Coordinate Structure Constraint *n.* (**CSC**) The phenomenon by which a coordinate structure is an **island**. More precisely, a dependency of certain sorts may not have one end inside one conjunct of a coordinate structure and the other end outside the coordinate structure. For example, a WH-dependency may not do so: **What did Lisa order e and Larry ordered chicken Kashmir?* **Across-the-board** phenomena constitute a systematic class of exceptions to the CSC. Ross (1967).

coordinating conjunction /kəʊˈɔːdɪneɪtɪŋ/ *n.* The traditional term for what is now usually called simply a **conjunction** (sense 1).

coordination /kəʊˌɔːdɪˈneɪʃn̩/ *n.* The linking of two or more elements as conjuncts in a **coordinate structure**.

copula /ˈkɒpjʊlə/ *n.* 1. A semantically empty formative, most often a verb, which in some languages serves to link a subject NP to a predicate which either is identified with the subject or characterizes the subject; an example is English *be* in *Lisa is a translator* and *She is my closest friend*. 2. Sometimes, by extension, a **quasi-copula**. *Adj.* **copular** or **copulative**.

copular sentence /ˈkɒpjʊlə/ *n.* A sentence consisting of a noun phrase combined with a predicate by means of a **copula**, such as *Lisa is a translator*.

copulative compound /ˈkɒpjʊlətɪv/ See **dvandva**.

copying language /ˈkɒpiɪŋ/ *n.* A formal language all of whose sentences have the form WW, where W is any string. Copying languages cannot, in general, be weakly generated by context-free grammars, a fact which has significant consequences for the analysis of **reduplication**; see, for example, Culy (1985).

core /kɔː/ *n.* 1. In some functional analyses of clause structure, that part of a clause represented by the arguments required by the valency of the verb, the subcategorized arguments plus the subject. See **layering** (sense 1). 2. See **core grammar**.

coreference /kəʊˈrefrəns/ *n.* The relation which obtains between two NPs (usually two NPs in a single sentence) both of which are interpreted as referring to the same extralinguistic entity. In linguistic representations, coreference is conventionally denoted by **coindexing**: *Lisa$_i$ said she$_i$ would come*. *Adj.* **coreferential** /ˌkəʊrefəˈrenʃl̩/.

core grammar *n.* In GB, an area of the theory of grammar, or a part of a particular grammar, delimited by some specific universal principles. The conception of core grammar has changed over the years; most recently, the term has been applied to those aspects of grammar regarded as being innate combined with the values assigned to **parameters** in particular languages. Cf. **marked periphery**. Chomsky (1977a).

Corepresentational Grammar /ˌkəʊreprɪzenˈteɪʃən̩l/ *n.* A theory of grammar proposed by Michael Kac (1975). Much as in LFG, the system provides two distinct and specialized representations of the syntactic structure of a sentence, one showing the ordinary constituent structure, the other showing various types of non-constituent information such as grammatical relations. A brief introduction is given in Kac (1980).

corpus (pl. **corpora**) /ˈkɔːpəs, ˈkɔːpərə/ *n.* A body of linguistic data from a particular language, in the form of recorded utterances or written texts, which is available for analysis.

correlative /kəˈrelətɪv/ *n.* 1. One of a pair of items expressing an **equative** construction, such as English *as . . . as, as many . . . as*. 2. In traditional grammar, a generic term for demonstratives, interrogatives and indefinites, such as *this, here, whence, whoever, everywhere, whenever* and *something*. This second sense is now obsolete.

correlative clause *n.* A relative clause construction in which the relative clause precedes the main clause and both are overtly marked, the relative clause by a WH-item and the main clause by a demonstrative, the whole thus being characterized by a structure along the lines of 'which one . . . that one'. An example from Gujerati:

[*je* dhobii maarii saathe aavyo] *te* DaakTarno bhaaii che
which washerman me with came that doctor's brother is
'The washerman who came with me is the doctor's brother.'

Cf. **adjoined relative clause**. Modification of 'co-relative', Avery Andrews (unpublished work); Downing (1974).

cosubordination /ˌkəʊsəbɔːdɪˈneɪʃn̩/ *n.* Any of various ways of combining clauses which appear to be syntactically intermediate between coordination and subordination. Examples include **clause chaining**, verb serialization (see **serial verb construction**) and the use of **switch-reference** systems. Olson (1981); Foley and Van Valin (1984).

counter-agent /ˈkaʊntərˌeɪdʒənt/ *n*. One of the **deep cases** recognized in some versions of Case Grammar, representing the force or agency against which an action is carried out, such as *the current* in *She swam against the current*.

counterexample /ˈkaʊntərɪɡˌzɑːmpl̩/ *n*. Any datum which, superficially at least, appears to be inconsistent with some proposed grammatical rule or principle, and which might therefore be interpreted as casting doubt on its validity. Chomsky has repeatedly stressed that the mere existence of such a datum does not in itself constitute a counterexample, but rather that only some particular proposed analysis of it can be regarded as a counterexample; this argument is reasonable enough in principle, but many linguists would claim that at least some data are so blatantly problematic that it is not unreasonable to regard them as *prima facie* counterexamples. It should also be pointed out that the dividing line between counterexamples and exceptions (irregularities) is far from clear: no one doubts the validity of the rule which says that English nouns form their plural by adding -*s*, in spite of the existence of a number of exceptions like *man*, *sheep* and *radius*; these are not regarded as counterexamples. Most linguists are comparatively reluctant, however, to admit the existence of mere exceptions to purely syntactic rules or principles.

counterfactual /ˌkaʊntəˈfæktʃʊəl/ *n*. or *adj*. See the discussion under **conditional sentence**.

counting grammar /ˈkaʊntɪŋ/ *n*. A formal grammar which permits the statement of rules and principles involving explicit reference to some number of categories or boundaries greater than one. For example, a statement that some dependency can hold over a maximum of two clause boundaries, or a rule referring to the third daughter of some node, could only be formulated in a counting grammar. The grammars of natural languages seem never to require such statements, and no contemporary theory of grammar explicitly permits them. See Berwick (1987) for some discussion.

count noun /kaʊnt/ *n*. A noun whose meaning is perceived to be a countable entity and which can be freely pluralized: *book*, *day*, *mistake*. Cf. **mass noun**.

CP /siː'piː/ *n*. In GB, the usual abbreviation for the maximal projection of the lexical category Complementizer, identified in that framework with the category S-bar. If the GB framework were ever to be formalized as a generative grammar using the rewrite rule format, CP would presumably be the **initial symbol**. Cf. **IP**.

cranberry morpheme /'krænbri/ *n*. 1. An apparent morpheme of no discernible intrinsic meaning which serves, sometimes in a unique instance, to distinguish meaning; the classic example is the *cran-* of *cranberry*. 2. By extension, a morph, usually of Latin origin, which occurs in a number of apparently related words and appears to be a morpheme but which has no identifiable meaning, such as the *-fer* of *refer*, *prefer*, *confer*, *defer*, *transfer*.

cross-categorial generalization /ˌkrɒskætəˈgɔːriəl/ *n*. A generalization which applies to more than one lexical category or to one-bar or maximal projections of more than one lexical category. For example, both verbs and prepositions in English, but not nouns and adjectives, permit following NP complements which must stand in the objective case. Many versions of the X-bar system attempt to provide for this by decomposing lexical categories into more primitive elements, the most usual such elements being called 'substantive' (or 'nominal') and 'predicative', represented as binary features [N] and [V], respectively (the **Platonistic features**). This decomposition, first proposed by Chomsky in unpublished work in 1974, effectively reduces all syntactic categories to mere subcategories of a single category. It has, however, proved to be one of the less successful aspects of the X-bar system. Cf. **cross-categorization**.

cross-categorization /ˌkrɒskætɪgəraɪˈzeɪʃn̩/ *n*. (also **cross-classification**) The phenomenon by which the syntactic categories which can appear as nodes in trees are simultaneously subject to generalizations which independently cut across them in such a way as to pick out different subclasses. For example, the verb *washing* in *Lisa is washing her car* is simultaneously a transitive verb and an *-ing* participle; it is therefore subject to all generalizations about transitive verbs, whether or not they are *-ing* participles, and also to all generalizations about *-ing* participles, whether or not they are transitive verbs. Cross-categorization phenomena are pervasive in syntax and are the principal motivation for the use of syntactic

features and for the representation of syntactic categories as **complex symbols**. The importance of cross-categorization was first explicitly noted by Bloomfield (1933).

crossed dependency /krɒst/ See **cross-serial dependency**.

crossover phenomena /'krɒsəʊvə fə,nɒmɪnə/ *n. pl.* A superficially diverse set of phenomena of which the following are examples, when these are regarded as constituting a unified set of facts. Observe that *I cut myself* is well-formed, while the corresponding passive **I was cut by myself* is (according to some) ill-formed. Observe also that *Who*ᵢ *said Lisa kissed him*ᵢ*?* is well-formed, while **Who*ᵢ *did he*ᵢ *say Lisa kissed?* is ill-formed. Postal (1971) proposed that these and other facts were examples of a general constraint which he called the **Crossover Constraint**, by which no NP can cross a coreferential NP during the derivation of a sentence (he was, of course, working within the framework of TG, in which just such crossovers would have been involved in the derivation of the ill-formed examples). In GB, most crossover violations (including those above) are excluded automatically by the principles of Binding Theory, though some are not. See **strong crossover**, **weak crossover**.

cross-serial dependency /,krɒs'sɪərɪəl/ *n.* A dependency involving pairs of items exhibiting the following general pattern:

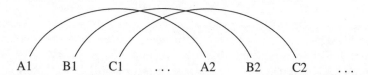

An example is the pattern exhibited in subordinate clauses in Swiss German, in which a sequence of object NPs is followed by a sequence of the verbs governing those NPs in matching order, each NP assuming the case form required by its verb (Shieber 1985):

Jan säit das mer d'chind   em Hans   es huus
Jan says that we the-children-Acc the Hans-Dat the-house-Acc
lönd hälfe aastriiche
let   help paint
'Jan says that we let the children help Hans paint the house.'

Such dependencies are interesting, because it can be proved that unlimited cross-serial dependencies cannot be even weakly generated by a context-free grammar; hence they provide the most striking evidence available that at least some natural languages are not context-free. See Shieber (1985) for discussion. Cf. **nested dependency**.

CSC See **Coordinate Structure Constraint**.

CSG See **context-sensitive grammar**.

CSL See **context-sensitive language**.

CS-PSG See **context-sensitive grammar**.

CS-PS-rule See **context-sensitive rule**.

CS-rule See **context-sensitive rule**.

c-structure /'siː,strʌktʃə/ *n*. In LFG, one of the two structures which together constitute the syntactic representation of a sentence. C-structure is represented as a constituent structure tree of the familiar sort. Cf. **f-structure**.

cumulative exponence /'kjuːmjʊlətɪv/ *n*. In morphology, the systematic realization of two or more grammatical categories by single unanalysable morphs. For example, in the inflection of nouns in Latin and in Russian, the categories case and number are regularly expressed by such morphs, so that the genitive plural, for instance, bears no resemblance either to the genitive singular or to the dative plural. Cf. **overlapping exponence**, **fused exponence**. Matthews (1974).

curly brackets /ˌkɜːli 'brækɪts/ See **braces**.

cycle /'saɪkl̩/ *n*. 1. See **transformational cycle**. 2. Any particular single application of the transformational cycle to a cyclic domain.

cyclic domain /'sɪklɪk/ *n*. Any subtree which is regarded as forming the domain for a single application of the **transformational cycle**. A cyclic domain is always dominated by a **cyclic node**.

cyclic node *n*. Any node in a tree which belongs to one of certain categories whose domains are designated as **cyclic domains** for the application of the **transformational cycle**. Most usually, the nodes S and NP are designated as cyclic nodes, though other suggestions have been made.

D

D See **determiner**.

DAG /dæg/ See **directed acyclic graph**.

dangling participle /'dæŋglɪŋ/ *n.* A **participle** which lacks an NP to which it can refer or which is separated from that NP by other material. Examples are [*Having said that,*] *there's another interpretation* and [*Driving down the highway,*] *a dog leapt out in front of me.* Dangling participles are vigorously condemned by prescriptivists, and are usually regarded as ill-formed by linguists, but they are far from rare in speech.

data /'deɪtə/, rarely /'dætə/ or /'dɑːtə/ *n. pl.* or *n.* 1. Traditionally, and still for most linguists, a corpus of utterances or written texts produced by native speakers, with respect to which a proposed grammatical description should be evaluated. 2. In the view of Noam Chomsky and his associates, the intuitions which native speakers have about their language, particularly about which strings do or do not correspond to well-formed sentences; in this view, accounting for these intuitions is a primary goal of linguistic investigation. The use of such intuitions as data has been severely criticized by many linguists on a number of grounds, most notably on the ground that the intuitions reported by speakers do not always correspond to their observed usage; see Labov (1975) for discussion. NOTE: traditionally, the form **data** is plural, with singular **datum**, but in much contemporary usage, **data** is an invariable mass noun (as in 'This data is interesting'), and the convenient singular **datum** must be replaced by some circumlocution such as 'piece of data'.

dative /'deɪtɪv/ *n.* or *adj.* 1. A case form typically indicating the individual who is the recipient of an action: Basque *neskari* 'to the girl' (*neska* 'the girl') in *Neskari eman diot* 'I gave it to the girl'. Dative forms are frequently also used in a wider sense; see **ethic construction**. 2. Denoting a grammatical pattern in which **direct objects** are distinguished from **indirect objects**, as opposed to **primary objects** from **secondary objects**. Cf. **dechticaetiative**. Sense 2: Blansitt (1984).

dative shift /ʃɪft/ *n.* (also **dative movement**) The phenomenon by which an underlying dative (indirect object) is realized as a direct object, the underlying direct object being realized as some kind of peripheral element. Dative shift is common in English, as illustrated by the pair *I sent the books to Lisa/I sent Lisa the books*, the second form showing dative shift. In languages with richer morphology, dative shift is often explicitly marked by an **applicative** verb form and/or by altered case marking on the two NPs. Occasionally the term 'dative shift' is extended to **applicative** constructions generally.

dative subject construction *n.* (also **affective construction**) A construction occurring in some languages in which an animate NP, usually an Experiencer, appears overtly in the dative (or another oblique) case, while another NP appears in the form usually associated with subjects. An example is the Basque *Joni liburua ahaztu zaio* 'John has forgotten the book', literally 'The book has forgotten to John', where *Jon* 'John' stands in the dative case and *liburua* 'the book' stands in the ordinary subject case. Dative subjects in some languages may exhibit at least some of the typical properties of subjects listed in Keenan (1976a) in spite of their overt oblique marking.

daughter /ˈdɔːtə/ *n.* A particular relationship which may hold between two nodes in a tree. If a node A immediately dominates a distinct node B, then B is a daughter of A. Cf. **mother**, **descendant**.

daughter-adjunction *n.* A type of **adjunction** in which the moving category becomes the daughter of an existing node without becoming the sister of any node. The following abstract example shows the node D being daughter-adjoined to the node C:.

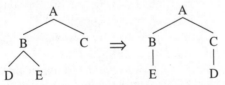

Daughter-adjunction has rarely been used in generative grammar.

Daughter-Dependency Grammar *n.* (**DDG**) A theory of grammar combining conventional constituent structure with dependency relations. Nodes are complex symbols bearing both categorial and dependency features; representations are monostratal, with vertical arcs expressing constituent relations and horizontal arcs expressing dependency relations. DDG was proposed by Richard Hudson (1976); in spite of its obvious appeal, the framework has been little developed, and its author has abandoned it in favour of the purely dependency-based approach **Word Grammar**. See Schachter (1980) for an introduction.

DCFL See **deterministic context-free language**.

DCG See **definite clause grammar**.

DDG See **Daughter-Dependency Grammar**.

dechticaetiative /dektɪˈsiːtiətɪv/ *adj.* Denoting a grammatical pattern in which **primary objects** are distinguished from **secondary objects**, rather than **direct objects** from **indirect objects**. Cf. **dative** (sense 2). Blansitt (1984).

decidability /dɪsaɪdəˈbɪlɪti/ *n.* 1. A property of a formal grammar for which a mechanical procedure exists that will determine in every case whether an arbitrary string is or is not a member of the language defined by the grammar. Almost all classes of formal languages are decidable in this sense, though the **recursively enumerable languages** are not. 2. Any similar property of a formal grammar, or of a class of formal grammars, involving the answer to some question about the language(s) defined by the grammar(s). See Partee *et al.* (1990) for a summary of the decidability properties of formal grammars.

decision procedure /dɪˈsɪʒn̩ prəʊˌsiːdʒə/ *n.* An explicit mechanical procedure for deciding whether some proposed grammar for a corpus of data is in fact the best possible grammar. Cf. **discovery procedure**, **evaluation procedure**. Chomsky (1957).

declarative /dɪˈklærətɪv/ *adj.* (also **indicative**) The mood category associated with the uttering of a statement which the speaker believes to be true. The declarative is the least marked of all the mood categories, and in most languages it is expressed by constructions and verb forms which carry no overt marking of mood, all other distinctions of mood being overtly marked in some way. See Palmer (1986) for discussion.

declension /dɪˈklenʃn̩/ *n.* 1. The inflection of a noun, pronoun, adjective or noun phrase for **case**, in languages exhibiting case distinctions. Such an item is said to **decline** (i.e., inflect for case). 2. A complete set of the case forms of such an item, representing the inflectional behaviour of the class it belongs to. A case language may have only one such class, as in Basque, in which virtually all NPs are inflected identically, or it may have several distinct such classes, as in Latin or Russian. 3. One of the declensional classes of nouns in languages exhibiting several such classes, such as the traditional five declensions of Latin nouns.

deep case /diːp/ *n*. In **Case Grammar**, any one of a set of **semantic roles** which are taken as the fundamental grammatical primitives in terms of which sentences are constructed. The list of deep cases recognized varies considerably from one presentation to another, as do the labels used; a fairly comprehensive list might include Agent, Patient, Theme, Experiencer, Goal, Recipient, Counter-Agent, Source, Path, Instrument, Result, Place, Time and Event. The assignment of particular NPs to particular deep cases is a matter of considerable controversy, and can often seem somewhat arbitrary: in an example like *Lisa filled the bucket with water*, the NP *the bucket* might be variously analysed as a Patient, a Place or a Goal, or perhaps even an Instrument, and similar uncertainty surrounds *water*. Deep cases also play a part in various contemporary theories of grammar, such as in Lexicase, and also in GB, where they are known as **theta roles**.

deep structure /diːp/ *n*. In most versions of **Transformational Grammar**, that representation of the structure of a sentence which is most remote from the surface and which is the structure directly generated by the rules of the **base** (sense 4), the **phrase structure rules** or **categorial rules**, with lexical items inserted. Deep structures serve as input to all the other components of the framework, particularly to the **transformations**. In GB, the equivalent structure is called **D-structure**. In TG, GB and various other **derivational** theories, the same or a similar level of structure is also variously called the **base** structure, the initial structure, the **remote structure** or the **underlying** structure.

default /dɪˈfɔːlt/ *n*. In a formal grammar employing features, a value which is automatically assigned to some feature by the framework whenever no other value is required by some statement in the grammar. The default value of a feature typically represents that value which is most frequent or least marked in the language. For example, the feature [PERSON] is often assigned the default value [3], since the vast majority of noun phrases in all languages are third person; doing this means that only the minority of non-third-person categories need be specifically marked. The use of such default values can greatly reduce the number of specific individual statements which have to be made in the grammar.

defective /dɪ'fektɪv/ *adj.* Denoting a lexical item which lacks some of the grammatical forms typically exhibited by members of its class. In English, for example, the verb *beware* has no finite forms and the modal *must* has no past tense; in Russian, certain verbs lack a first-person singular form; in Basque, the verb *-io-* 'say' has no non-finite forms; in Latin, the noun *vis* 'force' has no genitive or dative case forms, and the noun *natu* 'by birth' has no forms at all apart from the ablative singular.

definite /'defɪnɪt/ *adj.* Denoting a noun phrase which refers to some particular entity or entities and whose reference is seen as clearly established, or clearly establishable from the linguistic or extralinguistic context. Definite NPs are often divided into proper names, such as *Lisa* or *Paris*, and definite descriptions, such as *the new teacher*, *my mother*, *that dog* and *the girl you were talking to*. Cf. **indefinite**.

definite article *n.* A conventional label for a **determiner** most typically (though not necessarily exclusively) used in a noun phrase whose referent is assumed to be readily identifiable by the addressee, such as English *the*. Cf. **indefinite article**.

definite clause grammar *n.* (**DCG**) In computational linguistics, an implementation of a context-free grammar within a declarative system, such as PROLOG. Pereira and Warren (1980).

degree /dɪ'griː/ *n.* (also **grade**) The grammatical category by which adjectives and adverbs vary in form to express the presence of their associated characteristics to a greater or lesser extent, as illustrated by *big/bigger/biggest* and *slowly/more slowly/most slowly*. Further distinctions along the same dimension may be expressed lexically by **degree modifiers**, as in *very big* and *rather slowly*.

degree modifier *n.* (also **intensifier**) A lexical category, or a member of this category, whose members typically function as modifiers of an adjective or adverb and express the degree to which the quality expressed by that item is present. Examples include *very*, *too*, *so*, *rather*, *quite*, *fairly* and *extremely*, as in *very slow*, *too slow*, etc. NOTE: degree modifiers were assigned by traditional grammarians to the category Adverb, but they are now normally regarded by linguists as constituting a distinct category, though many reputable dictionaries and textbooks retain the older label.

deictic /'daɪktɪk/ *n.* (also **indexical**) Any lexical or grammatical item which serves to express a distinction within a **deictic category**, such as a personal pronoun, a demonstrative, a tense marking or an adverb like *here* and *then*.

deictic category *n.* Any **grammatical category** which serves to express distinctions in terms of orientation within the immediate context of an utterance. Deictic categories are those which make crucial reference to such factors as the time or place of speaking or the identity or location of the speaker, the addressee or other entities. Among the most frequent deictic categories are **person**, **tense** and **deictic position**.

deictic position *n.* A grammatical category occurring in perhaps all languages which serves to express distinctions of reference, particularly with respect to location. Deictic systems are almost always egocentric – that is, they express location primarily with reference to the speaker, though they may secondarily include reference to the addressee or to other entities. Deictic systems always include reference to distance, though they may also involve reference to other dimensions, such as direction, visibility, size, motion or previous mention. English has a simple two-way contrast between the notions 'near the speaker' (*here*, *this*) and 'away from the speaker' (*there*, *that*). Spanish exhibits a three-way contrast between 'near the speaker' (*aquí* 'here', *este* 'this'), 'a little way from the speaker' (*ahí* '(just) there', *ese* 'that (just there)') and 'far from the speaker' (*allí* '(over) there', *aquel* 'that (over there)'). In contrast, the three Japanese demonstratives *kono*, *sono* and *ano* have the respective meanings 'this (near the speaker)', 'that (near the addressee)' and 'that (away from both)'. Malagasy has a remarkable seven-term system which exclusively expresses differing degrees of distance from the speaker, plus elaborations involving visibility and other factors. The Australian language Dyirbal shows a rich deictic system involving such terms as *dayi* 'short distance upward', *daya* 'medium distance upward', *dayu* 'long distance upward', *balbala* 'medium distance downriver', *balbalu* 'long distance downriver' and *guya* 'across the river', among others. The most elaborate deictic systems known are those of Eskimo and Aleut, which include dozens of terms expressing such specific notions as 'that large or moving one way up there', 'that one outside, only partly visible' and 'that small one going away from the speaker'.

deixis /ˈdaɪksɪs/ *n*. Reference by a term forming part of a system expressing a **deictic category**: *you*, *now*, *there*, *this* or a past-tense marker. *Adj*. **deictic**. See Anderson and Keenan (1985).

deletion /dɪˈliːʃn̩/ *n*. 1. Any putative process which, in a **derivational** theory of grammar, removes some overt material from a sentence. Deletion processes were widely invoked in the Standard Theory of TG, and were the principal cause of the enormous power of that framework, as demonstrated by the **Peters–Ritchie results**. In the more recent descendants of that framework, deletion operations have been increasingly constrained, but are still present. In current versions of GB, certain deletion processes are permitted to apply between S-structure and LF. 2. By extension, a conventional label for any construction in which some material required for semantic interpretation is not overtly present, even in analyses and frameworks in which no deletion operation is proposed or permitted, as in **comparative deletion** or **unspecified object deletion**. *V*. **delete** /dɪˈliːt/.

deletion under identity /ʌndər aɪˈdentɪti/ *n*. A name sometimes given to instances of **ellipsis** in which the elided material is identical to other overt material in the sentence, as in *Lisa doesn't want to go, but Janet does*, where the continuation . . . *want to go* is said to be deleted under identity. See also **sloppy identity**.

demonstrative /dɪˈmɒnstrətɪv/ *n*. A **determiner** with a clear deictic function, such as *this* or *that* in English.

demotion /dɪˈməʊʃn̩/ *n*. In RG, any process in which a clause is restructured so as to move some NP into a lower-ranking position on the **Relational Hierarchy**, such as the demotion of an underlying subject to an oblique NP in passivization. The term is also sometimes used in a loose descriptive sense in frameworks in which it has no theoretical status.

denominal /dɪˈnɒmɪnl̩/ *adj*. In word formation, denoting a lexical item of another class derived from a noun or a nominal stem. For example, *mountainous* is a denominal adjective derived from the noun *mountain*.

deontic modality /diˈɒntɪk/ *n*. The area of **mood** concerned with permission, obligation and prohibition. Cf. **epistemic modality**.

dependency /dɪˈpendənsi/ *n.* 1. Any relation between two elements or positions in a sentence by which the presence, absence or
form of an element in one position is correlated with the presence,
absence or form of another element in another position. Typical
examples include **agreement, government** and **filler–gap dependencies** such as **topicalization** and **WH-Movement.** Dependencies are
conveniently divided into **local dependencies** and **unbounded
dependencies,** distinguished by the domain within which the dependency holds. The existence of dependencies in natural languages is
one of the two principal reasons that very simple theories of grammar, such as **regular grammars** or unelaborated versions of **context-
free grammars,** are inadequate for the characterization of natural
languages, the other reason being the existence of **inter-sentence
relations.** 2. In **dependency grammars,** a particular sort of relation
between two words in a sentence, by which one of them is linked to
the syntactic structure of the sentence as a whole solely by its
connection with the other one; the first is said to be dependent on
the second. In these frameworks, the syntactic structure of a sentence is seen as consisting primarily of such dependencies.

dependency grammar *n.* An approach to grammatical description
which is based, not on constituent structure, but on relations between individual words. Dependency grammars typically function in
terms of the subcategorization requirements of words, and often
attach considerable importance to grammatical relations; the existence of constituent structure is usually denied in favour of principles
of linearization applying to words. Sentence structure is usually
represented in terms of **dependency trees.** The first fully articulated
such framework was that of Tesnière (1959); the most recent proposal to use the name 'dependency grammar' is that of Mel'čuk
(1988). Certain other current theories of grammar are also versions
of dependency grammar, such as **Word Grammar** and **Lexicase.**

dependency tree *n.* In a **dependency grammar,** the graphical
device which is the usual means of representing syntactic structure.
A dependency tree consists of a set of nodes (usually individual
words) connected by arcs, each node being connected directly
upward to the node on which it is immediately dependent. At the
top of the tree is a unique node, the **governor** (or **controller**) on
which all other nodes ultimately depend; this is usually the verb.
Here is a dependency tree for the sentence *The police trapped the
frightened burglar behind the house:*

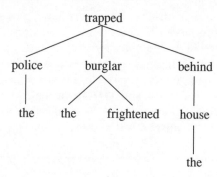

Tesnière (1959).

dependent marking /dɪ'pendənt ˌmɑːkɪŋ/ n. The grammatical pattern in which the relation between a head and a dependent of the head is morphologically marked on the dependent rather than on the head. Examples include the marking of a possessive relation on the possessor, rather than on the possessed, and the marking of grammatical relations by case forms on argument NPs, rather than by marking on the verb. Dependent marking is sometimes regarded as a typological characteristic of languages exhibiting it. Cf. **head marking**, and see Nichols (1986) for discussion. Van Valin (1985).

dependent verb See **medial verb**.

deponent verb /dɪ'pəunənt/ n. 1. In the grammar of Latin, a verb which exhibits exclusively passive morphology but which functions as an active verb, such as *uti* 'use', *loqui* 'speak' or *partiri* 'divide'. 2. A label occasionally used to denote any class of verbs in some language whose morphology is at odds with their syntactic behaviour, such as for the subclass of Basque intransitive verbs exhibiting transitive morphology.

derivation /ˌderɪ'veɪʃn̩/ n. 1. In word formation, the process of obtaining new words by adding affixes to existing words or stems, as illustrated by the formation of *happiness* and *unhappy* from *happy* or of *rewrite* and *writer* from *write*. Along with **compounding**, derivation is one of the two principal means of word formation in English and most other languages. 2. In a **derivational** theory of grammar, the process of obtaining a given **surface structure** from its **deep** (**underlying**, initial) **structure**, or a representation of the stages involved in doing this. *Adj.* **derivational**.

derivational /ˌderɪ'veɪʃənl̩/ adj. 1. Pertaining to **derivation** (sense 1) or to **derivations** (sense 2). 2. Denoting a theory of grammar in which the syntactic structure of a sentence is represented as an ordered sequence of formal objects (typically trees) related by the rules of the grammar. Typically in such a framework, two of the objects in the sequence are distinguished as being of special significance: the **deep** (initial, **underlying**) **structure**, which is the most abstract level of representation, and the **surface structure**, which is the least abstract level of representation; there may or may not be additional levels of representation, and some of these may or may not be distinguished as specially significant. The best-known derivational theories of grammar are **Transformational Grammar** and **Government–Binding Theory**, though others exist.

derivational constraint *n.* (also **global constraint**, **global rule**) In a **derivational** theory of grammar, a constraint that links two non-successive levels of representation. Absent from the Standard Theory of TG, derivational constraints were introduced by Lakoff (1970); while Lakoff's original formulation of them did not survive, certain aspects of them were reconstructed within the Revised Extended Standard Theory in the form of **traces**. Traces, which continue to be important in the GB framework, effectively permit a syntactic representation to 'remember' what has happened at earlier stages of a derivation, and hence derivational constraints are in some sense a part of GB.

derivational morphology *n.* (also **lexical morphology**) That branch of morphology dealing with **word formation**, particularly (but not exclusively) with **derivation** (sense 1). Cf. **inflectional morphology**.

descendant /dɪ'sendənt/ *n.* A relation which may hold between two nodes in a tree. If a node A dominates a distinct node B, then B is a descendant of A. Cf. **ancestor**, **daughter**.

descriptive /dɪ'skrɪptɪv/ *adj.* 1. Denoting a class of (usually intransitive) verbs or predicates which express states, qualities or relations, and sometimes also perceptions, rather than actions or events, particularly in languages in which such verbs and predicates show distinctive grammatical behaviour. Typical descriptive predicates are those with such meanings as 'be old', 'be fat', 'be black', 'be cousins' and 'hear'. A grammatically distinctive class of descriptive predicates is found in many North American languages, particularly Iroquoian languages. 'Descriptive' means about the same as **stative**, but is often preferred for labelling a formally distinct class, while the latter term is often preferred for denoting a semantic class of predicates, regardless of formal distinctions. Chafe (1967). 2. See **descriptivism**.

descriptive adequacy See under **adequacy**.

descriptivism /dɪ'skrɪptɪvɪzm̩/ *n*. The approach to grammatical characterization which holds that linguistic facts should be described as they are observed to exist. All serious linguistic approaches to grammar in this century have been descriptivist. Cf. **prescriptivism**. *Adj.* **descriptivist** /dɪ'skrɪptɪvɪst/ or **descriptive**.

desiderative /dɪ'sɪdərətɪv/ *adj*. 1. A **mood** category expressing the sense of 'wanting' or 'desiring'. In most European languages this notion is expressed by purely lexical means, but in some languages it is expressed grammatically, particularly by inflection of the verb. An example is the Japanese affix *-tai*, which derives adjectives from verb stems (*iku* 'go', *ikitai* 'wanting to go'); this is the ordinary means of expressing such meanings in Japanese. Latin has a class of desiderative verbs formed from simple verbs with the suffix *-urire*: *esurire* 'want to eat', from *edere* 'eat'. 2. A mood category expressing an unrealizable wish, as in the somewhat archaic English *Would that our leader still lived*. Sense 2: Jespersen (1924).

desinence /'desɪnəns/ *n*. An inflectional ending of a word.

destinative /'destɪnətɪv/ *n*. or *adj*. A distinctive case form found in certain languages which typically expresses an inanimate destination: Basque *kotxerako* 'for the car' (*kotxe* 'car') in *Kotxerako erosi dut hau* 'I've bought this for the car'.

Det /det/ See **determiner**.

determiner /dɪ'tɜːmɪnə/ *n*. (**Det** or **D**) A lexical category, or a member of this category, whose members typically occur within noun phrases and indicate the range of applicability of the noun phrases containing them. English determiners include the articles *the* and *a*, the demonstratives *this* and *that*, possessives like *my* and *your*, quantifiers like *many*, *few*, *no* and stressed *some*, and various other items like *either*, *which*, *both* and unstressed *some*. In most versions of the X-bar system, determiners are regarded as **specifiers** of nouns, but several analysts (such as Hudson 1984) have recently proposed that determiners might be better regarded as the heads of noun phrases, which would then be renamed 'determiner phrases'. Note: many analysts regard the quantifiers as forming a distinct lexical category from determiners, but this view, which is based chiefly on semantic criteria, is difficult to defend syntactically.

determiner phrase *n.* (**DetP** or **DP**) 1. The maximal projection of the lexical category Determiner, in frameworks in which such a projection is assumed to exist. 2. The preferred label for a **noun phrase** in analyses in which the determiner is regarded as the head of such a phrase. While still non-standard, this analysis has frequently been suggested as advantageous for a number of reasons (for example, by Hudson (1984)).

deterministic /dɪˌtɜːmɪˈnɪstɪk/ *adj.* Denoting a type of automaton or transition network in which, at every point, the path chosen is entirely determined by the current state and the next input character. Cf. **non-deterministic**, and see also **pushdown automaton** and **linear bounded automaton**.

deterministic context-free language *n.* (**DCFL**) Any one of the proper subset of **context-free languages** which are accepted by some **deterministic pushdown automaton**. Such languages have linear time recognition. The relevance of the DCFLs to natural languages has been little discussed; see Gazdar and Pullum (1985) for some comments.

DetP See **determiner phrase**.

deverbal /dɪˈvɜːbəl/ *adj.* In word formation, denoting a lexical item of another class derived from a verb or a verbal stem. For example, *realization* is a deverbal noun derived from the verb *realize*.

deviant /ˈdiːvɪənt/ *adj.* 1. See **ill-formed**. 2. Denoting a string which is either syntactically ill-formed or semantically uninterpretable, particularly in cases in which the decision as to which it is is difficult or controversial.

diachronic /daɪəˈkrɒnɪk/ *adj.* Pertaining to linguistic change across time. *Abstr. n.* **diachrony** /daɪˈækrəni/. Cf. **synchronic**.

diacritic feature /daɪəˈkrɪtɪk/ *n.* In some analyses, a morphological or syntactic feature attached to a particular lexical item or small group of lexical items and serving to denote that such items behave exceptionally with respect to some regular grammatical process. For example, the transitive verb *fit* might be marked with a diacritic feature to show that it fails to undergo passivization: *That suit fits you* but **You are fitted by that suit*.

dialect /'daɪəlekt/ *n*. 1. A distinctive variety of a language used by speakers in a particular geographical region or in a particular social group. 2. See **idiolect**. NOTE: this second usage, though widespread, is not recommended. *Adj*. **dialectal** /daɪə'lektl̩/.

diathesis /daɪ'æθɪsɪs/ *n*. The relation between the **semantic roles** (**deep cases, theta roles**) subcategorized for by a lexical verb or predicate and the surface expression of those roles as **grammatical relations**. Thus, for example, the verb *assault* requires an agent and a patient which, in the unmarked (active) case, are realized as subject and direct object, respectively. The term 'diathesis' expresses much the same notion as **voice**, but is typically used with reference to particular lexical items, while 'voice' is more commonly used in connection with the grammatical patterns involved in relating grammatical relations to participant roles. In LFG, the same relation is called the **lexical form** of the verb or predicate.

diminutive /dɪ'mɪnjʊtɪv/ *n*. 1. A derivational affix which may be added to a word to express a notion of small size, often additionally (or even instead) a notion of warmth or affection: Spanish *-it-*, *-ill-*. 2. A word formed by the use of such an affix: Spanish *gatito* 'kitten' (*gato* 'cat'), *palillo* 'toothpick' (*palo* 'stick'), *hijito* 'son' (affectionate) (*hijo* 'son', unmarked), *Juanita* 'Janey' (*Juana* 'Jane').

directed acyclic graph /daɪ,rektɪd eɪsɪklɪk 'grɑːf/ *n*. (**DAG**) A graphical representation of structure consisting of nodes linked by arcs in which every arc linking two nodes is directional and there are no loops. The conventional tree structures for sentences are DAGs, as are the feature matrices which constitute syntactic categories in GPSG. Graph theory.

direct object /daɪ'rekt/ *n*. (**DO**) The **grammatical relation** borne by an NP which occurs inside a verb phrase and which is the second obligatory argument of a transitive verb, most typically expressing a patient which undergoes the action of the verb. The presence of a direct object is what distinguishes a transitive verb from an intransitive one. Direct objects are typically distinguished from indirect and oblique objects, which also occur inside the VP, by such criteria as obligatory subcategorization by the verb, distinctive case marking in case languages (usually **accusative** in **accusative languages** and **absolutive** in **ergative languages**) and the ability to become the subject of a corresponding **passive**. There has been considerable controversy as to which NP should be regarded as the direct object in **double-object constructions** like *Lisa lent me this book*; at present there is perhaps something of a consensus in favour of the first NP (*me* in the example), though the issue cannot be regarded as settled. In GB, a direct object is referred to simply as an 'object', since indirect objects are not recognized in that framework. Cf. **subject**, **indirect object**, **primary object**, **secondary object**.

direct person marking See under **inverse person marking**.

direct speech /spiːtʃ/ *n*. The reporting of what someone has said by quoting her/his exact words, as in *'What time is it?', she asked* and *'There's a wasp on your back', she said quietly*. Cf. **indirect speech**.

disagreement /dɪsə'griːmənt/ *n*. Any of various phenomena in which an agreement morph assumes a form apparently inconsistent with the category it is supposed to be agreeing with. An example is the Spanish *Los norteamericanos somos sus amigos* the North-Americans we-are your friends 'We North Americans are your friends', in which the verb shows first person plural agreement even though the subject NP is third person plural.

disambiguation /ˌdɪsæmbɪgjʊ'eɪʃn̩/ *n*. Any procedure for selecting one of the meanings of an ambiguous string. This may be done in various ways, such as by adding extra words or paraphrasing or, in some cases, by adding referential indices. For example, the ambiguous string *Visiting relatives can be a nuisance* can be disambiguated by adding a second clause which is consistent with only one of the readings: *Visiting relatives can be a nuisance, especially when they drop in unexpectedly*. V. **disambiguate** /dɪsæm'bɪgjʊeɪt/.

discontinuous constituent /ˌdɪskən'tɪnjʊəs/ *n*. A constituent, or apparent constituent, which appears on the surface in two or more parts separated by material which is not part of the constituent, posing severe problems in drawing a tree structure. In the sentence *A student who'd actually done the reading turned up this morning*, the sequence *a student who'd actually done the reading* appears to be uncontroversially a constituent, but in the alternative form *A student turned up this morning who'd actually done the reading*, the same sequence is discontinuous. There is considerable evidence that discontinuous constituents need to be recognized in syntax, but at present no consensus exists as to how such sequences should be analysed; see Huck and Ojeda (1987) for some proposals in various frameworks. The existence of discontinuous constituents was implicitly recognized by the American structuralists; the first explicit treatment was proposed by Yngve (1960).

discourse /'dɪskɔːs/ *n*. A connected series of utterances by one or more speakers. Certain types of grammatical, lexical and phonological elements can be identified which typically serve to relate one utterance to another in some fashion, but, on the whole, attempts at extending the methods of grammatical analysis to the study of discourse, in the hope of constructing 'discourse grammars', have not been outstandingly successful.

discourse item *n*. Any lexical item or grammatical form which typically serves to relate one utterance to another in a discourse, or to relate the utterance in a particular way to the discourse as a whole. English has a number of such items, including *well*, *yes*, *surely*, *however*, *on the contrary*, *so* and *nevertheless*. Mandarin Chinese is reported as using a grammaticalized set of sentence-final particles for discourse purposes, including *le* 'currently relevant state', *ne* 'response to question', *ba* 'soliciting agreement', *ou* 'friendly warning', *a* or *ya* 'reduced forcefulness' and *ma* 'question'.

discovery procedure /dɪs'kʌvəri prəʊˌsiːdʒə/ *n*. An explicit mechanical procedure for extracting a grammar from a corpus of data. The attainment of such a procedure was, in principle at least, a major goal of the **American structuralists**. Cf. **decision procedure**, **evaluation procedure**. Chomsky (1957).

disjunct /'dɪsdʒʌŋkt/ *n*. One of the alternative elements combined in a **disjunction**.

disjunction /dɪs'dʒʌŋkʃn̩/ *n*. A **coordinate structure** which expresses a choice among alternatives, such as *coffee or tea*.

dislocation /dɪsləʊ'keɪʃn̩/ *n*. A construction in which an element is displaced from its normal position in the sentence, that position being occupied by a pro-form. English exhibits both left-dislocation, as in *This wine, I really like it*, and right-dislocation, as in *I really like it, this wine*. Right-dislocations are sometimes called 'afterthought constructions'. In spoken French, utterances involving dislocations in both directions are exceedingly common, as in *Jean, il l'a acheté, la voiture*, literally 'John, he's bought it, the car'. Cf. **topicalization**. Ross (1967).

displacement /dɪs'pleɪsmənt/ *n*. The occurrence of an element in a sentence in other than its canonical position, as in **preposing** and **dislocation**.

distal /'dɪstḷ/ *adj*. In a system of **deictic positions**, denoting that term expressing the greatest distance from the reference point, such as English *that* or *there*. Cf. **proximate**.

distribution /dɪstrɪ'bjuːʃn̩/ *n*. The full range of environments in which a lexical or grammatical form can occur.

distributive /dɪ'strɪbjʊtɪv/ *n*. 1. A lexical item, particularly a determiner, which is interpreted as referring separately and exhaustively to every single member of a group, such as *each*, *every*, *both* and *none*. 2. A phrase or inflected form involving a numeral and expressing a similar notion, such as *two each*, *two apiece*. Some languages have an inflected form for this purpose, such as Basque *-na*: *bina* 'two each', 'two apiece', 'two at a time' (*bi* 'two').

ditransitive verb /daɪ'trænsɪtɪv/ *n*. A verb which subcategorizes for two objects, such as *give*: *She gave me a kiss*.

DO See **direct object**.

domain /dəʊ'meɪn/ *n*. 1. (of a rule) The range of applicability of that rule. 2. (of a node in a tree) The complete subtree dominated by that node. See also **command domain**.

dominance /'dɒmɪnəns/ *n*. A relation which may hold between nodes in a tree. If a continuous downward path of whatever length can be traced from a node A to a node B, then A **dominates** B, and A bears the relation of dominance to B. By convention, a node dominates itself. The representation of dominance relations is one of the fundamental purposes of a tree diagram. Cf. **immediate dominance** and **proper dominance**, and see also **domain**, **ancestor** and **descendant**.

donkey sentence /'dɒŋki/ *n*. A sentence containing an anaphor whose antecedent is an indefinite NP whose reference is constrained by a quantifier elsewhere in the sentence; the classic example is *Any man who owns a donkey₍ᵢ₎ beats it₍ᵢ₎*. Such sentences pose unusually severe problems for most accounts of anaphora.

double-*ing* constraint /ˌdʌbəl'ɪŋ/ *n*. A constraint in English by which a verb which takes a complement VP in the *-ing* form may not itself appear in the *-ing* form: *It started to rain*, *It was starting to rain*, *It started raining*, but **It was starting raining*. Ross (1972a).

double negative /'dʌbḷ/ *n*. A construction in which one overt negative element appears within the scope of another without any independent function, such as *I didn't do nothing*. Long condemned by prescriptivist grammarians as 'illogical', such double negatives are regarded as non-standard in English but are very common in vernacular speech. In many other languages, however, double negatives (**negative concord**) are normal and obligatory, such as in Spanish: *No dice nada* 'He says nothing', literally 'he doesn't say nothing'; *Nunca veía a nadie en ninguna de las habitaciones* 'I never saw anybody in any of the rooms', literally 'I never saw nobody in none of the rooms'.

double-object construction *n.* A construction involving a **ditransitive verb** like *give* or *tell*, such as *Lisa gave me a kiss*. See the remarks under **direct object**.

double passive *n.* The construction in which passivization applies both in a matrix clause and in a complement clause, sometimes resulting in ill-formedness: *The city was allowed to be captured*; **The Duke was attempted to be killed*.

double perfect *n.* The construction, often regarded as ill-formed, in which both a matrix verb and its infinitival complement are marked for perfect aspect: *?She would have liked to have gone*.

down arrow /'daʊn ˌærəʊ/ *n.* In LFG, the symbol ↓, attached to a node in a tree to represent the functional structure (see **f-structure**) of that node. See the examples under **functional schema**, and cf. **up arrow**.

DP See **determiner phrase**.

D-structure /'diːˌstrʌktʃə/ *n.* In GB, the usual label for the initial (base-generated) level of the structure of a sentence, essentially what was formerly called **deep structure**.

dual /'djuːəl/ *n.* or *adj.* One of a set of contrasting **number** forms which serves to express exactly two of some entity. In English, the dual is a marginal phenomenon, illustrated by dual *both* contrasting with plural *all*, but in some languages nouns and/or pronouns are systematically inflected for singular, dual and plural numbers, as illustrated by Classical Arabic: *malikun* 'a king', *malikani* 'two kings', *malikuna* '(three or more) kings'.

dubitative /'djuːbɪtətɪv/ *adj.* A mood distinction, grammatically expressed in some languages, expressing the modal meaning 'perhaps it is so' or, in questions, 'can it be so?' For example, consider the behaviour of the Basque dubitative particle *ote*, one of a set of modal particles in that language:

> Pozik dago. 'She is happy.'
> Pozik ote dago. 'She might be happy.'
> Pozik al dago? 'Is she happy?'
> Pozik ote dago? 'Can she possibly be happy?'

dummy /'dʌmi/ *n.* (also **expletive**) A semantically empty element, most often a noun phrase, which is required for well-formedness in certain positions in certain structures. English makes extensive use of two such dummies, the *it* of *It's raining* and *It's nice to see you*, and the existential *there*, as in *There's a wasp on your back*. The infinitival *to* is also occasionally regarded as a kind of dummy, as in *You ought to go* (compare *You must go*), as is sometimes the complementizer *that*, as in *Lisa said that she would come*, though the label 'dummy' is not standard in these cases. See Bolinger (1977), however, for arguments that no so-called 'dummy' is ever truly devoid of meaning. Jespersen (1937: 102).

durative /'djʊərətɪv/ *adj.* An **aspect** form which expresses an action or state which is perceived as lasting for a certain length of time. The durative aspect is a subdivision of **imperfective** aspect, and it appears that few languages have a distinct form for representing durative aspect explicitly; often it is expressed only by a general imperfective form which is also used to express **habitual** or **progressive** aspect, though in English it is most usually expressed by the simple past or present forms, as in *I waited for an hour*. Durative contrasts most obviously with **punctual** aspect.

dvandva /'dvɑːndvə/ *n.* (also **copulative compound**) A type of compound word in which each element has an equal claim to be considered the head, as though the elements were joined by the word 'and': *Austria-Hungary*, *tragicomic*, *freeze-dry*.

dynamic /daɪ'næmɪk/ *adj.* Denoting a sentence, predicate, verb form or lexical verb expressing an action, movement or change: *Lisa peeled the potatoes*, *Lisa left the room*, *Lisa turned bright red*. The term 'dynamic' is a superordinate aspectual label contrasting with **stative**.

E

e /iː/ The conventional symbol for a **gap**, particularly an **empty category**: *Who did you say you saw* e *in town?*.

Earley algorithm /'ɜːli/ *n.* A particularly powerful and efficient parsing algorithm for context-free grammars; it always produces a result within time Kn^3 and space Kn^2, where K is a constant depending on the grammar and n is the length of the input string; if **ambiguous grammars** are excluded, it produces a result within time Kn^2. Earley (1970).

echo question /'ekəʊ/ *n.* A response to an utterance which takes the form of a question seeking confirmation of some part of that utterance and which, as far as possible, simply repeats that utterance. Echo questions in English are grammatically distinctive in that they do not undergo WH-fronting or inversion; if a WH-item is used, it must be stressed. For example, to the utterance *I saw Ignatz this morning*, a responding echo question might be *You saw Ignatz this morning?* or *You saw* **who?**

echo response *n.* Any response to an utterance which largely consists of repeating that utterance. For example, to the utterance *I saw Ignatz this morning*, a possible echo response would be *You saw Ignatz this morning*.

ECP /iː siː 'piː/ See **Empty Category Principle**.

ECPO /ɪ'ekpəʊ/ See **exhaustive constant partial ordering**.

effector /ɪ'fektə/ *n.* In some versions of **functional grammar** (sense 2), especially RRG, any NP which is in principle eligible to be an **actor**, whether or not it actually appears as the actor in a particular clause (it may be outranked by another NP which is present).

effectum /ɪ'fektəm/ *n.* A traditional label for a direct object NP which only comes into existence as a result of the action denoted in its clause, such as *the table* in *John built the table*. Cf. **affectum**.

egressive /ɪ'gresɪv/ See **conclusive**.

E-language /'iːlæŋgwɪdʒ/ *n.* (also **externalized language**) A language seen as a set of sentences. Cf. **I-language**. Chomsky (1986).

elative /'iːlətɪv/ *n.* or *adj.* 1. A case form, occurring in certain languages, typically used to express the notion '(motion) out of': Finnish *talosta* 'out of the house' (*talo* 'house'). 2. In languages with only two degrees of comparison for adjectives, the form expressing the greater degree: Arabic *ʔakbar* 'very great, greatest', from positive *kabir* 'great').

elision /ɪ'lɪʒn̩/ *n.* A very general term for the omission from an utterance of material which is required to complete the structure. For example, the utterance *Seems we have a problem* illustrates elision of the initial *it*. *V.* **elide** /ɪ'laɪd/.

ellipsis /ɪ'lɪpsɪs/ *n.* Any construction in which some material which is required for semantic interpretation and which could have been overtly present is absent but immediately recoverable from the linguistic context, particularly when that material is overtly present elsewhere in the sentence. For example, the sentence *Siobhan can't speak Spanish, but Lisa can* illustrates ellipsis of the repeated VP *speak Spanish* in the second clause. *Adj.* **elliptical** /ɪ'lɪptɪkl̩/; *V.* **ellipse** /ɪ'lɪps/. See also **deletion under identity**, **sloppy identity**.

Elsewhere Principle /'elsweə/ *n.* (also **Elsewhere Condition**) Another name for the **Proper Inclusion Principle**, used more in phonology than in syntax.

embedded question /ɪm'bedɪd/ See **indirect question**.

embedding /ɪm'bedɪŋ/ *n.* A structure in which one constituent is contained within another constituent, especially another constituent of the same category. The example *That book you lent me is very interesting* illustrates the embedding of the clause *you lent me* within a larger clause. Cf. **conjoining**, and see **recursion**.

emphasis /'emfəsɪs/ *n.* A very general term for any phenomenon which serves to draw particular attention to some element in a sentence or utterance, either to place that element in **focus** or to contrast it with some other element. Emphasis in spoken English is often achieved merely by stressing the emphasized element, but English and other languages also exhibit a range of grammatical means for expressing emphasis, such as particles, distinctive word order and **clefted** constructions.

empty category /'empti/ *n*. In GB, any of several abstract elements which have no overt phonetic realization but which are posited as occupying certain NP positions in sentences. Four types are currently recognized: **NP-trace**, **WH-trace**, **PRO** ('big PRO') and **pro** ('little pro'). These four types occur in distinct circumstances and have distinct properties. Several of the modules of GB make crucial reference to these empty categories, notably Binding Theory, Government Theory and Control Theory. See the individual entries for further information, and see under **Binding Theory** for a classification.

Empty Category Principle *n*. (**ECP**) In GB, one of the fundamental requirements of **Government Theory**. It states: a trace must be properly governed. Note that, in spite of its name, the ECP applies to only two of the four types of **empty category**. The chief function of the ECP is to place constraints on the movement of categories by the rule of **alpha movement**; it effectively allows a tree structure to 'remember' what has happened at earlier stages of a derivation, and it can be seen as GB's version of the older **derivational constraints**. See **proper government**.

empty morph *n*. In morphology, a morph which cannot be assigned to any morpheme. For example, in Basque *mendietan* 'in the mountains', *mendi* is the noun 'mountain', *-e-* is the usual form of the plural morpheme in oblique cases and *-n* is the usual form of the locative case, leaving *-ta-* unassigned as an empty morph.

empty node *n*. A node in a tree which, in some particular analysis, is postulated as being present even though no overt phonetic material is present to represent it. The **empty categories** of GB are examples of empty nodes, but the term is of wider applicability. For example, some analyses of such a sentence as *Lisa said she would come* postulate an empty COMP node in the complement clause: *Lisa said* [$_{S'}$[$_{COMP}$e] [$_S$*she would come*]]. An empty node is a syntactic null element; it must be distinguished from the case in which an item is posited as being syntactically present even though it is phonetically null. For example, some analyses of *French wine is expensive* would recognize the presence in the noun phrase of a lexical determiner which is an actual lexical item with zero phonetic realization; in such an analysis, the Det node in the NP is not empty.

empty word See **grammatical word**.

enclitic /en'klɪtɪk/ *n.* A **clitic** which is phonologically bound to a preceding host, such as *-n't* in *couldn't.* Cf. **proclitic**. Ancient Greek grammar.

endocentric /ˌendəʊ'sentrɪk/ *adj.* 1. Denoting a constituent which has a **head.** In many contemporary frameworks, every constituent must have a head, and this **endocentricity** is often regarded as the central requirement of the **X-bar system.** 2. In older usage, denoting a constituent whose distribution is, in principle at least, similar to that of its lexical head standing alone as a constituent. Thus, for example, the NP *these new books* is endocentric, since its lexical head *books* can form an NP with similar distribution: *These new books are interesting* vs. *Books are interesting.* Similarly, the AP *very big* is endocentric, since its distribution is similar to that of *big* standing alone. *Abstr. n.* **endocentricity** /ˌendəʊsen'trɪsɪti/. Cf. **exocentric**. Bloomfield (1933).

endocentric compound *n.* A **compound** which is a hyponym of the grammatical head: *armchair, airman, logbook, sky-blue, ice-cold, nosedive, spray-paint* or *tie-dyed.* Cf. **bahuvrihi**.

epicene /'epɪsiːn/ *adj.* In a language with a **gender** system showing a correlation with sex, denoting a noun which has an invariable gender but which can take referents of either sex. In French, for example, *écrivain* 'writer', *témoin* 'witness' and *contralto* 'contralto' are always masculine, even when referring to a woman, while *victime* 'victim', *personne* 'person' and *sentinelle* 'sentry' are always feminine, even when referring to a man. Cf. **common gender** (sense 1).

epiphenomenon (pl. **epiphenomena**) /'epɪfəˌnɒmɪnən, -ə/ *n.* 1. A superficially unified phenomenon which is actually the accidental result of the interaction of several independent principles. For example, Chomsky has often suggested that natural languages are epiphenomena, being little more than the more-or-less directly perceptible by-products of the underlying reality, the principles of universal grammar. 2. A surface generalization in a language which, in some proposed grammatical description, is regarded as an accidental consequence of the interaction of other independently required principles and hence as not deserving of its own formulation in the grammar. For example, in current versions of GB, the observation that a passive verb always has an underlying object as its subject is regarded as an epiphenomenon, since it results automatically from the interaction of the requirements of two modules, Case Theory and Theta Theory. *Adj.* **epiphenomenal** /ˈepɪfəˌnɒmɪnl̩/.

epistemic modality /epɪˈstiːmɪk/ *n.* The area of **mood** concerned with knowledge and belief, including at least the expression of possibility, probability and certainty (as perceived by the speaker), and, in some views, also the expression of the speaker's degree of commitment to what she/he says, as, for example, by the use of **evidentials**. Cf. **deontic modality**.

Equational Grammar *n.* An algebraic approach to grammatical characterization proposed by Gerald Sanders (1972). A brief introduction is provided in Sanders (1980).

equational sentence /ɪˈkweɪʒənl̩/ *n.* (also **equative**) A sentence in which one noun phrase is identified with another one: *Washington was the first American President.* An equational sentence can be turned round without infelicity: *The first American President was Washington.* Cf. **ascriptive sentence**.

equative /ˈekwətɪv/ *n.* or *adj.* 1. A construction in which one entity is characterized as having some property to the same extent as another entity, as in *Lisa's French is as good as Pierre's*, which illustrates the usual English equative construction. 2. See **equational sentence**.

Equi-NP Deletion /ˈekwi, ˈiːkwi/ *n.* (also **Equi**) An older name for a **control** construction. The name derives from the observation that, in a control construction, the second of two identical NPs required for semantic interpretation is absent, as though it had been deleted.

Equi-verb See **control verb**.

ergative /ˈɜːɡətɪv/ *n.* or *adj.* 1. The distinctive case form marking the subject of a transitive verb in morphologically **ergative languages** and contrasting there with the **absolutive**, used for intransitive subjects and direct objects. Various other names for this case are found in the literature, including 'agentive', 'active', 'transitive', 'operative', 'energetic', 'instructive', 'narrative' and 'relative'; these names should be regarded as obsolete, though some of them continue in use among specialists in particular ergative languages. Usually credited to Dirr (1912), but Alexis Manaster-Ramer has uncovered earlier uses by Sidney Ray, Johannes Schmidt and Alfredo Trombetti. Ray's unrelated locative use is from Latin *erga* 'next to, towards'; the modern sense is presumably from Greek *ergon* 'work'. 2. (more fully, **ergative–absolute**) Denoting a grammatical pattern in which subjects of intransitive verbs and direct objects of transitive verbs are treated identically for grammatical purposes, while subjects of transitive verbs are treated differently. Ergativity can be manifested morphologically (most typically, in the case marking of argument NPs and in verbal agreement) or syntactically (e.g., in the control of pronominalization or in the coordination of VPs). See Comrie (1978) or Dixon (1979). NOTE: this is now the established sense of the term 'ergative'; the following quite different senses are idiosyncratic at best, and should be avoided. 3. A label sometimes given to a canonical transitive clause whose subject is an agent, such as *John read the book*, as opposed to the non-ergative *John knew the truth*, or to the subject NP in such a clause. Anderson (1971). 4. A name sometimes given to the transitive pattern exemplified by the sentence *She opened the door*, as compared with the intransitive *The door opened*, or to the subject NP in the transitive construction, reflecting the observation that the patient NP *the door* functions indifferently as intransitive subject or as transitive object, with no change in the morphology of the verb or of the NP, much as happens regularly in morphologically ergative languages. This usage effectively equates ergatives with (a subclass of?) causatives; its utility is debatable, since the pattern is far from being fully productive in English: while a number of verbs participate in it (*dry, collapse, fly, drown*), some others show lexical suppletion (*die/kill, fall/drop, recover/cure*) and still others require various complex expressions (*get lost/lose, be born/bear, blush/make . . . blush, exist/bring . . . into existence*). Halliday (1967). 5. In GB, a label sometimes applied to those **unaccusative** verbs which can function both transitively and intransitively, such as *melt* in *The ice melted* and *John melted the ice*. Burzio (1981); Keyser and Roeper (1984). NOTE: the term 'ergative' has sometimes been misunderstood and applied in ways that are simply erroneous, particularly before 1970. A detailed account of the history of the term 'ergative' is given in Seely (1977). *Abstr. n.* **ergativity** /ɜːgəˈtɪvɪti/.

ergative language *n.* A language in which **ergative** (sense 2) morphology or syntax is prominent or predominant. In most ergative languages, as in Basque, ergativity is confined to the morphology, but some ergative languages exhibit extensive syntactic ergativity. In a few Australian languages, the best known of which is Dyirbal, the syntax operates almost exclusively on an ergative basis (Dixon 1972). Nevertheless, there are few if any languages which are exclusively ergative in their morphology and syntax. Ergative languages are much less common than **accusative languages**, but are far from rare. See Dixon (1979). Cf. **active language**, **accusative language**, and see **split ergativity**.

essential variable /ɪ'sentʃl̩/ *n.* A variable whose value may be any arbitrary string. Cf. **abbreviatory variable**.

essive /'esɪv/ *n.* or *adj.* A case form typically expressing the temporary state or character of some entity: Finnish *poikana* 'as a boy' (*poika* 'boy'). It may also be used as a complement of the verb 'be': Finnish *Isäni on pappina* 'My father is a priest' (*pappi* 'priest').

EST /iː es 'tiː/ See **Extended Standard Theory**.

ethic construction /'eθɪk/ *n.* A construction indicating that an individual is affected in some way by an action, such as *on me* in the English *The dog died on me*. It is very common for languages to use a dative form for this purpose; the construction is then called an **ethic dative**. An example is Basque *Ama hil zait* 'My mother has died', literally 'The mother has died to me'.

evaluation metric /ɪ,væljʊ'eɪʃn̩/ *n.* The set of criteria in terms of which an **evaluation procedure** is applied.

evaluation procedure /prəʊ'siːdʒə/ *n.* An explicit procedure for choosing among competing grammars in terms of some set of criteria constituting an **evaluation metric**. Cf. **discovery procedure**, **decision procedure**. Chomsky (1957).

evaluative /ɪ'væljʊətɪv/ *adj.* Denoting a mood-like category, grammaticalized in some languages, which serves to express the speaker's attitude towards a statement the truth of which she/he accepts; among the attitudes which may be so expressed are surprise, incredulity, disappointment, warning, approval or disapproval. For example, the Tibeto-Burman language Lisu exhibits a set of evaluative sentence-final particles, including (among others) *na* 'surprise', *lê* 'warning', *há* 'wonder', *xù* 'complaint', *læ* 'confirmation' and *mâ* 'expectation'. In the strict sense, the evaluative is not a mood, since the truth of the proposition expressed is not in doubt. See Palmer (1986) for discussion.

evasive /ɪ'veɪsɪv/ *adj.* Denoting a grammatical form used to avoid choosing between other forms marked for sex or gender, such as English *they* in examples like *Somebody has forgotten their umbrella*. Gotteri (1984).

eventive /ɪˈventɪv/ 1. *adj.* See **dynamic**. 2. *n.* (also **event**) In some versions of Case Grammar, a label for an NP which expresses an event, the verb in the same sentence typically being almost empty semantically. Examples include *an argument* in *They're having an argument* and *the assassination* in *The assassination took place in Berlin*.

evidential /ˌevɪˈdentʃl̩/ *n.* or *adj.* A grammatical category occurring in some languages by which all statements (and sometimes other sentence types) are overtly and obligatorily marked to indicate the source of the speaker's evidence for her/his utterance. A particularly rich system is that of the Papuan language Fasu, in which the English sentence *It's coming* has six distinct translations, distinguished as follows (Foley 1986):

> apere 'I see it.'
> perarakae 'I hear it.'
> pesareapo 'I infer it from other evidence.'
> pesapakae 'Somebody says so, but I don't know who.'
> pesaripo 'Somebody says so, and I know who.'
> pesapi 'I suppose so.'

Evidential systems, which are sometimes called **verification systems**, are sometimes regarded as forming part of the **mood** systems in languages exhibiting them. See Palmer (1986) for discussion. *Abstr. n.* **evidentiality** /ˌevɪdentʃiˈælɪti/.

exception /ɪkˈsepʃn̩/ *n.* A particular item or construction which is inconsistent with the statement of a grammatical rule. For example, the noun *man* is an exception to the rule that English nouns form their plural in *-s*, and the verb *go* is an exception to the statement that intransitive verbs cannot be passivized: *She is gone*. *Adj.* **exceptional** /ɪkˈsepʃənl̩/. Cf. **counterexample**, and see the discussion there.

exceptional case marking *n.* In GB, the ability of raising verbs to assign Objective Case to the NP subjects of non-finite complements, such as to *Lisa* in *I find Lisa charming* and *I consider Lisa to be my best student*. Such constructions cannot be handled by the ordinary machinery of Case Theory. See Haegeman (1991) for discussion.

excessive /ɪkˈsesɪv/ *n.* or *adj.* In some languages, an inflected form of an adjective, forming part of its system of comparison, which expresses a superabundance of the quality in question: Basque *handiegi* 'too big', from *handi* 'big'.

exclamation /ˌekskləˈmeɪʃn̩/ *n*. 1. One of the four **sentence types** of traditional grammar, typically expressing a more-or-less emotional comment on something and often characterized by a grammatically distinctive form. English examples are *What a nice day it is!* and *How lucky you are!* 2. Any utterance serving to express emotion, regardless of its grammatical form, which is often merely that of a word or a phrase, such as *What a bummer!, Hooray!, Shit!* or *No way! Adj.* **exclamative** /ɪkˈsklæmətɪv/.

exclamative *adj*. The **mood** category represented in an **exclamation** (sense 1).

exclusive first person /ɪkˈskluːsɪv/ *n*. In some languages, a distinct pronominal form expressing the meaning 'I and one or more others, excluding you' and contrasting there with an **inclusive first person**. In Hawaiian, for example, the exclusive first person dual *kaua* 'I and he/she' contrasts with inclusive *maua* 'I and you', and the exclusive plural *kakou* 'I and they' contrasts with inclusive *makou* 'I and you and he/she/they'.

Exclusivity Condition /ˌekskluˈsɪvɪti/ *n*. The requirement that, of any two distinct nodes A and B in a tree, one and only one of the following statements should be true: (a) A dominates B; (b) B dominates A; (c) A precedes B; (d) B precedes A. This condition is universally accepted, except by those few who advocate the use of **wild trees**, in which precedence is undefined.

exhaustive constant partial ordering /ɪgˈzɔːstɪv ˌkɒnstənt ˌpɑːʃəl ˈɔːdrɪŋ/ *n*. (**ECPO**) The property of a grammar in which the left-to-right ordering of sisters is always the same, regardless of the identity of the mother. Only a grammar possessing this property can be formulated in the **ID/LP format**. Gazdar and Pullum (1981).

exhaustive domination *n*. The relation which holds between a node in a tree and all of its daughters taken together. The complete sequence of constituents dominated by a single node is said to be 'exhaustively dominated' by that node, which is the mother of all of them.

existential sentence /ˌegzɪˈstentʃl̩/ *n*. A sentence which asserts the existence or non-existence of some entity, either in general or in a specified location: *There are no unicorns; There's a wasp on your back*. The entity whose existence is at issue is almost always represented by an indefinite noun phrase (obligatorily so in some languages). It is very common for languages to make use of a distinctive sentence pattern for this purpose, as does English, with its *There is*/*There are* construction.

exocentric /ˌeksəʊˈsentrɪk/ *adj*. 1. Denoting a constituent which has no **head**. The existence of exocentric constituents is prohibited in most versions of the **X-bar system**. 2. In older usage, denoting a constituent which contains no lexical head or which contains a lexical head which, when standing alone as a constituent, exhibits a substantially different distribution from the larger constituent. For example, the category Sentence is exocentric in most analyses, since either it has no lexical head (the LFG analysis), its lexical head is a verb which does not in general exhibit a distribution similar to that of a sentence (the GPSG analysis) or its lexical head is an abstract lexical category of unique distribution (the GB analysis). The category PP is regarded as exocentric in many analyses, on the ground that a PP has a distribution fundamentally different from that of a preposition standing alone, but this is debatable: *I knew her before the war* does not seem so different from *I knew her before*, if the analysis of *before* in the second example as an **intransitive preposition** is accepted. *Abstr. n.* **exocentricity** /eksəʊsenˈtrɪsɪti/. Cf. **endocentric**, and refer to the discussion there.

exocentric compound See **bahuvrihi**.

exophor /ˈeksəfɔː/ *n*. An **anaphor** (sense 1) whose antecedent lies outside the sentence containing the anaphor, and whose reference must therefore be determined from the linguistic or extra-linguistic context. For example, in the utterance *She left this note for you*, the pronouns *she* and *you* and the demonstrative *this* are all exophors. *Adj*. **exophoric** /eksəˈfɒrɪk/; *abstr. n*. **exophora** /ɪkˈsɒfərə/.

expansion /ɪkˈspænʃn̩/ *n*. The rewriting of a category as a string of categories by a phrase structure rule or an immediate dominance rule. For example, when the rule NP → Det N′ is applied, the NP node is expanded as a sequence of a determiner and an N-bar. The term was introduced by Wells (1947), drawing on earlier work by Harris, though Wells's conception of expansion was based upon the replacement of particular morphemes by longer sequences.

experiencer /ɪkˈspɪəriənsə/ *n*. The **semantic role** borne by an NP which expresses the animate NP who is the passive recipient of a sensation or a mental experience, such as *Lisa* in *Lisa has a headache* and *Lisa is happy*. Experiencer is one of the **deep cases** recognized in Case Grammar.

experiential /ɪkˌspɪəriˈentʃl̩/ *adj.* An aspectual category expressing the notion that an event occurred at least once during a certain
period up to a certain point in time. This is one of the functions of
the English perfect, as in *Mike has worked in Japan*, but some
languages have a distinctive form expressing this meaning, such as
the Japanese *-ta koto ga aru* construction, illustrated in the Japanese
translation of the preceding example, *Mike wa Nihon de hataraita
koto ga aru*.

explanatory adequacy /ɪkˈsplænətri/ See under **adequacy**.

expletive /ɪkˈspliːtɪv/ *n.* 1. See **dummy**. 2. A swear word, particularly one inserted into the middle of a phrase as a meaningless
emotional intensifier, as in *Where's that bloody cat?* The term is
derived from the language of poesy, in which it originally meant a word or
phrase inserted to fill out a line.

expletive infixation /ɪnfɪkˈseɪʃn̩/ *n.* The curious process by which
an expletive (sense 2) is inserted into the middle of a word, as in
fan-fuckin-tastic and the classic *down in Tumba-bloody-Rumba
shootin' kanga-bloody-roos*.

exponence /ɪkˈspəʊnəns/ *n.* The overt realization of a grammatical
distinction by a particular morph. See Matthews (1974) for
discussion.

exponent /ɪkˈspəʊnənt/ *n.* A morph which expresses some grammatical distinction. For example, in the Latin verb form *amat*
'he/she loves', the *-a-* is the exponent of imperfective aspect, while *-t*
is the exponent of the third person singular.

exponential time /ˌekspəˈnentʃl̩ taɪm/ *n.* In computational
linguistics, a characteristic of an **algorithm** for the application of
which the time required increases by some quantity raised to the
power n, where n is the length of the input string. For example,
certain non-linguistic problems, in the most efficient approach possible, require time $= k2^{cn}$, where k and c are constants. It has been
proved that transformational grammars of the type current in the
mid-1970s, when implemented in parsers, require exponential time
to parse input strings. Exponential time is an extremely undesirable
characteristic in an algorithm, since it generally means that the real
time required to obtain a result in a particular instance is impossibly
long for all but the shortest inputs. Cf. **polynomial time**, and see
Barton *et al.* (1987) for some discussion.

extended exponence /ɪk'stendɪd/ *n.* The phenomenon by which a single grammatical distinction is overtly expressed at two or more points within a word form. A simple example is the German noun plural *Wörter* 'words', plural of *Wort* 'word', in which plurality is simultaneously expressed by the vowel alternation and by the suffix. A more elaborate example is the Latin verb form *cucurristi* 'you (Sg) ran', a perfective form of the verbal root *curr-* 'run', in which perfective aspect is simultaneously expressed by the reduplication *cu-*, the suffix *-is-* and the choice of *-ti* to mark the second person singular. See Matthews (1972, 1974) for discussion.

Extended Projection Principle *n.* In GB, the requirement that a predicate must have a subject, especially when this is combined with the **Projection Principle**.

Extended Standard Theory *n.* (**EST**) The version of **Transformational Grammar** current in the mid-1970s, differing in a number of respects from the Standard Theory of a few years earlier, but most particularly in the way in which syntactic structures receive semantic interpretation. The EST was based on work by Noam Chomsky (1970, 1971) and more particularly by Ray Jackendoff (1972); it was conceived as a response to criticisms of the Standard Theory advanced by the proponents of **Generative Semantics** in the late 1960s. In the late 1970s, the EST underwent further modifications; the revised model, often called the **Revised Extended Standard Theory**, was in turn supplanted by **Government–Binding Theory** in the early 1980s. NOTE: the name 'EST' is sometimes found in the literature for the later development now usually called the 'REST'.

extension /ɪk'stenʃn̩/ *n.* Of a category, a second category which is consistent with the first but which is more fully specified. The category [NOUN][BAR 2][PERSON 3][NUMBER PLUR] (a third person plural NP) is an extension of the category [NOUN][BAR 2] (an NP).

external argument /ɪk'stɜːnl̩/ *n.* In GB, an argument of a verb lying outside its subcategorization frame, particularly a subject NP.

external conditions of adequacy See under **adequacy**.

externalized language See **E-language**.

external theta role *n.* In GB, a **theta role** which is assigned by a lexical head to its subject. Passives, raising verbs and unaccusative verbs are assumed to assign no external theta role, as a result of which the structures in which they appear undergo obligatory NP-Movement.

extraction /ɪk'strækʃn̩/ *n.* Any of various phenomena in which some element appears overtly in a position different from its canonical position. Examples include **WH-questions**, **relative clauses**, **topicalization**, **adverb preposing** and **dislocation**.

extraposition /ekstrəpə'zɪʃn̩/ *n.* 1. The construction in which a **sentential subject** appears in final position, the subject position being filled (in English) by the dummy *it*, as in *It surprises me that Gus is still hungry*. The complement clause in this position is said to be **extraposed**. 2. Any proposed process by which such a structure is derived from the corresponding **non-extraposed** structure, such as *That Gus is still hungry surprises me*. *V.* **extrapose** /ekstrə'pəʊz/. Jespersen (1961, VII:148); originally, the position, rather than the construction or the process.

extraposition from NP *n.* The construction in which a prepositional phrase or a relative clause which is understood as forming part of an NP is separated from the rest of that NP by intervening material: *A woman turned up who I used to work with in Liverpool* and *I bought a book this morning about hamsters*.

extraposition grammar *n.* In computational linguistics, an extension of a **definite clause grammar** which permits the recognition of non-adjacent sequences of elements which are more usually adjacent. A rule of the form S → NP . . . VP, for example, may be used to associate a VP with an apparent NP which is arbitrarily far away from it, as in the example *The book the professor recommended is good*.

extrinsic rule ordering /ɪk,strɪnzɪk 'ruːl ,ɔːdrɪŋ/ *n.* The requirement that certain rules in a grammar should apply in an order stipulated by the grammar. Extrinsic ordering was a regular feature of descriptions within the Standard Theory of TG, but few if any frameworks make use of it today.

F

factitive /'fæktɪtɪv/ 1. *adj*. Denoting a verb expressing a cause which produces a result, such as *make*, *build* or *kill*, or a clause containing such a verb. 2. *n*. In some versions of Case Grammar, a synonym for **result**.

favourite /'feɪvərɪt/ *adj*. An occasional synonym for **canonical**, especially in connection with clause structure.

f-command /'ef kə,mɑːnd/ *n*. In LFG, a relation which may hold between elements in an **f-structure**. It is stated as follows: an antecedent A f-commands a pronominal P iff (a) A does not contain P, and (b) every nucleus that contains A also contains P. Here **pronominal** is used in the LFG sense of an overt pronoun or reflexive, and **nucleus** in the LFG sense (sense 3). F-command is invoked to handle **binding** relations between NPs; it does much of the same work as **c-command** in GB, but it differs from the more familiar **command relations** in that it is defined over f-structures, rather than over constituent structures.

FCR See **feature cooccurrence restriction**.

f-description /'ef dɪ,skrɪpʃn̩/ *n*. In LFG, the set of requirements imposed by an annotated c-structure upon the corresponding f-structure. A c-structure and an f-structure may be independently well-formed, but they can only combine to provide the complete syntactic representation of a single sentence if the f-structure satisfies the f-description provided by the c-structure. See Sells (1985) for discussion.

feature /'fiːtʃə/ *n*. (also **syntactic feature**) Any one of the elements provided by a theory of grammar and available to make up part of the structure of a **category** (senses 1 and 2). A feature present in a category represents some characteristic of that category to which the rules of the grammar and the principles of the theory may refer. Typically, a feature may have a **value** which represents one of the competing possibilities for the realization of the category containing it; in some systems, the value of a feature may itself be a feature. A feature which has only two possible values is said to be 'binary'; an example is the feature [PLURAL] in English, which can only have the values [−] and [+], representing singular and plural number respectively. A feature which has more than two possible values is said to be 'multivalued' or 'n-ary'; an example is the feature [PERSON], which has the values [1], [2] and [3], representing first, second and third persons. Features are indispensable in syntax as a way of dealing with **cross-categorization**, and virtually all current theories of grammar make extensive use of them. They have long been used in syntax in a sporadic and *ad hoc* way, but explicit theories of features have only been developed in syntactic theory since about 1980, though features have been widely used in computational linguistics since the 1950s. See **complex symbol**, **cross-categorization**.

feature cooccurrence restriction *n*. (**FCR**) Any statement in a grammar or a theory of grammar which limits the possible combinations of features or their values within a single category (that is, on a single node). For example, the FCR [TENSE] > [VERB] requires that the feature [TENSE] may only be present in a category which also contains the feature [VERB]; in other words, only projections of the lexical category Verb may be marked for tense. Similarly, the FCR [+INV] > [+AUX, FIN] requires that an inverted category must be a finite auxiliary verb. Observe the following notational distinction: the FCR [X] > − [Y] requires that, when the feature [X] is present, the feature [Y] must be absent, while the FCR [X] > [−Y] requires that, when [X] is present, [Y] must also be present and carry the value [−]. Cf. **feature instantiation principle**.

feature instantiation /ɪnˌstæntʃiˈeɪʃn̩/ *n*. The assignment of a value to a feature by any means other than default assignment or stipulation by rule. It is convenient to think of instantiation as a kind of 'free choice' made by the grammar in generating sentence structures; instantiation is constrained, however, both by the **feature cooccurrence restrictions** and by the **feature instantiation principles**. For example, when some rule introduces a category NP into a structure, then, unless that particular rule itself stipulates a value for the feature [PLURAL], we are generally free to choose either [−] ('singular') or [+] ('plural') as the value of [PLURAL]; whichever value we choose is said to be instantiated on that NP. Now the value of [PLURAL] must also be instantiated on the noun which is the lexical head of that NP; this time, though, the choice is not free; the

Head Feature Convention (one of the feature instantiation principles) requires that the value instantiated on the noun must be the same as that instantiated on the whole NP.

feature instantiation principle *n.* Any of several principles which have the effect of constraining the values assigned to features on different nodes in a single structure. GPSG, the framework making the most explicit use of such principles, recognizes three: the **Head Feature Convention**, the **Foot Feature Principle** and the **Control Agreement Principle**. The function of these principles is to ensure that conflicting features do not appear in a structure. Cf. **feature cooccurrence restriction**.

feature matrix /ˈmeɪtrɪks/ See **complex symbol**.

feature value /ˈvæljuː/ *n.* Any one of the mutually exclusive possible specifications for a feature which it may assume in a particular instance; see the examples under **feature**.

feminine /ˈfemɪnɪn/ *adj.* A traditional label in certain **gender** languages for a gender class which shows some degree of semantic correlation with female sex. See the remarks under **gender**.

filler–gap dependency /ˈfɪlə ˈgæp/ *n.* Any **dependency** (sense 1) involving a **gap** and an overt element which is interpreted as occupying the position of that gap. Examples include **topicalization** and **WH-Movement**.

filter /ˈfɪltə/ *n.* A restriction on possible syntactic structures which applies only to a single level of structure (in a derivational theory, usually the most superficial one) and which has the effect of blocking certain structures regardless of their source. An example is the '*that-that* filter', which states that no English sentence may contain two consecutive occurrences of the complementizer *that*; this filter prevents the generation of structures like *[*That* [*that she smokes*] *bothers you*] *surprises me*, in contrast to extraposed versions like *That it bothers you* [*that she smokes*] *surprises me*. Cf. **constraint**. Filters were introduced by Perlmutter (1971), who called them 'surface-structure constraints'.

finite /ˈfaɪnaɪt/ *adj.* (also **tensed**) Denoting a form of a verb or auxiliary which can in principle serve as the only verb form in a sentence and which typically carries the maximum in morphological marking for such categories as tense and agreement permitted in a language. 2. Denoting a clause containing such a verb form. Cf. **non-finite**.

finite automaton See **finite-state automaton**.

finite closure *n.* The **closure** property exhibited by an operation which is not allowed to apply to its own output. For example, in a GPSG-type grammar, the (finite) set of immediate dominance rules is closed under the application of metarules.

finite language *n.* A language containing only a finite number of well-formed sentences. Since all natural languages appear to make use of **recursion**, linguists are confident that no natural language is a finite language.

finiteness result /'faɪnaɪtnəs rɪ,zʌlt/ *n.* A property of any formal theory of grammar which permits only a finite number of distinct grammars and hence only a finite number of languages. No existing theory of grammar is known to have this property. At times the possibility of a finiteness result has been regarded as an interesting question, but Pullum (1983) dismisses it on the ground that 'finite' in this context would most likely mean an inconceivably large number.

finite-state automaton /'faɪnaɪt,steɪt/ **(FSA)** (also **finite automaton**) or **finite-state transition network (FSTN)** *n.* The simplest type of automaton or transition network, consisting merely of a set of states (nodes) connected by directional arcs with actions or conditions attached, with no additional machinery. The languages generated or recognized by either the deterministic or non-deterministic FSAs are exactly the **regular languages**. NOTE: strictly, an FSTN is an abstract representation, while an FSA is an implementation of it for a particular purpose, but the difference is rarely significant.

finite-state grammar See **regular grammar**.

finite-state language *n.* **(FSL)** A language which can be recognized by a finite-state automaton; a **regular language**. Natural languages which exhibit unlimited **centre-embedding**, such as English, are demonstrably not finite-state languages.

first person /fɜːst/ *n.* The **person** category which includes reference to the speaker, as represented in English by the pronouns *I* and *we*. See also **exclusive first person** and **inclusive first person**.

flat structure /flæt/ See **non-configurational structure**.

flectional language /'flekʃənl̩/ See **inflecting language**.

floating quantifier /'fləutɪŋ/ *n*. A **quantifier** which appears in a position separated from the rest of the noun phrase of which it is understood to be part, as illustrated by *The players have all arrived*, in which the quantifier *all* has 'floated off' the subject NP *all the players*.

fluid intransitive /'fluːɪd/ *adj*. Denoting a pattern found in some **active languages** in which intransitive verbs and predicates can appear in either the agentive or the non-agentive pattern to express differing degrees of control over the action. For example, in the active language Eastern Pomo, the verb *ce:xélka* 'slip', 'slide' can take either agent subjects like *há:* 'I' (agent) or non-agent subjects like *wì* 'I' (non-agent) to express different meanings: *Há: ce:xélka* 'I'm sliding (on purpose)' but *Wì ce:xélka* 'I'm slipping (by accident)'. Dixon (1979).

focus /'fəukəs/ *n*. Special prominence given to some element in a sentence which represents the most important new information in that sentence or which is explicitly contrasted with something else. In English, focused elements are frequently marked only by stress, though **cleft** constructions are sometimes used. Some other languages variously mark focused elements by the use of particles, as in many Philippine languages, or by the use of word order, as in Basque, in which a focused element is placed directly before the verb.

folk etymology /'fəuk etɪ‚mɒlədʒi/ *n*. The process by which a word or phrase, usually one of seemingly opaque formation, is arbitrarily reshaped so as to yield a form which is considered to be more transparent. English examples include *sparrowgrass* (for *asparagus*), *Welsh rarebit* (for *Welsh rabbit*), *crayfish* (from French *écrevisse*) and *past master* (from *passed master*). A particularly striking example is Basque *zainhoria* 'carrot' (literally, 'yellow-root'), from Spanish *zanahoria*, of Arabic origin.

foot feature /fʊt/ *n*. In GPSG, any one of a designated set of features which are subject to the **Foot Feature Principle**. Foot features differ from the more numerous **head features** in that the former can in general be passed from a mother down to any daughter, not necessarily to a head daughter. The most frequently invoked foot features are those used to handle filler–gap dependencies and those used to mark constituents containing reflexives, reciprocals and WH-items and to control the agreement features required in these items.

Foot Feature Principle *n*. One of the **feature instantiation principles** of GPSG. Informally, it states: a foot feature present on any daughter must also be present on the mother.

foregrounding /'fɔːgraʊndɪŋ/ *n*. 1. A general term for any discourse phenomenon that provides special prominence for some part of a sentence or utterance, particularly for **focus**. 2. The effect of any discourse phenomenon which has the effect of carrying a narrative along, such as (it is claimed) transitive clause structure, telic and volitional verbs or punctual aspect. Hopper and Thompson (1980). 3. Any syntactic process which has the effect of moving a non-pivot NP into **pivot** position (usually subject position), such as the English passive. Foley and Van Valin (1984).

formal /'fɔːml̩/ *adj*. 1. Pertaining to grammatical forms, as opposed to the meanings or functions of those forms. In this sense, 'formal' contrasts with **functional**. 2. (of a grammar) Completely explicit; leaving nothing to be filled in by the reader.

formal complexity *n*. A synonym for **generative capacity**, often particularly for **weak generative capacity**. Cf. **computational complexity**.

formal grammar *n*. A fully explicit device which specifies, for a given initial set of elements (the 'vocabulary' or 'alphabet'), the complete set of strings of those elements which are in the language defined by the grammar. A grammar which is fully formal constitutes a linguistic use of what mathematicians and logicians call a 'formal system'. Most contemporary approaches to grammar purport to be formal in this sense, at least in principle, though in practice some frameworks are considerably more explicit than others; see, for example, the acid remarks in Pullum (1989).

formalism /'fɔːməlɪzm̩/ *n*. Any fully explicit notational device or set of such devices. The term can be applied, for example, to the **Kleene star**, to the **X-bar system** or to the entire framework of GPSG.

formal language *n*. A language generated by a **formal grammar**. A formal language may or may not resemble a natural language; one of the goals of grammatical investigation is the construction of grammars which generate formal languages resembling natural languages as closely as possible.

formal universal *n*. A **universal** of language which pertains to the form a grammar can take. The modules of GB, the **Head Feature Convention**, the **Theta Criterion**, the Binding Principles (see under **Binding Theory**) and the principle of **functional coherence** are all formal universals which have been proposed in one theory of grammar or another. Compare **substantive universal**.

formation /fɔːˈmeɪʃn̩/ *n*. 1. Any putative process by which some grammatical form is constructed from the grammatical resources of a language. 2. Any particular grammatical form, when regarded from the point of view of its structure.

formative /ˈfɔːmətɪv/ *n*. 1. A **morpheme**, particularly one which plays a part in syntax, such as the English complementizer *that* or possessive *-'s*. 2. In morphology, a bound form which is added to a **root** to derive a **stem**. For example, the Latin verb root *am-* 'love' takes the formative *-a-* (its 'thematic vowel') in all its forms; to this is added a further formative to derive each particular stem: *-ba-* to derive the imperfect stem *amaba-*, *-vi-* to derive the perfect stem *amavi-*, *-tu-* to derive the supine stem *amatu-*, *-nt-* to derive the participial stem *amant-*, and so on.

form class /ˈfɔːm klɑːs/ *n*. A general term for any class of items sharing morphological, and usually also distributional, characteristics. Examples include the class of nouns in English, the class of *-a*-stem verbs in Spanish and the class of **deponent verbs** in Latin.

form word See **grammatical word** (sense 1).

fragment /ˈfrægmənt/ *n*. 1. An utterance which consists only of a single phrase. Fragments are particularly common as responses to questions; for example, the question *Where's Lisa?* might be answered by a fragment such as *In the library* or *Visiting her aunt*. 2. See **grammar fragment**.

free /friː/ *adj*. The opposite of **bound**, in all senses of that term.

free form *n*. A form which can stand alone as a complete word, such as *book*, *went* or *under*. Compare **bound form**.

free morpheme *n*. A morpheme which can stand alone as a complete word, such as *book*, *green* or *go*. Compare **bound morpheme**.

free relative *n*. (also **headless relative**) 1. A **relative clause** which has no lexical head and which thus constitutes a noun phrase by itself: e.g., *whoever did that* in the sentence *Whoever did that is in* *trouble*. 2. Sometimes also an adverbial clause introduced by *whenever* or *wherever*, as in *I'll leave whenever Lisa leaves*.

free word order *n.* 1. The phenomenon, observable in certain languages, by which the individual words making up a sentence or a clause can be freely permuted into virtually any order without affecting either the well-formedness of the sentence or its propositional content. An example is the Australian language Dyirbal, in which the meaning 'The woman hit the man', most typically expressed as *bayi yara banggun dyugumbiru balgan*, literally 'the man the woman hit', can equally be expressed as *banggun balgan yara dyugumbiru bayi*, or as any other sequence of these word-forms. Free-word-order languages do not usually permit the mixing of words from different clauses. 2. By extension, and very commonly, the phenomenon, observable in certain languages, by which the major constituents of a clause (NPs, PPs, AdvPs, etc.) can be freely permuted with one another, and sometimes also with the verb, without affecting either the well-formedness of the sentence or its propositional content, though often with a difference in thematic structure. In Basque, for example, the meaning 'The students from Bilbao brought their new teacher some home-made sausage this morning' would most typically be expressed as *Gaur goizean Bilboko ikasleek irakasle berriari etxeko txorizoa ekarri diote*, literally 'today morning-in Bilbao-from students teacher new-to home-made sausage brought Aux', but many other orders are equally possible, such as *Etxeko txorizoa Bilboko ikasleek ekarri diote gaur goizean irakasle berriari*. However, the phrases *Bilboko ikasleek* 'the students from Bilbao', *irakasle berriari* 'to the new teacher' and so on can in no circumstances be broken up. It seems misleading to refer to languages like Basque as having free word order; ideally, the term would be restricted to languages like Dyirbal, and Basque should be said to have **free phrase order** (as suggested by Matthews (1981)), but this alternative term is little used, and in practice the label 'free word order' is applied indiscriminately to both cases.

frequentative /frɪˈkwentətɪv/ *n.* or *adj.* A synonym for **iterative**, though a few analysts draw a fine distinction between the two terms.

fronting /ˈfrʌntɪŋ/ See **preposing**.

FSA See **finite-state automaton**.

FSL See **finite-state language**.

FSTN See under **finite-state automaton**.

f-structure /'ef strʌktʃə/ *n.* (also **functional structure**) In LFG, one of the two grammatical structures which together are regarded as representing the syntactic structure of a sentence, the other being **c-structure**. An f-structure consists of a set of pairs of features ('attributes') and their values. Three kinds of values are possible: (1) an atomic symbol, such as [SG] in the specification [NUM SG]; (2) a **semantic form**, such as the value of PRED in [PRED 'love' ⟨(↑SUBJ) (↑OBJ)⟩]; (3) an f-structure, such as the value of SUBJ in

$$
\left[\text{SUBJ} \begin{bmatrix} \text{PRED} & \text{'woman'} \\ \text{DEF} & + \end{bmatrix} \right]
$$

F-structures are used in LFG to express most syntactic information other than constituent structure information, but most particularly to handle **grammatical relations**. F-structures are subject to the three requirements of **functional uniqueness**, **functional coherence** and **functional completeness**.

FUG /ef ju: 'dʒi:/ See **Functional Unification Grammar**.

full phrasal category /fʊl/ *n.* A **maximal projection**, particularly of one of the so-called **major lexical categories** (NP, VP, AP, PP). Cf. **intermediate phrasal category**.

full word See **lexical word**.

function /'fʌŋkʃn̩/ *n.* 1. Any formal expression which accepts some formal object(s) as input (its 'argument(s)') and returns some single formal object as its output (its 'value'). This basic mathematical notion is widely used for a range of purposes in a variety of theories of grammar. For example, the **f-structures** of LFG are functions, as are the feature matrices ('categories') of GPSG. 2. Any particular grammatical purpose which may be served by some form or construction. 3. See **grammatical function**.

functional /'fʌŋkʃən̩/ *adj.* 1. Pertaining to the communicative and social aspects of language use. 2. Pertaining to the grammatical purposes served by constituents, rather than to their form. For example, the functional category **adverbial** may be realized by a lexical adverb, a prepositional phrase, an infinitival complement or a subordinate clause. 'Functional' in this sense contrasts with **formal**

(sense 1). 3. Pertaining to **semantic roles** and/or to **grammatical relations**.

functional annotation /ænəʊˈteɪʃn̩/ See **functional schema**.

functional coherence /kəʊˈhɪərəns/ *n.* In LFG, a condition on the well-formedness of **f-structures**. It may be stated as follows: an f-structure is locally coherent iff the governable grammatical functions that it contains are governed by a local predicate; an f-structure is coherent iff all its subsidiary f-structures are locally coherent. The purpose of this constraint is to rule out structures containing additional elements which cannot be functionally interpreted; for example, it blocks *Lisa smiled me*, in which the NP *me* receives no functional interpretation (i.e., it is assigned no semantic role, since *smile* assigns only a Subject). Cf. **functional completeness**.

functional completeness /kəmˈpliːtnəs/ *n.* In LFG, a condition on the well-formedness of **f-structures**. It may be stated as follows: an f-structure is locally complete iff it contains all the governable grammatical functions that its predicate governs; an f-structure is complete iff all its subsidiary f-structures are locally complete. The purpose of this constraint is to rule out structures lacking required grammatical functions, such as *Lisa gave me*, which lacks one of the participant roles required by the verb *give*. Cf. **functional coherence**.

functional control *n.* The LFG term for cases of obligatory **control**. Obligatory control verbs like *try* and *seem* require their subject to be interpreted as the subject of their complement, as in *Lisa tried to fix the carburettor* and *Lisa seems to be happy*. Functional control is represented by arcs connecting attribute values in f-structure. Cf. **anaphoric control**.

functional grammar *n.* 1. Any approach to grammatical description which lays particular emphasis on the communicative and social aspects of language use and which consequently attempts to interpret grammatical forms largely in terms of these factors; a prominent example is **Systemic Grammar**. Explicit approaches which are functional in this sense are usually also functional in the second sense, though the reverse is not necessarily the case. 2. Any approach to grammatical description which attaches particular importance to **grammatical relations** (Subject, Direct Object, Complement, etc.) and/or to **semantic roles** (Agent, Patient, Goal, etc.), often downplaying the role of constituent structure in the process; examples are **Relational Grammar**, **Role-and-Reference Grammar**, **Systemic Grammar**. 3. (capitalized) A particular theory of grammar developed by Simon Dik and his colleagues in the 1980s, one of the most prominent examples of a functional grammar in the second sense. Dik's FG was introduced in Dik (1978); Dik (1980) gives a brief introduction, Siewierska (1991) a more substantial one. NOTE: LFG is in fact a functional grammar in sense 2, but its name derives at least partly from the importance in that framework of **functions** in the mathematical sense.

functional schema (pl. **schemata**) /'skiːma, 'skiːmətə or skiː'maːtə/ *n.* (also **functional annotation**) In LFG, one of the annotations on a node in a tree representing the way in which the **f-structure** of that node is integrated into the f-structure of the tree. For example, in the rule

$$S \rightarrow \quad NP \qquad VP$$
$$(\uparrow SUBJ) = \downarrow \qquad \uparrow = \downarrow$$

the functional schema on the NP (read 'up's subject is down') means that the f-structure of the NP (the down arrow) is passed up to the Subject part of its mother's f-structure (the up arrow), while that on the VP (read 'up is down') means that the f-structure of the VP is passed up to the f-structure of its mother; the latter notation indicates that the VP is the functional head of the S. Such schemata represent the principal way in which f-structures are linked to c-structures in LFG.

functional structure See **f-structure**.

Functional Unification Grammar *n.* (**FUG**) An approach to grammatical characterization proposed by Martin Kay (1982). FUG combines a functional approach to representing linguistic information with a unification approach to manipulating the grammar. All linguistic objects are represented by sets of functional descriptions consisting of attributes and their assigned values; functional descriptions are in the same format at all levels. Two functional descriptions either are incompatible or can be unified into a single description. FUG is not so much a theory of grammar as a framework within which various theories of grammar may be expressed in a uniform and computationally convenient way.

functional uniqueness /jʊ'niːknəs/ *n*. In LFG, a condition on the well-formedness of **f-structures**. It says: in a given f-structure, a particular attribute may have at most one value. This constraint prevents, for example, two different NPs from being assigned to the Subject function in one clause.

function word See **grammatical word** (sense 1).

fused exponence /fjuːzd/ *n*. The morphological phenomenon in which two or more morphemes which are in principle distinct are merged into a single morph by regular phonological processes. For example, the genitive plural of the Basque noun *gizon* 'man' is in principle formed by the addition of the oblique plural marker *-e-* followed by the genitive case ending *-en*, theoretically yielding **gizoneen*, but the phonologically regular merger of adjacent identical vowels yields the actual form *gizonen*, in which the plural and genitive morphemes are fused. Matthews (1974).

fused participle *n*. The use of a **gerund** with a preceding NP in the objective case, rather than in the genitive, as in *I dislike you eating peanuts in bed* (in the sense of 'I dislike your eating peanuts in bed'). Fowler and Fowler (1906).

fusion /'fjuːʒn̩/ *n*. The morphological phenomenon in which a word consists of several morphemes but in which no one-to-one correspondence can be established between morphemes and morphs. Examples include English *feet* (= {*foot*} + {Plural}) and *took* (= {*take*} + {Past}). Sapir (1921); Sapir's use of the term does not quite correspond to the definition given here.

fusional language /'fjuːʒən̩l/ *n*. A language in which **fusion** is prominent; an **inflecting language**.

future /'fjuːtʃə/ *n*. or *adj*. A **tense** form whose primary correlation is with future time. A pure future form is **predictive**, but very few languages seem to have such a form, most future tenses in languages which have them being also widely used to express volition. The future tense of Spanish, for example, is chiefly used for expressing promises and determination, other forms being preferred for simple predictions. English, it is perhaps worth pointing out, has no future tense; it uses a variety of 'present' (non-past) forms for expressing predictions, intentions, promises, determination, obligation, probability and inevitability.

future perfect *n*. A verb form combining future tense with perfect aspect, such as Latin *amavero* 'I shall have loved'.

fuzzy grammar /ˈfʌzi/ *n*. (also **non-discrete grammar**) An approach to grammatical characterization which makes crucial use of the idea that such notions as well-formedness, category membership and rule applicability are a matter of degree, rather than (as in most approaches) an absolute either/or matter. Instead of sharply distinguished categories, there are 'fuzzy categories' which shade into one another along continua called **squishes**; a lexical item can be characterized, for example, as '0.3 Noun', and a structure can be characterized as '0.6 well-formed'. Fuzzy grammar was introduced by George Lakoff (1973) and was developed in a series of papers by John Ross and others; its proponents addressed a wide variety of problematic data, but, not surprisingly, it has proved difficult to formalize in a useful way, and it seemingly attracts little interest at present. See Newmeyer (1986) for a brief summary with references.

G

gap /gæp/ *n.* A location in a sentence in which no element is overtly present even though some element appears to be in some sense grammatically required. The following examples illustrate gaps; the gaps posited are represented by the conventional symbol *e*: *Who were you talking to* e*?*; *That bird we saw* e *was a Carolina warbler*; *This book I can certainly recommend* e; *I can't speak French, but Lisa can* e; *Lisa speaks better French than Pièrre* e; *I bought three bottles of red wine and two* e *of white wine*; *I ordered beef Madras and Lisa* e *chicken Kashmir*; *Which papers did you file* e *without reading* e*?* Theories of grammar differ in their treatment of gaps: GB treats them as empty nodes present in the syntactic structure but unfilled by any lexical material; GPSG treats them as features on the mother node; LFG treats them as relations within **f-structures**. See also **filler–gap dependency**, **empty category**, **parasitic gap**.

gapping /'gæpɪŋ/ *n.* The phenomenon in which an apparent coordinate structure lacks a verb, and sometimes additional constituents, in all conjuncts but one (in English, the first one), the resulting structure appearing to consist of a coordination involving non-constituent sequences. Examples: *I ordered beef Madras and Lisa* e *chicken Kashmir*; *Elton gave the museum a pair of glasses and Rod* e e *a tee-shirt*; *Lisa is writing an essay on immigrants, Siobhan* e e e *on minority languages and Alison* e e e *on the French Academy*. Gapped constructions are notoriously difficult to analyse, and no completely satisfactory treatment is currently available. *Adj.* **gapped** /gæpt/. Ross (1967, 1970).

garden-path sentence /ˌgɑːdən ˈpɑːθ/ *n.* A sentence which is so constructed as to mislead the hearer into assigning an incorrect structure during processing, and hence perhaps into regarding the sentence as ill-formed when an unremarkable well-formed interpretation is available: *The horse shot from the stable fell over*. A garden-path sentence involves a **local ambiguity**, and it lacks the **prefix property**.

GB See **Government–Binding Theory**.

gender /'dʒendə/ *n.* 1. A **grammatical category** found in certain languages by which nouns are divided into two or more classes requiring different agreement forms on determiners, adjectives, verbs or other words: e.g., French *un vieux livre* 'an old book' but *une vieille maison* 'an old house', in which both the determiner and the adjective reflect the gender of the noun. The number of gender classes varies from a minimum of two to a maximum of about eight or ten; two or three is most usual. Gender may or may not be marked overtly on nouns; often only some nouns are overtly marked. There is usually some clear semantic basis for the gender classes in a gender language, typically involving such obvious notions as size, shape, animacy, humanness and sex, but sometimes involving more unexpected notions such as edibility or danger. In very few gender languages, however, is it possible to predict the gender of every noun from its meaning alone; the semantic correlation is usually much weaker than this. See Corbett (1991) for a detailed account. NOTE: most European languages other than English have gender systems showing some degree of correlation with sex; as a consequence, many non-linguists (and some linguists!) needlessly confuse gender with sex. This confusion should be avoided: sex is a matter of biology, while gender is a matter of grammar, and one which has no necessary connection with sex. (Most so-called 'feminine' nouns in French, for example (like *maison*), have no connection with the female sex.) 2. Sometimes, by extension, and as a result of the confusion just referred to, any grammatical or lexical distinction correlating with sex, such as English *he/she/it* or *duke/ duchess*. This extension seems objectionable and is probably best avoided.

generalization /ˌdʒenərəlaɪ'zeɪʃn̩/ *n.* A statement about the grammatical facts of a language, or about the facts of languages generally, which holds true in all cases or in nearly all cases. All contemporary theories of grammar consider it a major goal to identify generalizations (at least those which are 'linguistically significant'), to state them explicitly within grammars or theories of grammar and to explain them as far as possible by deriving them from fundamental principles. It is by no means obvious *a priori*, however, which generalizations are linguistically significant or even which generalizations exist at all; this last point arises partly because linguists disagree about how many exceptions can be tolerated before a proposed generalization must be abandoned and partly because **derivational** theories of grammar permit the stating of generalizations which hold at abstract levels of representation but not on the surface. See also **linguistically significant generalization**.

Generalized Phrase Structure Grammar /ˈdʒenərəlaɪzd/ *n.* (GPSG) A theory of grammar developed by Gerald Gazdar and his colleagues in the 1980s. The class of grammars permitted by GPSG is strongly equivalent to the class of context-free grammars, and GPSG represents the major attempt at characterizing natural languages in terms of context-free grammars. Among the distinctive characteristics of the framework are its **monostratal** representations of syntactic structure, its rejection of grammatical relations, its well-articulated theory of features, its acceptance of the **rule-to-rule hypothesis** and its separation of grammatical statements into a **metagrammar** (containing **metarules** and other generalizations about the rules of the grammar) and an **object grammar** (containing the rules which directly license local subtrees). GPSG makes no claims about psychological reality; the framework is designed purely to permit economical and insightful descriptions of linguistic phenomena. Its development signalled a return to the kind of formal explicitness which had been advocated by Chomsky in the 1950s but which had largely disappeared from syntactic theory in the intervening decades. The first major presentation of GPSG was Gazdar (1982); the most comprehensive statement of the framework is Gazdar *et al.* (1985). See Sells (1985) or Horrocks (1987) for a brief introduction. See also **Head-Driven Phrase Structure Grammar**.

generation /dʒenəˈreɪʃn̩/ *n.* The process by which a **generative grammar** enumerates and characterizes the sentences of a language. Such a grammar is said to 'generate' those sentences.

generative /ˈdʒenərətɪv/ *adj.* 1. Denoting any approach to grammatical characterization involving **generative grammar(s)**, in any sense of that term. 2. Denoting any approach to grammatical characterization which is fully explicit, which is completely formalized.

generative capacity /kəˈpæsɪti/ *n.* (also **power**) The range of sentences which can be generated by a particular class of grammars. We distinguish between **weak generative capacity**, in which the sentences are regarded merely as linear strings of elements, and **strong generative capacity**, in which the structures assigned to those strings are also considered; see the remarks under those entries.

generative grammar *n*. 1. A grammar for a particular language which at least enumerates and usually also characterizes (assigns structures to) all and only the well-formed sentences of that language. In the case of a language containing only a finite number of sentences, a mere list of these sentences would trivially satisfy the definition. The only generative grammars of any interest, however, are those which meet at least some of the conditions of **adequacy** which have been formulated; in any case, natural languages are agreed to contain an infinite number of sentences, and, since grammars are normally required to be finite, a generative grammar of a natural language must of necessity provide some more principled basis for characterizing sentences. In particular, such a grammar must provide machinery for treating **recursion**, the phenomenon which is chiefly responsible for the unlimited size of natural languages. Such a grammar differs from other approaches to grammatical description in that it is fully explicit, leaving nothing to be filled in by a human reader. The notion of a generative grammar in this sense was introduced by Chomsky (1957), and it has dominated work in syntax ever since (though see sense 4). Chomsky (1961). 2. Any particular theory of grammar which has as its goal the construction of such grammars for particular languages. 3. The enterprise of constructing such theories of grammar. 4. In the recent work of Noam Chomsky and his associates, an approach to grammatical characterization which focuses on the identification of universal **principles** of grammar. Generative grammar in this sense attaches little importance to the construction of generative grammars in sense 1. NOTE: the shift in the meaning of this term represented by sense 4 is rather more radical than it has sometimes been made to appear, since at least some of Chomsky's associates can be understood as maintaining that natural languages do not actually have grammars in sense 1.

Generative Semantics *n*. A version of **Transformational Grammar** which regards syntax and semantics as a single unified area of investigation and which regards the semantic structure of a sentence as its underlying syntactic structure, with the rules of syntax applying to such semantic structures in order to derive surface syntactic structures. The underlying structures posited are typically very abstract and involve a good deal of **lexical decomposition**; a classic example is the initial structure of the sentence *Floyd broke the glass*, roughly *Floyd do it Floyd cause become glass break*. Generative Semantics, which was called 'abstract syntax' in its early days, was proposed and developed in the late 1960s as an alternative to the

Standard Theory of TG; the key figures in its development were George Lakoff, James McCawley, John Ross and Paul Postal. The framework was eventually abandoned as impossibly ambitious, but many of its ideas had a lasting influence on the later development of generative grammar. See Newmeyer (1986) for an account of the rise and fall of the framework. Lakoff (1976); written 1963.

generic /dʒəˈnerɪk/ See **gnomic**.

genitive /ˈdʒenɪtɪv/ *n.* or *adj.* (also **possessive**) A distinctive case form typically marking a noun phrase which serves a possessive role within a larger noun phrase. Examples are *Lisa's* in *Lisa's new book* and Basque *Anaren* 'Ana's' in *Anaren bikini hori* 'that bikini of Ana's'. The genitive is unusual among case forms in that it does not normally express an argument or adjunct of the verb; nevertheless, in languages with well-developed case systems, it is usually integrated morphologically into the case system. See also **possession**.

gerund /ˈdʒerənd/ *n.* A traditional name for the *-ing* form of a verb in English when it serves as a **verbal noun**, as in *Swimming is good exercise*, *Lisa's going topless upset her father* and *I enjoy watching cricket*, or for a verbal noun in any language. The English gerund is always identical in formation to the **imperfective participle**, but it is none the less grammatically convenient to distinguish the two. Many analysts would restrict the term 'gerund' in English to *-ing* forms in which the verb retains its ability to take verbal arguments, adverbs and complements, as in *Deliberately bowling bouncers is unfair*, as contrasted with cases in which the *-ing* derivative functions straightforwardly as a noun, taking determiners, adjectives and other adnominals, as in *This deliberate bowling of bouncers is unfair*.

given /ˈgɪvən/ *adj.* (of the information conveyed by certain elements in an utterance) Assumed to be already known to the addressee, and hence serving only as a background for the remainder of the utterance, which expresses 'new' information. In the example *The opera you're thinking of is Turandot*, the NP *the opera you're thinking of* transparently expresses given information. *Abstr. n.* **givenness** /ˈgɪvənnəs/.

global /ˈgləʊbl̩/ *adj.* 1. Comprehensive, wide-ranging. This rather hazy adjective is much favoured by syntacticians, who are inclined to describe some proposal as a 'global' approach when they mean merely that they hope it will work in a variety of cases in a variety of languages. 2. Universal. 3. Pertaining to a complete sentence, rather than to only part of it; non-**local**. 4. In classical TG, pertaining to a complete derivation, rather than to a particular stage of representation.

global ambiguity *n.* An ambiguity present in a string of words corresponding to two or more complete sentences. Cf. **local ambiguity**.

global constraint (also **global rule**) See **derivational constraint**.

gloss /glɒs/ *n.* A translation of a word, phrase or sentence in another language, especially one which is intended merely as a guide to its approximate meaning or structure. A gloss of a single lexical item is enclosed in inverted commas, as when citing Basque *gizon* 'man'; the Basque example *Gizonak eman dit* man-Det-Erg give-PastPrt 3SgDO-Aux-1SgIO-3SgSubj 'The man gave it to me' illustrates the conventional manner of glossing complex expressions. *V.* **gloss**.

gnomic /'nəʊmɪk/ *adj.* (also **generic**) Denoting the aspectual form expressing a general or universal truth, as in *Rhubarb leaves are poisonous*, *Water boils at 100 degrees* and *The Romans wore togas*. Very few languages seem to have a distinctive form exclusively for expressing gnomic aspect; most often, as in English, the morphologically simplest form of verbs and sentences is used.

goal /gəʊl/ *n.* The **semantic role** borne by an NP expressing the end point of motion in an abstract or concrete sense, such as *London* in *I'm flying to London* and *that conclusion* in *How did you reach that conclusion?* Goal is one of the **deep cases** recognized in Case Grammar; it is sometimes conflated with Beneficiary.

governed /'gʌvənd/ *adj.* In any case of **government** (in senses 1 and 2 of that term), denoting the element which is subject to the requirements imposed by the second element, its **governor**.

governing category /'gʌvənɪŋ/ *n.* In GB, a specified local domain within which the principles of Binding Theory apply. The precise definition is somewhat complex and has undergone occasional modification; the following is given in Haegeman (1991): the governing category of an NP is the minimal domain containing that NP, its governor and an accessible subject. In the majority of instances, this statement can be reduced to the following: the governing category of an NP is the smallest NP or S containing that NP and its governor. See Haegeman (1991) for some explication of the unexplained complications.

government /'gʌvənmənt/ *n.* 1. Traditionally, any instance of a **dependency** in which the mere presence of one element (the governor) imposes some requirement upon the form assumed by a second element which is grammatically linked with it (the governed category). For example, a verb or a preposition which requires an object NP standing in the dative case is said to govern its object, or to govern the dative case. Certain instances of what are traditionally regarded as **agreement** are strictly instances of government, such as the concord in gender between an adjective and the noun it modifies; see the remarks under **agreement**. 2. In GB, a particular structural relationship which may hold between two nodes in a tree, and which is regarded as being of central importance in that framework. The precise definition of government has varied considerably over the years; a recent version (from Chomsky 1986) is the following: a node A governs a node B iff (a) A m-commands B; (b) no maximal projection intervenes between A and B; (c) A is a head. Government is essentially a special case of **c-command** (or, more recently, of **m-command**) in which certain additional requirements are met. It plays a crucial role in GB in the assignment of **Case** and in constraining the distribution of **empty categories**. The notion was introduced by Chomsky (1981) and significantly modified by Aoun and Sportiche (1982). See Haegeman (1991) for discussion, and see Barker and Pullum (1990) for an attempt at extracting the common core of the various definitions of government which have been offered; see also **proper government**. 3. See **lexical government**.

Government–Binding Theory *n.* (**GB**) The most prominent and influential contemporary theory of grammar, the direct descendant of the various versions of **Transformational Grammar**. GB differs radically from other approaches in its emphasis upon the elucidation of abstract universal **principles** of grammar; it devotes little attention to the writing of rules and the construction of grammars for particular languages, and indeed its proponents often maintain that there are no such things as rules of grammar, only the principles and the **parameters** whose values can vary from language to language within specified limits. GB is a **derivational** theory; the syntactic structure of a sentence is represented as an ordered series of trees, three of which are designated as being of special significance: **D-structure**, **S-structure** and **Logical Form** (**LF**). These representations make extensive use of null elements called **empty categories**. There is a single very general transformational operation called **Alpha Movement** whose intrinsic overgeneration is constrained by the requirements of each of a large set of semi-autonomous modules. The modules are **X-bar Theory** (concerned with basic constituent structure), **Theta Theory** (concerned with the argument structures of verbs), **Bounding Theory** (concerned with constraints on movement), **Government Theory** (concerned with the positioning of overt NPs and empty categories), **Case Theory** (concerned with the distribution of NP arguments), **Binding Theory** (concerned with the distribution of anaphoric items and empty categories) and **Control Theory** (concerned with the interpretation of clauses lacking overt subjects). Each of these modules has access to information provided by the other modules, and hence the modules are not 'informationally encapsulated' in the sense of Fodor (1983). GB was developed by Noam Chomsky and his associates; though certain aspects of the framework had been adumbrated in the 1970s, the Binding and Case components were first presented in Chomsky (1980), and the first full description of the whole system came in Chomsky (1981). Since its inception, GB has undergone various modifications, notably in Chomsky (1986). A brief introduction to GB is provided in Horrocks (1987); a more comprehensive presentation is Haegeman (1991).

Government Theory *n.* One of the modules recognized in GB. Its function is to ensure that certain types of structural relations hold between nodes in trees; its principal requirement is the **Empty Category Principle**.

governor /ˈɡʌvənə/ *n.* 1. In any case of **government** (in senses 1 and 2 of that term), the element whose presence imposes a requirement upon a second element, the governed category. 2. In GB, any one of certain categories designated as capable of bearing the relation of government to another category. In recent work, all heads are regarded as potential governors. 3. (also **controller**) In a **dependency tree**, the single word (normally the main verb) on which all the other words in the sentence ultimately depend.

GPSG See **Generalized Phrase Structure Grammar**.

grade /ɡreɪd/ See **degree**.

grammar /ˈɡræmə/ *n.* 1. The system by which the words and morphemes of a language are organized into larger units, particularly into sentences, perceived as existing independently of any attempt at describing it. 2. A particular description of such a system, as embodied in a set of rules. 3. The branch of linguistics dealing with the construction of such descriptions and with the investigation of their properties, conventionally divided into **morphology** and **syntax**. See also **traditional grammar**, **generative grammar**, **universal grammar**, **theory of grammar**. *Adj.* **grammatical**.

grammar fragment *n.* (also **toy grammar**) A small grammar which treats only a limited part of a language, intended as an illustration of some particular approach.

grammatical /grəˈmætɪkḷ/ *adj.* 1. Pertaining to **grammar**, in any sense of that term. 2. See **well-formed**. *Abstr. n.* (sense 2) **grammaticality** /grəmætɪˈkælɪti/.

grammatical category *n.* Any of various categories distinctions within which are expressed by variations in the form of lexical or phrasal constituents. Among the most frequently occurring grammatical categories are **person**, **number**, **gender**, **case**, **tense**, **aspect**, **mood**, **voice**, **degree** and **deictic position**, but other rarer ones exist. Grammatical categories are quite various in their nature. Some (the **deictic categories** like **person**, **tense** and **deictic position**) serve to express contextual features of an utterance. Others, like **mood** and **aspect**, express the speaker's perception of certain characteristics of the proposition embodied in her/his utterance. Still others, like **number** and **gender**, represent the grammaticalization of certain perceived semantic features of referents, or serve chiefly as **reference-tracking** devices. Yet others, like **voice** and **case**, serve largely to express aspects of the internal grammatical structure of a sentence, or to express the relative prominence of elements of the sentence. What they all have in common is that, when a grammatical category is present in a language, a choice among the available forms expressing distinctions within that category is *obligatory* in specified circumstances: one or another of the competing forms *must* be used. Thus, for example, in English, in which nouns are marked for number, one or the other of the two competing forms (singular or plural) must always be used; there is no possibility of avoiding the choice, even when the number distinction appears to be irrelevant.

grammatical function *n.* Another name for **grammatical relation**, preferred in certain frameworks, such as LFG.

grammatical morpheme *n*. A morpheme which has little or no semantic content and which serves chiefly as a grammatical element in morphology or syntax, such as *of*, *the*, the complementizer *that*, the *-ing* of gerunds and participles, Plural or Past tense. Cf. **lexical morpheme**.

grammatical relation *n*. (also **grammatical function**) Any one of several specific grammatical roles which a noun phrase can bear within its sentence. The most widely recognized grammatical relations are **subject**, **direct object**, **indirect object** and **oblique object**; some would add **genitive** and **object of comparison**, and some would also extend the concept to the grammatical roles played by categories other than NP, such as **predicate** or **complement**. As the name implies, grammatical relations are grammatical in nature, and are in principle quite independent of the **semantic roles** borne by those elements. Grammatical relations were identified very early in the history of European linguistics: Aristotle's division of sentences into subjects and predicates was perhaps the first step ever taken in syntactic analysis. Nevertheless, grammatical relations were largely ignored in twentieth-century linguistics until the 1970s, when a number of linguists, often working outside the then-current transformational mainstream, began to point out the syntactic importance of these relations; particularly influential was the paper by Keenan and Comrie (1977), which set up the **NP Accessibility Hierarchy**. At around the same time, Perlmutter and his colleagues were putting together **Relational Grammar**, a version of generative grammar in which grammatical relations were taken as the fundamental primitives. Today most theories of grammar incorporate grammatical relations in one way or another, though GPSG has nothing to say about them, and GB regards them in large measure as secondary and derived from constituent structure. Some recent work has proposed extending the conventional inventory of grammatical relations by adding such novel relations as **primary object** and **secondary object**.

grammatical word *n*. (also **empty word**, **form word**, **function word**) 1. A word with little or no intrinsic semantic content which primarily serves some grammatical purpose: *of*, *the*. 2. An occasional synonym for **word form**. This usage is natural enough, but it conflicts strongly with the better-established first sense, and is best avoided.

graph theory /grɑːf/ *n.* A branch of mathematics dealing with objects called graphs. A graph is simply a collection of points which may be connected by lines ('arcs'). A number of linguistic objects may be usefully regarded as graphs, the most important being **trees**. Graphs of linguistic interest are usually of the particular type called **directed acyclic graphs**.

group genitive /gruːp/ *n.* The English construction in which the possessive affix -'*s* is attached to a large NP in such a way that the affix is separated from the head noun of the NP. Examples include *The Wife of Bath's Tale*, *the woman you were talking to's husband*, *the south of France's population boom* and *that woman you're seeing's mother*. Jespersen (1933).

H

habitual /hə'bɪtʃʊəl/ *adj.* (also **consuetudinal**) The aspect category which expresses an action which is regularly or consistently performed by some entity. The habitual is a subdivision of the imperfective aspect. English has a distinct habitual form in the past tense only: the *used to* construction, as in *Lisa used to smoke*. Some other languages have a more systematic expression of habitual aspect, such as Spanish, which has a distinct habitual auxiliary *soler*: *Suele pasar por aquí* 'He usually comes this way'. See Comrie (1976) for discussion.

haplology /hæp'lɒlədʒi/ *n.* The morphological process in which one of two consecutive morphs of identical or similar form is dropped. For example, the Basque word for 'cider', a compound of *sagar* 'apple' and *ardo* 'wine', ought, by the usual rules of word formation, to have the form **sagar-ardo*, but the actual form is *sagardo*, in which one of the *-ar-* sequences has been dropped.

harmony /'hɑːməni/ *n.* In typology, the degree to which different typological characteristics correlate with one another in a consistent manner. For example, as was shown by Greenberg (1963), SOV word order, left-branching constructions, postpositions and case systems all tend strongly to correlate; a language exhibiting all of these shows a high degree of typological harmony.

hash mark /'hæʃ mɑːk/ *n.* A symbol used to denote that what follows is syntactically well-formed but semantically bizarre: *#Paul is a British trumpeter but a French cellist.*

HPSG See **Head-Driven Phrase Structure Grammar**.

head /hed/ *n.* 1. That element of a constituent which is syntactically central in that it is primarily responsible for the syntactic character of the constituent. For example, in the NP *these old books*, the noun *books* is usually regarded as the head (though see the alternative view suggested under **determiner phrase**). Traditional grammarians recognized a rather inexplicit and limited notion of heads; the notion was developed by the American structuralists and extended to most constituents. Early generative grammar effectively abandoned the notion for some years, but, since the rise of the X-bar system in the 1970s, the concept of a head has increasingly been seen as syntactically central. Today almost all constituents are generally regarded as **projections** of lexical heads. In the example above, the head of the NP would now usually be regarded as the N-bar *old books*, whose head in turn would be the noun *books*, which is the **lexical head** of the full noun phrase. There remains, however, considerable disagreement as to which categories are heads; see Muysken (1982) for a survey of conflicting views. It is usually assumed that a category has only one head, but coordinate structures are often analysed as containing as many heads as they have conjuncts. 2. In some views of morphology, a morpheme which is seen as playing a role in word formation comparable to that played by a syntactic head. For example, some would argue that the suffix *-ness* is the head of the word *happiness*. This non-standard view was advanced by Lieber (1980) and Williams (1981) and criticized by Zwicky (1985).

Head-Driven Phrase Structure Grammar /ˈhed drɪvn̩/ *n.* (**HPSG**) A theory of grammar developed in the mid-1980s by Carl Pollard and Ivan Sag from Pollard's earlier **Head Grammar**. HPSG is an eclectic framework which borrows heavily from other theories of grammar. It may be usefully viewed as a development of GPSG which is strongly influenced by categorial grammar and by LFG. HPSG makes heavy use of **unification**, and it is perhaps the most prominent and the best-developed of the various unification-based theories. Categories incorporate information about the categories they combine with, including subcategorization information, and hence very few rules are necessary, all important syntactic and semantic processes being driven by information in lexical entries. The framework is presented in Pollard and Sag (1987).

head feature *n.* A **feature** which, in some particular analysis, is designated as being subject to the **Head Feature Convention**. The great majority of syntactic features are normally treated as head features.

Head Feature Convention /kənˈventʃn̩/ *n.* (**HFC**) The requirement that a node in a tree must share certain feature specifications with its head daughter. This convention is invoked for a wide range of purposes, for example for guaranteeing that a plural noun phrase will have a plural noun as its head. The HFC is particularly associated with GPSG, the first framework to provide a completely explicit formulation of it, but all theories of grammar make use of it in one form or another.

Head Grammar *n.* (**HG**) A theory of grammar proposed by Carl Pollard (1984), consisting essentially of a hybrid of GPSG and categorial grammar. Head grammars, which incorporate **wrap** operations, characterize a well-defined set of languages which are a proper superset of the context-free languages; head grammars are, however, only 'mildly context-sensitive', and computationally they are only slightly less tractable than CF-grammars. The framework was later elaborated into **Head-Driven Phrase Structure Grammar**.

headless relative /'hedləs/ See **free relative**.

headline language /'hedlaɪn/ *n.* The syntactically distinctive style used in newspaper headlines, characterized by an absence of finite verbs and determiners, the use of the simple present to report recent past events and the extensive use of nouns modifying other nouns: *Bonn gives lead on Croats*, *PM to visit US* and *Railway station murder inquiry shock*.

head marking /'hed mɑːkɪŋ/ *n.* A grammatical pattern in which a relation between a head and a dependent of that head is morphologically marked on the head rather than on the dependent. Examples include possessive constructions marked on the possessed head rather than on the possessor (as in **construct state** and **izafet** constructions) and the marking of grammatical relations on the verb rather than by case forms on NP arguments. Head marking is sometimes regarded as a typological characteristic of languages exhibiting it. Cf. **dependent marking**, and see Nichols (1986) for some discussion. Van Valin (1985).

Head Parameter *n.* In GB, the proposed **parameter** by which a particular language chooses to put all its heads either to the left or to the right of their sisters. In fact, very few languages appear to conform straightforwardly to either pattern, and this proposal can only be maintained with considerable ingenuity.

heavy NP /'hevi/ *n.* A noun phrase which is very long. Heavy NPs often contain relative clauses or complement clauses, and they often show a tendency to occur at the end of the sentence, regardless of the canonical position of grammatically similar NPs. See **heavy NP shift**.

heavy NP shift /ʃɪft/ *n.* The phenomenon in which a **heavy NP** occurs at the end of its sentence in defiance of the canonical position of grammatically similar NPs. Heavy NP shift is observed very widely in the languages of the world. For example, in the SOV language Basque, an object NP normally precedes the verb, but an object which is a heavy NP usually follows its verb.

hedge /hedʒ/ *n.* An expression added to an utterance which permits the speaker to reduce her/his commitment to what she/he is saying: *I think*, *I suppose*, *I fancy*, *I would guess*, *I take it*, *it seems to me*.

hendiadys /hen'daɪədɪs/ *n.* The joining by a coordinating conjunction of two elements which properly stand in a subordinating relationship, such as *nice and warm* for 'nicely warm' or *try and do it* for 'try to do it'.

hesternal /'hestənl̩/ *adj.* Denoting a tense form occurring in certain languages which typically refers to events in the recent past, including 'yesterday' but not 'earlier today'. Both the Bantu language Kamba and the Carib language Hixkaryana, for example, have such a tense form, contrasting with a hodiernal past ('earlier today') and a remote past ('more than a few weeks ago'). Dahl (1985): Latin *hesternus* 'related to yesterday'.

heterocategorial head /ˌhetərəʊkætə'gɒriəl/ *n.* A **head** which is a projection of a different lexical category from its mother. For example, in *Drinking the water is not advised*, the VP *drinking the water* is arguably the head of an NP.

HFC See **Head Feature Convention**.

HG See **Head Grammar**.

hierarchical structure /haɪər'ɑːkɪkl̩/ See **configurational structure**.

hierarchy /'haɪərɑːki/ *n.* Any of various linear scales along which certain grammatical elements are ranked with respect to one or more grammatical processes. Among the most prominent are the **NP Accessibility Hierarchy** (the **Relational Hierarchy**) and the **Animacy Hierarchy**. Croft (1990) presents a summary of the principal grammatical hierarchies which have been recognized. *Adj.* **hierarchical** /haɪər'ɑːkɪkl̩/.

historic present /hɪ'stɒrɪk/ *n.* The use of a present-tense form with past time reference, as sometimes occurs in narratives with the function of adding vividness: *This guy comes in, right? He goes up to the bar and asks for a whisky.*

hodiernal /həʊdi'ɜ:nl̩/ *adj*. Denoting a tense form, particularly a past-tense form, occurring in certain languages which typically refers to events occurring on the day of speaking. A hodiernal past form occurs, for example, in Bengali, Kikuyu, Quecha, Zulu, Hixkaryana and European Spanish, and apparently occurred in seventeenth-century French, according to the Port Royal grammar. Dahl (1985): Latin *hodie* 'today'.

honorific /ɒnə'rɪfɪk/ *n*. or *adj*. A distinctive grammatical or lexical form used conventionally, and often obligatorily in certain contexts, to express respect towards someone other than the speaker. An example is the Japanese prefix *o-*, attached to nouns, adjectives and verbs in this function, as in *o-kirei* 'pretty' (respectful form; *kirei* is the unmarked form). More complex examples are provided by the Japanese honorific verbs: the ordinary verbs *ageru* 'give' and *miru* 'see', for example, have corresponding honorific forms *o-age ni naru* and *goran ni naru*, as well as more elaborate honorific forms.

hortative /'hɔːtətɪv/ *adj*. The mood category expressing an exhortation, typically represented in English by the distinctive structure illustrated in *Let's go* or *Let's see what can be done*.

host /həʊst/ *n*. The element to which a **clitic** or **affix** is phonologically bound.

hot news perfect /hɒt njuːz/ *n*. A particular function of the **perfect** aspect in English and some other languages, by which the perfect is used to express the present relevance of a recent past event: *The President has been shot.* See **perfect**. McCawley (1971).

hypallage /haɪ'pælədʒi/ *n*. Inversion of the normal order of words for rhetorical effect: *the trumpet's Tuscan blare.* Adj. **hypallactic** /haɪpə'læktɪk/.

hyperbaton /haɪ'pɜːbətən/ *n*. The use of an abnormal order of elements for rhetorical effect: *Us he devoured.*

hypercorrection /'haɪpəkə,rekʃn̩/ *n*. An error resulting from a confused attempt at avoiding another error, such as the use of *between you and I* by speakers taught to avoid the use of *me* in certain other circumstances. Adj. **hypercorrect** /'haɪpəkərekt/.

hyphen /'haɪfən/ *n.* A conventional symbol for marking the bound end of a **bound form**, as in the prefix *pre-* or the suffix *-ize*.

hypocorism /haɪ'pɒkərɪzm̩/ (also **hypocorisma** /haɪpəkə'rɪzmə/) *n.* A **diminutive**, particularly one used as an endearment or pet name, such as *Mikey* or *Lucykins*, or as a euphemism, such as *undies* or *hanky*. *Adj.* **hypocoristic** /haɪpəkə'rɪstɪk/.

hypotaxis /haɪpə'tæksɪs/ See **subordination**. Cf. **parataxis**.

hypothetic /hæpə'θetɪk/ *n.* or *adj.* A label sometimes applied to a verb form used typically or exclusively in **conditional sentences**.

hysteron proteron /ˌhɪstərɒn 'prɒtərɒn/ *n.* The inversion of the logical order of elements, as in *thunder and lightning* or in the baseball term *hit-and-run* (denoting a play in which the running precedes the hitting).

I

I The more recent symbol for **INFL**.

IA /aɪ 'eɪ/ See **Item-and-Arrangement**.

IC /aɪ 'siː/ See **immediate constituent**.

iconicity /aɪkə'nɪsɪti/ *n*. A direct correlation between a conceptual notion or distinction and its linguistic representation. Iconicity has not usually been considered a prominent feature of grammatical structures, but recently several linguists have pointed out interesting cases of it, notably Haiman (1985) and Bybee (1985). For example, it is suggested that the ordering of tense, aspect and mood markings with respect to a verb stem is most often iconic: aspect, which is conceptually most tightly bound to the verb, is morphologically marked closest to the verb stem, while mood, conceptually the least tightly bound, is marked furthest from the verb stem, with tense in between in both respects. *Adj*. **iconic** /aɪ'kɒnɪk/. See also **conceptual distance**.

IDC-command /aɪ diː siː/ *n*. (also **I-command**) One of the **command relations**. It states 'A node A IDC-commands another node B iff A's mother dominates B'. IDC-command is the most restrictive, or 'smallest', of all the command relations. Pullum (1986b).

idealization /aɪdɪəlaɪ'zeɪʃn̩/ *n*. The phenomenon by which a linguist constructing a grammar, or a theory of grammar, chooses to ignore certain complications or embarrassing observations in the raw data, for the sake of obtaining an elegant, economical and insightful account. All theory building in all disciplines necessarily involves some degree of idealization, and linguistics is no exception, but naturally there are controversies over the question of just how much idealization is permissible.

ideophone /'ɪdiəfəʊn/ *n*. One of a grammatically distinct class of words, occurring in certain languages, which typically express either distinctive sounds or visually distinctive types of action. In languages that have them, ideophones are usually as rigidly conventional in form as other words, though they may sometimes exhibit exceptional phonological characteristics, such as segments not otherwise attested. Here are a few of the many ideophones in the Carib language Apalai: *kute kute kute* '(frog) croak'; *pyh tere* 'jump into canoe'; *syrý tope topõ* 'falling into the water'; *kui kui* 'screaming'; *seky seky* 'creep up'; *tỹ tỹ tỹ* 'person walking'; *wywywywy* 'hammock swinging'; *uroruro* 'trees falling'; *tutututu* 'fast approach'.

idiolect /'ɪdiəlekt/ *n*. The speech of a particular individual. *Adj.* **idiolectal** /ɪdiə'lektl̩/.

idiom /'ɪdiəm/ *n*. An expression consisting of two or more words whose meaning cannot be simply predicted from the meanings of its constituent parts: *let the cat out of the bag*, *keep tabs on*, *a pig in a poke*. For semantic reasons, an idiom requires its own lexical entry in the lexicon, but many idioms participate in syntactic processes, as illustrated by the example *The cat has been let out of the bag*, in which the idiom has undergone passivization like any transitive structure. *Adj.* **idiomatic** /ɪdiə'mætɪk/.

idiom chunk /tʃʌŋk/ *n*. A portion of an **idiom** which is separated from the rest of the idiom in a particular sentence. In the example *The cat has been well and truly let out of the bag*, the phrase *the cat* is an idiom chunk constituting part of the idiom *let the cat out of the bag*.

ID/LP format /aɪ diː el 'piː ˌfɔːmæt/ *n*. A format for **categorial rules** in which these rules are separated into two sets of statements: a set of **immediate dominance rules**, specifying which mothers can have which daughters, and a set of **linear precedence rules**, specifying the left-to-right order of sisters. The ID/LP format appears to be essential, since the alternative is to provide rules specifying both types of information simultaneously, and this inevitably means that the same precedence information is stated over and over again in a number of distinct rules, with consequent loss of generalizations. For example, English has a large number of possible expansions for the category VP, such as VP → V, VP → V NP, VP → V PP, VP → V NP PP, among others, and in every one of these the verb precedes its sisters. This generalization is nowhere expressed in the traditional phrase structure format, but, in the ID/LP format, the ID rules simply state the possible daughters of VP, without stipulating any linear ordering, and then the LP rule V < X ('a verb precedes its sisters') provides the required generalization. In general, the ID/LP format can only be used in a grammar possessing the property of **exhaustive constant partial ordering**, but the ECPO property appears to be present in the grammars of most, and perhaps all, natural languages. Though various inexplicit proposals had previously been made by a number of linguists, the first fully explicit statement of the ID/LP format was given by Gazdar and Pullum (1981) within the GPSG framework; today, the format is widely employed in various other frameworks.

ID rule See **immediate dominance rule**.

IL /aɪ 'el/ See **indexed language**.

I-language /aɪ/ *n*. (also **internalized language**) A language seen as a set of rules and principles in the mind of a speaker, approximately the same notion as **competence**. Cf. **E-language**. Chomsky (1986).

illative /'ɪlətɪv/ *n*. or *adj*. A case form typically expressing the semantic notion of '(motion) into': Finnish *taloon* 'into the house' (*talo* 'house').

ill-formed /ɪl 'fɔːmd/ *adj*. (also **ungrammatical**, **deviant**) Denoting a syntactic structure which is not permitted by the rules of the grammar of a particular language. Ill-formedness is conventionally indicated by an asterisk preceding the string representing the structure, as in the example **Lisa smiled me*. Since a string normally carries less than complete information about the structure it is intended to represent, it may have to be supplemented by additional notational material, such as brackets, gaps or referential indices, to identify unambiguously the structure which is being characterized as ill-formed: **She put [on the dress]* and **Who$_i$ was she$_i$ talking to e?*

illocutionary force /ɪlə‚kjuːʃənri 'fɔːs/ *n*. The communicative intention of an utterance, which may be that of a request for action, a request for information, an order, a warning, a promise, an offer or a threat, or of many other possible such intentions. The illocutionary force of an utterance is in general independent of its grammatical form or **sentence type**. Austin (1962).

immediate constituent /ɪ'miːdiət/ *n*. (**IC**) A **constituent** of a category which is not a constituent of any unit which is itself a constituent of that category. When the **tree** representation of constituent structure is employed, 'immediate constituent' is simply a synonym for **daughter**.

immediate constituent analysis /ə'nælɪsɪs/ *n*. The exhaustive analysis of a sentence into a series of immediate constituents, all the way down to the individual words or morphemes which are its ultimate constituents, particularly when such analysis is regarded as displaying the fundamental syntactic structure of the sentence. The term is commonly applied to a representation of constituent structure in which nodes are not labelled for their syntactic category, though in some versions heads are recognized and constituents are classified as **endocentric**, **exocentric** or **coordinate**. IC analysis was unknown before the twentieth century; traditional grammarians had only a limited conception of phrases and never developed a clear notion of constituency. It is usually considered that IC analysis was introduced by Bloomfield (1917, 1933), and that Bloomfield was the first linguist ever to take an analytical view of sentence structure, in contrast to the earlier synthetic view, in which a sentence was regarded as an assembly of words. Perceval (1976) disputes this view, arguing that IC analysis was in fact introduced by the psychologist Wilhelm Wundt (1900), and that Bloomfield was merely developing Wundt's ideas. Bloomfield may well have been influenced by Wundt, but the analyses presented by Wundt appear in fact to be more reminiscent of dependency grammar than of constituency grammar, and Wundt's graphical representations look very much like dependency trees (with unlabelled arcs), half a century before Tesnière. But whatever Wundt may have intended, it was Bloomfield who introduced IC analysis into the linguistic mainstream, where it was picked up and developed by the American structuralists, notably by Wells (1947) and Nida (1960), and where it led ultimately to the development of our modern conception of constituent structure in the 1960s. See also **constituent structure** and **tree**.

immediate constituent diagram /ˈdaɪəgræm/ *n.* A **tree** exhibiting constituent structure, particularly one in which the nodes are unlabelled for their syntactic category.

immediate dominance *n.* The relation holding between a **mother** and its **daughter**. That is, a node A immediately dominates a distinct node B iff A dominates B and there is no other node intervening between them.

immediate dominance rule *n.* (**ID rule**) A **categorial rule** which specifies that a particular mother can have certain daughters but which specifies no left-to-right ordering of those daughters. See the discussion under **ID/LP format**.

imparisyllabic /ɪmpærɪsɪˈlæbɪk/ *adj.* (of a noun or verb in an inflected language) Having different numbers of syllables in different inflected forms, such as Latin *rex* 'king', genitive *regis*, etc. Cf. **parisyllabic**.

imperative /ɪmˈperətɪv/ *n.* or *adj.* (also **jussive**) The mood category associated with the uttering of commands, as in *Wash your hands!* Many languages have no specific grammatical form for this purpose, often employing (like English) the simplest possible form of the verb, but many others have a specialized imperative inflection of the verb, such as Spanish: *ven, venid, venga* and *vengan* are all specialized imperative forms of the verb *venir* 'come'.

imperfect /ɪmˈpɜːfɪkt/ *n.* or *adj.* A conventional label for a verb form which simultaneously expresses imperfective aspect and past time reference, such as Spanish *bebía* 'I used to drink', 'I was drinking'. NOTE: this term must not be confused with the distinct term **imperfective**.

imperfective /ɪmpəˈfektɪv/ *n.* or *adj.* A superordinate aspectual category making reference to the internal structure of the activity expressed by the verb, and contrasting with the **perfective**. The imperfective may be subdivided into various more specialized aspectual distinctions, such as **habitual**, **progressive** and **iterative**. See Comrie (1976) for discussion.

imperfective participle *n.* (also **present participle**) A **participle** marked for **imperfective** aspect, such as English *ironing* in *Lisa is ironing my shirts*, or a similar form in another language.

impersonal construction /ɪmˈpɜːsənl̩/ *n.* Any of various constructions occurring in certain languages in which the verb stands in an invariable third-person form (an 'impersonal verb') and the NP which might be regarded as the subject on semantic or psychological grounds stands in an oblique case; there may or may not be an additional NP standing in the canonical subject case. Some examples from Icelandic:

Mig   vantar   bókina.
me-Acc need-3Sg the-book
'I need the book.'

Mig   dreymir   allar nætur.
me-Acc dream-3Sg every night
'I dream every night.'

impersonal passive *n.* Any of various constructions involving an overt passive inflection on the verb and no lexical subject. In languages exhibiting them, impersonal passives are most typically derived from intransitive verbs, though not exclusively so. A simple example is the German *Gestern wurde getanzt* 'Yesterday there was dancing', literally 'Yesterday [it] was danced'. Oblique NPs may occur: the Turkish active *Hasan otobüse bindi* 'Hasan boarded the bus', in which the verb is intransitive and *otobüs* stands in the dative case, has a corresponding impersonal passive *Otobüse binildi* 'The bus was boarded', literally 'To the bus [it] was boarded'. Some languages even allow overt direct objects to occur in such constructions: The Russian transitive *Burja povalila derevo* 'The storm knocked down the tree', in which *burja* 'storm' is nominative and *derevo* 'tree' is accusative, has a corresponding impersonal passive *Burej povalilo derevo* 'The tree was knocked down by the storm', in which *burej* is instrumental and *derevo* is still accusative, there being no surface subject. There is some controversy over how far to extend the term 'impersonal passive'; some would extend it to constructions like the French *On vendit la maison* 'The house was sold', literally 'One sold the house', which differs from a canonical active transitive only in the presence of the impersonal subject pronoun *on*. See Siewierska (1984) for discussion.

implicational universal /ɪmplɪˈkeɪʃənl̩/ *n.* Any **absolute** or **relative universal** which is expressed in the form 'If a language has characteristic X, then it also has characteristic Y'. An example is: if a language has VSO basic word order, then it has prepositions (rather than postpositions). Implicational universals were introduced by Greenberg (1963) and have been most extensively developed by Hawkins (1983).

imprecative /ɪmˈprekətɪv/ *n.* An utterance, especially an obscene or blasphemous one, intended primarily to give offence: *Piss off!*; *Fuck you!* The distinctive syntax of these utterances is examined by James McCawley in his hilarious but very obscene 1971 paper, written under the pseudonym Quang Phuc Dong.

inalienable possession /ɪnˈeɪliənəbl̩/ *n.* A type of possessive construction in which the possessed item cannot in principle be separated from the possessor: *Lisa's eyes, John's parents, my name*. Some languages exhibit a distinctive grammatical form for inalienable possession. Examples from Hawaiian are alienable *ke ki'i a Pua* 'Pua's picture' (i.e., taken or painted by her), contrasting with inalienable *ke ki'i o Pua* 'Pua's picture' (i.e., of her), and *na iwi a Pua* 'Pua's bones' (e.g., which she is eating), contrasting with *na iwi o Pua* 'Pua's bones' (i.e., her own bones). Cf. **alienable possession**.

inanimate /ɪnˈænɪmət/ *adj.* Denoting a noun or noun phrase which is other than **animate**, such as one denoting a lifeless object, a plant, an abstraction or a nominalization.

inceptive /ɪnˈseptɪv/ See **inchoative**.

inchoative /ɪnˈkəʊətɪv/ *n.* or *adj.* (also **inceptive**, **ingressive**) A distinctive aspectual form expressing the beginning of a state or activity. Japanese, for example, has a productive verbal affix *-dasu* for expressing inchoative aspect: *hanashidasu* 'start to talk' (*hanasu* 'talk'), *tabedasu* 'start to eat' (*taberu* 'eat'), *furidasu* 'start to rain' (*furu* 'rain'). Latin has a class of inchoative verbs in *-sc-*: *tremescere* 'start to tremble' (*tremere* 'tremble'), *silescere* 'become silent' (*silere* 'be silent'), *obdormiscere* 'fall asleep' (*dormire* 'sleep').

inclusive first person /ɪnˈkluːsɪv/ *n.* A distinctive pronominal form occurring in some languages which expresses the meaning 'I and you (and possibly others)' and contrasting there with an **exclusive first person**. See examples under the latter entry.

incorporating language /ɪnˈkɔːpəreɪtɪŋ/ *n.* A language in which **incorporation** (sense 1 or 2) is prominent. Incorporating languages are most frequent in Siberia and in North America. NOTE: Comrie (1981) recommends restricting this term to languages displaying incorporation in sense 1 and labelling the others **polysynthetic**.

incorporation /ɪnˌkɔːpəˈreɪʃn̩/ *n.* 1. The grammatical process in which a single inflected word form contains two or more lexical roots. In the Siberian language Chukchi, for example, the English sentence 'The friends put a net' can be expressed either without incorporation as *Tumɣ-e kupre-n na-ntəvat-ɣʔan* friend-Erg net-AbsSg Prt-put-3Pl→3Sg or in the incorporated form *tumɣ-ət kopra-ntəvat-ɣʔat* friend-AbsPl net-put-3Pl, in which the noun meaning 'net' has been incorporated into the verb. Incorporation is not confined to object NPs; Chukchi also allows the incorporation of various oblique NPs into the verb. 2. The realization as affixes of lexical morphemes that could alternatively be expressed as separate words, there being no formal resemblance between the competing bound and free realizations. An example is the Siberian Yupik Eskimo sentence *aŋja-ʁḷa-ŋ-juɣ-tuq* boat-Augm-acquire-want-3Sg 'He wants to get a big boat'. This resembles the Chukchi case in that the morphemes 'acquire' and 'want' could instead be realized as separate words; it differs in that the bound forms of 'acquire' and 'want' bear no formal resemblance to the corresponding free forms, and hence the Eskimo sentence is one word consisting of a single lexical root (*aŋja-* 'boat') plus a number of derivational and inflectional affixes. NOTE: Comrie (1981) recommends that the term 'incorporation' be restricted only to the first sense, but in practice it is widely used also for the second. 3. A label occasionally applied to the formation of a **compound verb**. *V.* **incorporate** /ɪnˈkɔːpəreɪt/.

indefinite /ɪnˈdefɪnɪt/ *adj.* Denoting a noun phrase, or its associated determiner, which most typically expresses a non-specific or unidentified referent, such as the NP *a book* or the determiner *a* generally. In English, it is quite possible for an indefinite NP to have a specific referent: a speaker who says *I'm looking for a book* very probably has a specific book in mind, but cannot say *I'm looking for the book* unless she/he can assume that the addressee already knows which book is being referred to.

indefinite article *n.* A **determiner** most typically used in an NP with a non-specific or unidentified referent, such as English *a(n)* or unstressed *some*. Cf. **definite article**.

indefinite pronoun *n.* A traditional label for a pronoun which, even in context, has no specific identifiable referent: *something*, *anybody*, sometimes also *nothing*.

index (pl. **indices**) /ˈɪndeks, ˈɪndɪsiːz/ *n.* (also **referential index**) An annotation added to an element in a sentence, particularly to a noun phrase, to specify its reference. This is usually only necessary when two or more NPs occur in the same sentence, and the possibility arises that some of them may have the same referent. See examples under **coindexing**.

indexed grammar /ˈɪndekst/ *n.* One of a class of formal grammars resembling context-free grammars, but differing in that the number of categories permitted is infinite. In a conventional notation, an initially finite set of categories is expanded by the use of indices on non-terminal nodes; such a node may bear a linear sequence of indices of any length, and indices may be added to, or removed from, the left-hand end of the sequence (only) during the course of a derivation. When a rewrite rule is applied, the sequence of indices on the mother is automatically copied onto all non-terminal nodes; terminal nodes never carry indices. Rules of the form $A[i] \rightarrow W$, where W is a string, are allowed; such a rule can only be applied to a node A bearing the index [*i*] at its left-hand end, and its application results in the copying of the index sequence on A, minus [*i*], onto all non-terminal daughters. Rules of the form A → B[*i*], where B is a single non-terminal, are also allowed; the application of such a rule adds the index [*i*] to the left of the sequence on A and copies the result onto B. Null productions are also permitted. The following indexed grammar generates the language $\{a^n b^m c^n d^m: m,n > 0\}$:

S → T[k]	A[i] → aA	C[i] → cC
T → T[j]	A → B	C → D
T → T′	B[j] → bB	D[j] → dD
T′ → T′[i]	B[k] → e	D[k] → e
T′ → AC		

Here is the derivation tree for *abbcdd*.

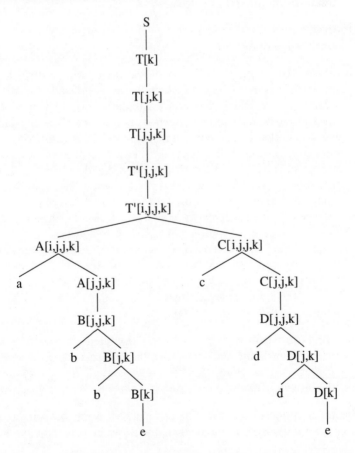

Indexed grammars are interesting because they are only slightly more powerful than context-sensitive grammars but are capable of handling **cross-serial dependencies**, as the grammar above illustrates; parsing them, however, requires exponential time. Various equivalent notations exist for them; the one used here is taken from Partee *et al.* (1990). See Gazdar (1985) for an introduction. Aho (1968).

indexed language *n.* (**IL**) A language generated by an **indexed grammar**. The indexed languages are a proper superset of the context-free languages and, if null productions are excluded, a proper subset of the context-sensitive languages; they are, in fact, **mildly context-sensitive**.

indexical /ɪn'deksɪkl̩/ *n.* or *adj.* See **deictic**.

indicative /ɪn'dɪkətɪv/ See **declarative**.

indirect command /ɪndaɪ'rekt/ *n.* The reporting of an order by **indirect speech:** *She told me to be careful.*

indirect object *n.* (**IO**) The **grammatical relation** expressing the entity which is the recipient or beneficiary of the action of the verb in sentences in which this entity is clearly distinct from a **direct object**. In some languages, such as Latin and Basque, indirect objects are clearly and consistently marked by a distinctive dative case form. In some other languages, however, the identification of indirect objects is more problematic. Consider the two English sentences *I gave Lisa the book* and *I gave the book to Lisa*. Traditional grammar regards *Lisa* as an indirect object in both sentences. Many contemporary analysts, however, disagree. Some hold that *Lisa* is an indirect object only in the first case, but an oblique object in the second. Others hold that *Lisa* is an indirect object only in the second case, but a direct object in the first. Still others maintain that English has no indirect objects at all, only direct objects and oblique objects. See Faltz (1978) and Ziv and Sheintuch (1979) for discussion.

indirect question *n.* (also **embedded question**) A question which forms a subordinate clause within a larger structure: *Lisa asked me* [*whether I was coming*], *Lisa wants to know* [*what she should do*] and *Can you tell me* [*where I can buy hamster food*]?

indirect speech /spiːtʃ/ *n.* The reporting of what someone else has said without using her/his exact words, as in *Lisa said she would* *come*. If this were expressed in direct speech, the result would be *Lisa said 'I'll come'*.

inessive /ɪnˈesɪv/ *n.* or *adj.* A case form occurring in certain languages which typically expresses the sense of English *in*: Finnish *talossa* 'in the house' (*talo* 'house'). The term 'inessive' is usually used to express a contrast with other cases expressing location, such as the **adessive**.

inferential /ɪnfəˈrentʃl̩/ *n.* or *adj.* A grammatically distinct form employed (usually obligatorily) in some languages to indicate that the speaker is drawing a conclusion from evidence. An example is the Turkish verbal affix *-miş*: compare *Ali geldi* 'Ali came' (I saw him) with *Ali gelmiş* 'Ali came' (I didn't see him, but I have good reason to believe he came). The inferential forms part of the **evidential** system in languages exhibiting it; see the discussion and further examples under that entry.

infinitive /ɪnˈfɪnɪtɪv/ *n.* A **non-finite** form of the verb occurring in some (but not all) languages and typically serving to express the meaning of the verb in the abstract, with no marking for or restriction in tense, aspect, mood or person (though some languages exhibit two or more infinitives distinguished in tense or aspect). The infinitive is often a distinctly inflected form, as in Spanish *venir* 'come'; English, however, uses the bare verb stem, as in the infinitive *come*. Infinitives are most often used as complements of other verbs, but can also have various other uses; they are commonly used as the citation forms of verbs in languages possessing them. NOTE: traditional grammar reserves the name 'infinitive' in English for a sequence such as *to come*, but this view is indefensible; see the remarks under *to*-**infinitive**.

infix /ˈɪnfɪks/ *n.* An **affix** which occupies a position in which it interrupts another single morpheme. In Tagalog, for example, the verbal root *sulat* 'write' (a single morpheme) exhibits such inflected forms as *sumulat* and *sinulat*, with infixes *-um-* and *-in-*. NOTE: it is very common to see the term 'infix' used merely to label a morpheme which comes between two other morphemes. For example, the Turkish verb stem *ye-* 'eat' forms an active infinitive *yemek* 'to eat' and a passive infinitive *yenmek* 'to be eaten'; some writers would label the passive marker *-n-* an 'infix', as though *yenmek* were directly derived from *yemek*, but the analysis is indefensible, and the Turkish passive marker is not a true infix, but merely a suffix which precedes certain other suffixes.

INFL /'ɪnfḷ/ *n.* (**I**) In GB, the abstract category which is posited as a locus of tense and agreement, and which in recent work is interpreted as a lexical category whose maximal projection I″ is identified with the traditional category Sentence. See Haegeman (1991) for discussion. Chomsky (1981).

inflecting language /ɪn'flektɪŋ/ *n.* (also **flectional language**) A language whose morphology is predominantly characterized by **inflection**, that is, by the direct variation in the forms of words for grammatical purposes by morphological processes other than mere **agglutination**. Examples are Latin, Ancient Greek and Russian. The label has often been regarded as of typological importance. Compare **isolating language**, **agglutinating language**. Schlegel (1818).

inflection /ɪn'flekʃṇ/ *n.* (also **inflexion**) 1. The variation in form of a single lexical item as required by its various grammatical roles in particular sentences. Distinctions of inflection reflect the various **grammatical categories** which occur in a language and the distinctions which are made within each. 2. A particular word form assumed by a lexical item in some grammatical environment. For example, *gave* and *given* are two inflections of the verb *give*. 3. A particular bound morph expressing an inflectional distinction. For example, one can speak of the English plural suffix *-s* or the past-tense suffix *-ed* as an inflection. NOTE: the spelling 'inflexion' is traditional in British English; the spelling 'inflection', traditional in American English, is now frequent also in British usage.

inflectional class /ɪn,flekʃənḷ 'klɑːs/ *n.* Any class of lexical items in a language whose members exhibit similar inflectional morphology, such as the class of nouns in English, of adjectives in French or German, of *-a*-stem verbs in Spanish or of *-o*-stem nouns in Latin.

inflectional morphology *n.* The branch of morphology dealing with the variation in form of words for grammatical purposes, as illustrated by *cat/cats* and *eat/eats/ate/eating/eaten*. Cf. **derivational morphology**.

ingressive /ɪn'gresɪv/ See **inchoative**.

inherent ambiguity /ɪn'herənt/ *n.* The property of a language which can only be generated by an **ambiguous grammar**. In other words, an inherently ambiguous language is one containing some strings which must necessarily receive two or more distinct analyses. Natural languages are usually assumed to be inherently ambiguous, but, as pointed out by Pullum (1984a), this assumption has more to do with our ideas about linguistically adequate descriptions than with any provable results about natural languages as sets of strings.

inheritance /ɪn'herɪtəns/ *n.* In certain theories of feature distribution in trees, the procedure by which a feature located on a node is automatically passed down to a daughter, usually the head daughter, if no conflicting requirement intervenes.

initial symbol /ɪˌnɪʃl̩ 'sɪmbl̩/ *n.* (also **start symbol**) In a formal grammar employing the **rewrite rule** format, the (normally unique) category symbol which is initially provided for expansion by the rules and which is *ipso facto* the category of the tree structure which results. In most systems this is the category S (Sentence), though in GB it would presumably have to be CP (S-bar). See also **centrality**.

insertion /ɪn's3:ʃn̩/ *n.* In a derivational theory of grammar, any procedure by which some element not previously present in a representation is added to that representation. An example is the insertion of the dummy *it* in some derivational accounts of extraposed sentences like *It surprises me that she has started smoking*.

instantiation /ɪnˌstæntʃi'eɪʃn̩/ See **feature instantiation**. *V.* **instantiate** /ɪn'stæntʃieɪt/.

instantiation of metavariables /'metəˌvɛəriəbl̩z/ *n.* In LFG, the formal procedure by which an annotated c-structure is matched up with a corresponding f-structure to provide a complete syntactic representation of a sentence.

instrument /'ɪnstrəmənt/ *n.* The **semantic role** borne by an NP which expresses the inanimate means by which something is done, such as *the key* in *Lisa opened the door with the key* and *The key opened the door*. Instrument is one of the **deep cases** recognized in Case Grammar.

instrumental /ɪnstrə'mentl̩/ *n.* or *adj.* A case form occurring in some languages which typically expresses the means by which something is done: Basque *lumaz* 'with a pen' (*luma* 'pen') in *Lumaz idatzi dut* 'I wrote it with a pen'.

intensifier /ɪn'tensɪfaɪə/ See **degree modifier**.

intensive reflexive /ɪn'tensɪv/ *n.* (also **intensive pronoun**) A **reflexive pronoun** which does not occupy an argument position in its sentence, but serves merely to intensify another overt NP with which it is coreferential, such as *herself* in *Lisa herself did it* or *Lisa did it herself.*

interfix /'ɪntəfɪks/ *n.* An empty morph occurring between a stem and a meaningful suffix. For example, the Russian proper name *Glinka* forms a relational adjective *Glinkovskij* or *Glinkinskij*, where *-skij* is the relational suffix and *-ov-* or *-in-* is an interfix. Dressler (1985).

interjection /ɪntə'dʒekʃn̩/ *n.* A lexical item or phrase which serves primarily to express emotion and which most typically fails to enter into any syntactic structures at all: *Ouch!*, *Hooray!*, *Yippee!*, *Damn!*, *Shit!*, *My God!* A few interjections, chiefly the profane and obscene ones, exhibit a very limited ability to enter into syntactic structures, as illustrated by *Damn the torpedoes!* and other coarse but familiar locutions.

intermediate phrasal category /ɪntə'miːdiət/ *n.* A category which is larger than a lexical category but smaller than a maximal projection, in other words, a one-bar projection (in most versions of the X-bar system), such as N-bar, V-bar, A-bar or P-bar. Cf. **full phrasal category**.

internal argument /ɪn'tɜːnl̩/ *n.* An **argument** of a verb which is located within a verb phrase, such as an object NP. Cf. **external argument**.

internal conditions of adequacy *n. pl.* See under **adequacy**.

internalized language /ɪn'tɜːnəlaɪzd/ See **I-language**.

interrogative /ɪntə'rɒgətɪv/ *n.* or *adj.* The **mood** category associated with questions. A few languages have distinctive verbal inflections for this purpose, but the interrogative mood is more commonly expressed by particles, by distinctive word order or merely by intonation.

interrogative pronoun *n.* A traditional name for a **WH-item** which is syntactically a pronoun: *who*, *what*.

inter-sentence relation /ɪntə'sentəns/ *n.* Any of various systematic relations between two sentence patterns of the general form 'If the language has a well-formed sentence of pattern A, it also has a well-formed sentence of pattern B involving the same lexical items'. Familiar examples in English include the relation between active and passive sentences and between extraposed and non-extraposed sentences. In his early writings, Chomsky laid great stress on the importance of expressing such relations by single statements in the grammar, and his rejection of phrase structure grammars was largely based on their presumed inability to express such relations; the transformations of early and classical TG were primarily formulated specifically to capture these relations. Transformational accounts proved to be inadequate, however; in particular, no satisfactory transformational description of the active/passive relation was ever formulated, and GB has now abandoned the attempt to express inter-sentence relations directly. Ironically, it was Gazdar's formulation of GPSG which provided the first adequate accounts of these relations through the agency of metarules. Several contemporary theories of grammar now express inter-sentence relations by means of lexical rules.

intractable /ɪnˈtræktəbl̩/ *adj*. Denoting a problem, or a class of problems, which is so difficult that no general solution can be found in a reasonable amount of time using a reasonable amount of resources. Fairly precise definitions of intractability can be provided by the discipline of **complexity theory**. In linguistics, intractability is chiefly an issue among computational linguists trying to develop efficient parsers: parsers based on certain theories of grammar can be proved to require **exponential time**, and hence to be in principle useless for practical purposes. Indeed, there is evidence that this is the case for *all* plausible theories of grammar, a result which leads some critics to suggest that such 'worst-case' results may be linguistically irrelevant. See Barton *et al.* (1987) for discussion.

intransitive /ɪnˈtrænsɪtɪv/ *adj*. 1. Denoting a verb, or a clause containing such a verb, which, intrinsically or in a particular instance, occurs without a direct object: *Lisa smiled*; *Lisa turned up at six o'clock*; *Lisa is eating*. 2. In GB, denoting a specified subclass of the class of intransitive verbs in sense 1, specifically those non-transitive verbs which are not assigned to the class of so-called 'ergative' (**unaccusative**) verbs. Thus the verb *melt* in *The ice melted*, which is classed as 'ergative', is not regarded as an intransitive, while *smile* is so regarded. Like so much GB terminology, this usage is objectionable, since it conflicts so starkly with the established sense of the term. Sense 2: Keyser and Roeper (1984).

intransitive preposition *n*. 1. A preposition-like adverbial which has no overt object NP, when this is regarded as belonging to the lexical category Preposition. An example is *before* in *What did you* *do before?*; comparison with *What did you do before the war?* suggests that *before* in the first example is an intransitive preposition. The analysis of such adverbials as prepositions is widely but not universally accepted; a difficulty is that very few prepositions show such behaviour. 2. A **particle** which forms part of a **phrasal verb**, when this is regarded as belonging to the lexical category Preposition. In an example like *She turned the light off*, the particle *off* is sometimes analysed as an intransitive preposition.

intrinsic rule ordering /ɪnˌtrɪnsɪk ˈruːl ɔːdrɪŋ/ *n.* Ordering of the rules in a grammar, not by mere stipulation of the analyst, but on the basis of some general principles. The clearest cases of intrinsic ordering are those in which rule B has nothing to apply to until rule A has applied first, so that rule A is intrinsically ordered before rule B, which otherwise has no function. Most discussions of rule ordering, however, have extended the concept of intrinsic ordering to embrace various other principles, such as the principle of maximum utilization, by which rules are ordered so as to allow each to apply to the largest possible number of cases. Rule ordering was a hot issue in the late 1960s and early 1970s, when grammars were typically written with large numbers of highly specific rules; the reduction in the number of rules in the more recent descendants of TG, and the development of non-derivational theories of grammar lacking any concept of ordering, have now rendered the rule-ordering controversies largely irrelevant.

intuition /ˌɪntjuːˈɪʃn̩/ *n.* Any linguistic judgement made by a native speaker about the grammatical facts of her/his language, such as, for example, a judgement about the well-formedness or lack of it of a particular example or about the possibility of coreference between two NPs in a sentence. From its earliest days, generative grammar has stressed the importance of intuitions as a source of linguistic data in preference to the recording of spontaneous utterances favoured by the American structuralists. This policy has been vigorously criticized on a number of grounds: the inconsistency of intuitive judgements, the observed discrepancies between intuitive judgements and spontaneous usage and, above all, linguists' practice of relying purely on their own intuitions in cases in which they have a theoretical stake in the outcome. See Labov (1975) for discussion.

inverse person marking /ˌɪnvɜːs ˈpɜːsn̩ mɑːkɪŋ/ *n.* A grammatical pattern exhibited in certain languages, notably those whose grammars feature a **chain-of-being hierarchy**, in which grammatical relations are morphologically marked on the verb, the relations borne by argument NPs being unmarked either by case forms or by linear order. Inverse person marking is particularly common in North American languages. The following examples from Navaho illustrate it. In Navaho, NPs are ranked on the hierarchy Human > Animal > Inanimate, and a lower-ranking NP may never precede a higher-ranking one in a sentence. When the agent/actor precedes the patient/goal, the verb carries the **direct** marker *yi*-; when the patient/goal precedes the agent/actor, the verb carries the inverse marker *bi*-:

> 'ashkii 'at'eed yiyiiltsa 'boy girl *yi*-saw'
> 'at'eed 'ashkii biiltsa 'girl boy *bi*-saw'
> 'The boy saw the girl.'

> *to dibe 'ayiil'eel 'water sheep *yi*-swept-off'
> dibe to 'abiil'eel 'sheep water *bi*-swept-off'
> 'The water swept the sheep off.'

Inverse constructions have often been described as 'passives', but in most cases there is little or no evidence for any similarity to the passive constructions of European languages.

inversion /ɪn'vɜːʒn̩/ *n*. 1. See **subject–auxiliary inversion**. 2. A general term for any phenomenon in which the canonical ordering of two elements is reversed. See Fowler (1965) for a catalogue of examples.

inverted commas /ɪnˌvɜːtɪd 'kɒməz/ *n. pl.* (also **quotes**) The conventional device for enclosing a **gloss**: Basque *etxe* 'house'.

IO /aɪ 'əʊ/ See **indirect object**.

IP /aɪ 'piː/ 1. *n*. In GB, the maximal projection of the abstract lexical category INFL, identified in that framework with the traditional category **sentence**. 2. *adj*. See **Item-and-Process**.

irrealis /ɪri'ælɪs/ *adj*. A label often applied in a somewhat *ad hoc* manner to some distinctive grammatical form, most often a verbal inflection, occurring in some particular language and having some kind of connection with unreality. Palmer (1986) recommends that this term should be avoided in linguistic theory on the ground that it corresponds to no consistent linguistic content.

irregular /ɪˈregjʊlə/ *adj*. Denoting a form which is not constructed according to the usual rules for items of its class: *feet*, *took*, *worse*. *Abstr. n.* **irregularity** /ɪˌregjʊˈlærəti/. Cf. **regular**.

island /ˈaɪlənd/ *n*. A constituent which is inaccessible to certain syntactic processes or relations, particularly **dependencies**, in that no dependency, or no dependency of a specified type, can have one end inside that constituent and the other end outside it. See further under **island constraint**. Ross (1967).

island constraint *n*. Any of various constraints on syntactic processes or dependencies having the general form 'No process or relation of type X may simultaneously involve elements both inside and outside a constituent of type Y'. The constituent Y is called an **island**. The first island constraint proposed was the **A-over-A Constraint** of Chomsky (1964). The classical island constraints were formulated by Ross (1967), including the **Coordinate Structure Constraint**, the **Complex NP Constraint**, the **Left-Branch Constraint**, the **Right Roof Constraint** and the **Sentential Subject Constraint**, among others. Since Ross's work, one of the central preoccupations of Chomsky and his associates has been the reduction of this large number of independent constraints to a smaller number of more general constraints, ideally to a single one; Chomsky (1973, 1981, 1986) represent major steps in this direction, and the **Subjacency Condition** of GB now successfully subsumes many, though not all, of Ross's constraints.

isolating language /ˈaɪsəleɪtɪŋ/ *n*. A language whose words are invariable in form, with each word typically consisting of a single morpheme. Such a language has no morphology; Vietnamese is a good example. See Horne (1966) for discussion, and compare **agglutinating language**, **inflecting language**. This notion was introduced by Schlegel (1818) as part of his three-way typology of languages, though the actual term 'isolating' was apparently not coined until much later.

Item-and-Arrangement /aɪtəm ænd əˈreɪndʒmənt/ *adj*. (**IA**) Denoting a rigidly distributional approach to grammatical characterization which involves no machinery other than lists of grammatical elements and statements of the positions in which they may appear. IA typically makes extensive use of **templates** and prohibits any appeal to grammatical processes deriving surface forms from underlying forms. It was a major feature of most **American structuralist** grammatical work, but it has been generally rejected in generative grammar on the ground that it prevents the formulation of generalizations. Cf. **Item-and-Process**. Hockett (1954).

Item-and-Process /'prəʊses/ *adj.* (**IP**) Denoting any approach to grammatical characterization which involves deriving surface forms from underlying representations by rules. The term was applied to early versions of generative grammar in recognition of one of the most prominent differences between it and earlier work by the American structuralists; it is no longer current. Cf. **Item-and-Arrangement**. Hockett 1954.

iterative /'ɪtərətɪv/ *n.* or *adj.* (also **frequentative**) An aspectual form expressing repetition of an action and constituting a subtype of **imperfective** aspect. English has no specific form for this, though the auxiliary *keep* is sometimes used for this purpose: *She kept writing me letters*. Some other languages, such as Hopi, have a distinct verbal inflection for the purpose.

izafet /ɪ'zɑːfet/ *n.* A term used in the grammars of certain languages to denote a construction in which a noun is possessed or modified by another noun or noun phrase, particularly when an overt marking of the relation occurs on the noun which is possessed or modified. An example is the Turkish *dil kurumu* 'language society', a compound of *dil* 'language' and *kurum* 'society', in which the syntactic relation is marked by the suffix *-u* on the head noun. Persian grammar.

J

jocular formation /'dʒɒkjʊlə/ *n.* A **neologism** deliberately coined for humorous effect, particularly one which is irregularly formed: *wasm* 'an outmoded doctrine'.

jussive /'dʒʌsɪv/ *n.* or *adj.* 1. See **imperative**. 2. More specifically, denoting an imperative form directed at someone other than the addressee, a 'third-person imperative'. In English, this sense is often expressed by the construction illustrated by the example *Let them eat cake!*, where this is interpreted as a command directed at 'them', and not as either the granting of permission or an order to the addressee. Some languages exhibit a distinct grammatical form expressing this meaning, as exemplified by Turkish *Gelsin!* 'Let him come!'.

K

k-command /keɪ/ *n.* One of the **command relations**. It states 'A node A k-commands another node B iff the lowest cyclic node properly dominating A also properly dominates B'. Lasnik (1976); originally 'kommand'.

Kleene star /ˈkliːn stɑː/ *n.* A notational device, conventionally an asterisk, used in the notation A* (a **regular expression**) to indicate a string of any number of items all belonging to the category A. The notation is borrowed from the mathematics of formal systems, in which it normally means a string of zero or more such categories, but many linguists use the notation to express a string of one or more such categories, which in mathematics would be expressed as A^+, since the notion 'zero or more' is only occasionally of linguistic use. Linguists with a mathematical or computational orientation usually stick to the established mathematical conventions; when encountering this device in linguistic works, you should check to see which way it is being used. Kleene (1956).

kommand /kəˈmɑːnd/ *n.* The original name for **k-command**.

L

labelled bracketing /'leɪbl̩d/ *n*. A manner of representing the constituent structure of a sentence in which each constituent is enclosed within a pair of square brackets labelled with the name of the category represented by that constituent. Here is an example, representing the sentence *Lisa bought that skirt in Paris*:

[$_S$[$_{NP}$[$_N$Lisa]] [$_{VP}$[$_V$bought] [$_{NP}$[$_{Det}$that] [$_N$skirt]] [$_{PP}$[$_P$in] [$_{NP}$[$_N$Paris]]]]]

labile verb /'leɪbaɪl/ *n*. (also **amphibious verb**) A lexical verb which can be construed either transitively or intransitively. At least eight classes may be recognized in English: (1) **absolute transitives** (*She is eating dinner*; *She is eating*); (2) **reflexive absolute transitives** (*She undressed the children*; *She undressed*); (3) certain **unaccusatives** (*She melted the ice*; *The ice melted*); (4) **mediopassives** (*They're selling my book*; *My book is selling well*); (5) certain verbs of perception (*She tasted the wine*; *The wine tasted good*); (6) certain **causatives** (*The horse was walking*; *She was walking the horse*); (7) certain verbs of motion (*She swam the Channel*; *She swam slowly*); (8) certain **progressives** (*They're reprinting my book*; *My book is reprinting*). See **pseudo-intransitive**.

landing site /'lændɪŋ saɪt/ *n*. In GB, a position to which a moving element moves, or which is in principle available for some element to move into.

language /'læŋgwɪdʒ/ *n*. 1. A **natural language**. 2. A **formal language**.

language-specific /spə'sɪfɪk/ *adj*. Denoting a characteristic of some particular language, or of certain particular languages, which is not typical of languages generally.

language type /taɪp/ *n*. Any of the various categories of language proposed in the various attempts at a linguistic **typology**; see the discussion under that entry.

layering /'leɪərɪŋ/ *n*. 1. Any of various **functional** (sense 2) views of clause structure in terms of the relative centrality of the elements of a clause. A typical such analysis regards a clause as consisting of a **nucleus** (the verb), a **core** (the arguments of the verb, including the subject) and a **periphery** (other elements). Layered analyses of this general sort have been a part of functional descriptions at least since the 1970s; details and terminology differ considerably, that used here being taken from Foley and Van Valin (1984). 2. A label sometimes applied to instances of multiple **self-embedding**, such as to a VP containing a sequence of ever-smaller VPs nested within it. 3. In some analyses, a label for the structure posited for a VP with multiple adjuncts. For example, the VP in the sentence *I wrote this book in six months on my word processor* might be assigned the layered structure [[[*wrote this book*] [*in six months*]] [*on my word processor*]].

LBA See **linear bounded automaton**.

leaf /liːf/ See **terminal node**.

learnability /lɜːnəˈbɪlɪti/ *n*. Of a proposed grammar, the degree to which that grammar could presumably be acquired by a child with normal exposure to language data in the form of utterances. Learnability has increasingly been an issue in the theory of grammar since the mid-1970s; one of the main driving forces behind the development of GB in particular has been the search to reduce the grammars of particular languages to a rich set of universal principles accompanied by a small number of parameter settings, in the hope that such an approach would serve to explain the impressive manner in which children learn languages. *Adj*. **learnable** /'lɜːnəbl̩/.

learned formation /'lɜːnɪd/ *n*. A word which is deliberately coined, not from elements of the contemporary language, but from elements of an earlier form of the language or from another classical language. For example, the English verb *break* can form a regular adjective *breakable*, but in many contexts it is more usual to employ the word *fragile*, a learned formation derived from Latin.

left-associative grammar /ˌleftəˈsəʊʃiətɪv/ *n*. In computational linguistics, a type of grammar which operates with a regular order of linear compositions. The approach is based on the building up and cancelling of **valencies** (sense 2); it is distinctive in that the history of the parse doubles as the linguistic analysis.

Left Branch Constraint /ˌleft ˈbrɑːntʃ/ *n.* An **island constraint** which states that, in English, an NP which is the left branch of a larger NP is an island. The constraint is invoked to explain the ill-formedness of such examples as **Which senator's did you meet* e *wife?*, in which the left branch of the NP *which senator's wife* has been moved. Ross (1967).

left-branching /ˌleftˈbrɑːntʃɪŋ/ *n.* or *adj.* A type of constituent structure in which modifiers appear to the left of their head, so that recursion of modifiers shows up in a tree diagram as repeated branchings to the left. The principal left-branching structure in English is the *-'s*-genitive, as illustrated by *Janet's boyfriend's mother's job*:

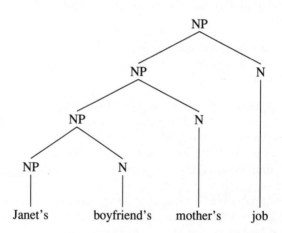

left-branching language *n.* A language in which left-branching structures predominate over right-branching ones. Most SOV languages are left-branching, such as Basque, Turkish and Japanese.

left-dislocation *n.* A **dislocation** in which some element is displaced to the front of the sentence, its normal position being occupied by an **anaphor** (sense 1), as in *Lisa, I like her*. Cf. **right dislocation**, **topicalization**. Ross (1967).

Leftness Condition /ˈleftnəs/ *n.* In GB, the requirement that a WH-trace cannot be coindexed with a pronoun to its left. This condition is invoked to rule out cases of so-called **weak crossover**, such as the following: **Who$_i$ does his$_i$ mother love* t$_i$? Such examples

are not blocked by the ordinary principles of Binding Theory.
Koopman and Sportiche (1982).

level /'levḷ/ *n.* 1. In a **derivational** theory of grammar, any one of the
ordered sequence of formal objects (usually trees) which represent
the structure of a sentence at each stage of its derivation and which,
taken all together, constitute the syntactic structure of the sentence.
Usually certain levels are designated as being of special significance;
in GB, for example, these are **D-structure**, **S-structure** and **Logical
Form** (LF). The term 'level' in this sense is a synonym of **stratum**.
2. In a non-derivational theory of grammar in which the structure
of a sentence consists of two or more formal objects described in
different terms, any one of these objects. Thus, for example, the
c-structure and the **f-structure** of a sentence in LFG would be
different 'levels' of representation. Cf. **stratum**. NOTE: Ladusaw (1988)
recommends restricting the term 'level' to the second usage, preferring **stratum**
for the first sense; this recommendation seems eminently worthwhile, but
prevailing usage in GB favours 'level' in the first sense.

lexeme /'leksiːm/ *n.* See **lexical item**.

lexical ambiguity /'leksɪkḷ/ *n.* An **ambiguity** deriving entirely from
the multiple meanings of a single lexical item, as in *This port is very
old*. Cf. **structural ambiguity**.

lexical category *n.* 1. (also **part of speech**, **word class**) Any one of
the dozen or so classes into which the lexical items of a language are
divided by their morphological and syntactic behaviour, such as
Noun, Verb, Adjective, Determiner and Preposition. Traditional
grammar recognized only about eight parts of speech, but all current theories of grammar have found it necessary to increase this
number by the addition of such non-traditional categories as
Determiner, Degree Modifier and Complementizer. There is as yet
no complete consensus as to precisely which lexical categories
should be recognized, though the divergence of views is not
dramatic. See Schachter (1985). 2. (also **major lexical category**)
In GB, any one of the four categories Noun, Verb, Adjective and
Preposition, which in that framework are regarded as having distinctive properties.

lexical decomposition /ˌdiːkɒmpə'zɪʃn̩/ *n.* The analysis, for
grammatical purposes, of lexical items as consisting of semantic
elements regarded as grammatical or functional formatives; a
famous example is the analysis of the verb *kill* as [DO[CAUSE

[BECOME[NOT[ALIVE]]]]]. Lexical decomposition was first proposed by Gruber (1965); it formed a major feature of **Generative Semantics**, and more recently it has been introduced into **Montague Grammar** (Dowty 1979) and **Role-and-Reference Grammar** (Foley and Van Valin 1984).

lexical entry /ˈentri/ *n.* In a grammar, that portion of the lexicon detailing the properties of a single particular lexical item. In addition to phonological and semantic information, the lexical entry includes at least such grammatical information as the lexical category, any subcategorization facts and any grammatical irregularities, both morphological and syntactic.

lexical exception *n.* A particular lexical item which fails to obey a generalization which applies to most other members of its class. For example, most transitive verbs in English can be passivized, but *fit* is an exception: *That suit fits you*, but not **You are fitted by that suit*. Thus *fit* is a lexical exception to passivization.

lexical form *n.* In LFG, that part of the lexical entry of a word, particularly a verb, which specifies the semantic roles required by that word and the grammatical relations (grammatical functions) by which they are realized. The verb *eat*, for example, has the lexical form

  eat, V, 'EAT ⟨(SUBJ)=Agent; (OBJ)=Patient⟩'

while its participle *eaten* has the lexical form

  eaten, V, 'EAT ⟨(BY-OBJ)=Agent; (SUBJ)=Patient⟩'

Lexical forms represent the formalization within LFG of the traditional notion of **diathesis**. Bresnan (1980).

Lexical-Functional Grammar *n.* (LFG) A theory of grammar developed by Joan Bresnan and Ronald Kaplan in the late 1970s and early 1980s; one of the three most influential contemporary frameworks. The name reflects two of the central characteristics of the framework. First, the role of the lexicon is considerably greater than in most other approaches; lexical entries are elaborate, with every single inflected form having its own lexical entry, and the lexicon does much of the work done by the syntax in other approaches. Second, grammatical relations (called 'grammatical functions') are primitives in LFG. The syntactic structure of a sentence consists of two formal objects, neither of which is derived from the other: the **c-structure**, which is a constituent structure tree of the familiar kind, and the **f-structure**, which carries non-constituent information such as the grammatical functions. Various conditions on well-formedness must be met by each of these objects separately, and further requirements apply to the match-up between them. The LFG languages include some non-indexed languages, and may not even be included in the context-sensitive languages; see Gazdar and Pullum (1985). LFG was introduced by Kaplan and Bresnan (1982); convenient introductions are given in Sells (1985) and Horrocks (1987).

lexical-functional language *n.* (**LFL**) A language defined by a particular **lexical-functional grammar**.

lexical gap *n.* The absence of a hypothetical word which would seem to fit naturally into the pattern exhibited by existing words. For example, English has sets of animal names like *stallion*, *mare*, *horse* and *buck*, *doe*, *deer*, but the set *bull*, *cow* lacks the obvious third term to complete the set.

lexical government *n.* The phenomenon by which certain syntactic rules or processes apply to structures containing certain lexical items but not to those containing other lexical items of the same class. For example, the putative process of **Dative Shift**, which relates pairs of sentences like *I showed the book to Lisa* and *I showed Lisa the book* applies only in the presence of certain lexical verbs, including *show* but not, for example, *demonstrate*: *I demonstrated my technique to Lisa*, but not **I demonstrated Lisa my technique*. This phenomenon constitutes a significant obstacle to the construction of grammars.

lexical head *n.* Of a syntactic category, the lexical item representing the lexical category from which that syntactic category is projected; informally, the lexical item which is the head of the head of the head . . . of the head of that syntactic category. For example, the lexical head of the NP *that chubby little hamster at the back of the cage* is the noun *hamster*.

lexical insertion *n.* In certain derivational theories of grammar in which the structure of a sentence is notionally regarded as being built up piecemeal, the process of selecting suitable lexical items from the lexicon and inserting them into a pre-existing syntactic structure.

Lexicalist Hypothesis /ˌleksɪkəlɪst haɪˈpɒθəsɪs/ *n.* The view that rules of syntax may not refer to elements smaller than a single word. The acceptance of this doctrine effectively removes word formation from the domain of syntax. See also the **Strong Lexicalist Hypothesis** and the **Weak Lexicalist Hypothesis**. Chomsky (1970); Jackendoff (1972).

lexical item *n*. (also **lexeme**) A word regarded as a comparatively abstract object which has a more-or-less consistent meaning or function but which can possibly vary in form for grammatical purposes. For example, the items *dog* and *dogs* are both particular forms of the lexical item DOG, and *take, takes, took, taking* and *taken* are all particular forms of the lexical item TAKE. A lexical item is a word in the sense in which a dictionary contains words, or in which the vocabulary of English contains so many words; in most (not all) theories of grammar, a single lexical item receives a single lexical entry. Cf. **word form**.

lexicality /leksɪ'kælɪti/ *n*. The requirement that all phrasal categories in a grammar should be projections of lexical categories. The term was coined by Kornai and Pullum (1990), who take it as the primary defining property of the **X-bar system**. As these authors point out, however, most versions of the X-bar system proposed in the literature violate this requirement by postulating various categories which do not participate in the system, such as Determiner, Tense, Particle, Conjunction, Auxiliary, Complementizer, Negative and even Sentence. In GB, at least, there is a growing tendency to adhere to the letter, though not the spirit, of lexicality by positing legions of ghostly nodes which have no independent motivation, for example by placing every determiner inside the structure $[_{D''}[_{D'}[_{D}\ ]]]$, even though D″ never contains any material other than the determiner itself. See also **endocentric**.

lexical morpheme *n*. A morpheme which primarily expresses real semantic content, such as *girl*, *green* or the *step-* of *stepmother*. Cf. **grammatical morpheme**.

lexical morphology See **derivational morphology**.

lexical NP *n*. In GB, an NP with overt phonetic content. Cf. **empty category**.

lexical rule *n*. A rule which derives lexical entries from lexical entries. Such rules are particularly important in LFG and in HPSG. A simple example is the purely morphological rule that derives English abstract nouns in *-ness*:

$$[[_{Adj} X]\ \text{-}ness]_N$$

A more elaborate example is the LFG rule for forming passives, which, ignoring the morphological marking, has the form

$$(\text{SUBJ}) \rightarrow \emptyset / (\text{OBL}_{\text{AG}})$$

$$(\text{OBJ}) \rightarrow (\text{SUBJ})$$

One of the most conspicuous trends in recent work in syntax is the increasing use of lexical rules to do work that was previously done by purely syntactic rules.

lexical word *n.* (also **full word**) A word with real semantic content, such as *green*, *kitchen* or *swim*. Cf. **grammatical word**.

Lexicase /'leksɪkeɪs/ *n.* A theory of grammar developed by Stanley Starosta in the 1970s and 1980s. Lexicase is a version of **dependency grammar** which makes extensive use of the basic ideas of **Case Grammar**; it is pithily described by Starosta as 'a panlexicalist monostratal dependency variety of generative localistic case grammar'. The most convenient introduction is Starosta (1988).

lexicon /'leksɪkən/ *n.* That part of the grammar of a language which includes the **lexical entries** for all the words and/or morphemes in the language and which may also include various other information, depending on the particular theory of grammar. The lexicon has traditionally been seen as the repository of miscellaneous facts forming part of no generalization, but recent theories of grammar have increasingly found it convenient to move ever larger quantities of information into the lexicon; even such seemingly impeccable syntactic generalizations as the active/passive relation are now stated in the lexicon in several frameworks, in the form of **lexical rules**. This growing importance of the lexicon is one of the most striking trends in recent work in syntax; it reaches its zenith in the framework called **Word Grammar**, in which almost every conceivable grammatical fact is stated only within lexical entries. See Andrews (1988) for a brief summary of just some recent suggestions.

lexico-syntactic /ˌleksɪkəʊsɪn'tæktɪk/ *adj.* Pertaining to the grammatical properties of individual words, or more particularly to subclasses of words. For example, the classification of nouns into grammatically significant gender classes in certain languages is a lexico-syntactic phenomenon.

lexis /ˈleksɪs/ *n.* The vocabulary of a particular language.

LF See **logical form**.

LFG See **Lexical-Functional Grammar**.

LFL See **lexical-functional language**.

liberation metarule /lɪbəˈreɪʃn̩/ *n.* In GPSG, a **metarule** which has the effect of providing structures in which several categories which would normally all occur as daughters of one particular mother are permitted to occur elsewhere, the object being to allow 'flatter' structures than would otherwise occur. For example, the metarule VP → W ⇒ S → NP, W has the effect of providing flat sentence structures in which all the categories that would normally occur as daughters of a VP node occur instead as daughters of S and sisters of the subject NP, there being no VP node in the sentence. Liberation metarules were introduced as a way of coping with flat structures within the GPSG framework. Pullum (1982).

licensing /ˈlaɪsənsɪŋ/ *n.* The phenomenon by which some grammatical configuration is explicitly permitted by some rule or component of the grammar which imposes restrictions on such configurations. *V.* **license** /ˈlaɪsəns/.

ligature /ˈlɪɡətʃə/ *n.* (also **linker**) A morpheme which in certain languages, notably Austronesian languages, is required to link certain specifiers or modifiers to a head noun within a noun phrase. Palauan, for example, requires a ligature in almost all NPs: *ngikey 'l ʔad* 'that man', literally 'that Ligature man', while Tolai requires one with adjectives: *a gege na davai* 'the crooked stick', literally 'the crooked Ligature stick'. Austronesian languages show a marked tendency to require a ligature below some (language-specific) cut-off point on a hierarchy of **bondedness**. The English possessive marker *-'s* may be regarded as a specialized ligature.

light verb /laɪt/ *n.* A verb with little or no semantic content of its own which combines with a (usually indefinite) direct object noun or NP which itself expresses a verbal meaning. In English, the most usual light verbs are *make*, *do*, *take*, *have* and *give*, as in such expressions as *have a look*, *take a drink*, *have a smoke*, *do a dance*, *give a shrug*, *make a move*, *give a kiss* and *have a wash*. Most light verb constructions in English have matching lexical verbs from which they differ, if at all, in an aspectual nuance: there appears to be little difference between *She gave him a kiss* and *She kissed him*, but there is a perceptible difference between *She took a drink* and *She had a smoke*, on the one hand, and *She drank* and *She smoked*, on the other. Light verbs occur in many languages other than English: Japanese *suru*, Turkish *etmek* and Basque *egin*, all meaning roughly 'do', for example, all serve to construct large numbers of verbal expressions with accompanying nouns, though in these languages, unlike in English, there is usually no alternative lexicalization available. Turkish *etmek* is in fact specialized in this function, while the Japanese and Basque verbs also serve as ordinary lexical verbs. Jespersen (1961, VI:117); revived by Cattell (1984).

linear bounded automaton /ˌlɪniə ˈbaʊndɪd/ *n.* (**lba**) A type of **automaton**, a kind of **Turing machine** which is limited to operating within the space defined by the original placement of the input on the tape. The languages defined by lbas are exactly the **context-sensitive languages** (if null productions are allowed), and are hence a proper superset of the languages defined by non-deterministic pushdown automata (the context-free languages) and a proper subset of the languages defined by Turing machines (the recursively enumerable languages). It is not known whether the deterministic lba languages are a proper subset of the non-deterministic lba languages.

linear grammar See under **regular grammar**.

linear precedence /ˈpresɪdəns/ *n.* (also **precedence**) A relation which may hold between two nodes in a tree, particularly (but not exclusively) between sisters. In trees as they are commonly conceived, of two nodes which are sisters, one of the two must come before (precede) the other in left-to-right order. The same is in fact true of any two nodes neither of which dominates the other, as required by the **Exclusivity Condition**. Phrase structure rules of the traditional kind incorporate linear precedence information as well as immediate dominance information, which leads to the loss of generalizations about linear precedence; the use of the **ID/LP format**, with its **linear precedence rules**, eliminates this problem.

linear precedence rule *n.* (also **LP rule**) In the **ID/LP format** for writing categorial rules, any rule which merely states that some category must precede some other category, when the categories in question are sisters. An example from English is the rule V < NP < X, which says that a verb precedes all its sisters, and that an NP precedes all its sisters except a verb.

linear time /taɪm/ *n*. The characteristic of a parser which requires only a time proportional to the length of the input string. This maximally desirable time property is achieved in the general case only by parsers based on grammars known or believed to be linguistically inadequate, such as **regular grammars** and **deterministic context-free grammars**.

linguistically significant generalization /lɪŋˌgwɪstɪkli sɪg-ˈnɪfɪkənt/ *n*. (**LSG**) Any generalization about the grammatical facts of a language which is, in the opinion of the linguist making the judgement, an important and independent fact about the language which needs to be separately expressed in the grammar. Inevitably, this is a subjective notion about which linguists can sincerely differ, and it is all too easy, when reading the literature, to suspect that, in practice, an LSG is a generalization which is conveniently expressible in somebody's particular theory of grammar. One might reasonably ask what a linguistically *in*significant generalization might look like; here is a possible example: no monosyllabic English verb which begins and ends with the same consonant forms its past tense by vowel change: *peep*, *cook*, *dread*, *suss*, *lull*, *maim* and so on all form their past tenses with the suffix *-ed*, unlike, say, *take*, *see* or *hang*. Few, if any, linguists have ever suggested that this generalization is anything other than an uninteresting accident, but there appears to be no principled basis for such a view, and there is no guarantee that the next theory of grammar to come along will not point to its ability to express this generalization readily as evidence of its advantages. See the remarks under **generalization**, and see also **epiphenomenon**.

linker /ˈlɪŋkə/ See **ligature**.

LIPOC /ˈlɪpɒk/ *n*. The **language-independent preferred order of constituents**, a putative universal preference for the ordering of the elements of a sentence. The LIPOC is postulated as a universal within **Functional Grammar** (sense 3); various formulations have been proposed, the most recent being the following, where '<' means 'precedes':

clitic < pronoun < NP < PP < subordinate clause

There are further statements about the ordering of elements within constituents, and the whole is considered subordinate to the requirements of thematic structure (sense 1), such as topicalization and focus. Dik (1978).

little pro /'lɪtl̩/ See **pro**.

L-marking /'elmɑːkɪŋ/ *n*. In GB, the property of being a complement of one of the lexical categories N, V, A or P. More specifically, A L-marks B iff A is a **lexical category** (sense 2) that theta-governs B.

local /'ləʊkl̩/ *adj*. Confined to a specified domain within a tree. Cf. **unbounded**.

local ambiguity *n*. An ambiguity which is apparent only when a substring of the full string is considered in isolation, and which in principle disappears when the whole string is considered. In the string *The guy who coaches my daughter is a professional*, the substring *my daughter is a professional* represents such a local ambiguity. Local ambiguities are always involved in **garden-path sentences**; they are a particular headache in the construction of **parsers**. Cf. **global ambiguity**.

local dependency *n*. A **dependency** which is confined within a specified domain. For example, case government by verbs or prepositions is confined to a single VP or PP node, and subject–verb agreement is confined to a single S node. Cf. **unbounded dependency**.

Localist Case Grammar /'ləʊkəlɪst/ *n*. A version of **Case Grammar** which takes as its fundamental grammatical elements a set of abstract locational elements, such as Location, Source, Path and Goal. The best-known such proposal is that of John Anderson (1971).

locality constraint /ləʊ'kælɪti/ *n*. (also **locality principle**) Any general principle of grammar which restricts the application of certain grammatical processes to a specified domain. Examples are the **Subjacency Condition** and the principle that limits government and Case assignment in GB to a c-commanded domain.

local subtree *n*. (also **local tree**) Any part of a tree consisting of a single node and the daughters of that node only; the unit of tree structure introduced by a single phrase structure rule or immediate dominance rule. Cf. **subtree**.

location /ləʊˈkeɪʃn̩/ *n.* (also **place**) The **semantic role** borne by an NP which expresses the place in which something exists or occurs. Location is one of the **deep cases** recognized in Case Grammar.

locative /ˈlɒkətɪv/ *n.* or *adj.* A case form occurring in some languages which typically expresses the place in, on or at which something exists or occurs: Turkish *masada* 'on the table' (*masa* 'table'), *Ankarada* 'in Ankara'. The term is commonly used in the grammars of languages having only a single such case, more specific terms being preferred with languages making finer distinctions, such as **inessive**, **adessive**.

Logical Form /ˈlɒdʒɪkl̩/ *n.* (**LF**) In GB, one of the three designated levels of syntactic representation recognized as having special significance. The notion of LF was introduced by Robert May in unpublished work in 1977, and its conception has changed over the years: originally it was seen as an essentially semantic level of representation, but now it is regarded as strictly syntactic. In current versions of GB, LF is regarded as being derived from S-structure primarily by the two operations of **WH-Movement** and **Quantifier Raising**, by which all WH-items and quantifiers are moved to the left margin of the sentence, where they can be interpreted as operators binding variables. For example, the sentence *Lisa greeted everybody* would have an LF roughly of the form [*everybody* [*Lisa greeted* x], parallel to the predicate calculus formula 'For all x, Lisa greeted x'. See May (1985) for a detailed account of LF.

logophoric pronoun /lɒɡəˈfɒrɪk/ *n.* A specialized pronominal form occurring always and only embedded under a verb of saying, thinking or perception and referring to the person whose speech, thoughts or perceptions are reported. Such pronouns are especially frequent in West African languages. In the following examples from Yoruba, the first shows an ordinary pronoun in the embedded clause, the second a logophoric pronoun:

o ri pe o ni owo
he$_i$ saw that he$_j$ had money
'He$_i$ saw that he$_j$ had money.'

o ri pe oun ni owo
he$_i$ saw that he$_i$ had money
'He$_i$ saw that he$_i$ had money.'

A few languages achieve the same effect by the use of distinctive verb forms, rather than distinctive pronouns. Hagège (1974).

long-distance dependency /ˌlɒŋ'dɪstəns/ See **unbounded dependency**.

long-distance reflexive *n*. A construction involving a **reflexive pronoun** which is not contained within the same clause as its antecedent. In English, this occurs only in restricted circumstances, as in the example *John$_i$ told Mary that perjuring himself$_i$ would be a mistake*. In some other languages, however, this represents the normal behaviour of reflexive pronouns, as in Chinese, Japanese and Korean. In the following sentence from Mandarin Chinese, for example, any one of the three NPs can equally serve as the antecedent of the reflexive pronoun *ziji* 'self':

> Zhangsan renwei Lisi shidao Wangwu xihuan ziji
> 'Zhangsan thinks Lisi knows Wangwu likes him(self).'

LP rule See **linear precedence rule**.

LR parser /el'ɑː/ *n*. A type of parser which recognizes exactly the **deterministic context-free languages**. See Chapman (1987) for an introduction.

LSG See **linguistically significant generalization**.

M

main clause /meɪn/ *n.* A **clause** which is not embedded under any other clause. Every well-formed sentence contains at least one main clause. Indeed, in current thinking, every well-formed sentence *is* a main clause. Traditional grammarians usually took the view that a subordinate clause embedded under a main clause was not itself part of that main clause, but most linguists today would adopt the opposite view.

main verb *n.* A traditional label for a non-auxiliary verb, particularly for one which occurs in a sentence together with one or more auxiliaries. For example, in *Lisa will be writing letters*, *writing* is the main verb.

major lexical category /ˈmeɪdʒə/ *n.* In some analyses, any one of the four lexical categories Noun, Verb, Adjective, Preposition, which are sometimes seen as having grammatical properties which distinguish them from the other (**minor**) lexical categories. In particular, it is often suggested that only major categories project phrasal categories within the X-bar system. See also **minor lexical category**.

mapping /ˈmæpɪŋ/ *n.* In the mathematics of formal systems, any explicit procedure by which each object in one set is systematically associated with some object or objects in another set (possibly the same set). In GB, for example, one may speak of the mapping of D-structures onto S-structures. Mathematicians distinguish between a mapping **onto** and a mapping **into**: in the former, every object in the second set is associated with an object in the first set; in the latter, this is not the case.

Marantz's Generalization /məˈrænts/ *n.* The observation that, in a construction in which an underlying indirect or oblique object has been promoted to direct object, the underlying direct object fails to exhibit the typical properties of a direct object – for example, it cannot trigger direct object agreement in the verb, nor can it undergo passivization.

Marcus parser /ˈmɑːkəs/ *n.* A parser proposed by Marcus (1980) which purports to parse English sentences using the then-current version of TG, the REST, as a basis. The Marcus parser has attracted a good deal of attention as the only functioning transformationally based parser ever constructed, but it has been criticized on the ground that it does not really use the REST framework for parsing: instead, it parses input by more conventional methods and then constructs an REST-style surface structure for the input.

marked form /mɑːkt/ *n.* 1. A form or construction differing from another with which it stands in a paradigmatic relationship (the **unmarked form**) by the presence of additional morphological material. For example, the lexical items *hostess* and *inconsistent* are marked with respect to *host* and *consistent*; plural *cats* is marked with respect to singular *cat*; and a passive construction like *Janet was arrested by the police* is marked with respect to the corresponding active *The police arrested Janet*. 2. A form or construction which is regarded as less central or less natural than a competing one on any of various grounds, such as lower frequency, more limited distribution, more overt morphological marking, greater semantic specificity or greater rarity in languages generally. For example, the noun *drake* is marked with respect to its superordinate *duck*; the uncommon adjective *nugatory* is marked with respect to its more frequent synonym *trivial*; the plural *brethren* is marked with respect to its more widely applicable synonym *brothers*; the intransitive passive construction illustrated in *Lisa is gone* is marked with respect to the nearly synonymous perfect *Lisa has gone*, since the latter applies to far more verbs than the former; and ergative morphology and syntax are marked with respect to accusative morphology and syntax, the former being far rarer in the languages of the world than the latter. The precise characterization of markedness is a matter of some controversy; see Eckman *et al.* (1986) and Tomić (1989) for discussion, and see Anderson (1989) for a history of the use of these terms. *Abstr. n.* **markedness**. The terms 'marked' and 'unmarked' were apparently introduced by Nikolai Trubetzkoy and Roman Jakobson, though the idea goes well back into the nineteenth century.

markedness shift /ˈmɑːkɪdnəs ʃɪft/ *n.* The historical process by which the more **marked** of two competing forms becomes less marked, and vice versa, as when a passive construction becomes more usual than the active, as seems to have happened in some Polynesian languages.

marked periphery /pə'rɪfəri/ *n*. In GB, that part of the grammar of a particular language which lies outside the **core grammar** and which is viewed as consisting of miscellaneous language-specific phenomena which cannot be straightforwardly accommodated within the principles of universal grammar. An English example is the **exceptional case marking** found in the accusative-and-infinitive construction, which cannot be handled by the ordinary principles of Case Theory. See the discussion under **core grammar**.

masculine /'mæskjʊlɪn/ *adj*. A conventional label in certain **gender** languages for a gender category which shows some degree of semantic correlation with male sex. See the remarks under **gender**.

mass noun /mæs/ *n*. A noun whose meaning is perceived to be anything other than a distinct countable entity, such as a substance (*wine*), a state of affairs (*happiness*), an activity (*sky-diving*) or a quality (*intelligence*). Mass nouns in English and other languages cannot usually be counted or pluralized in their primary senses, though many can be pluralized in special senses, such as 'variety', 'measure' or 'individual embodiment': *French wines* ('varieties of wine'), *two coffees* ('measures', of a type determined by the context), *an alien intelligence* ('embodiment'). Cf. **count noun**.

mate relation /meɪt/ *n*. A relation which holds between two nodes in a tree each of which bears a certain **command relation** to the other. The most familiar mate relation is the **clausemate** relation, which holds between two nodes each of which S-commands the other, but other command relations yield other mate relations: for example, two nodes which m-command (max-command) each other are max-mates, a notion involved in some definitions of **government** in GB. Barker and Pullum (1990).

mathematical linguistics /ˌmæθə'mætɪkl̩/ *n*. A branch of linguistics which studies the mathematical properties of language. The term was formerly understood as referring chiefly to statistically based approaches such as information theory; nowadays it normally refers to the study of formal grammars. See **Chomsky Hierarchy**, and see Perrault (1984) for a brief summary of some important results.

matrix clause /'meɪtrɪks/ *n*. (also **matrix sentence**) A clause which contains another clause embedded within it.

MAX-command /mæks/ See **m-command**.

maximal /'mæksɪml̩/ *adj.* Denoting any object which is in some sense the largest member of its class. The term is most often met in the phrase **maximal projection**, but it is also used in other ways: for example, one may speak of the 'maximal VP' in a particular tree, meaning the largest (highest) VP node among several nested VPs.

maximality /mæksɪ'mælɪti/ *n.* The requirement, adopted in some versions of the X-bar system, that every non-head daughter in a rule must be a maximal projection. Maximality is widely, though not universally, espoused by X-bar theorists; in principle, it is a very attractive constraint on possible rules, but, as pointed out by Kornai and Pullum (1990), the literature is full of analyses which hold to the letter, but not the spirit, of the requirement by positing ghostly nodes with no independent justification. Some analysts permit specified grammatical formatives to constitute the sole class of exceptions to Maximality, a position dubbed 'Weak Maximality' by Kornai and Pullum (1990). Kornai and Pullum (1990), but the idea goes back at least to Jackendoff (1977).

maximal projection *n.* In the **X-bar system**, the largest syntactic category which is formally related to some lexical category by the relation of **projection**, represented by the largest available value for the feature **bar**, and identified with the traditional **(full) phrasal category** associated with that lexical category. Assuming that the maximal bar-value is two, the maximal projection of the lexical category Noun, for example, is Noun-double-bar, represented as $\bar{\bar{\text{N}}}$, N'' or N^2; this category is identified with the category Noun Phrase. Other maximal projections are V'' (= VP), A'' (= AP) and P'' (= PP), and possibly others. Maximal projections as a class have certain identifiable properties: for example, only maximal projections can be **preposed**, and only maximal projections can serve as **complements**. See also **uniformity**.

m-command /em/ *n.* (also **MAX-command**) One of the **command relations**. It states 'A node A m-commands another node B iff the lowest maximal projection which properly dominates A also properly dominates B'. The notion was first defined by Aoun and Sportiche (1982), who called it 'c-command', intending that this relation should supplant the original definition of **c-command**; the name 'm-command' was proposed by Chomsky (1986) and is now usual, though one also encounters the name 'c-command in the sense of Aoun and Sportiche'.

medial verb /'miːdiəl/ *n.* (also **dependent verb**) One of the subordinate verb forms occurring in languages in which **clause chaining** is prominent.

mediopassive /mediəu'pæsɪv/ *n.* or *adj.* (also **middle**) A construction in which an intrinsically transitive verb is construed intransitively with a patient as subject and receives a passive interpretation: *This fabric washes easily, My new book is selling well.* In English, this construction is confined to a minority of verbs, and should perhaps be regarded as a purely lexical phenomenon, rather than as a syntactic one; in some other languages, however, such as Basque, the pattern is fully productive: every transitive verb can be so construed. See also **labile verb**. Nineteenth century, revived by Grady (1965); 'middle' is equally frequent, but it seems best to refrain from adding to the senses of that term; also 'passival' (Sweet 1892), 'activo-passive' (Jespersen 1961, III:347), 'patient-subject construction' (van Oosten 1977).

merging /'mɜːdʒɪŋ/ *n.* A synonym for **unification**, preferred in LFG.

metagrammar /'metə,græmə/ *n.* In certain theories of grammar, that part of a complete grammatical description which consists of statements that do not directly license subtrees but instead express generalizations about the rules of the grammar which *do* license subtrees, the **object grammar**. The division of a grammar into an object grammar and a metagrammar derives from van Wijngaarden's (1969) work in computation; the first theory of grammar to adopt it was GPSG.

metalanguage /'metə,læŋgwɪdʒ/ *n.* A language which is used to talk about another language, the **object language**. A metalanguage may be either a natural language or a formal language; the same is true of an object language. It is very common in linguistics to use a natural language, such as English, as a metalanguage to talk about the same natural language as the object language; when this is done, it is essential to distinguish the two clearly to avoid confusion. This is conventionally done by typographical means, such as by citing object language forms in italics or in inverted commas: compare *Men are beasts* with '*Men*' is an irregular plural. *Adj.* **metalinguistic** /,metəlɪŋ'gwɪstɪk/.

metarule /'metəruːl/ *n.* In GPSG, a statement which serves to express a generalization about the rules of the grammar. A metarule does not itself license local subtrees; instead it expresses a generalization about sets of local subtrees, particularly an **inter-sentence relation**, such as the active/passive or extraposed/non-extraposed relation. The following example relates inverted and non-inverted structures:

$$\text{VP} \rightarrow W \Rightarrow \text{S}[+\text{INV}] \rightarrow W, \text{NP}$$

This says that, for every rule in the grammar that expands the category VP as a string W, there is a corresponding rule that expands the category S as the same string W plus an NP, where the feature $[+\text{INV}]$ appears on the S. (Other statements in the grammar will take care of the linear ordering and ensure that the inverted verb is a finite auxiliary.) Metarules are usually constrained to apply only to immediate dominance rules which introduce lexical heads; they thus represent a kind of compromise between purely syntactic and purely lexical statements of such relations.

metavariable /'metəvɛəriəbḷ/ *n.* A variable whose possible values are other variables. The term is used in LFG to denote the **up arrow** and **down arrow** employed in **functional schemata** to represent f-structures which are themselves treated as variables.

metric /'metrɪk/ *n.* Any of various criteria which may be appealed to in deciding how successfully some proposed grammar meets some proposed level of **adequacy**.

middle /'mɪdḷ/ *n.* or *adj.* 1. In certain languages, notably Ancient Greek and Sanskrit, a distinctive verb form, contrasting with both active and passive, which serves to express that the subject is acting on herself/himself (reflexive) or for herself/himself; the middle forms part of the **voice** system of such languages. The term seems obviously appropriate for the construction illustrated by such English examples as *John is shaving* and *Lisa undressed*, but it is rarely so used. 2. By extension, in some analyses, denoting a clause containing only one argument NP, which is an actor: *John is waiting*, *The sun is shining*, *His popularity declined*, *Behave yourself!* Halliday (1976). 3. Denoting a transitive verb whose subject is not an agent, especially a **relational** verb (*have*, *deserve*), but sometimes also a verb of perception, cognition or emotion (*see*, *know*, *love*). 4. See **mediopassive**.

mildly context-sensitive /'maɪldli/ *adj.* Denoting any of various classes of formal grammars which define languages that are proper supersets of the **context-free languages** and proper subsets of the **context-sensitive languages**, specifically those grammars which can handle **cross-serial dependencies** limited to affecting two points, which have the **constant-growth property** and which allow parsing in **polynomial time.** Since there is considerable evidence that, at least in terms of **weak generative capacity**, no natural language requires more than slight additions to the power of context-free grammars, there is considerable interest in constructing mildly context-sensitive grammars; two attempts at doing this are **indexed grammars** and **tree-adjoining grammars.** Joshi (1985).

minimal /'mɪnɪml̩/ *adj.* Denoting an object which is in some sense the smallest of its class; in particular, often denoting a category in a tree which is the 'smallest' or 'lowest' of its type, such as the 'minimal' VP (the lowest VP in a set of nested VPs), or the 'minimal' maximal projection (the lowest of several embedded maximal projections).

minimality /mɪnɪ'mælɪti/ *n.* In GB, the requirement that, of several potential **governors** for a governed category, only the 'lowest' or 'closest' potential governor should actually govern that category.

minor lexical category /'maɪnə/ *n.* In some analyses, any lexical category other than the so-called **major lexical categories** of Noun, Verb, Adjective and Preposition. The minor categories are often assumed not to project phrasal categories, though this assumption has been challenged in some recent work, such as in Pollock (1989).

minor rule *n.* A generalization which applies only to a (typically small) subset of items in a language; an example is the inflectional pattern shown by certain English verbs, such as *sing/sang/sung*, *drink/drank/drunk*, *ring/rang/rung*, *stink/stank/stunk*, among others.

minor sentence type /taɪp/ *n.* A name sometimes given to any of various types of conventional utterances which do not have the structures of well-formed sentences, most usually lacking a finite verb. Some typical examples are *All aboard!*, *No smoking*, *Long live the King!*, *Yes*, *Ouch!*, *Good morning*, *Taxi!*, *This way, please*, *The more the merrier* and *Two spades*. Bloomfield (1933); Jespersen had previously called them 'inarticulate sentences' (1961, VII: 122).

mirror-image language /mɪrər'ɪmɪdʒ/ *n.* A formal language in which every string has the form WW⁻¹, where the string W⁻¹ is the exact reverse of the string W. Mirror-image languages can be generated by context-free grammars. Cf. **copying language.**

missing antecedent /'mɪsɪŋ/ *n.* The phenomenon in which a pronoun has no overt antecedent in its sentence, even though one appears to be required. An example is *I've never met a millionaire, but Lisa has, and she says he was a creep*, in which the antecedent of *he* is missing. Grinder and Postal (1971).

missing object construction *n.* The construction illustrated by examples like *Lisa is lovely to look at*, in which the infinitival VP has no object. This construction differs from *Tough*-Movement in that the seemingly related construction of the form *To look at Lisa is lovely* has a quite different sense. Schachter (1981).

modal /'məʊdl̩/ 1. *adj.* Pertaining to **mood** contrasts. 2. *n.* (also **modal auxiliary**) A lexical item, usually exhibiting the inflectional behaviour of a verb, which serves primarily to express a distinction of mood. English has a number of such modals, including *must, can/could, will/would, shall/should, may/might* and *ought*. See the remarks under **auxiliary** (sense 1).

modality /məʊ'dælɪti/ *n.* 1. A synonym for **mood**, often preferred for the expression of mood distinctions by lexical means or as a superordinate term when 'mood' is restricted to the expression of this category by verbal inflection. 2. A specific range of mood distinctions concerned with the speaker's estimate of the relationship between the actor and the accomplishment of some event. Modality in this sense is the category involved in distinguishing, for example, *can* ('knows how to'), *can* ('is physically able to') and *can* ('is permitted to'); it is also the category expressed by such verbs as *try, manage, fail* and *succeed*, and by aspectual verbs like *start, stop* and *continue* when these serve to express the speaker's view. Sense 2: Jakobson (1971).

modal preterite *n.* A past-tense form used to express unreal or counterfactual mood, rather than past time: *It's time you went to bed*; *If I spoke better French, I could work in Paris*.

mode /məʊd/ See **mood** (especially sense 2).

modification /mɒdɪfɪ'keɪʃn̩/ *n.* The relation which a **modifier** bears to its head.

modifier /'mɒdɪfaɪə/ *n.* Any category which serves to add semantic information to that provided by the head of the category within which it is contained, such as an adjective or a relative clause within an NP or an adverbial within a VP. Modifiers may be **restrictive** or

non-restrictive. In some versions of the X-bar system, a modifier is formally defined as a category which is a daughter of a one-bar projection and a sister of another. A modifier within an NP is often called an **attribute**. Cf. **specifier**, **complement**.

modular /ˈmɒdjʊlə/ *adj.* Denoting a theory of grammar in which each permitted grammar consists of a set of **modules**.

module /ˈmɒdjuːl/ *n.* In certain theories of grammar, any one of the several more-or-less autonomous components of a grammar. In a modular theory of grammar, each module of the grammar makes its own independent requirements as to well-formedness, and a well-formed structure is one which is licensed by every one of the modules independently. In some modular theories, such as Autolexical Syntax, the modules are 'informationally encapsulated' in the sense of Fodor (1983), meaning that no module has access to the representations provided by other modules; in other modular theories, such as GB, each module has access to information from other modules.

monad /ˈmɒnæd/ *n.* A formal object with no internal structure, such as the category NP in early generative grammar. *Adj.* **monadic** /mɒˈnædɪk/ Cf. **complex symbol**.

monostratal /mɒnəʊˈstreɪtl̩/ *adj.* 1. Denoting a manner of representing the syntactic structures of sentences in which a sentence is represented by a single formal object, typically an annotated tree structure, and no more abstract level of representation is recognized. 2. Denoting a theory of grammar in which such representations are exclusively employed, such as GPSG. Cf. **derivational** (sense 2). Perlmutter (unpublished work); Perlmutter (1984).

Montague Grammar /ˈmɒntəgjuː/ *n.* A system of formal semantics accompanied by a set of syntactic rules related to the semantic rules by the **rule-to-rule hypothesis**. This approach has been enormously influential in semantics; in spite of its name, it is essentially a theory of semantics, although the rule-to-rule aspect has been incorporated into at least one theory of grammar, GPSG. See Halvorsen and Ladusaw (1979) or Cooper (1980) for an introduction. *Adj.* **Montagovian** /mɒntəˈgəʊviən/. Montague (1970).

mood /muːd/ *n.* (also **modality**) 1. A grammatical category which expresses the degree or kind of reality of a proposition, as perceived by the speaker. Mood distinctions appear to be universally present in languages; they are variously expressed, often by inflection of the verb or by the use of specialized lexical items called **modals**. In many languages, the expression of mood is intimately bound up with the expression of **tense** and/or **aspect**; in others, however, its expression is sharply distinct. Of all the widely attested grammatical categories, mood is perhaps the most elusive; mood distinctions tend to shade off almost imperceptibly into expressions of the speaker's attitude and into clearly pragmatic factors, such as the speaker's perceived relationship to other people. Nevertheless, the existence of grammaticalized mood contrasts is beyond dispute. Various classifications of mood distinctions have been proposed, the most frequent being that between **epistemic** and **deontic modalities**. Foley and Van Valin (1984) propose a three-way contrast between **illocutionary force**, **status** and **modality** (sense 2); see these entries for explanations. **Evidential** and **evaluative** distinctions are also sometimes regarded as mood distinctions. NOTE: some analysts prefer to restrict the term 'mood' to distinctions expressed by inflection of the verb, and to use 'modality' as a superordinate label for the grammatical category as a whole. 2. Any one of the particular distinctions of mood occurring in a particular language. Among the more widely attested mood categories are **declarative**, **interrogative**, **imperative**, **jussive**, **subjunctive**, **conditional**, **hortative**, **desiderative**, **dubitative** and **necessitative**, though many others occur in one language or another. *Adj.* **modal**.

morph /mɔːf/ *n.* A piece of morphological material, consisting of a sequence of zero or more phonemes, considered *per se*, without any reference to its morphological status. A morph may represent a single morpheme, a sequence of two or more morphemes, a part of a morpheme or no morpheme at all. For example, the Basque noun *mendi* 'mountain' forms a locative plural *mendietan* 'in the mountains'; we can speak of the morph *-etan* occurring in this word without committing ourselves to any particular analysis of it. (For an analysis of this form, see under **empty morph**.)

morpheme /'mɔːfiːm/ *n.* (also **formative**) The minimal grammatical unit; the smallest unit which plays any part in morphology and which cannot be further decomposed except in phonological or semantic terms. A morpheme is an abstract unit which may or may not be realized by a fairly consistent stretch of phonological material. For example, a noun plural in English usually consists of two morphemes, a noun stem and the morpheme {Plural}; however, the realization of this sequence varies in ways which are both regular and irregular, as illustrated by such plurals as *cats*, *dogs*, *boxes*, *sheep, men, women, children, feet, mice, radii, formulae, criteria, indices, crises, cherubim* and *passers-by*. It is a widely used convention to enclose morphemes within braces; thus *feet* might be represented as {*foot*} plus {Plural}. Morphemes are variously classified as **free** or **bound**, or as **lexical** or **grammatical**. *Adj.* **morphemic** /mɔː'fiːmɪk/. Cf. **morph**, **allomorph**. The term was introduced by Baudoin de Courtenay (1895); after considerable variation in usage, the modern sense was established by Bloomfield (1933).

morpholexical rule /mɔːfə'leksɪkl̩/ *n.* A lexical rule which, for some morpheme, specifies all the allomorphs which that morpheme can assume in various grammatical environments. Lieber (1980, 1982).

morphological /mɔːfə'lɒdʒɪkl̩/ *adj.* 1. Pertaining to **morphology**. 2. An occasional synonym for **synthetic**. One may speak, for example, of a 'morphological causative' (one expressed by inflection of the verb) as opposed to an analytic or periphrastic causative.

morphology /mɔː'fɒlədʒi/ *n.* The branch of grammar dealing with the analysis of word structure, conventionally divided into **derivational morphology** (the study of word formation) and **inflectional morphology** (the study of the variation in form of single lexical items for grammatical purposes). See Matthews (1974) or Spencer (1991) for a comprehensive introduction. *Adj.* **morphological**.

morphosyntactic category /mɔːfəsɪn'tæktɪk/ *n.* Any morphologically distinguished class of forms which plays a part in syntax, such as the dative case, the feminine gender or the past tense.

morphosyntactic word *n.* A **word form** conceived as a realization of whatever grammatical distinctions are significant in the language in question. In Spanish, for example, finite verbs agree in person and number with their subjects: *canto* 'I sing', *cantas* 'you sing', *canta* 'he/she sings' and so on. But in the imperfect, the first and third person singular forms are identical: *cantaba* 'I was singing', *cantabas* 'you were singing', *cantaba* 'he/she was singing'; the first- and third-person forms *cantaba* are different morphosyntactic words, even though they might be regarded as identical word forms.

morphosyntax /mɔːfəʊ'sɪntæks/ *n.* The area of interface between morphology and syntax. Morphosyntax attracts attention chiefly in cases of morphosyntactic mismatch, in which the constituent structure required by the syntax is inconsistent with the word structure required by the morphology, as occurs in the various types of **bracketing paradoxes** (sense 1). *Adj.* **morphosyntactic**.

mother /'mʌðə/ *n*. A relation which may hold between two nodes in a tree. If a node A immediately dominates another node B, then A is the mother of B. Cf. **daughter**, **ancestor**.

Move-alpha /ˌmuːv 'ælfə/ See **Alpha Movement**.

movement chain /'muːvmənt tʃeɪn/ *n*. In GB, the combination of a moved constituent with its coindexed traces.

movement rule *n*. In a **derivational** theory of grammar, any rule that relates two sequential levels of representation in such a way that a constituent present in one place at one level is present in a different place at the other level. Movement rules were introduced into syntax by Chomsky (1957); the Standard Theory of TG recognized a very large number of movement rules, often quite elaborate and construction-specific. In GB only a single very simple and general movement rule is posited, the rule of **Alpha Movement**. Virtually all other theories of grammar reject the use of movement rules, and there have sometimes been suggestions that they could be dispensed with in GB as well.

multistratal /mʌltɪ'streɪtl̩/ *adj*. Denoting a manner of representing the syntactic structures of sentences, or a theory of grammar employing such representations, in which the structure of a sentence consists of two or more formal objects, particularly formal objects which are described in the same vocabulary. In practice, this term is usually a synonym for **derivational** (sense 2). TG, GB and RG are examples of multistratal frameworks. See **stratum**, **level**.

N

N See **noun**.

narrative /'nærətɪv/ *n.* or *adj.* A distinctive form, usually a verb form, found in certain languages (notably Bantu languages) which is confined to use in narratives (accounts of past events or stories) and which is often the only form which can occur there.

natural class /ˌnætʃərl̩ 'klɑːs/ *n.* 1. Formally, any class which can be characterized using less information than is required to characterize any part of it. Thus, for example, within the X-bar system, the natural class of maximal projections can be identified by the single feature specification [BAR 2], while any subclass of maximal projections can only be picked out by adding further feature specifications. 2. Informally, any class of linguistic objects which pattern grammatically in the same way and which therefore need to be referred to in the grammar as a single unitary class. For example, the class of verbs in English is a natural class, as is the class of transitive verbs and as is the class of ditransitive verbs. One of the more immediate goals of any theory of grammar is to provide a formalism that succeeds in representing natural classes in the second sense as natural classes in the first sense; failure to do this usually leads only to the endless labelling of things, a characteristic of much traditional grammatical description widely regarded as one of its great failings.

natural language *n.* 1. Any language which is, or once was, the mother tongue of a group of human beings. 2. By extension, any conceivable language which is consistent with the requirements of the theory of grammar and which hence might in principle be such a mother tongue.

natural-language processing /'prəʊsesɪŋ/ *n.* (**NLP**) The use of computers for handling various types of tasks involving natural languages, but most particularly for accepting natural-language input from human users and giving appropriate and useful responses. The central task of NLP is the construction of efficient **parsers**.

N-bar /en ˈbɑː/ *n.* In the X-bar system, the one-bar projection of the lexical category Noun, represented as N̄, N′ or N¹, and identified with the category which combines with a determiner to make up a noun phrase. The category is necessary to provide coherent analyses for NPs containing modifiers, such as *many students of linguistics*, analysed as [ₙₚ[Det*many*] [ₙ′[ₙ*students*] [PP*of linguistics*]]]. There is no traditional name for this category, though various labels such as 'nominal group' occasionally turn up in the literature.

necessitative /nəˈsesɪtətɪv/ *adj.* The mood category which expresses necessity or obligation, either deontic (as in *I have to go*) or epistemic (as in *That must be Lisa*). An example is the Turkish verb form *gitmeliyim* 'I have to go', an inflected form of *gitmek* 'go'. Jespersen (1924).

negation /nɪˈɡeɪʃn̩/ *n.* The presence of a **negative** (sense 1 or 2) in a sentence or constituent, or the addition of such an element, or the effect of that element when present. See Horn (1989); Payne (1985a).

negative /ˈnegətɪv/ *n.* 1. A grammatical element which, when added to a sentence expressing a proposition, reverses the truth value of that proposition. The usual English negative is *not* or *-n't*, as illustrated by the pair *I can speak French* and *I can't speak French*. A negative element is an **operator** which takes some part of its sentence as its scope; that scope may be the entire proposition, as in the last example, or only some part of it, as in the example *Aida was written by Verdi, not by Puccini*. The expression of negation varies widely among languages; Spanish uses a simple invariable *no*, while in Lugbara negative sentences exhibit a substantially different grammatical structure from their affirmative counterparts. 2. A lexical item or other element which can be analysed semantically as consisting of a negative in sense 1 plus another element serving as the scope of the negative. For example, English *nothing* can be analysed as *not* plus *something*, and *never* can be analysed as *not* plus *ever*; Latin *nolle* 'not want' can be analysed as *non* 'not' plus *velle* 'want'. 3. Denoting a sentence or constituent containing a negative element in either of the preceding senses.

negative concord *n.* The phenomenon by which the presence of an overt negative (sense 1) requires other elements in the sentence to be marked as negative. Spanish exhibits extensive negative concord: *No he visto nada* 'I didn't see anything', literally 'I didn't see nothing'; the form *No he visto algo*, without negative concord, is ill-formed. See the discussion under **double negative**.

negative polarity item *n.* Any of various items which can only occur within the scope of a **negative** (sense 1 or 2) and possibly also in certain other specified grammatical circumstances, notably in questions. English examples include *any*, *ever* and *at all*: *We don't have any wine*; *Do we have any wine?*; but *We have any wine*. Cf. **positive polarity item**. Klima (1964).

negative raising *n.* The phenomenon by which a negative element appears in a position in which it appears to have greater scope than is consistent with the interpretation of the sentence. An example is *I never want to see you again*, which appears to mean 'It is never the case that I want to see you again' (and can actually mean this), but which is commonly used to express the meaning 'I want never to see you again', with *want* outside the scope of the negative.

neologism /ni'ɒlədʒɪzm̩/ *n.* A newly coined word or phrase. Among the neologisms recorded in the 1989 edition of *The Longman Register of New Words* are *glasnost*, *wannabee*, *toyboy*, *fromage frais*, *intifada*, *wrinkly* (noun), *nutmeg* (verb, soccer term), *bonk*, *yuppify* and *geopathic*. *Adj.* **neologistic** /niɒlə'dʒɪstɪk/.

nested dependency /'nestɪd/ *n.* A **dependency** which is entirely contained within the two ends of another dependency, so that a series of nested dependencies looks like this:

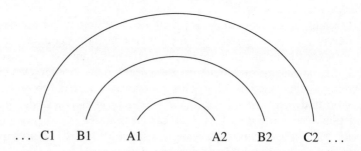

... C1   B1   A1   A2   B2   C2 ...

A familiar example of a nested dependency is **centre-embedding**. Unlimited nested dependencies cannot be weakly generated by a **regular grammar**, but they can easily be handled by a **context-free grammar**. Cf. **cross-serial dependency**.

nesting /'nestɪŋ/ *n.* An instance of **embedding** in which a category is embedded under, and interrupts, another instance of the same category.

network grammar /'netwɜːk/ *n.* A graphical representation of possible sentences (as strings) consisting of a set of points ('states') connected by arcs ('paths'); each arc is typically labelled with a word or formative which is added to the current string when that arc is traversed.

neuter /'njuːtə/ *adj.* A conventional label in certain **gender** languages for a gender category showing no particular semantic correlation with animacy or sex or, in some languages, for the single gender category showing no particular semantic correlation at all, representing the 'residue' category in such languages.

neutralization /ˌnjuːtrəlaɪˈzeɪʃn̩/ *n.* A synonym for **syncretism**, borrowed from phonology. *V.* **neutralize** /'njuːtrəlaɪz/.

nexus /'neksəs/ (pl. **nexus** or **nexuses**, but *not* *nexi) *n.* A superordinate term for the various ways of combining clauses into syntactic structures, such as **coordination**, **subordination** (embedding) and **cosubordination**. Foley and Van Valin (1984).

NICE properties /'naɪs ˌprɒpətiːz/ *n. pl.* A mnemonic label for the four principal properties distinguishing English auxiliaries from ordinary verbs: Negation (*Lisa doesn't smoke*), Inversion (*Does Lisa smoke?*), Code (*Lisa doesn't smoke, but Janet does*) and Emphasis (*Janet does smoke*). Huddleston (1976), deriving from the analysis in Palmer (1987, but originally 1974).

NL See **natural language**.

NLP See **natural language processing**.

NL vastness theorem /en el 'vɑːstnəs/ *n.* (also **vastness theorem**) The conclusion that the number of sentences in a natural language is transfinite, that is, greater than countably infinite. This conclusion

follows from the proposition that individual sentences can be trans-
finitely long, and may preclude the possibility of **constructive grammars** for natural languages. Langendoen and Postal (1984).

No-Crossing Condition /nəʊˈkrɒsɪŋ/ See **Non-tangling
Condition**.

node /nəʊd/ *n*. A labelled point in a tree which represents a constituent of the sentence represented by the tree. The label on the
node identifies the syntactic category to which the constituent belongs, and the internal structure of that constituent is shown by
the subtree dominated by that node. Nodes may be classified into
non-terminal nodes, **preterminal nodes** and **terminal nodes**. In the
tree below, the lexical items are terminal nodes; the lexical categories Det, N and V are preterminal nodes; all the other nodes
are non-terminals:

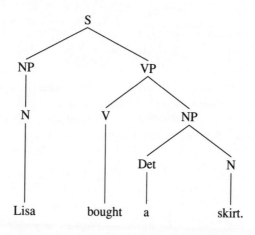

node admissibility condition /ədmɪsəˈbɪləti/ *n*. A way of interpreting a phrase structure rule or immediate dominance rule. A rule
interpreted as a node admissibility condition is considered to be, not
an instruction for expanding (rewriting) a category, but rather a
statement which licenses a local subtree. Such a view dispenses with
derivations and permits trees to be regarded as primitive objects: a
valid tree is merely one all of whose local subtrees are licensed by
rules. The generative capacity of a context-free grammar is unaffec-
ted by such a reinterpretation of its rules, but the same is not true of

a context-sensitive grammar: the context-sensitive grammar given below does not generate the tree shown if its rules are interpreted as rewrite rules, but it does if they are interpreted as node admissibility conditions.

A → B C

B → D / _ E

C → E / D _

McCawley (1968); McCawley credits Richard Stanley with the idea.

nominal /'nɒmɪnl̩/ 1. *adj.* Pertaining to nouns or to projections of nouns. 2. *adj.* In those versions of the X-bar system in which lexical categories are decomposed into the primitive elements [N] and [V], denoting any category which is [+N], in other words, nouns and adjectives. 3. *n.* See **nominalization**.

nominalization /ˌnɒmɪnəlaɪˈzeɪʃn̩/ *n.* 1. In morphology, a noun derived from a member of another lexical category, especially from a verb, such as *arrival* from *arrive*, *response* from *respond* and *swimming* from *swim* (as in *Lisa's swimming has improved*). 2. In syntax, a noun phrase derived from another category which is not a projection of the lexical category Noun, particularly from a verb phrase or a sentence. Examples include [*Lisa's going topless*] *upset her father*, [*To quit your job*] *would be a mistake* and [*That she smokes*] *surprises me*. NOTE: in English and in some other languages, the distinction between morphological and syntactic nominalizations is not always immediately clear. In particular, the English suffix *-ing* can be involved in either type: in *This constant smoking of marijuana has to stop*, *smoking* is clearly a morphological nominalization, as shown by the adnominal elements; in *Regularly smoking twenty cigarettes a day will ruin your health*, *smoking* is clearly the head of a syntactic nominalization of a VP, as shown by the object NP and the adverbials; but in *Smoking is bad for you*, *smoking* can be interpreted either way. See Comrie and Thompson (1985).

nominal sentence *n.* A label sometimes applied to a sentence containing no verb, particularly to a copular sentence in a language lacking an overt copula in some or all circumstances. An example is Turkish *Hasan büyük* 'Hasan is big', literally 'Hasan big'. The term has no theoretical significance.

nominative /'nɒmɪnətɪv/ *n.* or *adj.* 1. In a morphologically **accusative** language, the case form used for both subjects of intransitive verbs and subjects of transitive verbs. An example is English *I*, as in *I'm leaving* and *I've washed the car*. 2. In GB, the abstract Case assigned to a subject NP which is governed by the category INFL.

nominative–accusative language See **accusative language**.

non-argument binding See **A-bar binding**.

non-canonical complement /ˌnɒnkə'nɒnɪkḷ/ *n.* In GB, a category which is interpreted as a complement of a lexical head even though it is not a sister of that head. The most familiar examples are WH-items like *who* in such constructions as *Who did you see?* and *The woman who you saw is our MP*, in which *who* functions as a non-canonical complement of the verb *see* in each case.

non-canonical subject *n.* In GB, a category which is interpreted as the subject of some predicate even though it is not a sister of that predicate. Examples include *Who do you think did it?*, in which *who* functions as the subject of *did it*, and *She seems to be clever*, in which *she* functions as the subject of *be clever*.

nonce form /'nɒns fɔːm/ *n.* A word created accidentally or deliberately by an individual on a particular occasion, such as *disclude*, heard as the opposite of *include*.

non-configurational /ˌnɒnkənfɪgjʊ'reɪʃənḷ/ *adj.* Denoting a syntactic structure in which there is little or no downward branching of constituents, most categories instead simply being sisters. Some analysts have suggested, for example, that Basque sentences typically have non-configurational structures. If so, a Basque sentence like *Patxik Anari dirua dakarkio* Patxi-Erg Ana-Dat money-the-Abs he-is-bringing-it-to-her 'Patxi is bringing Ana the money' would have the following structure:

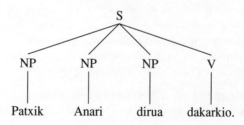

The existence of such non-configurational structures, which are also called 'flat structures', was first proposed by Hale (1981). Since that time the issue of non-configurationality has attracted enormous attention in the literature; at present, there is something of a consensus that such structures must be recognized for at least some constructions in at least some languages, but there is much less agreement as to which constructions and which languages, or as to what criteria should be invoked for recognizing such structures.

non-configurational language *n.* (also **W-star language**) A language in which non-configurational structures are prominent or predominant. The first such language to be identified was the Australian language Warlpiri (Hale 1981), but many others have since been proposed. Many of these proposals are controversial, but a particularly convincing case is that of the Australian language Nunggubuyu (Heath 1986).

non-deterministic /nɒndɪtɜːmɪˈnɪstɪk/ *adj.* Denoting an automaton or transition network in which, at some points, the choice of path is not completely determined by the current state and the next input character, and hence any implementation of which must successively try out all the available paths – effectively, an implementation must 'guess' one path at a time and then see if it leads to a successful conclusion. Cf. **deterministic**.

non-discrete grammar /nɒndɪˈskriːt/ See **fuzzy grammar**.

non-finite /nɒnˈfaɪnaɪt/ *adj.* Denoting any form of a verb which cannot serve as the only verb in a simple sentence. Non-finite forms typically include **participles**, **infinitives** and **verbal nouns**; these typically differ from **finite** forms in lacking the ability to be marked for tense or agreement. Cf. **finite**.

non-local conditions on trees /nɒnˌləʊkl̩ kənˈdɪʃn̩z/ *n. pl.* Any of various grammatical statements about well-formed tree structures whose domain is larger than a **local subtree**. A simple example is the requirement that a reflexive in English must have a c-commanding antecedent: *Janet examined herself* but **Herself examined Janet*. Other examples include **filler–gap dependencies**, such as those involved in WH-fronting. Theories of grammar differ markedly in their treatment of non-local conditions; in

GPSG, for example, *all* non-local conditions are interpreted as connected series of strictly local dependencies (**paths**, or **chains**); GB treats filler–gap dependencies in the same way, but permits other non-local conditions to be stated directly in the grammar.

non-modal auxiliary /nɒn'məʊdl̩/ *n.* An **auxiliary** which carries no expression of **mood**, such as English perfect *have* or progressive *be* in examples like *Lisa has quit smoking* and *Lisa is working on her translation*. Cf. **modal** (sense 2).

non-recurrent alternation /ˌnɒnrɪ'kʌrənt/ *n.* An instance of **allomorphy** which is confined to a single morpheme, such as the *man/men* alternation in English.

non-restrictive /ˌnɒnrɪ'strɪktɪv/ *adj.* Denoting a **modifier**, such as an adjective or a relative clause, whose presence is not required for identification of the referent of the noun phrase containing it, but which serves merely to add extra information. In English, non-restrictive adjectives often have reduced stress: *The yellow 'boat came into view* (the hearer already knows what boat is meant), and non-restrictive relative clauses regularly have comma intonation: *The woman, who was smiling, sat down* (the hearer already knows which woman is meant). Cf. the examples under **restrictive**. In some languages, the distinction between restrictive and non-restrictive modifiers is more overtly marked. In Spanish, for example, restrictive adjectives usually follow the noun, while non-restrictive adjectives usually precede: *la negra silueta* 'the black silhouette' (i.e., the only silhouette under discussion, which happens to be black), but *la silueta negra* 'the black silhouette' (as opposed to other silhouettes of different colours).

Non-tangling Condition /ˌnɒn'tæŋglɪŋ/ *n.* (also **No-Crossing Condition**) The requirement that the lines in a tree which connect mothers to daughters should not cross. This requirement was rejected in the implicit representations adopted by American structuralists in the 1940s and 1950s, but it has been almost universally accepted within generative grammar since the work of Noam Chomsky in the 1950s. Occasionally, however, someone proposes that the requirement should be rejected, particularly to allow the analysis of discontinuous constructions. For example, James

McCawley, the foremost contemporary opponent of the Non-tangling Condition, advocates the use of trees such as the one below (McCawley (1982); this particular example also violates the Single Mother Condition, though not all of McCawley's examples do so):

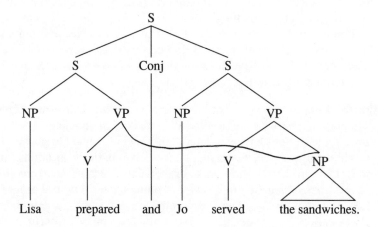

non-terminal node /ˌnɒnˈtɜːmɪnl̩/ *n.* Any node in a tree which dominates at least one other node. Frequently a node which is a lexical category and which dominates only a lexical item is called a **preterminal node**, rather than a non-terminal. Cf. **terminal node**.

notational convention /nəʊˈteɪʃənl̩ kənˌventʃn̩/ *n.* Any notational device which, in some system, is understood as having some particular interpretation. For example, the phrase structure rule S → NP VP is conventionally understood as meaning 'an S node in a tree may have the two daughters NP and VP, in that order'. Similarly, the notation X* is conventionally understood as meaning 'a linear string of any number of occurrences of a single category'.

notational variant /ˈvɛəriənt/ *n.* 1. Any notational convention which is interpreted as having exactly the same meaning as some other notational convention. For example, the notations NP, N″ and N^{max} are all understood as meaning 'the maximal projection of the lexical category Noun', and are hence notational variants of one another. 2. By extension, the relation which holds between any two formal systems which have exactly the same **generative capacity**. For example, the most familiar class of **categorial grammars** has the same generative capacity as the class of **context-free grammars**, and the two formalisms are hence notational variants.

notional definition /ˌnəʊʃənl̩ defɪ'nɪʃn̩/ *n*. Any definition of a linguistic category or element which appeals crucially to its meaning. An example is the traditional definition of a noun as 'the name of a person, place or thing'. Widely used in traditional grammar, notional definitions are rejected by all current theories of grammar as unworkable. (For example, the adjective *red* is surely the name of a colour, while it is difficult to see that the noun *arrival* is the name of anything if the verb *arrive* is not.)

noun /naʊn/ *n*. (**N**) One of the principal **lexical categories**. This category appears to be universally present in languages; while prototypical nouns have meanings denoting individual physical entities like *dog* and *tree*, words that behave grammatically as nouns can in fact exhibit a very wide range of meanings, such as *edge*, *colour*, *beauty*, *arrival*, *ancestry* or *absence*. Among the most typical properties of nouns in languages generally are inflection for number, classification for gender and, above all, the ability to occur with determiners inside noun phrases. NOTE: traditional grammar often included adjectives in the category Noun, distinguishing 'nouns substantive' (nouns) from 'nouns adjective' (adjectives). This use is obsolete. *Adj*. **nominal**.

noun class /klɑːs/ *n*. In a language exhibiting **gender**, any one of the gender classes into which nouns are divided.

noun classification /klæsɪfɪ'keɪʃn̩/ *n*. The phenomenon, occurring in certain languages, by which nouns are divided into a number of semantically based classes by the occurrence of **classifiers** in certain types of noun phrases, each noun typically requiring one of the set of classifiers. Dixon (1986) identifies three respects in which noun classification systems typically differ from systems of **noun classes** (gender classes): (1) the number of noun classes is usually small, often two or three and rarely more than eight or ten, while the number of classifiers is typically much larger, often many dozens; (2) classifiers are always free forms, while gender is never marked by free forms, either being marked on nouns only by bound forms or not being marked on nouns at all; (3) gender systems always require agreement on some elements other than the nouns themselves, while classifiers never require agreement. To these a fourth difference may be added: nouns in gender systems are always exhaustively classified for gender, while in a classifier language some nouns may take no classifier at all.

noun-complement clause *n.* A clause which serves as a complement to a head noun within a noun phrase, as in the example *the rumour* [*that the Martians have invaded*].

noun phrase *n.* (**NP**) One of the principal **syntactic categories**, and one which appears to be perhaps universally present in languages. Functionally, a noun phrase may be defined as any category which can bear some **grammatical relation** within a sentence, such as subject, direct object, indirect object or oblique object. Structurally, a noun phrase is regarded in most versions of the X-bar system as the maximal projection of the lexical category Noun, N″, with a noun as its lexical head. This view, which works well in most circumstances, runs into difficulties with NPs containing pronouns, such as *she*, *this*, *something* and *little old me*; as a consequence, many analysts, beginning with Hudson (1984), have suggested that NPs should rather be regarded as the maximal projections of the category Determiner (with pronouns then being assigned to this category) and hence renamed Determiner Phrases. This revised view is not currently standard. Noun phrases were not recognized by traditional grammar; the first explicit use of the term occurred in Harris (1951), though some earlier American structuralists apparently had some kind of implicit grasp of the notion.

NP /en 'piː/ *n.* 1. See **noun phrase**. 2. (italicized) In **complexity theory**, the class of problems soluble in polynomial time on a nondeterministic Turing machine. Such problems can only be solved by making guesses and testing each guess to see if it is a solution; on an ordinary computer, this requires **exponential time**. The class of problems in *NP* is believed to be a proper superset of the class of problems in *P* (sense 4), though this is yet to be proved. See Barton *et al.* (1987) for discussion.

NP Accessibility Hierarchy /ək,sesə'bɪləti/ *n.* A hierarchy of **grammatical relations** proposed by Keenan and Comrie (1977), as follows:

Subject < DO < IO < Oblique object < Genitive < Object of comparison

This hierarchy has proved to be of importance in the grammars of a large number of languages; such processes as passivization, relative clause formation and causative formation make crucial reference to it. The identification of this hierarchy greatly stimulated recognition of the importance in syntax of grammatical relations, which had previously been widely neglected, and spurred the development of theories of grammar in which grammatical relations play a central role, including RG, LFG and the various frameworks known as **functional grammars** (sense 2). RG incorporates a modified version of the Keenan–Comrie hierarchy under the name **Relational Hierarchy**.

NP-**complete** /en piː kəm'pliːt/ *adj*. Denoting any problem which is *NP*-**hard** and also in *NP* (sense 2). *NP*-complete problems are soluble, so far as is known, only by algorithms running in **exponential time**, and are hence computationally intractable.

NP-**hard** /en piː hɑːd/ *adj*. Denoting any problem which is as difficult to solve as any problem in *NP* (sense 2).

NP-Movement *n*. In GB, the name given to those instances of **Alpha Movement** in which a noun phrase is moved from one argument position to another. NP-Movement is invoked in constructions involving passives, raising verbs and unaccusative verbs, in all of which the NP occupying a surface subject position is analysed as underlyingly occupying a different position. Thus *Janet was arrested* e is derived from an underlying e *was arrested Janet*; *Lisa seems* e *to be happy* from underlying e *seems Lisa to be happy*; and *The ice melted* e from underlying e *melted the ice*. NP-Movement is forced in all these instances by the requirements of Case Theory and Theta Theory. See **Burzio's Generalization**, and cf. **WH-Movement**.

NP-trace *n*. In GB, the coindexed empty category left behind by an NP which has been moved by **NP-Movement**. For example, the initial structure e *seems Lisa to be happy* is converted to *Lisa$_i$ seems* e$_i$ *to be happy*, in which the symbol e$_i$ represents the NP-trace left behind by the movement of *Lisa*, with which it is coindexed.

n-tuple /en 'tjuːpl/ *n*. (also **tuple**) In the characterization of formal systems, a set of *n* distinct formal objects or (more usually) specified classes of formal objects. If (as is often the case) the objects are given in a specified order, we have an 'ordered *n*-tuple'. An (ordered) *n*-tuple with two members is called an (ordered) pair; one with three members is a triple; with four, a quadruple, and so on.

nucleus /'njuːkliəs/ (pl. **nuclei** /'njuːkliaɪ/) *n.* 1. That part of a constituent consisting of its head and those elements for which the head subcategorizes, but excluding any adjuncts. Cf. **periphery** (sense 1). 2. The central element in a clause, a verb or predicate, considered in isolation. 'Nucleus' in this sense is one of the terms involved in analysing a clause in terms of **layering**. Cf. **core**, **periphery** (sense 2). 3. In LFG, any part of an **f-structure** consisting of a Predicate and its subcategorized arguments. *Adj.* **nuclear** /'njuːkliə/.

null element /'nʌl ˌeləmənt/ *n.* (also **zero**) An element which, in some particular description, is posited as existing at a certain point in a structure even though there is no overt phonetic material present to represent it. For example, many linguists would argue that the plural form *sheep* consists of two morphemes, the noun stem *sheep* and a null plural suffix Ø. Most approaches to grammatical description recognize the existence of at least some null elements, and the problem of how to limit their use in a principled way has long been a bone of contention: both structuralist (sense 2) and generative approaches have sometimes indulged in the proliferation of zeros, even to the extent of positing zeros which contrast with other zeros; see, for example, Chomsky and Lasnik (1977). As an example of the possible utility of null elements, consider the sentences (a) *She said that she would come* and (b) *She said she would come*, the second of which lacks an overt complementizer. At least three analyses of the (b) sentence are possible, all of which have been advocated on occasion. (1) The (b) sentence contains no Comp node. This analysis avoids the use of null elements, at the price of postulating an additional syntactic structure. (2) The (b) sentence contains a Comp node, which is empty. This analysis requires only one structure, but posits a syntactic null element, an empty node. (3) The (b) sentence contains a Comp node which is filled by a complementizer that happens to have the phonetic shape Ø. This analysis pushes the null element out of the syntax altogether and into the phonology. The extensive use of null elements is particularly characteristic of GB; see **empty category**. The Indian grammarian Paṇini was the first to use null elements, but their modern use derives primarily from Bloomfield (1933).

null production /prə'dʌkʃn̩/ *n.* A phrase structure rule which rewrites a category as a null element, such as the rule NP → *e*. Null productions were expressly rejected in Chomsky's (1957) definition of phrase structure rules, but most contemporary views of phrase structure admit the existence of such rules in context-free grammars. The name derives from mathematical linguistics, in which 'production' is the usual term for 'rewrite rule'.

null-subject language *n*. (also **pro-drop language**) A language in which **pro-drop** occurs.

Null-Subject Parameter See **Pro-Drop Parameter**.

number /ˈnʌmbə/ *n*. The grammatical category, most often associated with nouns and pronouns, whose primary correlation is with the number of distinguishable entities. English has a simple two-way number contrast between **singular** and **plural** (*dog*/*dogs*; *child*/ *children*; *radius*/*radii*), but some other languages exhibit more elaborate number systems involving **dual**, **trial** and **paucal** forms as well as singular and plural. Except perhaps in pronoun systems, number is not universally present in languages; Chinese and Japanese are two examples of languages in which number contrasts are generally absent.

O

object /'ɒbdʒɪkt/ *n.* (**O**) 1. A generic term for any noun phrase occupying an argument position other than subject. Objects are conventionally divided into **direct objects**, **indirect objects** and **oblique objects**. 2. In GB, the usual term for **direct object**. *Adj.* **objective**.

object grammar *n.* In a theory of grammar recognizing the existence of a **metagrammar**, that part of the grammar consisting of the rules which directly license trees. In such an approach, of which GPSG is the most prominent example, all generalizations about the rules of the object grammar are extracted and stated separately in the metagrammar.

object-initial language /ˌɒbdʒɪkt ɪ'nɪʃl̩/ *n.* A language in which, in the most usual order of elements in a sentence, the object NP comes first, preceding both the subject and the verb. Object-initial languages were long thought to be non-existent and perhaps even impossible, but a number of them are now known, all of them spoken in the Amazon basin. The first such language to be identified was the Carib language Hixkaryana, studied by Derbyshire (1961, 1979). Hixkaryana, like many other Amazonian languages, has Object–Verb–Subject order, but some Amazonian languages, like Apurinã, exhibit Object–Subject–Verb order. See Derbyshire and Pullum (1981, 1986) and Pullum (1981) for further information.

objective /ɒb'dʒektɪv/ *adj.* Denoting a case form which serves in general to mark non-subject NPs of various types, such as direct objects, indirect objects and objects of prepositions. An example is the objective form of English personal pronouns, like *me*, *him* and *us*.

objective genitive *n.* A construction involving a nominalization of a transitive verb accompanied by a possessive NP or a PP with *of* which is interpreted as the object of that verb, as in *the prime minister's assassination* or *the destruction of the city*. Cf. **subjective genitive**.

object language *n*. A language which is under discussion. An object language may be a formal language, as in the mathematics of formal systems, but in linguistics it is more usually a natural language. The point of the term is that we often discuss a natural language in another natural language, or even in the same natural language; for example, we often discuss the grammar of English in ordinary English, and it is essential to distinguish the English which is under discussion (the object language) from the English which we are using to discuss it (the **metalanguage**). Failure to make this distinction leads to hopeless confusion; see the discussion under **metalanguage**.

object of comparison *n*. The **grammatical relation** borne by an NP which is the **standard** in a comparative construction, such as *Lisa* in *taller than Lisa*.

oblique /ə'bliːk/ *adj*. 1. Denoting an argument NP which is neither a subject nor a direct object (nor, in some analyses, an indirect object; this point is controversial and possibly language-specific). Oblique NPs in English are realized as objects of prepositions; in some other languages, they may be objects of postpositions or case-marked NPs. This use is currently standard. 2. In the traditional grammatical descriptions of Latin and Greek, denoting any case form of a noun other than the nominative or vocative. This use is not current in grammatical theory.

oblique clause See **adverbial clause**.

oblique object *n*. (OO) A noun phrase which is **oblique** in sense 1.

observational adequacy /ɒbsə'veɪʃənl̩/ See under **adequacy**.

obviative /'ɒbviətɪv/ *n*. or *adj*. One of a set of third-person pronominal forms occurring in certain languages and used exclusively for the second or later third-person entity to be mentioned in a discourse, the first such entity to be mentioned being referred to by one of a contrasting set of **proximate** forms. Obviative forms are often misleadingly called 'fourth-person' forms. The proximate–obviative distinction is particularly common in North American languages.

of-**insertion** *n*. In certain derivational analyses, the putative process which is responsible for the presence of *of* in nominalizations like

Lisa's refusal of the offer, when this is regarded as being derived
from an underlying sentence like *Lisa refused the offer*.

OO /əʊ 'əʊ/ See **oblique object**.

open class /'əʊpən klɑːs/ *n*. A **lexical category** whose membership
is typically large and which can easily accept new members. In
English, for example, the categories Noun, Verb and Adjective are
all open classes. Cf. **closed class**.

open function *n*. In LFG, a complement or an adjunct containing
an empty argument position which must be controlled by an NP
located outside it. Examples: [*Having arrived early,*] *Lisa decided to
take a stroll*; *She tried* [*to fix the carburettor*]. The notations XCOMP
and XADJUNCT are used to represent such functions in LFG. Cf.
closed function.

operator /'ɒpəreɪtə/ *n*. Any grammatical element which bears a
scope relation to some part of its sentence. Examples include determiners and quantifiers, negation, tense, aspect and mood.

optative /'ɒptətɪv/ *adj*. 1. The mood category expressing realizable
wishes or hopes, as exemplified by the rather formal English *May
we succeed*. Some languages exhibit a distinct grammatical form for
this purpose. 2. The conventional name for a morphologically distinct set of verb forms in Ancient Greek and Sanskrit serving a
variety of purposes, including the optative in sense 1.

optionality /ɒpʃən'ælɪti/ *n*. In the X-bar system, the requirement
that all and only the non-head daughters of a category must be
optional – that is, that no category may have an obligatory daughter
other than its head. Of all the suggested constraints upon X-bar
structures, this is perhaps the one which is most difficult to maintain
and the one which is most frequently violated in practice. Kornai and
Pullum (1990), but the notion is much older.

OSV language /əʊ es 'viː/ *n*. A language whose basic word order is
Object–Subject–Verb, such as the Amazonian language Apurinã.
See **object-initial language**.

overgeneration /ˌəʊvədʒenə'reɪʃn̩/ *n*. The phenomenon by which
some component of a grammar which builds structure permits, in
isolation, the existence of a number of ill-formed structures. These
unwanted structures must be prevented from occurring ('filtered
out') by the requirements of other components of the grammar. *V*.
overgenerate /əʊvə'dʒenəreɪt/.

overlapping exponence /əʊvə'læpɪŋ/ *n*. The realization in a particular case by a single morph of two or more morphemes which are usually realized separately in a language. In Spanish, for example, finite verb forms usually contain separate morphs for expressing tense/mood and for expressing the person/number of the subject, but the first person singular present indicative forms like *como* 'I eat' show a single morph -*o* realizing both these categories. Cf. **cumulative exponence**. Matthews (1974).

OVS language /əʊ viː 'es/ *n*. A language whose basic word order is Object–Verb–Subject, such as the Carib language Hixkaryana. See **object-initial language**.

P

P 1. See **preposition, postposition**. 2. The conventional abbreviation for **phrase** in such symbols as NP (= noun phrase), VP (= verb phrase), etc. 3. An abbreviation for **patient** in the **SAP** analysis of clause structure. 4. (italicized) In **complexity theory**, denoting the class of problems soluble in polynomial time on a deterministic Turing machine. Membership in *P* is widely taken as a hallmark of efficient computability: if a problem is not in *P*, it cannot be efficiently computed. This is so because all problems not in *P* have (so far as we know) only exponential time algorithms, and can only be solved by enumerating all possible solutions and testing them one by one. Cf. *NP* (sense 2).

PA See **pushdown automaton**.

paradigm /'pærədaɪm/ *n*. The full set of inflected forms exhibited by some class of lexical items, such as the declensional forms of a class of nouns or the conjugated forms of a class of verbs, often as represented by the forms of a single typical item. *Adj*. **paradigmatic**.

paradigmatic relation /ˌpærədɪg'mætɪk/ *n*. Any relation between two or more linguistic elements which are in some sense competing possibilities, in that exactly one of them may be selected to occupy some particular position in a structure. For example, the various determiners which might occur within a particular NP stand in a paradigmatic relation; the various verb forms from which the verb form in a particular sentence is chosen do the same; the various case forms of NPs in case-marking languages do likewise; and the active and passive constructions for transitive verbs may also be said to stand in a paradigmatic relation. Cf. **syntagmatic relation**. The notion of a paradigmatic relation was introduced by the Swiss linguist Ferdinand de Saussure in the first decade of the twentieth century; it represents a generalization of the traditional notion of a **paradigm**.

paralanguage /'pærəˌlæŋgwɪdʒ/ *n*. The use of non-verbal elements in speech, such as intonation, expressions and gestures, in such a way as to affect the meaning of an utterance. *Adj*. **paralinguistic** /pærəlɪŋ'gwɪstɪk/.

parallel construction /'pærəlel/ *n.* A construction, particularly a coordinate construction, all of whose parts stand in the same syntactic relation to the rest of the sentence. The example *I like to read fantasy novels in the bathtub and to experiment in the kitchen* illustrates a parallel construction; the possibly ill-formed ?*I like to read fantasy novels in the bathtub and experimenting in the kitchen* illustrates a non-parallel one. *Abstr. n.* **parallelism**.

parallelism /'pærəlelɪzm̩/ *n.* 1. The use of the same construction in consecutive sentences for rhetorical effect, as in *I came; I saw; I conquered.* 2. See **parallel construction**.

parameter /pə'ræmɪtə/ *n.* In GB, any one of various putative universal statements permitting a specified degree of variation within languages. The idea is that any one language selects just one of the small number of choices permitted by the theory of grammar. Examples include the **Head Parameter**, the **Adjacency Parameter** and the **Pro-Drop Parameter**. *Adj.* **parametric** /pærə'metrɪk/.

paraphrase /'pærəfreɪz/ *n.* Either of two sentences which are structurally or lexically different but which are related in that they have approximately the same meaning. Paraphrases are particularly invoked as a way of identifying particular readings of **ambiguous** strings. For example, the two readings of the ambiguous string *The target was not hit by many arrows* could be singled out by the paraphrases *The target was missed by many arrows* and *The target was hit by few arrows*. *Adj.* **paraphrastic** /pærə'fræstɪk/.

parasitic gap /pærə'sɪtɪk/ *n.* A gap whose antecedent is identical to that of a second gap occurring in the same sentence, and which could not occur in the absence of that second gap. In the following examples, the parasitic gap is denoted by the symbol e_p: *What articles did John file e without reading* e_p *?*; *This kind of food you have to cook e before you can eat* e_p; *Which boy did Mary's talking to* e_p *bother e most?* The phenomenon was first pointed out by Ross (1967); Perlmutter reportedly suggested the name 'sympathetic deletion', but the term 'parasitic gap', apparently coined independently by Taraldsen (1980) and Engdahl (1983), is now standard.

parasynthesis /pærə'sɪnθəsɪs/ *n.* A type of word formation in which a phrase is combined with an affix, as in *red-haired*. *Adj.* **parasynthetic** /pærəsɪn'θetɪk/.

parataxis /pærə'tæksɪs/ *n.* 1. Traditionally, the coordination of clauses (and, rarely, of phrases) without the use of overt conjunctions; **asyndeton**, as in *I'm ready; let's go.* 2. Occasionally, the coordination of clauses, with or without the use of overt conjunctions. Cf. **hypotaxis**. *Adj.* **paratactic** /pærə'tæktɪk/.

parentheses /pə'renθəsiːz/ *n. pl.* (also **round brackets**) 1. An **abbreviatory convention** in which two rules which differ only in that one of them contains an extra term absent from the other are collapsed into a single **rule schema**. For example, the two rules VP → V NP and VP → V NP PP could be collapsed into the schema VP → V NP (PP). 2. A similar notational convention used for combining example sentences one of which differs from the other only in the presence of an additional element, as illustrated by the example *She filled (up) my glass.* Parentheses can be combined with an **asterisk** in two ways: the representation *Who did you say (*that) turned up* indicates that the sequence is ill-formed only if *that* is present, while *The thing *(that) interests me is this* indicates that the sequence is ill-formed only if *that* is absent. Cf. **braces**.

parenthetical /pærən'θetɪkl̩/ *n.* A word, phrase or sentence which interrupts a sentence and which bears no syntactic relation to that sentence at the point of interruption. In the following examples, the parentheticals are variously set off by commas, parentheses or dashes: *Lisa was, in the opinion of every one of us, the most desirable woman in England*; *His performance (to be perfectly blunt) was disastrous*; *Postal's analysis – he was, of course, working in the TG framework – depends crucially on crossover*. (The last example illustrates a parenthetical within a parenthetical.) Parentheticals present formidable difficulties of analysis; see Espinal (1991) for a summary of analytical proposals. The term 'parenthesis' is traditional, but 'parenthetical' is now usual in linguistic usage.

parisyllabic /pærɪsɪ'læbɪk/ *adj.* In an inflected language, denoting a noun or verb all or most of whose inflected forms contain the same number of syllables, such as Latin *vis* 'force', accusative *vim*, etc. Cf. **imparisyllabic**.

parse /pɑːz/ 1. *vt.* To assign a grammatical structure to (a string of words). Parsing may be a classroom exercise, but nowadays it is more usually carried out by computer programs called **parsers**. 2. *vi.* To be assigned a grammatical structure, especially successfully by the action of a parser. 3. *n.* The grammatical structure assigned to a string of words by the action of a parser.

parser /ˈpɑːzə/ n. A computational device, most usually a computer program, that is capable of reading a string of words representing a well-formed sentence and of assigning a suitable grammatical structure to it, usually as an intermediate step in assigning a meaning to the string. The construction of efficient parsers is a central activity in **natural-language processing**.

parse tree n. A **tree** (sense 1), particularly one which is assigned to an input string by the action of a **parser**.

partially productive /ˈpɑːʃəli/ adj. Denoting a grammatical process, particularly a process involved in word formation, which can sometimes be extended to new instances, but which cannot be freely applied in all instances without producing questionable or unacceptable results. An example is the process by which the suffix *-less* derives adjectives from nouns: *tieless, braless, shoeless, friendless, homeless, windowless, treeless* and *carless* sound familiar enough, but *houseless, vestless, penless, forkless* and *cigaretteless* all sound rather strange, and *breakfastless, underwearless, paintless, bushless* and *smell-less* all border on the impossible.

participant role /pɑːˈtɪsɪpənt/ n. A **semantic role** which represents an entity which participates more or less directly in the situation expressed in the clause, especially an Agent, Patient, Recipient or Experiencer.

participial relative clause /pɑːtɪˈsɪpiəl/ n. A construction containing a participle which functions like a relative clause but which lacks both a relative pronoun and a finite verb, as illustrated by *The woman [wearing the white miniskirt] is John's wife* and *The vegetables [sold here] are not very fresh*. A participial relative is one type of **reduced relative clause**.

participle /ˈpɑːtɪsɪpl̩/ n. Any of various non-finite verb forms which can act as the heads of verb phrases functioning as adjectival or adverbial modifiers. English exhibits an imperfective participle (or 'present participle') in *-ing* and a passive participle (or 'past participle') of variable formation, as illustrated in the examples *The woman lighting a cigarette is Lisa*; *Arriving at work, I found a message waiting for me*; *The child rescued from the well is now in hospital*; *Exhausted by his efforts, he tumbled into bed*. The label 'participle' is also usually extended to non-finite forms which do not function in this way but which serve to combine with auxiliaries in the formation of periphrastic verb forms; an example is the English perfect participle, such as *finished* in *Lisa has finished her translation*. (The perfect participle and the passive participle are usually identical in form in English, but it is convenient to distinguish them syntactically.) *Adj.* **participial**.

particle /'pɑːtɪkl̩/ *n.* (**Prt**) 1. Traditionally, any lexical item which exhibits no inflectional morphology and hence is invariable in form; the term is only used in connection with languages in which the open classes Noun, Verb and Adjective do inflect. 2. In the grammar of English, one of the preposition-like items which occur in **phrasal verbs**, such as the second item in each of *make up*, *put down*, *take off*, *look at* and *run down* (= *depreciate*). 3. A label typically applied to some more-or-less well-defined class of uninflected words in the grammar of some particular language when no more obvious label presents itself.

particle movement *n.* A name, derived from classical TG usage, for the putative process which relates structures in which phrasal verbs are continuous to those in which they are discontinuous, illustrated by *She turned on the light* and *She turned the light on*.

partitive /'pɑːtɪtɪv/ *n.* or *adj.* 1. A case form occurring in some languages which typically expresses a part of a whole, and often related notions, such as an entity only partly affected by an action, such as Finnish *maitoa* '(some) milk' (*maito* 'milk') in *litra maitoa* 'a litre of milk', and *kirjoja* '(some) books' in *Hän pani kirjoja pöydälle* 'He put some books on the table'; cf. *Hän pani kirjat pöydälle* 'He put the books on the table', where *kirjat* '(the) books' is in the accusative. 2. Any form or construction serving a similar purpose, such as French *du vin* '(some) wine' in *J'ai acheté du vin* 'I've bought some wine'.

part of speech /pɑːt əv 'spiːtʃ/ *n.* The traditional name for a **lexical category**.

passive /'pæsɪv/ *n.* or *adj.* 1. A construction in which an intrinsically transitive verb is construed in such a way that its underlying object appears as its surface subject, its underlying subject being either absent (a 'short passive') or expressed as an oblique NP (a 'long passive', or 'passive-with-agent'), the construction usually being overtly marked in some way to show its passive character. Typical English examples include *Esther has been promoted* and *The GPSG framework was developed by Gerald Gazdar*. The passive is a **voice** category. 2. A verb form used in such a construction. See

Siewierska (1984) or Keenan (1985a) for discussion, and see also **impersonal passive** and **mediopassive**.

passive participle *n.* That non-finite form of a verb which serves as the head of a passive VP, such as *admired* and *lost* in *Lisa is admired by everybody* and *The expedition got lost in the mountains*. In English, the passive participle is almost always identical in form to the **perfect participle**, both traditionally being called the 'past participle', but some speakers distinguish the two for a few verbs: *I haven't proved it* vs. *It hasn't been proven*; *Lisa has never showed a taste for red wine* vs. *This result has never been shown*.

past /pɑːst/ *n.* or *adj.* The **tense** category correlating primarily with past time. As is usual with grammatical categories, the correlation is typical rather than exceptionless, as illustrated by such English examples as *If I spoke better French, I could get a better job* and *It's time you went to bed*, in which past-tense forms refer to non-past time. English has only a single past tense, but some other languages have more elaborate systems; see under **tense**.

past anterior /æn'tɪərɪə/ *n.* A tense form expressing a time which is past with respect to another past time. English has no specific form for this, usually employing only a simple past, as in *I finished the book before Lisa arrived*, though the **pluperfect** is sometimes used instead: *I had finished the book before Lisa arrived*.

past participle *n.* A traditional label for what is more accurately called the **perfect participle** or **passive participle**.

past perfect See **pluperfect**.

path /pɑːθ/ *n.* 1. The **semantic role** borne by an NP which expresses the stretch of territory through which concrete or abstract motion occurs, such as *the bridge* in *We crossed the bridge to the far side* and *Bangkok* in *We flew to Sydney via Bangkok*. Path is one of the **deep cases** recognized in Case Grammar. 2. (also **chain**) In certain theories of grammar, a sequence of nodes in a tree which are regarded as linked in some way, the two end points of the sequence often constituting the two ends of a dependency, particularly an unbounded dependency. See McCloskey (1988) for some discussion of paths in recent work. 3. In graph theory, any continuous route through a graph in which no node occurs twice.

patient /'peɪʃn̩t/ *n.* The **semantic role** borne by an NP which expresses the entity undergoing an action, such as *the roof* in *I've* *repaired the roof* and *The roof collapsed*. Patient is one of the **deep cases** recognized in Case Grammar, and one of the **theta roles** recognized in GB; it is often conflated with Theme.

patient-subject construction See **mediopassive**.

PATR /'pætə/ *n*. A formal language for expressing grammars in computational terms, consisting of a context-free rule formalism supplemented with a powerful feature system. PATR is not designed to make restrictive claims about possible grammars; instead, it is so constructed as to allow a wide variety of formalisms to be expressed in a uniform manner. PATR was first proposed by Rosenschein and Shieber (1982); its modified version PATR-II was presented by Shieber *et al.* (1983). A convenient brief introduction is given in Shieber (1986).

paucal /'pɔːkl̩/ *n*. or *adj*. In some languages, a distinct **number** form for nouns, expressing the idea of 'a few of' and contrasting with both singular and plural forms, and sometimes with other forms. For example, the Semitic language Tigre distinguishes singular *färäs* 'horse', paucal *ʔäfras* 'a few horses' and plural *ʔäfresam* 'horses'. The paucal is sometimes called the 'little plural'.

pda /piː diː 'eɪ/ See **pushdown automaton**.

Penthouse Principle /'pent̩haʊs/ *n*. The putative principle that no syntactic process may apply solely in subordinate clauses. Ross (1973b).

per cent sign /pə'sent̩ saɪn/ *n*. A conventional symbol indicating that the grammatical status of what follows varies depending on the speaker making the judgement. Sometimes the variable judgements are predictable in terms of the speaker's social or geographical background; at other times individual judgements vary in a seemingly arbitrary manner. Examples are *% You need your hair cutting*; *% The beer here is lousy any more*; *%I ain't seen him*; and *%I ran into Janet while enjoying herself at the disco*. The first of these is consistently adjudged well-formed by speakers from certain areas of England, but not by other speakers; the second is well-formed only for speakers from certain parts of the northeastern United States; the third is well-formed only for speakers of certain non-standard dialects; the fourth is variously adjudged well-formed or ill-formed by speakers in a seemingly unpredictable manner. Cf. **question mark**.

percolation /ˌpɜːkəˈleɪʃn̩/ *n.* (also **trickling**) 1. The process by which a syntactic feature present on a node in a tree is notionally passed either upward or downward in accordance with some principle of **feature instantiation**, so that it also appears on other nodes where its presence is required. 2. A similar notional process sometimes postulated as occurring within words as part of word formation.

perfect /ˈpɜːfɪkt/ *n.* or *adj.* 1. A distinctive **aspect** most typically expressing a state resulting from an earlier event, as in *Lisa has gone out* (i.e., she is not here now). In English and other languages, the same form is used also to express other related but distinct aspectual notions, such as the **experiential** (e.g., *Lisa has worked in Paris*), present relevance of a recent event, the **hot news perfect** (e.g., *The President has been shot*) and the 'perfect of persistent situation' (e.g., *Lisa has been working for an hour*). Dahl (1985) makes a distinction between 'perfect' and **resultative** aspects; see the remarks under the latter term. The perfect is somewhat anomalous among aspectual forms, and its precise characterization is a matter of some controversy; see Comrie (1976) for one view and Dahl (1985) for another. The perfect aspect can be combined with any tense; the examples above all illustrate the **present perfect**, but the **past perfect (pluperfect)** and **future perfect** also exist. Note that the unmodified term 'perfect' is often loosely applied to the present perfect. NOTE: it is important not to confuse the 'perfect' aspect with the **perfective** aspect; they are entirely distinct, in spite of the unfortunate similarity in their names, which results from the accident that Latin happened to use the same form in both functions. 2. In certain European languages, such as French and German, a conventional label for a verb form which is constructed in the same way as the English perfect, and which historically may have had the same function, but which now functions chiefly as a past tense.

perfect infinitive *n.* An **infinitive** form marked for perfect aspect, such as Latin *amavisse* 'to have loved' or its English translation.

perfective /pəˈfektɪv/ *n.* or *adj.* A superordinate aspectual category involving a lack of explicit reference to the internal temporal consistency of a situation, and contrasting principally with the **imperfective**. In English, perfective aspect is chiefly expressed by the simple past-tense form, as in *The hamster climbed up behind the bookcase* and *Lisa learned French in Caen*. See Comrie (1976) for discussion.

NOTE: be careful not to confuse 'perfective' aspect with **perfect** aspect; they are entirely distinct.

perfect participle *n*. The English participle which combines with the auxiliary *have* to form the **perfect**, such as *finished* in *Lisa has finished her master's*, or a similar form in another language. In English, the perfect participle is almost always identical to the **passive participle**.

perfect progressive passive *n*. A verb form simultaneously marked for perfect and progressive aspects and passive voice: *My house has been being painted for two weeks now*. Some English speakers find these ill-formed.

performance /pəˈfɔːməns/ *n*. The actual linguistic behaviour of particular individuals on particular occasions. Performance contrasts chiefly with **competence**; such phenomena as slips of the tongue, memory lapses, interruptions and processing difficulties arising from length or complexity are specifically assigned to the domain of performance phenomena, which are usually seen as lying outside the scope of the competence theories of generative grammar. Chomsky (1965).

periphery /pəˈrɪfəri/ *n*. 1. That part of a constituent consisting only of adjuncts, excluding the head and the elements for which the head subcategorizes. Cf. **nucleus**. 2. In an analysis of clause structure in terms of **layering**, the least central elements in a clause, typically everything other than the verb and its arguments. 3. See **marked periphery**. *Adj*. **peripheral** /pəˈrɪfərəl/.

periphrasis /pəˈrɪfrəsɪs/ *n*. 1. The use of **periphrastic** forms. 2. Saying something in a roundabout way, as in the use of *negative growth situation* for 'recession', or of *The answer to your question is in the affirmative* for 'yes'. *Adj*. **periphrastic**.

periphrastic /perɪˈfræstɪk/ *adj*. Denoting a construction, especially one involving a verb, in which one or more **auxiliary** words are used to express grammatical distinctions, as opposed to the direct inflection of the lexical item involved. An example is the English verb form *will be eaten*; compare its Latin equivalent *edetur*, which involves no periphrasis.

perlative /ˈpɜːlətɪv/ *n*. or *adj*. A case form typically expressing the path over which some movement takes place.

person /'pɜːsn̩/ *n.* A **deictic** grammatical category which primarily distinguishes among entities in terms of their role, if any, in a conversational exchange. The three-way distinction among **first person** (the speaker), **second person** (the addressee) and **third person** (everyone and everything else) appears to be universally expressed in languages. The expression of person is often intersected by the expression of other grammatical categories, such as number, sex and gender, but no clear example is known of a language which exhibits more than this three-way person contrast. The **proximate/obviative** contrast found in some languages has sometimes been described as representing a contrast between third person and 'fourth person', but this is misleading.

personal pronoun /'pɜːsənl̩/ *n.* One of a typically small and closed set of lexical items with the principal function of distinguishing among individuals in terms of the deictic category of **person** but often also expressing certain additional distinctions of number, animacy, sex, gender or other categories. The English personal pronouns are *I, we, you, he, she, it* and *they*. Most other languages have comparable sets of personal pronouns, though the particular distinctions expressed vary significantly from one language to another, and some languages have only first- and second-person personal pronouns, using demonstratives or other deictic items for third-person reference. Some languages, however, particularly in southeast Asia, make little or no use of personal pronouns; the function of personal pronouns in these languages is chiefly performed by lexical nouns or noun phrases. For example, in Malay proper names and such nouns as *tuan* 'sir', *guru* 'teacher', *tukang* 'craftsman', *amah* 'nurse' and *'mak* 'grandmother' are used more frequently than personal pronouns.

perspective /pə'spektɪv/ *n.* The category invoked to account for the contrast between grammatically distinct sentences which describe the same state of affairs. Examples include such pairs as *She banged the hammer against the wall* and *She banged the wall with the hammer*; *Janet met Elroy at the pub* and *Elroy met Janet at the pub*; *Lisa sent Larry a letter* and *Larry got a letter from Lisa*; *The result surprised me* and *I was surprised at the result*. The notion of perspective is important in most **functional grammars** (sense 2), particularly **Functional Grammar** (sense 3). The term derives from the Prague School's use of 'functional sentence perspective'; the shortened form was introduced by Charles Fillmore (1977).

Peters–Ritchie results /ˌpiːtəz ˈrɪtʃi rɪzʌlts/ *n. pl.* A series of
proofs, by the mathematical linguists Stanley Peters and Robert
Ritchie, demonstrating first that transformational grammars of the
type proposed in the **Standard Theory** of Transformational
Grammar are weakly equivalent to the **unrestricted grammars** (in
other words, they can weakly generate any languages which can be
generated at all), and second that this result continues to hold even
if the most severe restrictions are placed upon the base rules. The
Peters–Ritchie results confirm the enormous power of transformations as they were conceived in the 1960s and, even though they
apply only to weak generative capacity, they are widely credited
with providing much of the motivation behind the attempts at
restricting the power of transformational frameworks which have
characterized the work of Chomsky and his associates since the
early 1970s. Peters and Ritchie presented their results in Peters and
Ritchie (1971, 1973). An outline of their first proof is given in Partee
et al. (1990), and also in Bach (1974); a simpler version of the more
complex second proof is provided in Bach and Marsh (1987).

phantom category /ˈfæntəm/ *n.* A syntactic category which is
postulated as existing in the grammar of a language and which
serves as the basis of certain generalizations, but which never
appears in a tree structure representing a sentence of the language.
For example, Welsh has VSO word order, and a category VP does
not appear as a continuous sequence in Welsh sentences; some
analyses, however, postulate the existence of a category VP in
Welsh, in terms of which such requirements as subcategorization
may be stated, even though no VP node ever appears in a tree. The
notion is particularly associated with GPSG, in which the VP rules
serve as input to the metarules which serve in turn to produce the
rules which actually license local subtrees. Gazdar and Sag (1981).

phrasal category /ˈfreɪzl̩/ *n.* 1. Any syntactic category which is a
one-bar or greater **projection** of a lexical category. Phrasal categories are usually divided into **maximal projections** (or **full phrasal
categories**) such as Noun Phrase (N-double-bar), Prepositional
Phrase (P-double-bar) and so on, and **intermediate phrasal categories**, such as N-bar, P-bar and so on. 2. Sometimes more specifically a synonym for **maximal projection** (**full phrasal category**).

phrasal genitive *n.* The English possessive construction involving
the simultaneous use of the preposition *of* and the possessive *-'s*, as

in the example *a friend of Lisa's*. Jespersen (1961, VII:300); the terms 'prepositional genitive' and 'post-genitive' have also been used.

phrasal verb *n.* A lexical verb, particularly in English, which consists of a simple verb combined with one or more **particles**, the meaning of the whole being typically unpredictable from the meanings of its constituent elements. Examples include *make up, take off, turn on, put down, walk out, take in, give up, ring up, put up with* and *do away with*. Phrasal verbs present notorious difficulties of analysis, not least because many (not all) of them permit the particle to be optionally separated from the simple verb: *She took off her dress* or *She took her dress off*. Quirk *et al.* (1972) distinguish phrasal verbs from **prepositional verbs**; see the remarks under that entry. According to Fowler (1965:451), the name was coined by the lexicographer Henry Bradley.

phrase /freɪz/ *n.* 1. A synonym for **constituent**. In this sense, any constituent, even a clause, may be regarded as a phrase. 2. A synonym for **maximal projection**, particularly in such category labels as Noun Phrase, Verb Phrase, Prepositional Phrase, etc. In this sense the term 'phrase' contrasts with **clause**. 3. Traditionally, and very loosely, a label applied to any string of words which someone wants to consider, regardless of its syntactic status. In this sense, 'phrase' may be regarded as the syntactic equivalent of the morphological term **morph**; the alternative term 'sequence' seems preferable.

phrase marker /ˈmɑːkə/ See **tree**.

phrase structure *n.* (**PS**) See **constituent structure**.

phrase structure grammar *n.* A formal grammar consisting entirely of **phrase structure rules**. Such a grammar may be either a **context-free grammar** or a **context-sensitive grammar**; see these last two entries for discussion. See Manaster-Ramer and Kac (1990) for a survey of the use of this term.

phrase structure rule *n.* (**PS-rule**) A **rewrite rule** which rewrites exactly one category as a string of zero or more categories (or, in some conceptions, as a string of one or more categories). If no environment is specified for the application of the rule, it is a **context-free rule**; if an environment is specified, it is a **context-sensitive rule**. See these last two entries for discussion and examples.

picture noun /'pɪktʃə/ *n.* One of a small group of English nouns which have the unusual property of permitting reflexive pronouns to occur inside prepositional phrases of which they are the heads, as in *Lisa sent me this picture of herself.* Cf. **Lisa smiled at the man beside herself.* Other picture nouns include *story*, *photograph*, *song* and *poem.* Picture-noun reflexives pose difficulties for many accounts of reflexivization. Gruber (1967).

pied-piping /paɪd'paɪpɪŋ/ *n.* The phenomenon in which a preposition whose object is a WH-item appears in a fronted position immediately preceding its object: *From where does this come?*; *The woman to whom you were speaking is my sister.* In many languages pied-piping is obligatory, but in English it is optional and largely confined to formal styles, the colloquial language preferring non-pied-piped forms like *Where does this come from?* and *The woman you were speaking to is my sister.* V. **pied-pipe** /paɪd'paɪp/. Ross (1967).

pivot /'pɪvət/ *n.* 1. In a comparative construction, the grammatical formative which serves to relate the comparative form to the standard, such as English *than* in examples like *taller than Lisa.* 2. In a syntactic structure, the NP which is grammatically most central, typically exhibiting such properties as the ability to coordinate, to control anaphora or deletion and to be realized as a null element in control structures. In the majority of languages, the pivot is simply the grammatical subject, but in some languages, particularly those exhibiting syntactic ergativity, the pivot is typically the patient NP in a transitive clause (see, for example, Dixon 1972 on Dyirbal), and some analysts prefer the non-committal descriptive term 'pivot' to avoid controversy about the proper use of the term 'subject' in such languages. Heath (1975).

place /pleɪs/ See **location**.

Platonistic features /pleɪtə'nɪstɪk/ *n.* The features [±N],[±V], used in some versions of the X-bar system for decomposing the major lexical categories, most often as follows: [+N, −V] = Noun, [+N, +V] = Adj, [−N, +V] = Verb, [−N, −V] = Preposition. Chomsky (unpublished work, 1974).

pleonastic /pliːə'næstɪk/ *adj.* Involving the use of words or morphemes which are redundant, in that they merely repeat information already expressed elsewhere. Consider, for example, the Basque verb form *dituzte* 'they have them', as compared with *du* 'he has it': here -*te* marks the plurality of the subject, while both -*it*- and -*z*- mark the plurality of the object, which is therefore expressed pleonastically. *Abstr. n.* **pleonasm** /'pliːənæzm̩/.

pluperfect /pluːˈpɜːfɪkt/ *n.* or *adj.* (also **past perfect**) A traditional label for a verb form expressing past tense and perfect aspect: *Lisa had finished the translation by ten o'clock.*

plural /'plʊərəl/ *n.* or *adj.* In a language with grammatical distinctions of **number**, that number category typically used to refer to the largest possible number of entities. In English and most other European languages, the plural contrasts only with the **singular**, and hence usually carries the meaning 'two or more'; in languages with a singular and a **dual**, the plural expresses 'three or more'; in those with singular, dual and **trial**, the plural expresses 'four or more'; in those with a **paucal**, the plural expresses 'more than a few'.

plurale tantum /plʊəˌraːleɪ ˈtæntəm/ (pl. **pluralia tantum** /plʊəˈraːliə/) *n.* A noun which is invariably plural in form but singular in sense: *scissors, tongs, pliers, pants, jeans, culottes, spectacles, binoculars.* Most of those occurring in English fall into three well-defined semantic groups, exemplified by *scissors, pants* and *spectacles.* In English, such nouns are counted with the aid of the word *pair*: *a pair of scissors, two pairs of jeans.* NOTE: the singular **plurale tantum** is rarely used, the plural form of the term being far commoner.

plus sign /'plʌs saɪn/ *n.* In the notation A$^+$, a notational convention indicating a string of one or more occurrences of the category A. Cf. **Kleene star**, and refer to the remarks there.

PO /piː ˈəʊ/ See **primary object**.

polarity item /pəʊˈlærɪti ˌaɪtm̩/ *n.* Any item which is either a **positive polarity item** or a **negative polarity item**.

polarity reverser /rɪˈvɜːsə/ *n.* Any element which, when added to a context requiring a **positive polarity item**, converts it to one requiring a **negative polarity item**: *not, hardly.*

polar question /'pəʊlə/ *n.* A question which expects one of two possible responses, especially a yes–no question like *Are you ready?*

polynomial time /pɒlɪˌnəʊmiəl ˈtaɪm/ *n.* The property of an **algorithm** which always delivers a result within a number of steps, and hence (in computational terms) a time, which is proportional to some positive power of the length of the input string. For example, the **Earley algorithm** for context-free grammars always succeeds within time Kn^3, where K is a constant and n is the length of the string. **Deterministic** polynomial time is an attractive characteristic in an algorithm, since it generally means that results for inputs of reasonable lengths can be obtained in a conveniently short time. Cf. **exponential time**, and see Barton *et al.* (1987).

polysyndeton /pɒlɪ'sɪndɪtn̩/ *n.* A **coordinate structure** involving a series of overt **conjunctions**: *Lisa and Jo and Siobhan and Siri.*

polysynthetic /pɒlɪsɪn'θetɪk/ *adj.* A label sometimes applied to word forms, or to languages employing such word forms, consisting of an unusually large number of bound morphemes, some of them with meanings or functions that would be expressed by separate words in most other languages. In a polysynthetic language, very often a complete sentence seems to consist of a single such word. Polysynthetic languages are particularly frequent in North America; the Iroquoian languages are well-known examples. Müller (1880); earlier linguists had used the term **incorporating**, but this last term is now usually given a more specific meaning.

polysystemism /pɒlɪ'sɪstəmɪzm̩/ *n.* An approach to grammatical characterization which views the structure of a language, not as a single integrated system (as in most approaches), but as a collection of independent but overlapping systems. The term is particularly applied to the work of the British linguist J. R. Firth. *Adj.* **polysystemic** /pɒlɪsɪs'tiːmɪk/.

portmanteau morph /pɔːt'mæntəʊ/ *n.* A single morph which represents two or more morphemes. An example is the morph *-o* in the Latin verb form *amo* 'I love': here *am-* is the verb root, and *-o* simultaneously expresses the categories first person, singular, present, active, indicative, all of which are in general overtly marked on Latin verb forms. Hockett (1947).

portmanteau word See **blend**.

positive /'pɒzɪtɪv/ *adj.* Denoting the simplest form of an adjective or adverb, contrasting with such other forms as the **comparative** and the **superlative**.

positive polarity item *n.* Any lexical or grammatical item which is confined to occurring in non-negative contexts, such as unstressed *some*: *We have some wine*, but **We don't have some wine.* Cf. **negative polarity item**.

possession /pə'zeʃn̩/ *n.* A general name for any relation between two noun phrases by which the second in some sense 'belongs to' the first. Possession is expressed in two main ways: (1) by a possessive construction, in which both NPs involved typically form a single larger NP, as in the English *Lisa's eyes* or the French *les vins d'Alsace*; (2) by a predication of possession, as in the English *Lisa has a car*. A typology of possessive constructions is given in Croft (1990).

possessive /pə'zesɪv/ See **genitive**.

possessive pronoun *n.* (also **possessive adjective**) A **determiner** which functions as the possessive form of a pronoun: *my*, *your*, *their*. See also **absolute possessive**.

POSS-*ing* /pɒs'ɪŋ/ *n.* A construction involving a **gerund** whose subject is a possessive NP: *Lisa's going topless upset her father*; *I don't like John's driving*. There is a potential contrast between such pairs as *I don't like John's driving on the motorway* and *I don't like John driving on the motorway*, but speakers of English differ in their views of these constructions. Some perceive a difference of meaning (roughly, 'manner of driving' vs. 'fact of driving'), others regard the first as a mere formal variant of the second, still others find only the first well-formed and yet others find only the second well-formed. Cf. **ACC-*ing***, and see the remarks under **gerund**. Rosenbaum (1967).

postcedent /pəʊst'siːdənt/ *n.* A label occasionally applied to an **antecedent** which follows its anaphor, as in **backward pronominalization**. The term seems to be without theoretical significance and is rarely used.

postmodifier /pəʊst'mɒdɪfaɪə/ *n.* Any **modifier** which follows its head, such as *in a miniskirt* in *a girl in a miniskirt*. The term is not usually considered to have any theoretical significance.

postposition /pəʊstpə'zɪʃn̩/ *n.* (**P**) A lexical item which is identical to a **preposition** in every respect except that it follows its object NP. Postpositions are rare in European languages (though English has at least one, *ago*, as in *five years ago*), but they occur to the exclusion of prepositions in a number of other languages, such as Japanese and Basque. A Japanese example: *Chichi wa boku ni tokei o kureta* father Topic me to watch DO gave 'My father gave me a watch', where *wa*, *ni* and *o* are all postpositions. Postpositions are consistently preferred to prepositions in **SOV languages**, as first pointed out by Greenberg (1963), though they also occur elsewhere. The term **adposition** is used as a cover term for both prepositions and postpositions.

potential /pə'tentʃl/ *adj.* The mood category expressing ability or possibility. An example is Turkish *yapabilirim* 'I can do it', an inflected form of *yapmak* 'do'. Jespersen (1924).

power /'pɑʊə/ See **generative capacity**.

PP See **prepositional phrase**.

precede-and-command condition /prɪˌsiːd ənd kə'mɑːnd/ *n.* A constraint on **backward pronominalization**, which states that a pronoun may not both precede and S-command its antecedent. Hence *After she*ᵢ *came in, Janet*ᵢ *sat down* is well-formed, since *she* does not S-command *Janet*, but **She*ᵢ *sat down after Janet*ᵢ *came in* is ill-formed, since *she* both precedes and S-commands *Janet*. In GB, this constraint is subsumed under **binding theory**. Langacker (1969).

precedence /'presɪdəns/ See **linear precedence**.

predicate /'predɪkət/ *n.* 1. That constituent of a sentence, most typically a verb phrase, which combines with the subject NP to make up the complete sentence. Examples: *Lisa* [*enjoyed the film*]; *Your photographs* [*are ready*]; *I* [*have already finished marking your essays*]. In some languages, certain types of sentences can have predicates which, superficially at least, are of categories other than VP, as in the Turkish example *Hasan büyük* 'Hasan is big', in which the predicate has the surface form of an adjective phrase. Aristotle. 2. A verb, or a complex structure consisting of a verb or auxiliary plus a closely bound meaningful element, when this is considered as a linguistic unit which can or must combine with specified **arguments** or **participant roles** to make up a clause. Examples of predicates in this sense are *die*, *kill*, *melt*, *be happy* and *turn red*. Predicates in this sense can be classified in various useful ways. Grammatically, they may be classified in terms of their **valency**, the number and types of arguments which they require. There are also grammatically relevant semantic classifications, the best-known of which is that of Vendler (1967). 3. In formal logic, an element which must combine with a specified number of arguments to make up a well-formed expression; the linguistic use of 'predicate' in sense 2 is directly derived from this logical usage.

predicate complement See **complement** (sense 2).

predicate nominal *n.* A traditional name for a noun phrase in predicate position, particularly in a copular sentence, such as *a translator* in *Lisa is a translator*.

predication theory /predɪ'keɪʃn̩/ *n.* The area of syntax which deals with the possible structures or functions of **predicates** (sense 2).

predicative /prɪ'dɪkətɪv/ *adj.* Denoting an element which occurs inside a **predicate** (sense 1), such as the adjective phrase *too big* in *This is too big*.

predictive /prɪ'dɪktɪv/ *adj.* A label occasionally applied to a future tense form which can only be used to make predictions and which cannot be used to express intentions. Very few languages are known to have such a specialized form. Dahl (1985).

prefix /'priːfɪks/ *n.* An **affix** which precedes the root, stem or base to which it is bound, such as the English derivational affixes *re-* and *un-*, the Japanese honorific *o-* or any of the large set of inflectional affixes found in Swahili (for an example, see under **agglutination**). The prevalence of prefixes over suffixes is strongly characteristic of **VSO languages** and, to a lesser extent, of **SVO languages**, as first pointed out by Greenberg (1963).

prefix property /'prɒpəti/ *n.* The property of a sentence, regarded as a **string**, which has no initial proper substring which is also a sentence. A **garden-path sentence** like *The diners hurried through their meal were annoyed* lacks the prefix property, since the initial proper substring *The diners hurried through their meal* is also a sentence.

premodifier /ˌpriː'mɒdɪfaɪə/ *n.* An *ad hoc* label for any modifier which precedes its head. The term is usually considered to have no theoretical significance.

preposing /ˌpriː'pəʊzɪŋ/ *n.* (also **fronting**) Any of various constructions in which a constituent is placed at the beginning of a sentence or clause, as in **WH-Movement** or **adverb preposing**.

preposition /ˌprepə'zɪʃn̩/ *n.* (**P**) A lexical category, or a member of this category, which typically combines with a noun phrase to make a larger constituent, a **prepositional phrase**, which in turn can typically occur inside a verb phrase or inside an N-bar. English examples include *to, from, with, of, under* and *in front of*, as in *to Lisa, from Paris, with great enthusiasm, of the game, under an*

umbrella and *in front of the post office*. Prepositions usually constitute a **closed** lexical category. Both etymologically and in practice,
the term 'preposition' is restricted to a lexical item which precedes
its object NP, the term **postposition** being used for a comparable
item which follows its object NPs, and **adposition** being used as a
superordinate label. *Adj.* **prepositional**.

prepositional phrase /ˌprepəˈzɪʃənl̩/ *n.* (**PP**) A phrase consisting
of a preposition and a noun phrase serving as its object: *in the
garden, with Lisa, in front of the post office*. In most versions of the
X-bar system, the category PP is regarded as the maximal projection
of the lexical category Preposition, P″. Prepositional phrases can
contain specifiers: *just behind the house* and *way over the limit*.

prepositional specifier *n.* A lexical item which modifies a prepositional phrase and is, in some analyses, regarded as the **specifier** of
the category PP: [*straight*] *into the hole*, [*way*] *over the limit*, [*just*]
behind the house, [*miles*] *up the river*.

prepositional verb *n.* A complex verb resembling a **phrasal verb**,
but distinguished, according to Quirk *et al.* (1972:815), by the
following criteria (here *call on* is a prepositional verb, *call up* a
phrasal verb): (1) unstressed particle (*They ˈcall on the man*; *They
call ˈup the man*); (2) absence of particle shift (**They call the man
on*; *They call the man up*); (3) separability (*They call early on the
man*; **They call early up the man*); (4) pied-piping (*the man on
whom they called*; **the man up whom they called*).

preposition stranding *n.* The construction in which a preposition
appears with no overt object NP, that NP being realized elsewhere
in the sentence, usually by **WH-Movement**. An example is *Who
were you talking to?* See also **pied-piping**.

prescriptivism /prɪˈskrɪptɪvɪzm̩/ *n.* An approach to grammatical
characterization one of whose primary objects is the identification of
forms and usages which are considered by the analyst to be 'correct'
and the proscribing of forms and usages felt to be 'incorrect'. The
criteria invoked in such an approach are necessarily those selected
by the analyst and are hence essentially subjective; they typically
include appeals to 'logic', to aesthetic factors, to tradition and/or to
literary usage; not infrequently, they also include appeals to the
grammatical facts of other languages which are regarded as having
greater prestige. Prescriptivism was strongly characteristic of a good
deal of the work published on the grammar of English and of other

European languages during the eighteenth, nineteenth and early twentieth centuries, particularly of the textbooks prepared for use in schools. Among the best-known prescriptivist statements about English are the insistence on *It's I* and the rejection of *It's me*, the condemnation of sentence-final prepositions and the condemnation of the so-called **split infinitive**. Most modern linguists would probably accept that some degree of prescriptivism is necessary for educational purposes, but all would vigorously reject prescriptivism as a basis for grammatical characterization. *Adj.* **prescriptivist** /prɪ'skrɪptɪvɪst/. Cf. **descriptivism**.

present /'prezənt/ *n.* or *adj.* The **tense** category occurring in some languages which is most regularly used to refer to actions or states in progress at the moment of speaking, or which at least includes this function as one of its major uses. The term is sometimes used to label a tense form of rather wider applicability than this; in English, for example, the name 'present' is regularly used for the tense which would more explicitly be called the 'non-past', as it contrasts only with a past tense.

presentative /prɪ'zentətɪv/ *adj.* Any of various constructions which serve to introduce a new element into a discourse, such as the American English pattern illustrated by *There was this bus coming up the road*.

present participle *n.* In English and some other languages, the traditional name for what is more properly called the **imperfective participle**, such as *writing* in *Lisa is/was writing letters*.

present perfect *n.* A verb form simultaneously marked for present tense and perfect aspect, such as that in *I have eaten dinner*. The present perfect is sometimes loosely called the 'perfect'.

presumptive /prɪ'zʌmptɪv/ *n.* or *adj.* The **mood** category associated with a supposition, as in the example *He is probably rich*. Very few languages appear to have a distinctive form for expressing this mood explicitly. See Palmer (1986) for discussion.

preterite /'pretərɪt/ *n.* or *adj.* A past-tense verb form which is unmarked for aspect: *saw, loved*.

preterminal node /ˌpriː'tɜːmɪnl̩/ *n.* A node in a tree which dominates nothing but a lexical item. Cf. **non-terminal node**, **terminal node**.

preverb /'priːvɜːb/ *n.* Any of various particle-like morphemes occurring in a number of languages which most typically occur immediately before a verb. Examples are Hungarian *ki* 'out' (*megy* 'go', *kimegy* 'go out') and *be* 'in' (*jön* 'come', *bejön* 'come in') and German *aus* 'out' (*gehen* 'go', *ausgehen* 'go out') and *zu* 'to' (*kommen* 'come', *zukommen* 'approach'). Some preverbs in some languages can in certain circumstances be separated from an associated verb; this is true of both Hungarian and German, as illustrated by German *Er kam auf dem Auto zu* 'He approached the car'. Preverbs in some languages serve to express oblique relationships in lieu of case marking, as in Winnebago *Kook-ra ho-nanchin-je-enan* box-Def in-stand-Aux-Declarative 'It is standing in the box', in which the preverb *ho-* expresses the locative relation of *kookra* 'the box'.

primary object /'praɪməri/ *n.* (**PO**) The union of direct objects in simple transitive clauses with indirect objects in ditransitive clauses, when this grouping functions as a grammatical natural class, contrasting with direct objects in ditransitive clauses (**secondary objects**). The PO/SO contrast is widespread in the languages of the world, occurring, for example, in Swahili, Huichol, Ojibwa, Palauan and (arguably) English. Languages exhibiting this pattern are labelled **dechticaetiative** by Blansitt (1984); in such languages, POs typically control such processes as verb agreement and passivization. Dryer (1986); various other terms are found in the literature in a similar sense, including 'principal object' and 'prime object'.

primitive /'prɪmɪtɪv/ *n.* In a formal system, any one of the minimal elements in terms of which the system is constructed, and which cannot be defined in terms of any other elements in the system. All other elements used in the system must be defined in terms of the primitives.

principal parts /ˌprɪnsɪpl̩ 'pɑːts/ *n. pl.* In the grammar of an inflecting language, a conventional list of certain selected forms of a lexical item, especially a verb, from which all the remaining forms can generally be constructed by rule. The principal parts of an English verb are conventionally the infinitive, the past tense and the perfect participle ('past participle'): *eat, ate, eaten; go, went, gone; drive, drove, driven.* Those of a Latin verb are the first person singular present indicative active, the infinitive, the first person singular perfect indicative active and the supine: *amo, amare,* *amavi, amatum* 'love'; *ago, agere, egi, actum* 'drive'; *fero, ferre, tuli, latum* 'bear'.

principle /'prɪnsɪpl̩/ *n.* Any statement in a theory of grammar which is conceived as having universal validity, subject at most to minor adjustments for the grammars of particular languages. Some examples are the **Theta Criterion** and the **Projection Principle** of GB and the **Control Agreement Principle** and the **Head Feature Convention** of GPSG. The identification of such universal principles is one of the chief motivating forces of recent work in syntax and is in particular the central goal of GB; it is the most important respect in which recent work differs from earlier approaches to grammatical investigation, including earlier generative approaches.

principles-and-parameters *adj.* Denoting the approach to grammatical characterization advocated in GB, in which the (core) grammar of a particular language is regarded as consisting of a set of universal **principles** plus the language-specific settings for a small number of **parameters**.

Priority-to-the-Instance Principle /praɪˌɒrəti tə ðiː 'ɪnstəns/ See **Proper Inclusion Principle**.

privative /'prɪvətɪv/ *adj.* Denoting an affix expressing the notion 'without', such as the *a-* of *amoral* or the *-less* of *topless*.

PRO /prəʊ/ *n.* (also **big PRO**) In GB, the **empty category** posited as existing in the overtly vacant subject position of the infinitival VP complements of **control verbs**, as illustrated by *Lisa wants* [PRO *to learn Dutch*] and *Lisa decided* [PRO *to stop smoking*]. Within the Binding Theory of GB, PRO is analysed as [+anaphoric, +pronominal], and is hence subject to the conflicting requirements of Principles A and B, a conflict which can only be resolved if PRO is ungoverned. The module of GB postulated to deal with the very considerable problem of finding a referent for PRO is called **Control Theory**. Most frameworks other than GB deny the existence of any element occupying the position of PRO, preferring instead to recognize simple VP complements without subjects.

pro /prəʊ/ *n.* (also **little pro**) In GB, the **empty category** posited as existing in the overtly vacant subject position in certain languages exhibiting the phenomenon of **pro-drop**. For example, the sentence *Viene* 'He/She is coming' in the pro-drop language Spanish would be analysed as [pro *viene*]. Little pro is regarded as an ordinary personal pronoun in most respects, apart from its lack of phonetic content.

proclitic /ˌprəʊˈklɪtɪk/ *n.* A **clitic** which is phonologically bound to a following host, such as French *je* 'I' in *je vais* 'I'm going'. Cf. **enclitic**.

pro-constituent /ˈprəʊkənˌstɪtʃʊənt/ *n.* (Also **pro-form**). See **anaphor** (sense 1).

pro-drop /ˈprəʊdrɒp/ *n.* The phenomenon in which an argument position of a verb, particularly subject position, can be left empty. The pro-drop language Spanish allows well-formed sentences like *Viene* 'He/She is coming', whereas non-pro-drop French and English require overt subject NPs: **Vient*; **Is coming*.

pro-drop language See **null-subject language**.

Pro-Drop Parameter *n.* (also **Null-Subject Parameter**) In GB, the parameter by which the grammar of a language may permit or prohibit **pro-drop**.

production /prəˈdʌkʃn̩/ *n.* A synonym for **rewrite rule**, preferred in mathematical and computational linguistics.

productive /prəˈdʌktɪv/ *adj.* Denoting a grammatical pattern, particularly a morphological pattern, which can be more or less freely applied to any item meeting its requirements, including elements newly added to the language. For example, the formation of abstract nouns in English with the suffix *-ness* is productive, as almost any adjective can undergo it: *happiness, hopelessness, crash-worthiness*. (Certain adjectives with Latin and Greek suffixes are systematic exceptions to this process, such as *variable, topical* and *thematic*, but this fact does not alter the essential productiveness of *-ness*.) Similarly, the passive construction in English is productive for transitive verbs: the appearance of the new transitive verb *access* immediately permits a passive, as in *That utility can be accessed from the main menu*. Cf. **unproductive, partially productive**.

pro-form /ˈprəʊfɔːm/ (also **pro-constituent**) See **anaphor** (sense 1).

progressive /prəˈgresɪv/ *n.* or *adj.* (also **continuous**) The **aspect** category which refers specifically to an action or event which is in progress at the moment of time serving as the reference point for the utterance. English expresses this regularly by means of its *be . . .-ing* construction, as in *Lisa is/was/will be writing letters*.

Progressive aspect is a subdivision of **imperfective** aspect. Comrie (1976) distinguishes 'progressive' from 'continuous', using 'continuous' to mean 'non-habitual' and 'progressive' as a subcategory of 'continuous', but this possibly useful distinction is not widely made, the two terms being generally regarded as synonymous.

progressive passive *n.* A verb form marked simultaneously for progressive aspect and passive voice: *My house is being painted.* This construction was regarded as ill-formed in English until fairly recently. See also **perfect progressive passive**.

projection /prə'dʒekʃn̩/ *n.* 1. In the X-bar system, any non-lexical syntactic category which is regarded as systematically related to a lexical category which regularly occurs as its lexical head. For example, the categories Noun Phrase (N-double-bar) and N-bar are regarded as projections of the lexical category Noun, which usually occurs as the lexical head of both. Such a projection differs formally from its related lexical category only in respect of the value assigned to the feature [BAR]. 2. The relation which holds between the rules of a grammar and the trees which are licensed by that grammar. The set of well-formed trees is said to be **projected** from the rules of the grammar. 3. In certain theories of grammar, notably GB, a formal relation which holds between the lexical entries of lexical items and the grammatical structures in which those lexical items appear, by which certain properties of the lexical entries, especially their subcategorization properties, must be maintained in the grammatical structures. One says that the syntactic representations are projected from the lexicon. 4. Loosely, any of various other relations which may exist between two objects or sets of objects. For example, one may speak of the 'projection' of a language from a particular corpus of data from that language. In this sense, 'projection' means roughly 'extrapolation'.

Projection Principle *n.* One of the fundamental principles of GB. It states that representations at each syntactic level are projected from the lexicon, in that the subcategorization and theta-marking properties of a lexical item must be maintained and satisfied at every level of representation. This principle has far-reaching consequences; perhaps more than any other single factor it is responsible for the major differences between GB and the earlier versions of TG. It greatly enhances the role of the lexicon in syntax, since it effectively asserts that some position in syntactic structure will exist if, and only if, some lexical item requires it to exist (or 'licenses' it).

This principle also rules out many of the particular analyses advanced within the earlier framework, such as all those involving the movement of subject NPs into non-subject NP positions which did not exist at earlier stages of the derivation. Indeed, the Projection Principle in isolation would rule out movement rules altogether; the limited range of movement operations still recognized in GB is made possible only by the permitted existence of **empty categories**, whose occurrence is strictly regulated by the various other components of the framework, and by the special provision made for the presence of the non-subcategorized subject position by the **Extended Projection Principle**.

prolative /'prəʊlətɪv/ *n.* or *adj.* 1. See **benefactive**. 2. A traditional term for an infinitival complement of a verb or auxiliary like *want*, *must* or *start*.

prolepsis /prəʊ'lepsɪs/ *n.* The use of a modifier which only becomes appropriate through the action of the verb, as in *paint it green*. *Adj.* **proleptic** /prəʊ'leptɪk/.

promotion /prəʊ'məʊʃn̩/ *n.* In RG, any of various syntactic processes by which some NP is moved from a lower- to a higher-ranking position within the **Relational Hierarchy**, such as from direct object to subject during passivization. The term is also used informally for the same purpose in frameworks in which such operations receive no formal recognition. Cf. **demotion**.

pronominal /prəʊ'nɒmɪnl̩/ 1. *adj.* Pertaining to **pronouns**. 2. *n.* In GB, any of the various types of NP analysed in that framework as possessing the feature specification [+p] and hence as subject to Principle B of the **Binding Theory**, by which it must be free in its governing category. The only overt NPs in this class are personal pronouns like *you* and *they*, but the two empty categories called **pro** and **PRO** are also included. 3. A synonym for **pronoun**, especially in LFG.

pronoun /'prəʊnaʊn/ *n.* The lexical category, or a member of this category, whose members typically function as noun phrases in isolation, not normally requiring or permitting the presence of determiners or other adnominals, and whose members typically have little or no intrinsic meaning or reference. Pronouns are conventionally divided into several distinct classes, including **personal pronouns** (*I*, *they*), **reflexive pronouns** (*herself*), **demonstrative pronouns** (*this*), **indefinite pronouns** (*something*, *anybody*), interrogative pronouns (*who*, *what* in questions) and **relative pronouns** (*who*, *which* in relative clauses). *Adj.* **pronominal**.

proper constituent /'prɒpə/ *n.* A constituent of a category which is not identical to that category. Every category is necessarily a constituent of itself, but it is never a proper constituent.

proper dominance *n.* The relation which holds between a node A and a distinct node B which A dominates. The term is necessary because, by definition, a node always dominates itself, but it never properly dominates itself.

proper government *n.* In GB, an important relation which may hold between two nodes in a tree. There are two cases to be considered: **antecedent government** and **theta government**. A node A antecedent-governs a node B iff A governs B and A is coindexed with B. A node A theta-governs a node B iff A assigns a theta role to B. The notion of proper government is crucial in the statement of the **Empty Category Principle**. Observe that antecedent government is a special case of **government**, while theta government is a quite different relation.

Proper Inclusion Principle /ɪn'kluːʒn̩/ *n.* (also **Elsewhere Principle**, **Priority-to-the-Instance Principle**) The principle that, in any conflict between a more specific and a more general requirement of the grammar, the more specific one always takes priority. Thus, for example, the statement that the English noun *man* has the irregular plural *men* takes precedence over the general rule for forming plurals in English. Sanders (1974); the principle itself was explicitly expressed by the Indian grammarian Paṇini.

proper noun *n.* A noun whose only function is to refer to a designated entity, such as *Lisa*, *Paris*, *Neptune* or *Greta Scacchi*. Cf. **common noun**.

proposition /prɒpə'zɪʃn̩/ *n.* The semantic content of a statement. By extension, a yes–no question may be interpreted as having the form 'Is the proposition *p* true?', while a WH-question may be interpreted as having the form 'For which value of x is the proposition *p* true?' For example, the question *Does Lisa smoke?* may be interpreted as 'Is the proposition *Lisa smokes* true?', while *What did Lisa see?* may be interpreted as 'For which value of x is the proposition *Lisa saw x* true?'

proscription /prəʊˈskrɪpʃn̩/ *n.* In a **prescriptivist** approach to grammar, any statement which prohibits the use of some form or construction, such as the prescriptivist 'rule' forbidding the ending of a sentence with a preposition. *V.* **proscribe** /prəʊˈskraɪb/.

pro-sentence /ˌprəʊˈsentəns/ *n.* A lexical item which typically functions in isolation as a complete utterance: *yes, no.*

prospective /prəʊˈspektɪv/ *n.* or *adj.* An aspectual form which typically expresses the notion that some event is imminent, such as English *be going to* or *be about to*. The prospective forms the future analogue of the perfect; it differs from other aspects of the future in that it does not necessarily express either a prediction or an intention. A few languages have a productive inflected form for expressing just this meaning, such as Basque *-(t)zorian*: *hiltzorian* 'on the point of death' (*hil* 'die'). See Comrie (1976) for discussion.

protasis /ˈprɒtəsɪs/ *n.* (also **antecedent**) In a **conditional sentence**, the clause whose truth value determines the truth value of the other clause. In English, a protasis is introduced by *if*, as in *If I see Lisa, I'll tell her*. Cf. **apodosis**.

pro-verb /ˈprəʊˌvɜːb/ *n.* An occasional synonym for **pro-VP**. This use, which is not recommended, is modelled on the traditional form 'pronoun' for what is actually a pro-NP.

pro-VP /ˌprəʊ viː ˈpiː/ *n.* A **pro-form** whose antecedent is a VP, such as *do so* or *do it* in examples like *I asked Lisa to proofread the typescript, and she did so/did it.*

proximate /ˈprɒksɪmət/ *adj.* 1. In a **deictic system**, the term expressing the closest position to the reference point, normally the speaker, such as English *here* or *this*, and contrasting with **distal** and possibly other terms. 2. In certain languages, a subdivision of the third person used for reference to the first third person entity mentioned in a particular discourse, and contrasting with the **obviative**. See the remarks under the latter entry.

Prt See **particle**.

PS (**phrase structure**) See **constituent structure**.

pseudo-cleft sentence /ˈsjuːdəʊkleft/ *n.* (also **WH-cleft**) A marked construction in which the non-focused constituents are extracted from their logical positions and preceded by a WH-item, this sequence being connected by a copula to the focused constituent, which comes last. The unmarked sentence *John bought a car yesterday* has the corresponding pseudo-cleft *What John bought yesterday was a car*. Cf. **cleft sentence** and **reverse pseudo-cleft**.

pseudo-intransitive /ˌsjuːdəʊɪn'trænsɪtɪv/ *adj*. Denoting an intransitive construction involving a **labile verb** which appears to be intrinsically transitive. Lyons (1968).

pseudo-passive /ˌsjuːdəʊ'pæsɪv/ *n*. or *adj*. 1. A label sometimes applied to a passive construction in which the verb is intransitive and the subject is underlyingly the object of a preposition: *This bed was slept in by George Washington*; *My begonias have been trampled on by the children*; *The eradication of disease has been dreamt about for centuries*. The subset of intransitive verbs appearing in this construction is approximately the class known as **unergatives**. 2. See **impersonal passive**.

PS-rule See **phrase structure rule**.

psychological reality /saɪkə‚lɒdʒɪkl̩ ri'ælɪti/ *n*. The putative characteristic of a grammar, or of a part of a grammar, which is consistent with what is known about human mental processes. The best-known work addressing this issue is Halle *et al.* (1978).

psych-verb /saɪk/ *n*. A verb expressing a psychological state, particularly one which, in English, is typically construed in the passive with a following preposition other than *by*: *be surprised at*, *be disgusted with*, *be excited about*, *be interested in*. Postal (1971).

punctual /'pʌŋktʃʊəl/ *n*. or *adj*. The **aspect** category expressing an action or state which is confined to a single instant of time, as in the example *Hillary reached the summit of Everest*. The punctual is a subdivision of the **perfective**. See Comrie (1976) for discussion.

purpose clause /'pɜːpəs/ *n*. An adverbial clause which expresses the purpose of an action, such as the bracketed sequences in the examples *Lisa is learning Spanish* [*to improve her job prospects*] and *Lisa bought a word processor* [*so that she could work more efficiently*].

purposive /'pɜːpəsɪv/ *n*. or *adj*. A case form occurring in certain languages which primarily expresses the purpose of an action. Such a case form occurs most noticeably in certain Australian languages; an example is Yidiny *-gu*, as in *yingu waguuja galing minyaagu* 'The man is going out for meat', where *minyaagu* 'for meat' is a purposive. Dixon (1980).

pushdown automaton /ˈpʊʃdaʊn/ *n*. (**pda**) An extension of a **finite-state automaton** equipped with a pushdown stack that permits the system to remember where to resume after a named subnetwork has been traversed. The non-deterministic pushdown automata accept exactly the class of **context-free languages**, while the deterministic pdas accept only the **deterministic context-free languages**.

pushdown stack /stæk/ *n*. A computational device consisting of a linear storage space in which any number of items may be stored. An item placed in the stack is said to be 'pushed' and must go on top of any items already in the stack; only the topmost item may be removed from the stack ('popped'), and hence the stack operates on the principle of 'last in first out'. Such a stack provides a convenient way of handling recursion in languages.

Q

quantifier /'kwɒntɪfaɪə/ *n*. A **determiner** whose meaning expresses some notion of quantity: *many, lots of, few, some, no*. Some analysts regard quantifiers as forming a distinct category from determiners, but this distinction is difficult to justify in syntactic terms.

quantifier floating /'fləʊtɪŋ/ *n*. The phenomenon in which a quantifier occurs separated from the rest of the noun phrase of which it is semantically a part. An example is *The students have all arrived*, in which the quantifier *all* has 'floated' off the NP *all the students*.

quantifier raising *n*. In GB, a process which is posited as occurring between S-structure and Logical Form, by which quantifiers are assumed to be moved to the leftmost position in a sentence, where they can be interpreted as binding variables in the sentence in much the same way as do quantifiers in predicate calculus. For example, the sentence *Lisa charms everybody* has the Logical Form *Everybody$_i$ Lisa charms e$_i$*, in which the quantifier *everybody* has been raised.

quasi-copula /'kweɪsaɪ ˌkɒpjʊlə/ *n*. A lexical verb which links a subject NP to a nominal or adjectival predicate but which, unlike a true copula (such as *be*) has real semantic content, often aspectual, modal or perceptual: *She remained healthy; She grew stronger; She stood firm; It went wrong; She seemed happy; It proved a failure; It tastes good; It looks a simple task*.

queclarative /kwɪ'klærətɪv/ *n*. An utterance which has the form of a question but the force of a statement, most often an emphatic or sarcastic statement. Examples: *Who speaks Polish around here?* (meaning 'Nobody speaks Polish around here'); *Is she clever!* (meaning 'She's clever'); *Isn't this nice?* (variously meaning 'This is very nice' or 'This isn't nice at all'). Sadock (1971).

question /'kwestʃən/ *n*. One of the traditional **sentence types**, corresponding to an utterance which, in principle at least, requires a linguistic response from the addressee. The most familiar types of questions are **WH-questions** like *Who were you talking to?* and

yes–no questions like *Do you smoke?*, but other types exist, such as *Is this a snark or a boojum?*

question mark /mɑːk/ *n.* A conventional symbol indicating that the grammatical status or acceptability of what follows is uncertain, in that speakers cannot decide or disagree unpredictably in their judgements. An example is *?I saw Janet while enjoying herself*, concerning which different English speakers either are uncertain or differ in their judgements in a way that seems to be entirely unpredictable in terms of their geographical or social background. The combinations '??' and '?*' are sometimes used to denote increasing degrees of doubtfulness. Cf. **per cent sign**. Early 1960s; the first published use was apparently that by Gleitman (1965).

quotative /ˈkwəʊtətɪv/ *n.* or *adj.* An explicitly marked form occurring in some languages which expresses the fact that the speaker has not personally witnessed what she/he is describing but is quoting what someone else has told her/him, and which is obligatory in this circumstance. The formal expression of this category varies widely: Hixkaryana *hati* is a particle forming part of the verification system (see **evidential**) of that language; Japanese *soo da* is a specialized predicate taking a finite clause as complement; Turkish *miş* is a verbal affix. In some languages, the formal expression of the quotative is identical to that of the **inferential**; this is true of Turkish, but not of Hixkaryana or Japanese. The term 'quotative' is recommended by Dahl (1985) from among the various terms found in the literature.

quotes /kwəʊts/ See **inverted commas**.

R

raising /ˈreɪzɪŋ/ *n.* Any of various phenomena in which some linguistic element appears in a higher clause than is semantically appropriate. See examples under **subject raising** and **negative raising**.

raising verb *n.* A lexical verb or predicate which typically appears in a syntactic structure in which its surface subject is logically or semantically the subject of its complement clause. A familiar example is *seem*: in *Lisa seems to be happy*, the NP *Lisa* is semantically the subject of *be happy* but grammatically the subject of *seem*. Other raising verbs and predicates in English include *appear*, *tend* and *be likely*. See also **subject raising**.

reading /ˈriːdɪŋ/ *n.* One of the possible interpretations of an ambiguous string.

readjustment /riːəˈdʒʌstmənt/ See **restructuring**.

realis /rɪˈælɪs/ *adj.* A label occasionally employed to label a verb form typically used to refer to an event or a state perceived as actually occurring or having occurred, and contrasting with **irrealis**; see the remarks under that entry.

realistic grammar /rɪəˈlɪstɪk/ *n.* Any attempt at grammatical characterization which is, or purports to be, psychologically real, in the sense that it is consistent with what is known about mental processes.

realization /rɪəlaɪˈzeɪʃn̩/ *n.* Any surface form which is regarded as representing some more abstract structure, particularly when the surface form is significantly different from the proposed abstract structure. For example, the surface form *won't* is sometimes taken to be a realization of the underlying sequence *will not*.

reanalysis /riːəˈnæləsɪs/ *n.* 1. See **restructuring**. 2. The historical process by which a well-formed surface string comes to be interpreted as having a different structure from formerly, as when the earlier English *It will be* [*easy for us*] *to do that* was reanalysed as *It* *will be easy* [*for us to do that*], leading to the innovating structure *For us to do that will be easy*.

recipient /rɪˈsɪpiənt/ *n*. The **participant role** borne by an NP which expresses the (usually animate) entity which receives some concrete or abstract object, such as *Lisa* in *I gave Lisa the book* and *Lisa received a letter*. Recipient is one of the **deep cases** recognized in Case Grammar, though it is sometimes conflated with Goal or with Beneficiary, or with both.

reciprocal /rɪˈsɪprəkl̩/ *n*. An **anaphor** (sense 1), or a construction involving such an anaphor, expressing the action of two entities on each other, or of several entities on one another. The most familiar English reciprocal anaphor is *each other*: *Janet and Elroy are not speaking to each other*.

recognition /rekəɡˈnɪʃn̩/ *n*. The task faced by an **automaton** in deciding whether some particular string does or does not form part of some particular language. Recognition does not necessarily involve the assignment of a correct structure, or even of any structure, to the string, and hence the 'recognition problem', as it is called, is purely a matter of **weak generative capacity**. Cf. **generation**, and see also **parser**.

recoverability constraint /rɪkʌvərəˈbɪlɪti/ *n*. In some derivational theories of grammar, a proposed constraint by which no overt material may be deleted from a tree in the course of a derivation unless it is explicitly recoverable from the resulting surface structure.

recurrent alternation /rɪˈkʌrənt/ *n*. An instance of **allomorphy** which affects a number of morphemes in the same way. An example is the *e/a* alternation in Turkish, which affects a number of morphemes identically: plural -*ler*/-*lar*, dative -*e*/-*a*, locative -*de*/-*da*, ablative -*den*/-*dan*, habitual -*er*/-*ar* and so on. Matthews (1974).

recursion /rɪˈkɜːʒn̩/ *n*. The phenomenon by which a constituent of a sentence dominates another instance of the same syntactic category; equivalently, the phenomenon by which the rules of a formal grammar permit a category to have another instance of the same category as a descendant. Some simple examples: *Lisa said that she would come* (S embedded under S); *the story of my life* (NP embedded under NP); *under the boughs of an ancient cypress* (PP embedded under PP); *started to learn Dutch* (VP embedded under VP). Recursion is pervasive in natural languages, and, in general, there is no principled limit to the number of instances of recursion which may occur within a single category: *I'm reading a book about the reasons for the development of computers with the capacity for high-speed manipulation of virtual objects under the control of users with no previous experience of* . . . Recursion is the principal reason that the number of sentences in a natural language is normally taken to be infinite. *Adj.* **recursive**; *V.* **recurse** /rɪˈkɜːs/.

recursive language /rɪˈkɜːsɪv/ *n.* A formal language for which an **algorithm** exists that will always determine whether an arbitrary string is in the language or not within a finite but unbounded number of steps. The recursive languages are a proper superset of the context-sensitive languages.

recursively enumerable language /rɪˌkɜːsɪvli ɪˈnjuːmərəbḷ/ *n.* (also **r.e. language**) A formal language for which a procedure exists that will always determine whether an arbitrary string is in the language, if it is, within a finite but unbounded number of steps. Failure to obtain a positive result within a given number of steps may mean either that not enough steps have yet been performed to determine that the string is in the language or that the string is not in the language, but there is no way of deciding which. The mathematical linguist Robert Wall once informally characterized r.e. languages by saying 'If it's there, we'll find it eventually, but it might take a while.' The r.e. languages are characterized by the class of **unrestricted grammars** and are accepted by **Turing machines**.

recursive transition network *n.* (RTN) A **transition network** consisting of a number of subnetworks, each labelled with the name of a syntactic category, and equipped with a pushdown stack which enables the system to jump to a specified subnetwork and to remember where to return to after traversal of the subnetwork is completed. RTNs constitute an extension of finite-state transition networks (see **finite-state automaton**). Cf. **augmented transition network**.

reduced clause /rɪˈdjuːst/ *n.* 1. A sequence with the distribution and meaning of an adverbial clause but lacking both a subject NP and a finite verb; it typically consists of a relative adverb and a predicate expression. Examples: [*When in Rome,*] *do as the Romans do*; *Please make corrections* [*where necessary*]; *Edison discovered thermionic emission* [*while working on something else*]. 2. A **small clause**, particularly in sense 1. NOTE: there is at present no consensus as to whether or how the terms 'reduced clause' and 'small clause' should be distinguished.

reduced relative clause *n.* Any of various constituents which function like relative clauses but which lack both a relative pronoun and a finite verb. Examples: *The woman [wearing the white mini-skirt] is Lisa* (an **adverbial relative clause**); *Neptunium was the first artificial element [to be created]*; *The footprints [in the snow] were sharp and clear.*

redundancy /rɪ'dʌndənsi/ *n.* The phenomenon by which the same information is expressed more than once in a single sentence or utterance. For example, in the sentence *I saw Lisa yesterday*, the past-tense marking on the verb redundantly repeats the indication of past time carried by the adverb *yesterday*. Redundancy is pervasive in natural languages; information theorists have shown that it actually increases the efficiency of communication by helping to ensure that a message may be correctly understood even when parts of it are not successfully transmitted. *Adj.* **redundant** /rɪ'dʌndənt/.

redundancy rule *n.* Any rule of grammar which, instead of building structure, places constraints on the range of possible structures which may be built by the structure-building rules. The term is most often used in morphology, where a statement like 'No English word may begin with more than three consecutive consonants' is called a 'lexical redundancy rule'.

reduplication /rɪ,djuːplɪ'keɪʃn̩/ *n.* The morphological phenomenon in which some morphological material is repeated within a single form for lexical or grammatical purposes. Reduplication is a common phenomenon in the languages of the world, taking a variety of forms and serving a variety of purposes. Malay, for example, uses reduplication for several purposes: adverb formation (*baik* 'good', *baik-baik* 'well'), indefinite plurality (*bunga* 'flower', *bunga-bunga* 'flowers') and word formation (*mata* 'eye', *mata-mata* or *memata* 'policeman'). Certain Latin verbs form their perfect stems by reduplication: *curr-* 'run', perfect stem *cucurr-*. Chukchi derives certain absolutive case forms by reduplication: *nute-* 'tundra' (stem), absolutive *nutenut*. Tagalog uses reduplication as part of its verbal inflection: *sulat* 'write', future *susulat*. Turkish uses it to express 'and so forth': *Ali-Mali* 'Ali and the others'. Yiddish-influenced American English uses it to express dismissal: *Jaguar-Schmaguar!* Unlimited reduplication cannot be weakly characterized by context-free grammars; see Pullum (1984a) for discussion. *V.* **reduplicate** /rɪˈdjuːplɪkeɪt/; *adj.* **reduplicative**.

reduplicative compound /rɪˈdjuːplɪkətɪv/ *n.* A **compound** whose formation involves **reduplication**: Malay *mata-mata* 'policeman' (*mata* 'eye').

Reed–Kellogg diagram /ˌriːdˈkelɒg daɪəgræm/ *n.* A graphical device for indicating certain aspects of the syntactic structure of a sentence. The construction of Reed–Kellogg diagrams ('diagramming sentences') was a regular feature of the teaching of English grammar in American schools until about 1960. Such diagrams incorporate a mixture of information about constituent structure, dependency relations and grammatical relations. A typical example is shown below, representing the sentence *The police trapped the frightened burglar just behind the house*:

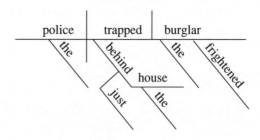

Apparently introduced by Clark (1863), but modified and popularized by Reed and Kellogg (1877).

reference /ˈrefrəns/ *n.* The phenomenon by which some noun phrase in a particular utterance or sentence is associated with some entity in the real or conceptual world, its **referent**. Reference is a semantic phenomenon, but its expression is often grammaticalized in important ways; see under **reference tracking**.

reference-dominated language /ˈdɒmɪneɪtɪd/ *n.* A language in which discourse factors are regularly syntacticized in clause-internal grammar, and which consequently structures clauses in terms of a **pivot** (sense 2), which is normally the grammatical subject. English is a reasonable example of such a language. Cf. **role-dominated language**, and refer to the remarks there.

reference tracking /'trækɪŋ/ *n.* Any grammatical mechanism which permits the hearer of an utterance to retrieve from the form of that utterance information as to which entity is being referred to at each point in the discourse. Foley and Van Valin (1984) distinguish four major types of reference-tracking mechanisms: **pivot/ voice** systems; **switch-reference** systems; **gender** systems; and the inference systems of East Asian languages. This last type of system is hardly grammatical in nature at all, being characterized primarily by the extensive use of null anaphora and by heavy appeal to sociolinguistic conventions such as the use of **honorific** forms. See also Comrie (1989) for a brief summary of some major reference-tracking devices.

referent /'refrənt/ *n.* The entity in the real or conceptual world which is associated with a noun phrase in a particular sentence or utterance. For example, the NP *Abraham Lincoln* would in most (not all) contexts be understood as picking out a particular tall, bearded man who was born in Kentucky, who served as President of the USA during the American Civil War and who was assassinated in 1865: this individual is the referent of that NP.

referential index /ˌrefə'rentʃl/ *n.* (also **index**) A notational device, conventionally a subscript, attached to a noun phrase in a representation of a sentence in such a way that any single subscript, in any number of occurrences, indicates that all NPs bearing it are to be understood as having the same **referent**. In the example *After she$_i$ arrived, Lisa$_i$ asked her$_j$ to give her$_i$ an account of herself$_j$*, the indices indicate which NPs are to be taken as coreferential; a different set of indices could be attached to the same string of words to give a different interpretation. In some frameworks, referential indices are regarded as part of the syntactic representation of a sentence.

referring expression /rɪˌfɜːrɪŋ ɪk'spreʃn̩/ *n.* A noun phrase which is understood as having some identifiable entity as its **referent**.

reflexive /rɪ'fleksɪv/ *adj.* 1. Denoting a construction in which two noun phrases are understood as having the same **referent**, such as *Lisa washed herself carefully* or *Lisa prefers to do her own decorating*. 2. Denoting any grammatical form which is typically used in such constructions, such as a reflexive verb form or a **reflexive pronoun**.

reflexive absolute transitive *adj.* Denoting the construction in which an intrinsically transitive verb is construed intransitively with a reflexive sense: *She undressed*; *She is washing*. See **labile verb**.

reflexive passive *n.* A construction which has the semantic force of a passive, but which has the apparent surface form of a transitive active construction with the underlying direct object appearing as the surface subject and the direct object position occupied by a reflexive pronoun. An example from Spanish is *Sus novelas se publicaron en Madrid* 'His novels were published in Madrid', literally (it would seem) 'His novels published themselves in Madrid' (note that *publicaron* 'published' is third person plural, agreeing with *sus novelas*). Reflexive passives in fact present considerable difficulties of analysis: consider the further Spanish example *Se les acusó* 'They were accused', in which the pronoun *les* 'them' stands in the object form and the verb is third singular, and the structure of the sentence is far from clear.

reflexive–patient-subject construction *n.* The construction in which a transitive verb has a patient as its subject and a stressed reflexive pronoun as its object: *This car practically drives itself.* Lakoff (1977).

reflexive pronoun *n.* A pronoun which must normally take as its antecedent another noun phrase in the same sentence, most often (in English) the subject NP of its clause. Examples are *herself* and *ourselves*, as in *Lisa looked at herself in the mirror*. In most circumstances in English, the use of such a reflexive is obligatory to express coreference within a clause: the example *Lisa looked at her in the mirror*, with a non-reflexive pronoun, does not permit coreference. Certain constructions are exceptional, however: the sentence *Lisa set the book down beside her* can have the same interpretation as *Lisa set the book down beside herself*. A reflexive most usually occupies an argument position in the sentence, but this is not so in sentences with so-called 'intensive' reflexives, such as *Lisa herself did it* and *Lisa did it herself*. The informal English of many speakers permits a seemingly anomalous use of reflexives without antecedents, as in *This paper was written by Lisa and myself*, where conservative speakers would require . . . *by Lisa and me*; such occurrences are probably best regarded as not true reflexives at all, but as mere emphatic forms of personal pronouns.

regular /ˈregjʊlə/ *adj.* Denoting a grammatical form or construction which is entirely typical of the most usual pattern exhibited in a language. The term is not confined to morphology, but it is most often used there: one speaks, for example, of the English verb *love* as a 'regular verb', since its inflection follows exactly the pattern exhibited by most English verbs. *Abstr. n.* **regularity** /regjʊ'lærɪti/. Cf. **irregular**.

regular expression /ɪk'spreʃn̩/ *n.* An expression, consisting of a sequence of categories, constructed by the use of **concatenation** (ab), of union (a+b) or of the **Kleene star** (CA*).

regular grammar *n.* Any formal grammar employing the **rewrite rule** formalism in which every rule has one of the forms A → *a* B or A → *a*, where A and B represent non-terminal symbols and *a* represents a terminal symbol. Such a grammar effectively generates sentences one word at a time, assigning in the process an untenable constituent structure. Here is a fragment of a regular grammar:

1	S	→	*the* A
2	A	→	*very* A
3	A	→	*old* B
4	A	→	*happy* B
5	B	→	*man* C
6	B	→	*woman* C
7	C	→	*drank* D
8	D	→	*his* E
9	D	→	*her* E
10	E	→	*tea* F
11	E	→	*coffee* F
12	F	→	*quietly*

Thanks to the presence of the recursion permitted by rule 2, this particular fragment actually generates an infinite number of strings, though the variety is severely limited. The class of regular grammars is exactly equivalent to the class of **finite-state grammars**, which constitute merely a notational variant employing the graphical device of **transition networks** in place of the rewrite formalism. The set of languages weakly defined by the regular grammars is a proper subset of the set of **context-free languages**. Only rarely have regular grammars been seriously proposed as grammars of natural languages (one case being Reich (1969)); the proof sketched in Chomsky (1957) that regular grammars cannot weakly generate unlimited centre-embedding has usually (with some tidying up) been regarded as sufficient to exclude them from consideration. NOTE: the definition and the example actually represent the class of 'right-linear grammars', in which strings are generated from left to right; if the first type of rule is replaced by the form A → B *a*, the result is a 'left-linear grammar', which generates strings from right to left. The two classes are weakly equivalent, but the two types of rule must not be combined in a single grammar, or the result is no longer a regular grammar.

regular language *n.* A language defined by a **regular grammar**; a **finite-state language**.

r.e. language /ɑːˈriː/ See **recursively enumerable language**.

relation /rɪˈleɪʃn̩/ *n.* 1. Formally, a two-place **predicate** (sense 3). Elements of English which may conveniently be interpreted as relations include *is taller than*, *loves*, *is the father of* and *has visited*. 2. More generally, any linguistically significant connection between two objects or classes of objects. Relations in this general sense are conventionally divided into two classes, **syntagmatic** and **paradigmatic**. 3. See **grammatical relation**. *Adj.* **relational**.

relational adjective /rɪˈleɪʃənl̩/ *n.* An adjective derived from a noun which has no semantic content beyond that present in the noun and which serves only to provide a form of the noun which can act as a modifier: *telephonic* from *telephone* and *Glaswegian* from *Glasgow*. In English, relational adjectives are few and little used in comparison with the frequency of compounding: we prefer to say *Glasgow telephone system*, rather than *Glaswegian telephonic system*. Languages in which compounding is poorly developed, such as the Romance languages and the Slavonic languages, typically make extensive use of relational adjectives: Spanish, for example, has *alimentación infantil* (literally, 'infantile food') for *baby food* and *novela policíaca* (literally, 'policical novel') for *detective story*.

Relational Grammar *n.* (**RG**) A theory of grammar developed by David Perlmutter and Paul Postal in the 1970s. RG differs from all other approaches in taking **grammatical relations** like Subject, Direct Object and Indirect Object as its primitives and in assigning no particular importance to constituent structures of the familiar kind. The three relations just enumerated are distinguished as **terms** and are conventionally labelled as 1, 2 and 3, respectively. In addition to the terms, certain other relations are distinguished, including **oblique objects** and the highly original concept of a **chômeur** (see below). These relations are crucially ordered in the **Relational Hierarchy**, and most syntactic operations are interpreted as the promotion and demotion of NPs along this hierarchy; for example, passive formation typically involves the 'advancement' (promotion) of a 2 to a 1, with the consequent demotion of the original 1 to the distinctive non-term status of a 'chômeur', a label applied to an NP which has been ousted from term status in the course of an operation. The framework is, therefore, obviously derivational in conception, in that a sentence is viewed as having different structures at different stages (or 'strata'), but, in contrast with what happens in transformational theories, the syntactic structure of a sentence is represented by a single formal object called a 'stratal diagram', in which all strata are depicted simultaneously. RG represents the first major attempt at incorporating grammatical relations into syntactic theory; its influence has been widely acknowledged, but the framework itself has now been largely superseded by other approaches, such as LFG, which, while accepting the importance of grammatical relations, also insist upon the necessity of constituent structure representations. Much of the early work in RG remained for years unpublished, but most of it is now collected in Perlmutter (1983b) and Perlmutter and Rosen (1984). See Perlmutter (1980) for a brief introduction, Blake (1990) for a more substantial one. **Arc Pair Grammar** represents a distinctive variant of RG.

Relational Hierarchy *n.* In RG, a hierarchy of the principal grammatical relations recognized in that framework, usually given as follows:

   Subject > Direct Object > Indirect Object > Oblique > Chômeur

Almost all syntactic operations in RG are interpreted as the movement of NPs up and down this hierarchy, and much of the content of the framework derives from restrictions placed upon such movement. The Relational Hierarchy has much the same form as the independently derived **NP Accessibility Hierarchy**, and incorporates some of the same insights.

relational structure *n.* The structure of a sentence or a clause from the point of view of the **grammatical relations** borne by the various NPs in it.

relational verb *n.* A transitive verb which expresses a stative relation: *have, involve, need, deserve, depend on.* Quirk *et al.* (1972: 96).

relation-changing rule /rɪˈleɪʃn̩ ˌtʃeɪndʒɪŋ/ *n.* In RG, any putative syntactic operation which changes the grammatical relation borne by a particular NP in a sentence, such as the operation deriving a passive structure from an active one. On occasion, the term is also used informally in frameworks in which the concept has no formal status.

relative adverb /'relətɪv/ *n.* An adverb which serves to introduce a relative clause, such as *where* and *when* in *the street where I live* and *the day when I first met you.*

relative clause *n.* A type of clause, most often a subordinate clause, which serves to modify a noun phrase. In English and many other languages a relative clause is usually a constituent of the noun phrase whose head it modifies, but some languages employ quite different formal expressions in which this is not the case. Relative clauses are conventionally divided into two types, differing in their semantics and sometimes also in their formal expression. The first type is the **restrictive** relative clause, in which the clause is essential for identification of the referent of the NP; an example is *Lisa is applying for the job* [*I told her about*], in which the clause identifies the job in question. The second type is the **non-restrictive** relative clause, in which the clause merely adds further information about the NP, without being required for identification, as in *Lisa,* [*who speaks excellent French,*] *is applying for a job in Paris.* For some discussion of the variety of relative clause constructions in the languages of the world, see Keenan (1985b); see also **adjoined relative clause**, **correlative clause**, **strategy**.

relative pronoun *n.* A pronoun which serves to link a relative clause to the noun phrase of which it forms a part, such as *which* and *whose* in the examples *This is the book which I was telling you about* and *Any student whose thesis is late will be penalized.* Opinion is divided as to whether the item *that*, which also performs the same function in cases like *This is the book that Lisa wants*, is best regarded as a relative pronoun or as a **complementizer**, with the second view perhaps predominating. See also **relative adverb**.

relative tense *n.* A tense form whose temporal point of reference is determined by its syntactic relation to another tense form, such as the English gerund: in examples like *Before leaving, she checked the house* and *Before leaving, you'll have to see the boss*, the time reference of *leaving* is determined by its relation to the time reference of the main clause (past in one case, future in the other). Cf. **absolute tense**, **absolute-relative tense**. See Comrie (1985a) for discussion.

relative universal *n.* (also **statistical universal**) A universal statement which holds good for the great majority of languages but not for all. For example, the statement 'Subject precedes Object in basic word order' holds for all but a tiny minority of languages.

Relativized A-over-A Principle /'relətɪvaɪzd/ *n.* A modified version of the **A-over-A Constraint** with improved coverage. Bresnan (1976).

remote structure /rɪ'məʊt/ *n.* In derivational theories of grammar, a representation which is far removed from surface structure, often simply the **deep structure**.

REST /ɑːr iː es 'tiː/ See **Revised Extended Standard Theory**.

restricted distribution /rɪ'strɪktɪd/ *n.* The property exhibited by an item which does not occur in the full range of environments typically exhibited by members of its class. For example, the English noun *headway* is restricted to occurring as the object of the verb *make*: *We're making headway*; *Some headway has been made*; but **We need more headway*; **We've achieved some headway*. Though most adjectives in English occur in both attributive and predicative position, some are restricted to attributive position (*major, key, topmost, main, mere*), while others are restricted to predicative position (*asleep, afraid, glad, well*).

restrictive /rɪ'strɪktɪv/ *adj.* Denoting a modifier (such as an adjective or a relative clause) or an appositive whose presence is essential for identifying the referent of the noun phrase. In the example *the Spanish settlements in America*, the adjective *Spanish* is restrictive; compare the non-restrictive *poor* in *my poor mother*. For further examples, see under **relative clause** and **appositive**. Cf. **non-restrictive**.

restructuring /riː'strʌktʃərɪŋ/ *n.* (also **readjustment**, **reanalysis**) In some derivational theories of grammar, any of various putative processes posited as applying to change the syntactic structure of a sentence, often in a seemingly somewhat *ad hoc* way, for the specific purpose of accounting for some unexpected data. For example, the active sentence *George Washington* [*slept* [*in this bed*]] has a seemingly unexpected (pseudo-)passive *This bed was slept in by George Washington*, leading some analysts to propose that the active structure can undergo restructuring to *George Washington* [[*slept in*] [*this bed*]], permitting passivization to apply normally.

result /rɪ'zʌlt/ *n.* (also **factitive**) One of the **deep cases** recognized in some versions of Case Grammar, representing an NP whose referent only comes into existence as a result of the action of the verb, such as *this translation* in *Lisa did this translation*.

resultative /rɪˈzʌltətɪv/ *n.* or *adj.* An aspectual form expressing a state resulting from an earlier event. This term is often regarded as a synonym for **perfect**, but Dahl (1985) makes a case for distinguishing the two. He points out that English *He is gone* and *He has gone*, both expressing a present state resulting from an earlier action, differ in that only the first can accept the adverb *still*: *He is still gone* vs. **He has still gone*. Dahl proposes to restrict the term 'resultative' to the first form, which seems to focus more strongly on the present state, and to use 'perfect' exclusively for the second, in which the earlier action appears to be more prominent. (The first construction is marginal in English, but in Swedish both constructions are fully productive.)

resumptive pronoun /rɪˈzʌmptɪv/ *n.* (also **shadow pronoun**) 1. In certain types of relative clause constructions, an overt pronoun which occurs within the relative clause in its 'logical' position, instead of a gap. In English, resumptive pronouns are confined to those cases in which the presence of the more usual gap would violate some **island constraint**, as in the example *That's the woman that I didn't know if she was coming or not*, in which *she* is a resumptive pronoun. In some other languages, such as Welsh, resumptive pronouns are regularly used in most or all relative clauses. 2. In a **left-dislocation**, the pronoun which occurs in the non-dislocated part of the sentence and is coreferential with the dislocated NP, such as *her* in *Lisa, I really like her*.

retained object /rɪˈteɪnd/ *n.* A traditional label for the underlying direct object in a **dative-shifted** or **applicative** construction in which another NP has taken over the surface realization of a direct object, particularly in a passive structure, such as *this book* in *I was given this book for Christmas*.

reverse pseudo-cleft /rɪˈvɜːs/ *n.* A construction identical to a **pseudo-cleft** except that the order of the two major elements is reversed. Thus, the pseudo-cleft *What I need is a pint of beer* has the corresponding reverse pseudo-cleft *A pint of beer is what I need*.

Revised Extended Standard Theory /rɪˈvaɪzd/ *n.* (**REST**) The version of **Transformational Grammar** current in the late 1970s and deriving from the **Extended Standard Theory** of a few years earlier. The REST differs greatly from its immediate precursor; among its major innovations are the following: (1) the introduction of **traces** into syntactic representations; (2) the acceptance (in principle) of the **X-bar system** as a theory of base rules; (3) an enormous reduction in the power of transformational rules, with the whole clanking transformational apparatus of earlier years reduced to the single rule of **Alpha Movement**; (4) the increased attention paid to formulating constraints on rules, rather than formulating the rules themselves; (5) the downgrading of the earlier **surface structure** and the recognition of a new, slightly more abstract designated level of representation called **shallow structure**, viewed as the exclusive input to the semantic rules; and (6) the recognition of an entirely new level of representation called **Logical Form**. No single publication can be cited as the source of the REST, though Chomsky (1973, 1977a) and Chomsky and Lasnik (1977) perhaps deserve special mention in this connection. In the literature of the time, the REST was often referred to as the 'EST', but a later generation of linguists has usually seen the two frameworks as quite distinct. At the beginning of the 1980s, further major modifications in the REST led to its replacement by the very different framework called **Government–Binding Theory**. See Newmeyer (1986) for some account of the history of the REST.

rewrite rule /'riːraɪt/ *n.* The most usual formalism for expressing a structure-building process in a formal grammar. In its most general form, a rewrite rule is simply an instruction to rewrite some string of categories (conventionally given on the left of an arrow) as some other string of categories (on the right); the only general restriction is that the left side may not be null. Since, in the most general case, any arbitrary string can be rewritten as any other arbitrary string, the derivation of a terminal string from an initial symbol cannot, in general, be represented as a tree, but only as a sequence of strings, and hence the rewrite rule formalism is most appropriate to discussions of **weak generative capacity**: consider, for example, the impossibility of interpreting the rule A B d E → d A C c E d as an unambiguous tree. When, however, sufficiently severe restrictions are placed upon the permitted rules, the sequence of strings may be replaced by the more informative constituent structure trees. This is true of the subset of rewrite rules called **context-free rules**, and, providing certain precautions are taken, it is also true of the less restricted subset called **context-sensitive rules**.

R-expression /'ɑːrɪkˌspreʃn̩/ *n.* In GB, any overt noun phrase which is not a pronoun (in the traditional sense of that term). More precisely, an R-expression is an overt NP analysed as [–a, –p] and hence subject only to Principle C of the Binding Theory, namely, that it be free (unbound) in all domains. Typical R-expressions are *Lisa*, *the dog*, *the last chapter of the book* and *Janet's cigarettes*. The name is derived from the phrase 'referring expression', used in semantics for the largest class of NPs, but the GB usage is not synonymous with the semantic sense.

RG See **Relational Grammar**.

rheme /riːm/ *n.* A synonym for **comment**, preferred in the phrase 'theme and rheme'.

rhetorical question /rɪˈtɒrɪkl̩/ *n.* A question which does not expect a response from the addressee.

right-branching /ˌraɪt ˈbrɑːntʃɪŋ/ *n.* A type of constituent structure in which modifiers and complements appear to the right of their heads, so that recursion of these elements shows up in a tree diagram as repeated branching to the right. English has a large number of such structures; the example below shows the effect of the recursion of prepositional phrases inside noun phrases:

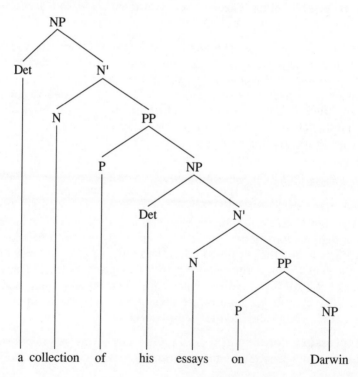

right-branching language *n.* A language in which right-branching constructions predominate over left-branching ones. Most VSO and SVO languages, including English, are right-branching. Cf. **left-branching language**.

right dislocation *n.* A construction in which some constituent occurs at the end of the sentence, its canonical position being occupied by a **pro-form**: *She's very clever, Lisa.* Right dislocations are sometimes called 'afterthought constructions'. Cf. **left dislocation**. Ross (1967).

right-node raising *n.* (also **shared-constituent coordination**) A construction consisting of an apparent coordination of two sentences in which each sentence lacks its rightmost constituent, and a single further constituent appears on the right which is interpreted as filling both gaps: *Lisa prepared, and Siobhan served, the cucumber sandwiches.* Right-node-raised constructions present formidable difficulties of analysis.

Right Roof Constraint /ruːf/ *n.* (also **Rightward Movement Constraint**) The constraint, in English and some other languages, by which some element of a sentence which occurs further to the right than its expected 'logical' position cannot occur more than one clause boundary to the right of that position. Thus, for example, *That [it surprises you] [that Lisa smokes] is amusing* is well-formed, but **That [it surprises you] [is amusing] [that Lisa smokes]* violates the Right Roof Constraint and is ill-formed. Ross (1967).

right wrap *n.* An operation upon strings, defined as follows: if a functor category XP of the form $[_{XP}X\ W]$ is right-wrapped around another category Y, where X and Y are single elements and W is a (possibly empty) string, the result is the string X Y W. Right wrap was defined as a way of dealing with certain types of **discontinuous constituents**, such as those illustrated in *persuaded Lisa to leave*, *easy problem to solve* and *too hot to eat.* Right wrap was introduced by Emmon Bach (1979) within the framework of Categorial Grammar, but it has sometimes been extended to other systems, notably HPSG.

role /rəʊl/ *n.* Any of various semantically or pragmatically based functions ascribed to some element in a sentence or an utterance, particularly to a noun phrase. The most prominent group of roles in syntax is the set of **semantic roles** recognized in some theories of grammar, but several others exist, especially in the various kinds of **functional grammar** (all senses), such as **actor** and **undergoer**.

Role-and-Reference Grammar *n.* (**RRG**) A theory of grammar developed by William Foley and Robert Van Valin in the 1980s, incorporating a number of insights gained by functionally oriented linguists. RRG is a **functional grammar** in senses 1 and 2 of that term; it is formulated in terms of the communicative purposes which need to be served and the grammatical devices which are available to serve those purposes. Among its distinguishing characteristics are a variety of **lexical decomposition** based upon the Montague-style predicate semantics of Dowty (1979), an analysis of clause structure in terms of **layering** (sense 1), mapping from 'logical' structures into monostratal syntactic representations and the use of a set of **participant roles** organized into a hierarchy from which the highest-ranking available role in a clause assumes the special superordinate role of **actor** and a second argument, if present, may assume the superordinate role of **undergoer**. RRG is unusual among theories of grammar in the extent to which it is structured to provide equal treatment for the grammars of languages which are very different from English: such phenomena as non-configurationality, verb serialization, split ergativity and switch-reference systems receive analyses which are no less natural than analyses of the facts of English. Like most functional theories of grammar, however, RRG has (so far, at least) received comparatively little formalization. The most comprehensive presentation is Foley and Van Valin (1984); convenient brief introductions are Van Valin and Foley (1980) and Van Valin (1991).

role-dominated language /'rəʊl ˌdɒmɪneɪtɪd/ *n.* A language which lacks a consistently identified grammatical **pivot** in terms of which clauses are organized, sometimes regarded as a significant typological category. Cf. **reference-dominated language**. Van Valin and Foley (1980).

root /ruːt/ *n.* 1. A node in a tree which has no mother. Only one such node is normally permitted to occur in a tree, as required by the **Single Root Condition**; in most frameworks this is always the node S (for 'sentence'), though **tree-adjoining grammars** recognize the existence of a set of auxiliary (non-terminal) trees with other roots. 2. In morphology, the simplest possible form of a lexical morpheme, upon which all other bound and free forms involving that morpheme are based. For example, the Latin verb meaning 'love' has the root *am-*, from which are formed the various stems, such as present *ama-* and perfect *amav-*, which in turn serve as bases for the construction of inflected forms like *amat* 'he loves' and *amavi* 'I have loved'. Similarly, the Arabic verb meaning 'write' has the triconsonantal root *ktb*, from which all other forms are derived by various layers of affixation. Cf. **stem**, **base**.

round brackets /ˌraʊnd ˈbrækɪts/ See **parentheses**.

RRG See **Role-and-Reference Grammar**.

RTN See **recursive transition network**.

rule /ruːl/ *n.* Any statement expressing a linguistically significant generalization about the grammatical facts of a particular language, especially when formulated within the formalism of some particular formal description. The notion of a grammatical rule is one of the most ancient conceptions in grammatical investigation. Most modern theories of grammar draw a sharp distinction in principle between generalizations, which are expressed by rules, and non-general facts, which are expressed by other means, notably by **lexical entries** in the **lexicon**. There is considerable controversy, however, over just where the line should be drawn, and one of the most conspicuous tendencies of recent work has been the steady movement of statements formerly expressed by rules into the lexicon. For some discussion, see under **generalization**, and see also **partially productive** and **metarule**.

rule-governed *adj.* Denoting the presumed property of human linguistic behaviour by which most phenomena can be readily seen as instances of the interaction of a relatively small number of generalizations expressible by rules. The view of linguistic behaviour as rule-governed is pervasive among grammarians, in whose formal descriptions rules play an accordingly prominent part. Objections have often been raised by those who prefer to see linguistic behaviour as more 'creative' than rule-governed, but such objections are more typical of non-linguists than of linguists.

rule of construal See **construal, rule of**.

rule ordering /ˈɔːdərɪŋ/ *n.* In a derivational theory of grammar, any convention or stipulation by which some rule or rules must apply before others in the course of a derivation. In the earlier versions of TG, rule ordering was a major issue, but in GB its importance has been greatly reduced: the only significant ordering requirement is the principle of the **transformational cycle**, apart from the stipulation that certain rules, such as **Quantifier Raising**, apply only in the derivation of Logical Form from S-structure. In a non-derivational framework, the issue does not even arise. See **extrinsic** and **intrinsic rule ordering**.

rule schema /'skiːmə/ (pl. **schemata** /skiː'mɑːtə/) *n.* Any statement which collapses two or more rules of grammar by means of some **abbreviatory convention**.

rule-to-rule hypothesis /haɪ'pɒθəsɪs/ *n.* The doctrine that every rule of syntax that builds structure should be matched by a semantic rule which interprets that structure. The idea was introduced by the logician Richard Montague (1970); it is accepted in certain current theories of grammar, notably GPSG, but is rejected by most others.

S

S 1. The conventional abbreviation for **sentence** (senses 2 and 3). 2. A conventional abbreviation for **subject** in the 'subject–verb–object' analysis of **basic word order** types. 3. A conventional abbreviation for 'intransitive subject' in the **SAP** analysis.

sandhi /'sændi/ *n.* Any of various phenomena in which the form of a word or morpheme is modified by the presence of an adjoining word or morpheme: *would* + *you* → ['wʊdʒuː]; Latin *reg-* 'king' (stem) + *-s* (Nominative) → *rex* (i.e., *reks*). Sanskrit grammar.

SAP /es eɪ 'piː/ A tripartite classification of the principal NP arguments in transitive and intransitive clauses. An intransitive clause is viewed as having a single argument, the subject (S). A transitive clause is seen as having two arguments, the agent (A) and the patient (P) (or in some versions the object O), either one of which may be identified with S for grammatical purposes, producing either an **accusative** pattern (A = S) or an **ergative** pattern (P = S). Dixon (1972).

S-bar /es'bɑː/ *n.* The conventional label for the category which forms a **complement clause**, such as the bracketed sequence in the example *Lisa said* [*that she would come*]. An S-bar typically consists of a complementizer and a sentence. Originally, the name was intended as a purely *ad hoc* label: S-bar was not considered to be a projection of the category S within the X-bar system. In recent years, however, the category has been reanalysed in various ways within various frameworks. In GB, S-bar is now identified with CP, the maximal projection of the lexical category Complementizer. In GPSG, all three of VP, S and S-bar are regarded as V-double-bar, the maximal projection of the category Verb, with additional features being invoked to distinguish them. LFG, in contrast, continues to regard the category S-bar as having no particular relation to any other category.

Scale-and-Category Grammar /ˌskeɪl ənd 'kætəgri/ *n.* An early name for **Systemic Grammar**. Halliday (1961).

S-command /'eskəmɑːnd/ *n*. One of the **command relations**, the first to be identified. It states 'A node A S-commands another node B iff the lowest S which properly dominates A also properly dominates B'. Langacker (1969); originally simply **command**.

scope /skəʊp/ *n*. That portion of a particular sentence which is interpreted as being affected by an **operator** present in that sentence, such as a quantifier or a negative. For example, the sentence *Everybody loves somebody* has two distinct interpretations. In one of them, the scope of *somebody* lies within the scope of *everybody*, and the sentence can be paraphrased as 'Everybody has somebody or other that she/he loves'; in the other, the scope relations are reversed, and the sentence can be paraphrased as 'There is some particular individual whom everybody loves'. This is an example of a 'scope ambiguity', which can arise when two or more scope-bearing elements are present in the same sentence.

scrambling /'skræmblɪŋ/ *n*. In some analyses within derivational theories of grammar, the putative process which is responsible for the surface ordering of elements occurring in sentences in languages with **free word order**. Never adequately formalized, the idea has been generally abandoned in more recent theories of grammar, though the term is still occasionally used informally to denote free word order in general. Ross (1967).

secondary object /'sekəndri/ *n*. (**SO**) The direct object in a ditransitive clause, in circumstances in which this is treated differently from a direct object in a simple transitive clause, this latter being treated like the indirect object in a ditransitive clause. Cf. **primary object** and see the discussion there. Dryer (1986); the term 'subsidiary object' is also found.

second person /'sekənd/ *n*. That category of **person** which includes reference to the addressee, but not reference to the speaker. English uses only the single pronoun *you* in this function, though other languages often have more elaborate systems of second-person forms, such as European Spanish, with its four-way distinction among *tu*, *usted*, *vosotros* and *ustedes*; these forms variously contrast in both number and intimacy.

selection(al) restriction /sə'lekʃən(l̩) rɪˌstrɪkʃn̩/ *n*. Any of various semantic constraints reflected in the ability of lexical items to combine in syntactic structures. For example, while *Lisa wrapped the box of chocolates in tissue paper* is unexceptional, the syntactically identical #*Lisa wrapped the orbit of Neptune in tissue paper* is semantically bizarre because it violates a selectional restriction holding between the verb *wrap* and its object. Astoundingly, these restrictions were for a few years in the mid-1960s regarded as syntactic facts to be expressed in grammars; most theories of grammar no longer attempt this. Cf. **subcategorization**. Katz and Fodor (1963).

self-embedding /self/ *n*. The phenomenon by which a category is contained within a larger category of the same type, such as an NP within a larger NP; see the examples given under **recursion**.

semantax /sə'mæntæks/ *n*. A name sometimes given to syntax and semantics taken together, when they are regarded as a single unified area of investigation, as in **Generative Semantics**. The term is now rarely used.

semantic form /sə'mæntɪk/ *n*. In LFG, any lexical item that contains the value PREDicate in its lexical entry. A semantic form that subcategorizes for one or more functions is a **lexical form**.

semantic function See **semantic role**.

semantic network *n*. (also **associative network**) A network or a directed graph which is given a particular semantic interpretation. Nodes represent concepts and arcs represent relations between concepts.

semantic role *n*. (also **deep case**, **semantic function**, **theta role**) Any one of several semantic relations which a noun phrase may bear in its clause, classified from the point of view of the involvement of the entity denoted by that NP in the situation expressed by the clause, independently of its grammatical form. Among the most widely recognized are Agent, Patient, Experiencer, Recipient, Theme, Beneficiary, Instrument, Goal, Source, Place, Time and Path; the first few of these, denoting the more obvious participants in a situation, are sometimes called **participant roles**. Semantic roles are fundamental in **Case Grammar**, where they are known as **deep cases**; they are also important in GB (where they are known as **theta roles**) and in many versions of **functional grammar** (sense 2). Gruber (1965); made prominent by Fillmore (1968).

semantics /sə'mæntɪks/ *n*. The branch of linguistics dealing with the meanings of words and sentences. The relation between syntax and semantics and the location of the dividing line between them have long been matters of controversy. Several extreme positions have been maintained. One, associated with **Generative Semantics**, holds that syntax and semantics are not distinct at all, but constitute a unified area of investigation. Another, associated, for example, with the **Standard Theory** of TG, holds that the two are sharply distinct, with syntactic structures being primary and the semantics serving only to interpret syntactic structures. A third, arguably represented by some versions of **functional grammar** (sense 1) and of **cognitive grammar**, is that the two are distinct but that the syntax serves only to realize underlying semantic structures. Most linguists today would probably advocate some kind of intermediate position in which the two areas are distinct and make independent requirements but in which the dividing line is somewhat blurred and each area can have effects upon the other. *Adj.* **semantic** /sə'mæntɪk/. Bréal (1911).

semelfactive /seməl'fæktɪv/ *n.* or *adj.* An **aspect** category expressing an action or event which is perceived as happening exactly once, as in one reading of the example *Lisa sneezed*. The semelfactive is a subdivision of **perfective** aspect. Few languages seem to employ a distinctive form for this function, though Hopi is possibly one which does.

sentence /'sentəns/ *n.* 1. Traditionally, any **utterance** or written sequence of words which is regarded as capable of standing alone to express a coherent thought. 2. In generative grammar, the syntactic category which is taken as the largest category capable of syntactic characterization, all of its component parts being bound together by the rules of syntax and its entire structure being **well-formed**; in a framework employing the **rewrite rule** formalism, the category is represented by the **initial symbol** S. It is important to understand that a sentence in this linguistically central sense is an abstract linguistic object; cf. **utterance**. In the X-bar system, the category S is variously regarded as the maximal projection of the lexical category Verb (the GPSG analysis), as the maximal projection of the abstract lexical category INFL (the GB analysis) or as a projection of no category at all (the LFG analysis). The structural definition of the category 'sentence' was introduced by Bloomfield (1933). 3. In a syntactic structure, any constituent dominated by the initial symbol S; a **clause**. 4. In the oxymoron 'ill-formed sentence', an ill-formed structure which approximates to a sentence and which typically departs from well-formedness only in one or two identifiable respects. 5. In a formal grammar, any **string** which is generated by the grammar. *Adj.* **sentential**.

sentence adverb *n.* A lexical item typically having the approximate distribution, and often the form, of an **adverb**, but behaving semantically not as a modifier of the verb or VP but as an operator upon the entire proposition. Sentence adverbs in English variously express distinctions of modality, evaluation, illocutionary force and perhaps other notions; examples include *possibly, certainly, undoubtedly, hopefully, fortunately, frankly, confidentially* and *briefly*. There is a case for recognizing sentence adverbs as a distinct lexical category, but they are more usually regarded as specialized members of the category Adverb.

sentence type /taɪp/ *n.* One of the four traditional classes of sentence, in a classification which attends only to surface form and not to discourse function, the four types being **statements, commands, questions** and **exclamations**, conventionally associated with the four **mood** categories **declarative, imperative, interrogative** and **exclamative**.

sentential relative clause /sen'tentʃl̩/ *n.* A relative clause whose antecedent is a complete sentence, as in the example *England have beaten the West Indies, which amazes me*.

sentential subject *n.* An S-bar which occupies the subject position in its clause, as in the example [*That Lisa has quit smoking*] *surprises me*.

Sentential Subject Constraint *n.* An **island constraint** which states that a WH-dependency may not reach inside a sentential subject, as illustrated by the example **Who does* [*that Lisa saw* e *in town*] *surprise you?* Ross (1967).

sequence of tenses /'siːkwəns/ *n.* The phenomenon, occurring in English and some other languages, by which the tense of a finite verb in a matrix clause places constraints on the tense of a finite verb in a complement clause. In English, the rule is simply that a past tense in the main clause must be followed by a past tense in the complement clause: *Lisa says she wants a BMW*; *Lisa said she wanted a BMW*; but ??*Lisa said she wants a BMW*.

serial verb construction /'sɪəriəl/ *n.* (also **verb serialization**) A construction in which what appears to be a single clause semantically is expressed syntactically by a sequence of juxtaposed separate verbs, all sharing the same subject or agent but each with its own additional arguments, without the use of overt coordinating conjunctions. Here are two examples, from the West African languages Yoruba and Vagala, respectively:

ó mú ìwé wá
he took book came
'He brought the book.'

ù kpá kíyzèé mòng ówl
he take knife cut meat
'He cut the meat with a knife.'

Serial verb constructions are particularly common in West Africa, in eastern and southeastern Asia and in New Guinea. See Sebba (1987).

shadow pronoun /'ʃædəʊ/ See **resumptive pronoun**.

shallow structure /'ʃæləʊ/ *n*. In the **Revised Extended Standard Theory**, a designated level of syntactic representation which follows the application of all transformations but precedes the application of deletion rules and filters. The S-structures of GB are roughly equivalent to the shallow structures of the REST.

shared-constituent coordination /ʃɛəd/ See **right-node raising**.

short passive /ʃɔːt/ See **agentless passive**.

simple sentence /'sɪmpl/ *n*. A traditional label for a sentence consisting of only a single clause. The term 'simplex sentence' is occasionally found in more recent work for the same notion. Cf. **compound sentence**, **complex sentence**.

simultaneous-distributive coordination /sɪməl,teɪnɪəs dɪ'strɪbjʊtɪv/ *n*. A construction involving two coordinate structures whose conjuncts are explicitly paired off in order: *Lisa and Larry drank whisky and brandy, respectively*. Kac *et al.* (1987).

Single Mother Condition /'sɪŋgl/ *n*. The requirement that each node in a tree, apart from the root, should have exactly one **mother**. The Single Mother Condition is almost universally accepted in generative grammar, but see Sampson (1975) and McCawley (1982) for arguments against it. Sampson (1975).

Single Root Condition *n*. The requirement that a tree should have exactly one **root** (sense 1). This condition is universally accepted.

singular /'sɪŋgjʊlə/ *n.* or *adj.* In a language with distinctions of **number**, that number category which is normally employed to refer to a single entity in circumstances in which entities can be distinguished and counted. The singular is overwhelmingly the morphologically simplest form in such languages, as illustrated by English *cat*, *child*, *box*, compared with the corresponding plural forms *cats*, *children*, *boxes*. Cf. **plural**.

sister /'sɪstə/ *n.* A relation which may hold between two nodes in a tree. If a node B and a node C are both immediately dominated by the same node A (in other words, A is the **mother** of both), then B and C are sisters.

sister-adjunction *n.* In certain derivational theories of grammar, a type of **adjunction** in which the moving category becomes a sister of another specified category. In the abstract example below, the moving category D becomes a 'right sister' of E:

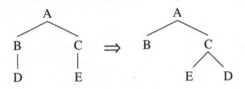

Sister-adjunction was widely employed in classical TG, but it is not recognized at all within GB, in which **Chomsky-adjunction** is the only permitted form of adjunction.

slash /slæʃ/ *n.* 1. In GPSG, the feature which appears on a node to indicate that a gap is present somewhere in the domain of that node, the value of SLASH in a particular instance representing the type of gap required. For example, the abbreviated feature specification VP[SLASH NP] represents a VP containing a 'missing' NP somewhere inside it; such a node label would appear, for example, on the VP node in the sentence *Who did you see?*, in which the VP beginning with *see* lacks an NP in object position. The use of this feature represents the normal GPSG manner of handling **filler–gap dependencies**. 2. (also **solidus**) A notational convention often used to abbreviate two or more examples of data which differ only at a single point. An example is *Lisa$_i$ set the book down beside her$_i$/ herself$_i$*, abbreviating the two sentences *Lisa$_i$ set the book down* *beside her*_i and *Lisa*_i *set the book down beside herself*_i. The slash in this use is a typographically simpler alternative to **braces** (sense 2).

slash category *n*. In earlier versions of GPSG, a type of derived syntactic category representing a familiar category containing a gap. An example is VP/NP, representing a VP node containing an empty NP position. In early GPSG, such a category was regarded as distinct from the category VP, but in all more recent formulations, the category VP/NP, now represented as VP[SLASH NP], is regarded merely as a VP carrying a particular feature specification.

Slash Principle *n*. In GPSG, a principle proposed to account for a number of **island constraints**. The principle says that a SLASH feature specification appearing within a category must appear also within a head daughter or a complement daughter. This principle accounts for the **Subject Condition**, the **Adjunct Island Condition** and parts of the **Complex NP Constraint**.

slash termination /tɜːmɪˈneɪʃn̩/ *n*. In GPSG, any procedure which is employed to place a lower limit on the downward spread of a SLASH feature through a tree and thereby to guarantee that the lower element involved in a SLASH dependency is present in a suitable position. Slash termination is usually done by metarule, though other devices have sometimes been employed, such as ID rules.

slifting /ˈslɪftɪŋ/ *n*. The construction in which a complement clause precedes its matrix clause: *Lisa is coming, I think*. Ross (1973a): 'S(entence)-lifting'.

sloppy identity /ˈslɒpi/ *n*. Any of various instances of **deletion under identity** in which the deleted material is not strictly identical to the overt material supporting the deletion. Examples include *Juliet has quarrelled with her boyfriend, and so has Flaminia* (in the reading of '. . .quarrelled with Flaminia's boyfriend') and *The ringleader was hanged and his followers imprisoned*. Ross (1967).

slot-and-filler /ˌslɒt ənd ˈfɪlə/ *adj*. Denoting an approach to grammatical characterization which employs **substitution frames** as diagnostics. A series of such frames is constructed, each containing a single gap or 'slot', on some convenient, if usually rather *ad hoc*, basis, and items are classified on the basis of their ability to 'fill' particular slots. Thus, for example, the frame *This new _____ is good* might serve to identify the class of nouns, while *_____ is good* might serve to identify the class of noun phrases. Slot-and-filler approaches represent a development of the distributional emphasis of American structuralism; the best-known framework employing it is **Tagmemics**, but the single most ambitious attempt at using it to characterize the grammar of English is represented by Fries (1952). While most linguists would probably agree that a slot-and-filler approach can occasionally be useful as a heuristic device, few if any would defend the approach as a promising basis for a theory of grammar.

sluicing /'sluːsɪŋ/ *n.* The construction in which most of an embedded WH-question is deleted under identity, as in *Someone is sweet on you, and I can tell you who*. Ross (1969).

small clause /smɔːl/ *n.* 1. Any of various constituents resembling a clause but lacking a finite verb, particularly a **participial relative clause**, an **adverbial participle** or a **gerund**. Examples: *The woman [wearing glasses] stood up*; *[Wanting to make a good impression,] she chose her outfit carefully*; *[Lisa's going topless] upset her father*. See **reduced clause**, and refer to the remarks there. Williams (1975). 2. A sequence of an NP in objective case and a following predicate, when this is considered a constituent. Examples: *I consider [her intelligent]*; *I want [you in my office]*; *She ordered [the room to be cleaned]*; *She made [us do it]*. The analysis of such sequences as constituents is accepted in GB but rejected in most other frameworks, including GPSG and LFG. Stowell (1981); Chomsky (1981).

SO /es 'əʊ/ See **secondary object**.

solidus /'sɒlɪdəs/ See **slash** (sense 2).

source /sɔːs/ *n.* The **semantic role** borne by an NP which expresses the start point of motion in an abstract or concrete sense, such as *the mountain* in *We walked down from the mountain* and *The mountain began to spew out clouds of smoke*. Source is one of the **deep cases** recognized in Case Grammar.

SOV language /es əʊ 'viː/ *n.* A language in which the normal order of elements in a sentence is Subject–Object–Verb, such as Japanese, Turkish, Basque or Quechua. SOV languages universally tend to show certain typological characteristics, such as postpositions, case systems and left-branching structures in which modifiers (even relative clauses) precede their heads, as was first pointed out by Greenberg (1963).

specifier /'spesɪfaɪə/ *n*. In some versions of the X-bar system, a cover term for any category which occurs as the daughter of a maximal projection and the sister of a one-bar projection and which serves in some (often rather ill-defined) sense to delimit the range of applicability of the maximal projection. Conventionally, determiners are regarded as the specifiers in noun phrases, degree modifiers in adjective phrases and prepositional specifiers in prepositional phrases: [[*these*] *old clothes*], [[*very*] *proud of her success*], [[*straight*] *into the hole*]. The identification of specifiers in verb phrases, if indeed they exist at all, is a matter of considerable controversy. Cf. **modifier**, **attribute**, **complement**. Chomsky (1970).

split antecedent /splɪt/ *n*. The phenomenon in which an **anaphor** (sense 1) has as its **antecedent** a non-existent noun phrase consisting of the coordination of two or more NPs occurring separately in the sentence. Examples are *Janet convinced Elroy that they should get married* and *Janet persuaded Elroy* PRO *to make love*, in which the antecedent of *they* and of PRO is in each case the conjunction of *Janet* and *Elroy*. Split antecedents provide difficulties for most approaches to anaphora and to control.

split ergativity *n*. A grammatical pattern in which ergativity is manifested in some classes of sentences in a language but not in others. In split-ergative languages, ergativity may be confined to sentences whose subject is of a particular type (e.g., inanimate or non-pronominal), to sentences involving particular combinations of NPs (e.g., inanimate subject plus animate object), to particular tenses or aspects (usually, past tense or perfective aspect) or to a wide range of other circumstances. Split ergativity is in fact quite common; the great majority of ergative languages appear to exhibit a split of one type or another. Languages in which ergativity is confined to sentences involving volitional actions have been given the special name **active languages**. Silverstein (1976).

split infinitive *n*. The traditional label for the English construction in which the formative *to* is separated from a following infinitive by an adverb or a negative, as in the example *I decided to really give it a go*. The name is a misnomer, since the sequence *to give* is not an 'infinitive' nor even a constituent (all current analyses agree that the sequence *give it a go* is a constituent, a VP), and hence nothing is 'split'. Traditional grammarians of a prescriptivist bent have for generations strongly condemned this construction, in spite of the fact that it is the normal English form; their insistence on placing the adverb somewhere else ignores the unnaturalness and even the occasional impossibility of reordering examples like *She decided to gradually get rid of the teddy bears she had been collecting for years*.

split-intransitive *adj.* Denoting a grammatical pattern in which intransitive clauses are divided into two types differing in their grammatical realization, most usually in the case assigned to the subject NP, particularly in languages in which the choice is entirely determined by the identity of the lexical verb or predicate. The most usual type of split intransitivity is that occurring in **active languages**, but other types occur, such as in Basque, in which a semantically arbitrary subclass of intransitive verbs requires transitive morphology. Cf. **fluid-intransitive**. See Merlan (1985) for discussion. Dixon (1979).

Split-Morphology Hypothesis /haɪˈpɒθəsɪs/ *n.* The doctrine that **inflectional morphology** and **derivational morphology** are fundamentally different and should be treated separately in the grammar. Long accepted by most morphologists, this doctrine is rejected by the proponents of the **Strong Lexicalist Hypothesis**.

split objectivity /ɒbdʒekˈtɪvɪti/ *n.* The grammatical pattern in which some grammatical processes are sensitive to the **direct object/ indirect object** contrast while others are sensitive to the **primary object/secondary object** contrast. Among languages exhibiting split objectivity are Southern Tiwa, Mohawk, Tzotzil and Yindjibarndi. Dryer (1986).

***spray/load* verb** /spreɪ ˈləʊd/ *n.* One of a small class of English verbs with the distinctive grammatical property of taking two internal arguments, either of which may appear as a direct object, the other appearing as some kind of oblique object, as in *She sprayed paint on the wall/She sprayed the wall with paint*; *They loaded hay onto the wagon/They loaded the wagon with hay*. Other members of this class include *crowd, cram, smear* and *sprinkle*. All the members of this class seem to share a certain semantic property, roughly that of moving a substance or a collection of objects into a receptacle or onto a surface. The existence of this class was reportedly first noted by Barbara Hall Partee in unpublished work; the first published discussion was in Fillmore (1968), and the name was coined by Levin and Rappaport (1986).

squish /skwɪʃ/ *n.* A continuum of (especially lexical) category membership, by which membership of a category is regarded as a matter of degree, rather than as an either/or proposition. For example, the word *newspaper* in *This newspaper headline* might be regarded as lying somewhere on a noun–adjective continuum. Squishes are fundamental in **fuzzy grammar**; they represent much the same notion as **clines**. Ross (1972b).

S-structure /'esstrʌktʃə/ *n.* In GB, one of the three designated levels of the representation of the syntactic structure of a sentence. S-structure represents the result of the application of Alpha Movement and of the Case assignment rules, but is itself subject to certain further operations, notably the raising and deletion operations involved in deriving both the LF-structure and the surface phonetic realization. S-structure is roughly equivalent to the **shallow structure** of the REST.

stacking /stækɪŋ/ *n.* The occurrence of multiple adjectives or multiple relative clauses attached to a single head noun: *a pretty little white house*; *a card that is exposed during the deal which is picked up by the receiving player*. *Adj.* **stacked** /stækt/.

standard /'stændəd/ *n.* In a **comparative** construction, that element to which some other element is compared. In English, the standard is normally marked by a preceding formative *than*. Thus, in the example *Lisa speaks better French than Sue* (*does*), *Sue* is the standard.

Standard Theory *n.* The version of **Transformational Grammar** proposed by Noam Chomsky (1965), differing considerably from the original transformational framework sketched out in Chomsky (1957). The Standard Theory dominated work in syntactic theory in the late 1960s, but, under pressure from the advocates of **Generative Semantics**, it was substantially modified, giving rise to what became known as the **Extended Standard Theory**, which was in turn followed by the **Revised Extended Standard Theory** and then by the **Government–Binding Theory**. Until very recently, however, the Standard Theory dominated textbooks of syntax, and there are a number of textbooks still in print which present what is essentially the Standard Theory with a few accretions from more recent work.

starred form /'stɑːd fɔːm/ *n.* A sequence marked with an **asterisk** and hence regarded as ill-formed: **She smiled me*.

start symbol /'stɑːt ˌsɪmbəl/ See **initial symbol**.

statement /'steɪtmənt/ *n.* One of the fundamental **sentence types** of traditional grammar, having the form of an assertion that some proposition is true. An example is *Lisa is a translator*.

statistical universal /stə'tɪstɪkl̩/ See **relative universal**.

stative /'steɪtɪv/ *n.* or *adj.* Denoting a form or construction which expresses a state of affairs, rather than an event. English does not always distinguish statives from dynamic passives. The sentence *The window was broken*, for example, is ambiguous between a stative reading and a dynamic reading, though the addition of adverbials may force one or the other reading: *The window was broken by John* (dynamic); *The window was broken all week* (stative). Many other languages, however, have explicit stative constructions: in German, *Das Fenster war gebrochen* can only have a stative reading (i.e., 'it had a hole in it'), while *Das Fenster wurde gebrochen* is strictly dynamic (i.e., 'the window got broken'). 'Stative' is a superordinate aspectual category contrasting with **dynamic**.

stative verb *n.* A lexical verb whose meaning expresses a state, rather than an event, such as *know, want, understand, fear* or *like*. Stative verbs in English are distinguished by their inability to appear in the progressive aspect in ordinary circumstances: **Lisa is knowing/understanding/liking French*. (Some of them can, however, appear in the progressive in special senses or constructions: *Lisa is understanding more French every day*; *Lisa is liking French* (where *French* is understood as 'the course in French which she is pursuing').)

status /'steɪtəs/ *n.* A synonym for **mood** in the narrowest possible sense of that term, sometimes preferred to distinguish the central notion of 'degree or kind of reality' from other notions frequently regarded as modal in nature, such as **illocutionary force**, **evidential** and **evaluative** distinctions and **modality** in sense 2 of that term. Whorf (1956).

stem /stem/ *n.* In morphology, a bound form of a lexical item which typically consists of a **root** to which one or more morphological **formatives** have been added and which serves as the immediate **base** for the formation of some further form or set of forms. For example, the Latin verb *amare* 'love', whose root is *am-*, has an imperfect stem *amaba-* from which are derived the various imperfect forms *amabam* 'I used to love', *amabas* 'you used to love', *amabat* 'he/she used to love' and so on; it also has a perfect stem *amav-* from which are derived *amavi* 'I loved', *amavisti* 'you loved', *amavit* 'he/she loved' and so on. Bauer (1983) reserves this term for a form to which inflectional affixes are directly added, preferring 'base' elsewhere.

stranding /'strændɪŋ/ *n.* Any of various phenomena in which some element of a sentence occurs in the absence of an associated element which would normally accompany it and which is required for its interpretation. A familiar example from English is **preposition stranding**, in which a preposition occurs with no overt following object, as a result of WH-Preposing (see **WH-Movement**). Examples are *Who were you talking to?* and *That Rolls she arrived in is hired*, in which the prepositions *to* and *in* are stranded. In all varieties of Eskimo, a noun phrase containing an adjective can often be optionally realized in a form in which the head noun of the NP is incorporated into the verb, leaving the adjective stranded but still bearing any case marking or agreement morphs; see examples under **incorporation**.

strategy /'strætədʒi/ *n.* Any of several conceivable constructions which might in principle be used for performing some grammatical function, particularly one which is used in a particular language. For example, the formation of relative clauses is accomplished in a variety of ways in the languages of the world: the relative clause may be finite or non-finite (participial); it may or may not be embedded within the clause containing its head; if embedded, it may precede or follow its head; it may or may not contain a relative pronoun; it may or may not carry a special marker of subordination; it may represent the relativized NP within itself either as a gap or as a resumptive pronoun; and so on. The particular construction used by a language is said to represent the 'relativization strategy' of that language.

Stratificational Grammar /strætɪfɪ'keɪʃənl̩/ *n.* A theory of grammar in which linguistic structure is regarded as consisting of a number of distinct autonomous levels called 'strata', the relation between the representation in one stratum and that in the next less abstract stratum being conceived as one of realization in every case. The framework has been criticized as being so excessively unrestrictive as to be consistent with any conceivable set of facts at all, but, whatever its merits or shortcomings, it has been severely hampered by its typographically nightmarish graphical representations, which are arguably the most awkward such representations ever seriously proposed. The framework was proposed by Sidney Lamb (1966); see Lockwood (1972) or Sullivan (1980) for an introduction.

stratum /'streɪtəm/ (pl. **strata** /'streɪtə/) *n*. 1. In Relational Grammar, any one of the several levels of organization typically postulated as forming part of the syntactic structure of a sentence. 2. More generally, in any theory of grammar in which the structure of a sentence is regarded as consisting of two or more representations employing the same vocabulary, any one of those representations. NOTE: this usage is recommended by Ladusaw (1988); compare **level** (sense 2).

strict c-command /strɪkt/ *n*. A synonym for **c-command**, sometimes used to make it clear that **m-command** is not the relation being referred to. See the remarks under **c-command**.

strict subcategorization See **subcategorization**.

string /strɪŋ/ *n*. A sentence, or part of a sentence, regarded as a linear sequence of elements, without regard for any further levels of structure. In the early days of generative grammar, sentences in natural languages were almost invariably regarded as strings, or more precisely as sequences of strings. Only gradually did generative grammarians abandon this conception in favour of regarding sentences primarily as two-dimensional tree structures, and even today sentences are still regarded as strings in mathematical linguistics for purposes of investigating the **weak generative capacity** of classes of grammars. See under **tree** for further information.

string equivalence /ɪ'kwɪvələns/ See **weak equivalence**.

stringset /'strɪŋset/ *n*. A language, particularly a formal language, regarded as a set of **strings**. The stringset defined by a grammar is equivalent to the **weak generative capacity** of that grammar.

strong conditions of adequacy See under **adequacy**.

strong crossover /strɒŋ/ *n*. A conventional label for those instances of **crossover phenomena** which do not involve genitives and which are felt to be grossly ungrammatical; an example is **Who$_i$ does he$_i$ think e$_i$ did it?* In such an example, the WH-trace is A-bound by the pronominal, and hence the structure is ruled out by Principle C of the **Binding Theory**. It is also, however, ruled out by the **Leftness Condition**. Cf. **weak crossover**.

strong equivalence /ɪ'kwɪvələns/ *n*. The relation which holds between two grammars which have the same **strong generative**

capacity – that is, they generate exactly the same sets of strings and assign exactly the same sets of structures to those strings. Two grammars exhibiting strong equivalence are said to be **strongly equivalent**. Cf. **weak equivalence**.

strong generative capacity *n.* (of a particular formal grammar) The set of strings and their associated structures generated by that grammar. Cf. **weak generative capacity**.

Strong Lexicalist Hypothesis *n.* The doctrine that rules of syntax may make no reference whatever to the morphological structure of word forms, not even to inflectional morphology. Proponents of this doctrine reject the **Split-Morphology Hypothesis**, the idea that inflection is distinct from derivation; they reject the use of **paradigms** and emphasize the syntagmatic aspects of word structure, almost to the extent of espousing an **Item-and-Arrangement** view of morphology. Cf. **Weak Lexicalist Hypothesis**. See Spencer (1991) for discussion.

strong verb *n.* In certain languages, notably the Germanic languages (including English), a verb which inflects by internal vowel change, rather than by affixation: *sing*, *sang*, *sung*; *write*, *wrote*, *written*. Cf. **weak verb**.

structural ambiguity /ˈstrʌktʃərl̩/ *n.* An **ambiguity** involving the assignment of two or more syntactic structures to a string. See examples under **ambiguity**.

structural description /dɪˈskrɪpʃn̩/ *n.* In a formal grammar, a representation of the structure assigned to a particular string by the rules of the grammar.

structuralism /ˈstrʌktʃərəlɪzm̩/ *n.* 1. Any approach to linguistic description which views the grammar of a language primarily as a system of relations. Structuralism in this sense derives largely from the work of the Swiss linguist Ferdinand de Saussure. Virtually all twentieth-century approaches to linguistics are structuralist in this sense, in contrast with the predominantly atomistic approach of much nineteenth-century linguistics, in which a language was seen primarily as a collection of individual elements. In the words of Lepschy (1982), structuralism is marked by its emphasis on abstraction and generality, while prestructuralist approaches were characterized by an emphasis on the concrete and the particular. 2. (also **American structuralism**) A particular approach to linguistic description developed in the United States in the 1940s and 1950s. The

American structuralists (or 'post-Bloomfieldians') drew their inspiration from the work of Leonard Bloomfield, though it is clear that Bloomfield would not have approved of some of their more extreme positions. The framework was characterized by an extremely narrow view of what constituted scientific investigation and by a remarkable set of dogmatic principles which have been rejected by almost all other approaches. Among these principles were the doctrine of the 'separation of levels', by which no morphological analysis could be undertaken until the phonological analysis was complete, and no syntactic analysis could be undertaken until the morphological analysis was complete, and the complete rejection of any appeal to processes in linguistic description in favour of a rigidly distributional view of linguistic elements often referred to as the 'Item-and-Arrangement' framework. In rejecting most of these doctrines, the early generative linguists came to use 'structuralist' as a term of abuse; they rejected the structuralist programme *en bloc* as a merely 'taxonomic' one, that is, as one concerned only with labelling and classification, and not with explanation. Nevertheless, the achievements of the American structuralists were considerable: their concern for explicitness, for precision and for generality helped pave the way for generative linguistics; their development of the notion of constituent structure influenced the later development of syntax far more than is often recognized; and their enormous respect for primary linguistic data, at the expense of theoretical elegance, deserves more credit than it is sometimes accorded. See Huddleston (1972) and Stark (1972) for accounts of American structuralism, and see Newmeyer (1986) for an account of the confrontation between structuralist and generative linguistics. *Adj.* **structuralist** /'strʌktʃərəlɪst/.

structure /'strʌktʃə/ *n.* The set of **syntagmatic relations** holding among the elements of a sentence or some distinguishable subpart of a sentence – in other words, the particular way those elements are put together to make up that sentence or subpart. Cf. **system**.

structure dependence /'strʌktʃə dɪˌpendəns/ *n.* The seemingly universal property by which the rules of grammar operate in terms of syntactic structures (especially constituent structure) and not in terms of the linear sequence of words or of their phonological shapes. It is because of this property of structure-dependence that we do not find rules of grammar referring to notions like 'the fourth word in the sentence' or 'a word of three syllables'. *Adj.* **structure-dependent** /'strʌktʃə dɪˌpendənt/.

Structure-Preservation Constraint /prezə'veɪʃn̩ kən,streɪnt/ *n*. The requirement, in some **derivational** theories of grammar, that operations which change a syntactic representation during the course of a derivation may not alter the identity or location of labelled nodes in the tree. For example, if an NP node is present at some point at one level of representation, it must be present at the same point at all levels of representation; it may not disappear, turn into a PP node or move to a different location where no NP node was present at an earlier level of representation. The requirement of structure preservation, which is fundamental in GB, was introduced by Emonds (1970); it played a major part in curtailing many of the wilder excesses of derivations in the classical theory of TG.

subcategorization /,sʌbkætəgəraɪ'zeɪʃn̩/ *n*. (also **strict subcategorization**) The phenomenon by which the members of a single **lexical category** do not all exhibit identical syntactic behaviour. For example, some verbs ('transitive verbs' like *kill* and *build*) take direct objects, while others ('intransitive verbs' like *die* and *smile*) do not; some verbs (*say*, *decide*) permit a following *that*-complement clause; some (*enquire*, *wonder*) permit a following *whether*-complement clause; others (*kill*, *die*, *speak*) permit neither; still others (*ask*, *consider*) permit both. Subcategorization facts are complex and often arbitrary, and the subcategories required for various grammatical purposes overlap almost endlessly; subcategorization phenomena represent the principal area in which syntax is forced to get to grips with the properties of individual words. Syntacticians have been slow to devise elegant treatments of subcategorization; the **subcategorization frames** of earlier generative grammar were clumsy and involved a good deal of redundancy. While GPSG, at least, has succeeded in formulating a simple and economical mechanism for treating subcategorization, many linguists, instead of building subcategorization requirements into the syntax, have preferred to take the radical step of doing precisely the opposite, leading to the development in the 1980s of theories of grammar, such as Word Grammar and HPSG, in which virtually *all* syntactic information is squeezed into the subcategorization requirements of lexical items.

subcategorization feature *n*. In some theories of grammar, notably GPSG, a feature which is used to express the subcategorization requirements of certain lexical items. GPSG uses features with arbitrary names, usually just numbers, for this purpose; features are present in lexical entries and are introduced into tree structures on

lexical nodes. For example, the rule VP → V[7], NP introduces a
simple transitive structure with the subcategorization feature [7] on
the V node, and every verb in the lexicon which can appear in that
structure carries the feature [7] as part of its lexical entry. Such
features constitute perhaps the most elegant treatment of subcategorization facts currently available.

subcategorization frame /freɪm/ *n.* A device for treating the
subcategorization requirements of lexical items, consisting simply of
a statement in the **lexical entry** for that item of the sisters it requires
or permits. Thus, for example, the lexical entry for the verb *see*
might include the frame [V, _____ NP], meaning that this verb can
be inserted into a V node immediately followed by an NP, as in *Lisa
saw me*. Similarly, the verb *tell* might have the frame [V, _____ NP
S'[-WH]], allowing it to appear in structures like *Lisa told me that
she would come*. Such frames were regularly used in TG, and they
are still widely used in GB, in spite of a number of drawbacks. For
one thing, they make it difficult to specify the *absence* of a category:
what is to stop the verb *see* from appearing with two following NPs,
as in **Lisa saw me the book* (cf. *Lisa gave me the book*)? For
another, they are highly redundant, in that they merely repeat
information already provided by the rules of the grammar, as
pointed out by Heny (1979): the rule VP → V NP, for example, says
that a verb can be followed by an NP, information which is repeated
endlessly in the lexical entry of every simple transitive verb.

subcategory /ˈsʌbˌkætəgri/ *n.* Any one of the various overlapping
subclasses of a lexical category which must be recognized in a
grammar. Two examples are the subcategory of adjectives appearing in **attributive** position (*big, pretty, major, topmost*, etc.) and the
subcategory appearing in **predicative** position (*big, pretty, awake,
asleep*, etc.). A few subcategories have traditional names ('transitive verb', 'count noun'), but most do not.

subdeletion /ˈsʌbdɪˌliːʃn̩/ *n.* (also **comparative subdeletion**) A
label applied to the absence, in certain types of comparative constructions, of a quantifying or qualifying element in the constituent
serving as or containing the standard of comparison. In the following example, the symbol '*e*' represents the subdeleted quantifier:
I own more board games than I own e *books*. V. **subdelete** /ˈsʌb-
dɪliːt/. Cf. **comparative deletion**. Bresnan (1976).

Subjacency Condition /sʌbˈdʒeɪsənsi kənˌdɪʃn̩/ *n.* In GB, the
principal requirement of **Bounding Theory**. It says: no single appli-

cation of a movement rule may cross more than one bounding node. The bounding nodes in English have usually been taken to be NP and S, though NP and S-bar have been proposed for other languages and occasionally also for English. The Subjacency Condition was introduced by Chomsky (1973) as a way of combining some of Ross's **island constraints**; it has generally been regarded as a success, though it had the surprising consequence of forcing what were previously regarded as unbounded movement rules, like WH-Preposing, to be reinterpreted as **successive cyclic** rules.

subject /'sʌbdʒɪkt/ *n*. (S) 1. The most prominent of the **grammatical relations** which a noun phrase may bear in a clause. In most, but not all, languages subjects are prominent and readily identified; the subject forms the grammatical **pivot** in terms of which its clause is structured and in terms of which it is related to other clauses in the discourse. Subjects most typically exhibit a large number of grammatical, semantic and discourse properties, as exhaustively summarized in Keenan (1976a). Among these are the following: subjects represent entities with independent existence; subjects control coreference, including reflexives, pronouns and null anaphors; subjects control switch-reference systems; subjects control verb agreement; subjects are topics in unmarked constructions; subjects are the targets of advancement processes; subjects can be relativized, questioned and clefted; subjects undergo raising; subjects receive minimal case marking; subjects are agents in unmarked constructions. While few of these properties may be unique to subjects in a given language, a subject may usually be identified by the fact that it exhibits more of them than any other NP. Languages in which subjects are prominent (the majority) are variously called **subject-prominent** or **reference-dominated**. 2. In some analyses, a constituent of a phrase which plays a role somewhat analogous to the subject of a sentence. For example, in the phrase *Lisa's refusal of the offer*, *Lisa's* is sometimes regarded as the subject of the NP. Sense 2: Jackendoff (1977).

subject–auxiliary inversion *n*. The variety of **inversion** in which an auxiliary precedes a subject NP, as in *Is she coming?*, *What would you like?* and *Never have I seen such a mess*.

Subject Condition /kən'dɪʃn̩/ *n*. An **island constraint** which states that a WH-dependency may not cross the boundary of a subject NP. This condition is invoked to account for the ill-formedness of examples like *Who was a picture of e on the table?*, as opposed to *Who is that a picture of e?*

subjective genitive /səb'dʒektɪv/ *n.* A possessive NP or a prepositional phrase with *of* which is interpreted as the subject of a nominalized verb. Examples are *Lisa's* in *Lisa's arrival* and *Buffalo's* in *Buffalo's defeat of Philadelphia.* Cf. **objective genitive**.

subject-prominent language /'prɒmɪnənt/ *n.* A language in which grammatical **subjects** are readily identifiable and play an important role in the syntactic organization of sentences. The majority of the world's languages, including English, are subject-prominent; this property is sometimes regarded as typologically important. Cf. **topic-prominent language**, **reference-dominated language**. Li and Thompson (1976).

subject raising *n.* (also **raising**) The phenomenon in which an NP which is semantically the subject of a lower predicate appears on the surface as the subject of a higher predicate. An example is *Lisa seems to be happy*, in which the NP *Lisa* is semantically the subject of the predicate *be happy* but functions grammatically as the subject of *seem*.

subjunctive /sʌb'dʒʌŋktɪv/ *n.* or *adj.* A traditional label for a set of morphologically distinctive verb forms occurring in certain languages, especially European languages, which are largely confined to certain types of subordinate clauses and which often serve to express such **mood** categories as remoteness, unreality or possibility. European languages differ in the extent to which the subjunctive forms genuinely contrast with indicative forms; in the majority of circumstances in the majority of these languages, the subjunctive form is obligatory in most circumstances in which it is possible at all, and it serves merely as a redundant expression of certain types of subordination: in Spanish, for example, the subjunctive is obligatory after most matrix verbs of wanting, advising, permitting, prohibiting, ordering, hoping and the like, as well as after subordinators like 'before', 'when', 'as soon as' (in certain circumstances) and, interestingly, in a complement of *el hecho de que* 'the fact that'. English has lost the morphological subjunctive which it once had, but the term is still sometimes applied to certain distinctive forms occurring in North American speech and in formal varieties of British English: *if I [were] you . . .; I suggest she [do] it; I recommend this [be] done.*

subordinate clause /sə'bɔːdɪnət/ *n.* A traditional label for any **clause** which is embedded under a higher clause. Subordinate clauses are of several types, the most important being **adverbial clauses**, **complement clauses** and **relative clauses**.

subordinating conjunction /sə'bɔːdɪneɪtɪŋ/ *n.* The traditional term for a **subordinator**. This traditional name is now little used in linguistics, since it leads to potential confusion with the term **conjunction**.

subordination /sə,bɔːdɪ'neɪʃn̩/ *n.* (also **hypotaxis**) The phenomenon by which one clause, the **embedded clause** or **subordinate clause**, forms a constituent of a larger clause, the **matrix clause**.

subordinator /sə'bɔːdɪneɪtə/ *n.* A lexical category, or a member of this category, whose members serve to introduce **adverbial clauses**. English examples include *before*, *after*, *when*, *while*, *if*, *although*, *because* and *whenever*. The traditional name for these items, 'subordinating conjunctions', is still occasionally used. Many analysts regard subordinators as specialized members of the category Preposition.

substantive /'sʌbstəntɪv/ 1. *n.* A traditional, but now virtually obsolete, synonym for **noun**. Some traditional grammarians also included pronouns in the class of substantives. 2. *adj.* (also **nominal**) In those versions of the X-bar system in which lexical categories are decomposed into the binary features [N] and [V], denoting any category which is [+N], in other words, nouns and adjectives.

substantive universal /səb'stæntɪv/ *n.* Any formal object which is universally present in grammars, or at least universally available. Examples include the categories Noun and Verb Phrase and the features [PLURAL] and [FINITE]. Cf. **formal universal**.

substitution frame /sʌbstɪ'tjuːʃn̩ ˌfreɪm/ *n.* Any one of the diagnostic strings used in a **slot-and-filler** approach to grammatical characterization. See the examples under that entry.

substring /'sʌbstrɪŋ/ *n.* Any part of a **string** which is under consideration.

subsumption /səb'sʌmptʃn̩/ *n.* The relation which holds between a more general category A and a more specific category B when B contains all of the features of A and some additional features besides: in this case, A is said to 'subsume' B. For example, the category NP[PLUR +] (a plural NP) subsumes the category

NP[PLUR +] [PERS 3] (a third person plural NP). Cf. **extension**.
V. **subsume** /səb'sjuːm/.

subtraction /səb'trækʃn̩/ *n.* Any morphological process involving
the removal of part of a root. In Fijian, for example, verbal roots
are rendered intransitive by subtraction of a final consonant: *kaut-*
'carry', intr. *kau*; *yawak-* 'go away', intr. *yawa*; *rai-* 'see', intr. *rai*;
saum- 'repay', intr. *sau*.

subtree /'sʌbtriː/ *n.* Any part of a tree consisting of a single node
and all the material dominated by that node. Cf. **local subtree**.

succession /sək'seʃn̩/ *n.* The characteristic of a grammar formulated
in terms of the X-bar system in which every non-terminal node of
the form X^n has a daughter of the form X^{n-1}. Succession is widely
assumed to be a desirable characteristic, but it is violated in one way
or another in nearly every published analysis involving the X-bar
system: such familiar rules as $N'' \rightarrow S'$ and $N' \rightarrow A'' \ N'$ are
inconsistent with succession. Kornai and Pullum (1990) use the term
'Weak Succession' for the condition that every non-terminal of the
form X^n should have a daughter of the form X^m, where *m* is less
than or equal to *n*. Kornai and Pullum (1990).

successive cyclicity /sək͵sesɪv sɪ'klɪsɪti/ *n.* In certain derivational theories of grammar, the phenomenon by which an
unbounded dependency is interpreted as resulting from a series
of local movement rules, each obeying constraints on boundedness.
The successive cyclic interpretation of WH-Movement was one of
the chief consequences of the introduction of the **Subjacency Condition** into later versions of TG. *Adj.* **successive cyclic**.

suffix /'sʌfɪks/ *n.* An **affix** which follows the root in the form
containing it. English examples include the noun plural suffix *-s* (as
in *cats*) and the derivational suffixes *-er* (as in *writer*) and *-ness* (as in
happiness). Cf. **prefix**, **infix**, **circumfix**, **superfix**.

Super-Equi /'suːpər͵ekwi/ *n.* A name formerly applied to cases of
optional **control** crossing more than one clause boundary, such as in
the example *Lisa_i thought it would be easy e_i to learn French*. The
name reflects the old **Equi-NP Deletion** analysis of control constructions crossing only one clause boundary. Grinder (1970).

superessive /suːpər'esɪv/ *n.* or *adj.* (also **supraessive**) A case form
expressing the semantic notion of 'on' or 'on top of'.

superfix /'suːpəfɪks/ *n.* (also **suprafix**) A suprasegmental (stress or tone) distinction which serves as the sole exponent of a grammatical distinction, conveniently, if somewhat abstractly, regarded as an affix. A simple example is the stress contrast distinguishing certain noun–verb pairs in English, such as *record* (N)/*record* (V) and *contest* (N)/*contest* (V). A more elaborate example is provided by the Zairean language Ngbaka, in which the four major tense/aspect forms of all verbs are marked solely by tones: falling, level, falling–rising and rising:

Form 1	Form 2	Form 3	Form 4	
wà	wā	wǎ	wá	'clean'
gbɔ̀tɔ̀	gbɔ̄tɔ̄	gbɔ̌tɔ̌	gbɔ́tɔ́	'pull'

Welmers (1973) provides some even more striking examples of overt pronouns and prefixes which consist solely of tones with no associated segments; such tones simply 'muscle in' on the following syllable in one way or another. NOTE: the form 'suprafix' is preferred by those linguists with a knowledge of Latin, but, they being a minority these days, 'superfix' is far more frequent in use.

superlative /sʊ'pɜːlətɪv/ *n.* or *adj.* In languages exhibiting three degrees of comparison for adjectives and/or adverbs, that form expressing the highest degree of comparison: e.g., English *biggest* (from *big*), *worst* (from *bad* or *badly*) and *most beautiful* (from *beautiful*). Cf. **positive**, **comparative**, **excessive**, **elative**.

supine /'suːpaɪn/ *n.* 1. In the grammar of Latin, a distinct non-finite form derived from one of the participial stems of a verb and serving to express certain types of complements. In the familiar Latin phrase *mirabile dictu* 'wonderful to tell', *dictu* is the supine of the verb *dicere* 'tell'. 2. In the grammars of certain other languages, a conventional label for a non-finite form whose functions are more or less reminiscent of those of the Latin supine. The term has no general linguistic significance.

suppletion /sə'pliːʃn̩/ *n.* The use of two or more distinct stems for forming the inflections of a single lexical item: *go/went*, *person/people*, *bad/worse*. Adj. **suppletive** /sə'pliːtɪv/.

supraessive /suːprə'esɪv/ See **superessive**.

suprafix /'suːprəfɪks/ See **superfix**.

surface structure /'sɜːfɪs/ *n.* 1. In various **derivational** theories of grammar, that level of syntactic representation which is least abstract and which typically serves as the input to the phonological rules. In the Standard Theory of Transformational Grammar, the surface structure of a sentence was simply the tree that resulted from the application of all the transformational rules; it contained no record of its own derivational history, and it served as input to the phonological rules, but not to the semantic rules. In the Extended Standard Theory, surface structure served as part of the input to the semantic rules, along with the **deep structure**. In the Revised Extended Standard Theory, surface structure was enriched by the presence of null elements called **traces**, which allowed it to 'remember' certain aspects of its derivational history, and it became the sole input to both phonological and semantic rules; in that framework, it contrasted with a slightly more abstract level of representation called **shallow structure**. In Government–Binding Theory, the old shallow structure, now renamed **S-structure**, has come to be regarded as one of the three principal designated levels of representation, along with **D-structure** and **Logical Form**, and surface structure (now often called 'surface form') is apparently regarded as having no particular syntactic significance, though it still serves as input to the phonological rules. 2. A label sometimes applied to a tree representing the constituent structure of a sentence even in frameworks which are not derivational. Chomsky (1965).

SVO language /es viː 'əu/ *n.* A language in which the normal order of elements in a sentence is Subject–Verb–Object, such as English, French or Swahili. SVO languages universally tend to show many of the same typological features as VSO languages, though not so consistently, as first pointed out by Greenberg (1963).

switch function /swɪtʃ/ *n.* A grammatical device found in many languages which serves to track a particular participant across clauses and to indicate the possibly varying grammatical or semantic relations borne by that participant. English uses a switch-function system, as illustrated by the example *Lisa went to the library and ∅ asked for a biography of Thomas Hardy and ∅ was given this one.* Cf. **switch reference**. Foley and Van Valin (1984).

switch reference *n.* A grammatical device found in certain languages which serves to track a particular grammatical or semantic relation across clauses and to monitor whether the participants bearing that relation are the same or different. Such a system encodes simultaneously the relative discourse reference of two NPs in consecutive clauses and the grammatical relations of those NPs. Switch reference is particularly common in North American languages. The following examples, from Lakhota, illustrate the use of the two conjunctions *na* and *čha* in determining the reference of subject and object NPs; the first is the 'same-reference' conjunction, the second the 'switch-reference' conjunction:

Ø-ʔį   na Ø-Ø-kté
3Sg-arrived and 3Sg-3Sg-killed
'Hei arrived and killed himj.'

Ø-ʔį   čha Ø-Ø-kté
'Hei arrived and hej killed himi.'

Cf. **switch function**. Jacobsen (1967).

syllepsis /sɪ'lepsɪs/ See **zeugma** (sense 2).

swung dash /swʌŋ 'dæʃ/ *n*. The symbol '~', used to separate alternative and equivalent grammatical forms: *proved ~ proven*.

syncategorematic item /sɪŋkætəgərɪ'mætɪk/ *n*. A lexical item which belongs to no **lexical category** or, equivalently, which belongs to a category of which it is the only member. English lexical items which are often treated as syncategorematic include *not*, infinitival *to*, *even* (as in *Even James enjoyed the party*) and *please*. Formal logic.

synchronic /sɪŋ'krɒnɪk/ *adj*. Referring to the description of a language at a particular moment in time (not necessarily the present moment). *Abstr. n.* **synchrony** /'sɪŋkrəni/. Cf. **diachronic**.

syncretism /'sɪŋkrətɪzm̩/ *n*. (also **neutralization**) The morphological phenomenon in which two or more morphosyntactically distinct forms of a lexical item are formally identical. In Latin, for example, genitive and dative case forms of nouns are usually distinct (*amicus* 'friend', genitive *amici*, dative *amico*), but in -*a*-stem nouns they exhibit syncretism (*puella* 'girl', genitive/dative *puellae*). *Adj.* **syncretic** /sɪŋ'kretɪk/.

syndeton /'sɪndɪtən/ *n*. A coordinate structure involving the explicit use of coordinating conjunctions like *and*. *Adj.* **syndetic** /sɪn'detɪk/; *abstr. n.* **syndesis** /'sɪndɪsɪs/. Cf. **asyndeton**.

synesis /'sɪnɪsɪs/ *n*. Agreement with sense rather than with form, as in *The Cabinet are divided on this issue*.

syntactic blend /sɪn'tæktɪk/ *n.* An utterance which switches part-way through from one well-formed structure to another, the whole being ill-formed; an example is **It's my car is the problem.* See **anacoluthon, zeugma, apo koinou construction**.

syntactic category *n.* Any formal object which is available to serve as a node in a tree. In early generative grammar, syntactic categories were usually regarded as **monads** with no internal structure and were usually represented by purely mnemonic names or symbols like V or NP. In virtually all contemporary work, however, syntactic categories are analysed as **complex symbols** with representations like [+N] [–V] [BAR 2] [+PLURAL] [3 PERSON], and symbols like NP are regarded purely as typographical abbreviations. See Gazdar *et al.* (1988) for a very general formalization of the notion of a syntactic category.

syntactic feature See **feature**.

syntagm /'sɪntæm/ *n.* (rarely **syntagma** /sɪn'tægmə/) An occasional synonym for **construction**. NOTE: in many European languages, this word is used as the exact equivalent of the English word **phrase**. *Adj.* **syntagmatic**.

syntagmatic relation /sɪntæg'mætɪk/ *n.* Any relation holding be-tween two elements which are simultaneously present in a single structure, such as that between a verb and its object. Cf. **paradig-matic relation**. Saussure (1916).

syntax /'sɪntæks/ *n.* The branch of grammar dealing with the organ-ization of words into larger structures, particularly into sentences; equivalently, the study of sentence structure. *Adj.* **syntactic, syntac-tical** /sɪn'tæktɪk,-l̩/. NOTE: the form **syntactical** is traditional, but contem-porary usage among linguists favours **syntactic**.

synthetic /sɪn'θetɪk/ *adj.* Denoting a pattern in which grammatical distinctions are expressed by variation in the forms of words, rather than by the use of additional auxiliary words. Examples include English *eat, eats, ate, eating* and Basque *gizona* 'the man', *gizonari* 'to the man', *gizonarekin* 'with the man', *gizonak* 'the men', etc. Cf. **analytic**.

synthetic language *n.* A language characterized by a high fre-quency of **synthetic** structures, whether **inflecting** or **agglutinating**. Examples include Latin, Arabic, Turkish, Basque and Georgian. See Horne (1966) for discussion. Schlegel (1818).

system /'sɪstəm/ *n.* A very general term for an organized set of competing possibilities among the grammatical or lexical elements of a language, often considered together with a set of statements for choosing among these possibilities. For example, one might speak of the 'pronoun system' of a language, meaning the complete inventory of pronouns occurring in it and the rules for choosing among them, or one might speak of the 'verbal system' of a language, meaning the complete set of possible verb forms and the rules for using them. The notion of a system was introduced by Ferdinand de Saussure; it represents an elaboration of the traditional notion of a **paradigm**, but differs in that it emphasizes the relations among the elements, rather than the elements themselves.

Systemic Grammar /sɪ'stiːmɪk/ *n.* A theory of grammar developed by Michael Halliday and his colleagues during the last several decades. First introduced in Halliday (1961), the framework was originally called **Scale-and-Category Grammar**. Systemic Grammar sees a grammatical system as a network of interrelated systems of classes; entry conditions define the choices which can be made within each system; these choices become increasingly specific ('delicate') as the analysis proceeds. Systemic Grammar is a **functional grammar** in sense 1 of that term; it attaches overriding importance to the elucidation of communicative function, and its analyses incorporate a great deal of communicative, pragmatic and sociolinguistic information of a sort not commonly encountered in other approaches. Its proponents have particularly stressed its utility in the analysis of texts, an area beyond the scope of most other theories of grammar, and indeed Systemic Grammar is so different from other approaches in its motivation and objectives that direct comparison is almost impossible. The most convenient brief introduction is Morley (1985); a more detailed introduction is Butler (1985). A rigorous formalization is provided in Patten and Ritchie (1987).

system network *n.* In Systemic Grammar, a body of interrelated rules which, taken together, specify the set of well-formed categories available in the grammar.

T

t See **trace**.

TAG /tiː eɪ 'dʒiː/ See **Tree-Adjoining Grammar**.

Tagmemics /tæg'miːmɪks/ *n*. A framework for grammatical description developed by Kenneth Pike and his colleagues. Tagmemics is a **slot-and-filler** approach which is primarily designed to allow fieldworkers to reduce corpora of data to coherent descriptions efficiently; it is particularly associated with the Summer Institute of Linguistics, an association of missionary linguists devoted largely to Bible translations. See Cook (1969) or Jones (1980) for an introduction.

tag question /'tæg ˌkwestʃən/ *n*. A question which immediately follows a statement and which serves to seek confirmation, either explicitly (as in *She's Irish, isn't she?*) or rhetorically (as in *She's Irish, is she?*). The formation of tag questions in English is notoriously complex, most other languages managing with an invariable tag like Spanish *¿no?*

tag statement /'tæg ˌsteɪtmənt/ *n*. A statement which immediately follows another statement and which serves to reinforce that first statement, as in *She's Irish, she is*.

TAL /tiː eɪ 'el/ See **tree-adjoining language**.

tangling /'tæŋglɪŋ/ *n*. The phenomenon in which the arcs in a tree connecting mothers to daughters are permitted to cross, in violation of the **Non-tangling Condition**; see the example under this last entry.

taxonomy /tæk'sɒnəmi/ *n*. Any proposed system for labelling and classifying grammatical elements. All approaches to grammatical description necessarily incorporate some taxonomic elements, but the term 'taxonomic' has particularly been used by generative linguists as a term of abuse for the work of the **American structuralists** (see **structuralism**), which they regard as excessively concerned with classification at the expense of explanation. *Adj.* **taxonomic** /tæksə'nɒmɪk/.

telic /'tiːlɪk/ *adj.* Denoting an activity which has a recognizable goal the achievement of which would necessarily bring the activity to an end, as in the examples *Lisa is cleaning the fridge* and *We drove to Canterbury*. 2. Denoting a verb or predicate which, intrinsically or in a particular case, exhibits this semantic property, such as the verbs in the preceding examples. Cf. **atelic**. See Comrie (1976) for discussion. Garey (1957).

template /'templeɪt/ *n.* A general pattern for the formation of word forms belonging to some lexical category in a particular language. A template consists of a linear sequence of 'slots' or 'positions', each of which can or must be filled by one (or occasionally more than one) of a specified class of morphemes. For example, Young and Morgan (1980) propose an analysis of Navaho verb forms in terms of ten positions, as follows: (1: theme) (2: iterative) (3: distributive) (4: direct object) (5: subject) (6: theme) (7: mode/aspect) (8: subject) (9: classifier) (10: stem); in any particular Navaho verb form, some (though not all) of these positions will be filled by appropriate morphemes. The template approach to inflectional morphology seems particularly appropriate for many North American languages; it was highly developed by the American structuralists, and formed much of the inspiration for their **Item-and-Arrangement** view of morphology generally.

temporal clause /'tempərl/ *n.* An **adverbial clause** which expresses some notion of time. Temporal clauses in English are usually introduced by one of the subordinators *before*, *after*, *since*, *while*, *when* and *whenever*. Examples: *The phone rang* [*while she was in the bath*]; [*Before Lisa came to Brighton*] *she lived in Dorset*.

tense /tens/ *n.* 1. The **grammatical category** which correlates most directly with distinctions of time. Tense is a frequent category in the languages of the world, but is far from universal, Chinese being an example of a language which lacks tense entirely. Tense distinctions are very frequently marked on finite verbs. English exhibits a minimal tense system with a two-way contrast between past and non-past forms, as illustrated by *Lisa lives in France* vs. *Lisa lived in France*; *Lisa is smoking* vs. *Lisa was smoking*; *Lisa has finished her essay* vs. *Lisa had finished her essay*; *Lisa says she will come* vs. *Lisa said she would come*. English lacks a distinctive future tense. A few languages, of which the New Guinea language Hua is the best-known example, have a two-term system contrasting future and non-future. Latin and the Romance languages show a three-term tense system with past, present and future tenses, though the use of the future is highly restricted in some of these languages. Some languages exhibit more elaborate tense systems, distinguishing, for example, recent past and remote past tenses. The New Guinea language Yimas has a remarkably rich system of seven tenses: four past tenses, distinguishing varying degrees of remoteness, a present, a near future and a remote future (Foley 1986). See Comrie (1985a) for discussion, and see also **absolute tense** and **relative tense**. 2. Any particular tense form exhibited by a particular language, such as the English past tense. NOTE: traditional grammar often uses the term 'tense' in a very loose manner that covers not only distinctions of tense but also those of **aspect** and sometimes even further distinctions. Thus, Latin is sometimes said to have six 'tenses', when in reality it has three tenses which intersect with two aspectual categories to produce six distinct sets of forms. It would be very convenient to have an unambiguous term for referring to any single one of the tense–aspect–mood distinctions made in a single language, but no such term appears to be in use.

tensed /tenst/ *adj.* Denoting a clause, a VP or a verb which is **finite** and which is therefore marked for tense.

term /tɜːm/ *n.* In RG, any one of the grammatical relations Subject, Direct Object or Indirect Object, regarded as fundamental in that framework and usually designated as 1, 2 and 3, respectively. Other relations are regarded as 'non-terms'.

terminal node /'tɜːmɪnl̩/ *n.* (also **leaf**) A node in a tree which dominates no material; this is usually a lexical item.

terminal symbol /'sɪmbl̩/ *n.* In a formal grammar employing the **rewrite rule** format, a symbol which cannot be rewritten by any of the rules in the grammar and which hence can only ever appear as a terminal node in a tree.

TG See **Transformational Grammar**.

TGG See under **Transformational Grammar**.

***that*-trace effects** /ðæt'treɪs ɪˌfekts/ *n. pl.* Another name for the phenomena covered by the **Complementizer–Gap Constraint**.

thematic relation /θɪ'mætɪk/ *n.* (also **thematic role**) 1. Traditionally, and still currently, the contribution made by some element of a sentence to the information content of that sentence. The most widely recognized thematic relations are **topic**, **comment** and **focus**.

2. In GB, another name for **theta role**. See the comment under **thematic structure** (sense 2).

thematic structure *n.* 1. The structure of a sentence seen from the point of view of the distribution of information within it. The most important thematic notions are **topic**, **comment** and **focus**. 2. In GB, the set of **theta roles** (**semantic roles**) assigned by a verb or predicate. An example is the thematic structure of the verb *kill*, represented as [1(external):Agent; 2(internal):Patient]. NOTE: this choice of terminology in GB is extremely unfortunate, to say the least, as it leads to immediate potential confusion with the long-established first sense.

theme /θiːm/ *n.* 1. In morphology, an older synonym for **base** (sense 1), now little used. 2. A synonym for **topic** (sense 1), contrasting with **rheme** (= **comment**). 3. The **semantic role** borne by an NP expressing an entity which is in a state or a location or which is undergoing motion, such as *the ball* in *The ball is dirty*, *The ball is on the table* and *She threw me the ball*. Theme is one of the **deep cases** recognized in Case Grammar. It is not easy to draw a line between Theme and Patient, and some analysts conflate the two.

theory of grammar /ˈθɪəri/ *n.* 1. The branch of linguistics which investigates the characterization of the grammars of natural languages, which tries to determine the properties which such grammars can have. 2. Any particular proposal as to the nature of possible grammars for natural languages. Among the most influential of such proposals are **Government–Binding Theory**, **Lexical-Functional Grammar** and **Generalized Phrase Structure Grammar**, but many others exist.

Theta Criterion /ˈθiːtə kraɪˌtɪəriən/ *n.* (also **θ-Criterion**) In GB, the requirement that the arguments of a verb in a syntactic structure and the theta roles required by the verb's lexical entry must match up on a one-to-one basis.

theta government *n.* In GB, one of the two instances of **proper government**; see the discussion under that entry.

theta role *n.* (also **θ-role**) In GB, the usual term for one of the **semantic roles** recognized in that framework and assigned by verbs and predicates to their arguments by the requirements of **Theta Theory**. The proponents of GB have been remarkably unforthcoming about precisely which theta roles are posited in the framework, but at least Agent, Patient and Goal are generally recognized, and some of the other semantic roles recognized in **Case Grammar** are at least occasionally invoked.

Theta Theory *n.* (also **θ-Theory**) In GB, the module which deals with the valency requirements of verbs. It incorporates a set of participant roles called **theta roles**, whose proper distribution in sentence structures is mediated chiefly by the **Projection Principle** and the **Theta Criterion**. Chomsky (1981).

third person /θɜːd/ *n.* That category of **person** which includes no reference to the speaker or to the addressee. The English pronouns *he*, *she*, *it* and *they* are all third person in reference, as are the overwhelming majority of noun phrases in all languages.

third-person imperative *n.* An **imperative** directed at someone other than the addressee; see examples under **jussive** (sense 2).

TMA /tiː em 'eɪ/ An abbreviation for 'tense–mood–aspect', often used when speaking in general terms of the (frequently interrelated) formal expression of these three grammatical categories.

tmesis /'tmiːsɪs/ *n.* Separation of the elements of a compound word by other material, as in *what things soever* for *whatsoever things*, or in *She took her dress off*, as opposed to *She took off her dress*.

to-**infinitive** /tuː/ *n.* A conventional label for an infinitival verb phrase preceded by the formative *to*, as in *Lisa wants to buy a BMW*. In traditional grammar, such a sequence as *to buy* was regarded as a single form, the so-called 'infinitive' of the verb *buy*, but this analysis is rejected by all contemporary theories of grammar: all possible tests point to the conclusion that the sequence *buy a BMW* is a constituent (a verb phrase), and hence to the conclusion that *to buy* is not a constituent of any kind. Cf. **bare infinitive**.

top–down /ˌtɒp 'daʊn/ *adj.* Denoting an approach to generating or parsing sentences in which one begins with the S node at the top, expands this into a suitable set of daughters, expands each of these into a further set of constituents, and so on, until the individual words are reached. Cf. **bottom–up**.

topic /'tɒpɪk/ *n.* 1. (also **theme**) That element of a sentence which is presented as already existing in the discourse and which the rest of the sentence (the **comment**) is in some sense 'about'. In English and in many other languages, the topic is most often realized as the grammatical subject in the unmarked case; the choice of a topic which is not the subject is usually accompanied by a marked construction of some kind. See examples under **topicalization**. 2. In Philippine languages, a conventional label for an overtly marked NP which exhibits some, but not all, of the typical properties of subjects and which contrasts in those languages with an **actor** (sense 2), an NP exhibiting the remaining subject properties. See Schachter (1976) for discussion.

topicalization /ˌtɒpɪkəlaɪˈzeɪʃn̩a/ *n.* The phenomenon in which some element of a sentence is singled out as the **topic** by the use of a marked construction. In English, this is done by preposing the topicalized element: [*This book*] *I can't recommend*; [*In the park*] *stood a bronze statue*.

topic-prominent language /ˈtɒpɪkˌprɒmɪnənt/ *n.* A language in which **topics** are overtly marked and play a prominent role in the grammatical organization of sentences, sometimes regarded as a typologically important notion. Chinese and Japanese are two well-known examples. Cf. **subject-prominent language**. Li and Thompson (1976).

***Tough*-Movement** /tʌf/ *n.* The phenomenon in which the underlying direct object of a verb in a complement of certain predicates is realized as the surface subject of that predicate. For example, the sentence *It is hard to please Lisa* can be alternatively realized as *Lisa is hard to please*, the latter structure illustrating *Tough*-Movement of the underlying direct object *Lisa*. The phenomenon was first discussed by Rosenbaum (1967); the name was coined by Postal (1971), and reflects the observation that most of the English predicates permitting it are semantic expressions of ease or difficulty, like *tough*, *hard* and *easy*. The name 'object-to-subject raising' is also occasionally found in the older literature.

toy grammar /tɔɪ/ See **grammar fragment**.

trace /treɪs/ *n.* 1. (*t*) In the REST and in GB, a putative empty category left behind in a particular location by the movement of some element out of that position. The use of traces allows a tree to 'remember' earlier stages of a derivation, and traces can be regarded as a formalization of certain aspects of the earlier **derivational constraints**. GB recognizes two types of traces: **NP-traces** and **WH-traces**; see examples under those entries. Chomsky (1975b). 2. In natural-language processing, a record of the steps involved in the construction by a parser of a parse for a particular input.

tractable /ˈtræktəbl̩/ *adj.* In complexity theory, denoting a problem or class of problems which can be solved using a reasonable amount of computational resources; specifically, in computational linguistics, denoting a grammar or class of grammars capable of serving as the basis of a **parser** which gives results in a reasonable amount of time. *Abstr. n.* **tractability** /træktə'bɪlɪti/.

traditional grammar /trə'dɪʃənl̩/ *n.* A label applied loosely to the entire body of grammatical description in Europe and America during the whole period before the rise of modern linguistics in the twentieth century, but particularly to the descriptions presented in school textbooks in the nineteenth and early twentieth centuries. The term is often used with clear pejorative connotations, reflecting the sometimes inadequate nature of traditional descriptions and the overtly **prescriptivist** orientation of the school texts, but it should not be forgotten that traditional grammar represents the fruits of more than two thousand years of serious grammatical investigation, or that many of the categories and analyses of traditional grammar have been incorporated with only minor modifications into our current theories of grammar. Certain contemporary approaches, such as that presented in Quirk *et al.* (1985), can also be characterized as traditional in their outlook, even though they are considerably more linguistically sophisticated than earlier traditional descriptions.

transducer /trænz'djuːsə/ *n.* A **transition network** which is capable of dealing with two or more strings simultaneously, and which can hence handle such tasks as comparison, translation and simultaneous generation.

transform /'trænsfɔːm/ *n.* A general term for any structure or string which is regarded as derived in some way from another structure or string regarded as more basic.

transformation /ˌtrænsfə'meɪʃn̩/ *n.* 1. In the work of Zellig Harris (notably Harris 1957), a formal, static, non-directional statement expressing a systematic relation between two sentence patterns regarded as linear strings of elements, such as between active and passive structures in English. In Harris's conception, neither structure is regarded as being more basic or as being derived from the other. 2. In the early work of Noam Chomsky and his associates, such as Chomsky (1957), a formal, directional statement expressing a systematic relation between two sentence patterns regarded as linear strings of elements, such as between active and passive structures in English. In this conception, one of the structures is regarded as basic and the other is regarded as derived from it by the action of the transformation, which is seen as an operation upon strings. 3. In the period from about 1965 to about 1976, a formal, directional statement expressing a systematic relation between two subtrees, in which one such subtree is regarded as basic and the other as derived from it by the action of the transformation, which is seen as an operation upon subtrees. In this conception, the structures of the subtrees involved are permitted to be specified in virtually unlimited detail. 4. Since about 1976, a formal, directional statement similar to that described in sense 3, but differing in that very severe constraints are placed upon the possible characterization of the subtrees involved, typically to the extent that nothing may be specified beyond the requirement that some category should be present somewhere both before and after the application of the transformation. NOTE: this brief attempt at characterizing the varying interpretations which have been attached to the term 'transformation' neglects a number of details, such as the existence in Chomsky (1957) of an entirely separate set of 'generalized' or 'double-base' transformations, which had the function of combining two separate sentences into a single sentence. *Adj.* **transformational**.

transformational cycle /trænsfə'meɪʃən̩/ *n.* (also **cycle**) In the **Standard Theory** of Transformational Grammar, the chief principle governing the application of most transformational rules to trees. Certain nodes, called **cyclic nodes**, are designated as having a special status, and the subtree dominated by a cyclic node is called a **cyclic domain**. When transformations are applied to a tree, all the rules subject to the cycle must apply first to the lowest cyclic domain in the tree, then to the next higher one, and so on, until the rules have applied to the highest available domain, each particular application of the rules to a particular domain being called a single **cycle**. Most usually, the categories S and NP are designated as cyclic nodes, though other suggestions have been made. The principle of the transformational cycle (usually called simply the 'cycle') is retained in GB, though it seems to be regarded as less central than formerly. In the Standard Theory, certain rules, notably WH-Movement, were regarded as exempt from the requirements of the cycle, but in GB all transformations are subject to it. Fillmore (1963).

Transformational Grammar *n.* (**TG**) (more fully, **Transformational Generative Grammar**, or **TGG**) A theory of grammar conceived by Noam Chomsky in the 1950s and elaborated by Chomsky and others during the succeeding decades. Chomsky's ideas were originally laid out in the massive and forbidding work *The Logical*

Structure of Linguistic Theory, completed in 1955 but not published until 1975. The theory was brought to the attention of linguists by Chomsky's 1957 book *Syntactic Structures*, which offered a brief and programmatic sketch of the framework. Chomsky's ideas were received with politeness but little interest by most established linguists; however, they were taken up with enormous enthusiasm by a younger generation of linguists, and within a few years TG had become the orthodox mainstream in American linguistics. The changeover was accompanied by a great deal of bitterness, as described in Newmeyer (1986). In 1965 Chomsky published *Aspects of the Theory of Syntax*, in which he presented a version of TG that was greatly revised from the early one and far more comprehensive; the theory described in *Aspects* quickly became known as the Standard Theory of TG. (For years, students of linguistics referred to the 1957 and 1965 books affectionately as 'The Old Testament' and 'The New Testament'.) TG was the first explicitly generative approach to grammar in modern times, and for many years the only one; it revolutionized the study of linguistics in general and of syntax in particular. TG was astonishingly powerful (see **Peters–Ritchie results**), but it proved to be remarkably bad at analysing a wide range of grammatical phenomena; in time, it underwent numerous and substantial modifications (the **Extended Standard Theory** and the **Revised Extended Standard Theory**), and it was finally supplanted in the early 1980s by its direct descendant **Government–Binding Theory**. For further information, see these terms and also **Standard Theory**, **Generative Semantics**. See Newmeyer (1986) for a historical account of the development of TG.

transition network /træn'zɪʃn̩/ *n.* A mode of graphical representation of possible sentence structures conceived purely of strings of elements. It consists of points, representing states, connected by directed arcs, representing transitions between states; each arc is typically, though not necessarily, labelled with a potential sentence element.

transition network grammar *n.* A type of **network grammar** which uses **transition networks** to exhibit the range of possible surface structures. See Woods (1970).

transitive /'trænsətɪv/ *adj.* Denoting a verb, or a clause containing such a verb, which subcategorizes for a direct object NP. Some transitive verbs absolutely require a direct object: *assassinate*, *destroy, undergo, prefer.* Others (**absolute transitives**) can optionally appear without an overt direct object; examples are *eat, understand, kill* and *paint.* A few transitive verbs can do this only by receiving a reflexive interpretation, such as *wash* and *undress.* Very many transitive verbs, the so-called **unaccusative** verbs, can be freely used as intransitives; examples are *sink, melt, roll* and *collapse.* Finally, some transitive verbs can be used intransitively with a passive interpretation in the **mediopassive** (or 'middle') construction; examples are *sell, wash* and *cook.* In English, most transitive verbs can undergo passivization, though there are a few apparent exceptions, such as *fit, suit* and *weigh* (one sense); the transitive status of these verbs is questionable.

transitive adjective *n.* An adjective which requires or permits a following complement, usually expressed in English by a prepositional phrase but in some other languages by a suitably case-inflected NP. Examples: *proud of her success, delighted with her results, devoid of significance, anxious about the decision, frightened of snakes.*

transitive verb phrase *n.* (**TVP**) A label sometimes applied to certain discontinuous sequences consisting of a verb and another element separated from it by a direct object NP, when these are regarded as forming discontinuous constituents. Examples: *Lisa [persuaded] me [to go]; She [made] the children [clean up the mess]; I [consider] her [a friend]; We want to [paint] the bathroom [white]; I [regard] her [as very clever]; She [inserted] a coin [into the slot].* See **right wrap.** Bach (1979).

translative /'trænslətɪv/ *n.* or *adj.* A case form occurring in some languages which typically expresses a state into which something changes, such as Finnish *vedeksi* 'into water' (*vesi* 'water') in *Lumi muuttui vedeksi* 'The snow turned to water'.

transparency /træns'pærənsi/ *n.* In GB, the property of a node which fails to act as a **barrier.** *Adj.* **transparent** /træns'pærənt/.

tree /triː/ *n.* 1. (also **tree diagram, tree structure, parse tree, phrase marker**) A graphical representation of the constituent structure of a sentence in which each constituent is represented by a node label which indicates its syntactic category and the immediate constituents of each category are linked to it by lines ('arcs'). Here is an example representing the sentence *Lisa bought that blue skirt in Paris*:

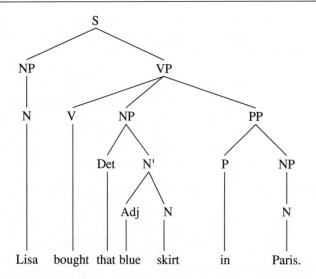

The formalization of trees is far from being a trivial matter. Trees as they are commonly conceived are subject to a number of conditions, the most important being the **Single Root Condition**, the **Single Mother Condition**, the **Exclusivity Condition** and the **Non-tangling Condition**. Other conceptions are possible, however; see McCawley (1982) for a formalization which rejects two of these conditions. Though American linguists had earlier used representations equivalent to trees with no labels on the nodes, the first modern trees to be published were those in Chomsky (1956, 1957), in which works trees were rejected as inadequate; this rejection resulted from the overriding concern of early generative linguists with representing sentences as sequences of **strings**. Though Eugene Nida (1960) made extensive use of trees with unlabelled nodes, trees continued to be very rare in syntactic work published in the early 1960s, and it is significant that E. R. Gammon, in his detailed 1963 survey of graphical representations of syntactic structure, makes no mention of trees in the modern sense (though he does include Nida's unlabelled trees). In 1964, Paul Postal (1964a) was still dismissing trees as in principle inferior to strings, though interestingly it was in that same year that Jerrold Katz and Postal published the first work to make extensive use of trees. Chomsky made very sparing use of trees in his influential 1965 book, but by this time trees were being widely used to represent sentence structure. Nevertheless, as late as 1968, James McCawley still found it necessary to protest against the prevailing tendency to regard trees as secondary to strings, and it has been only slowly and gradually that linguists have become sufficiently familiar with **graph theory** to realize that trees can be usefully regarded as primitives in their own right, and not as inferior reflections of strings. NOTE: McCawley (1988) points out that, strictly speaking, a **tree structure** (an abstract linguistic object) is distinct from a **tree diagram** (a graphical representation of a tree structure), but the distinction is rarely important in practice, and is usually ignored. 2. Any of various other graphical representations of sentence structure which are reminiscent of (botanical) trees, particularly a **dependency tree**.

Tree-Adjoining Grammar /ˈtriː ədʒɔɪnɪŋ/ *n.* (**TAG**) One of a class of formal grammars in which trees are taken as primitive elements which can be combined into larger structures. A TAG consists of a set of initial trees, each dominated by the symbol S, a set of auxiliary trees, each containing at the bottom another instance of the category which is its root, and the operation of adjunction, which inserts an auxiliary tree into another tree. Adjunction is performed by excising from the matrix tree a subtree dominated by a node X, replacing the excision by the auxiliary tree (which must be dominated by a node of category X) and inserting the excised subtree under the other instance of X in the auxiliary tree. Here is an example, showing the adjunction of the auxiliary tree B into the matrix tree A to produce the result C:

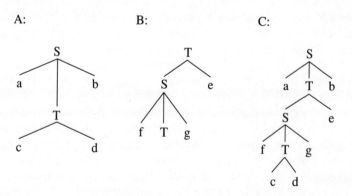

Dependencies are treated by joining two related nodes with an arc which is preserved in all adjunctions; such arcs may be 'stretched' without limit and may cross. Simple TAGs are weakly, but not strongly, equivalent to context-free grammars. TAGs enhanced by the use of local context-dependence for adjunction are 'mildly' context-sensitive; the languages they describe constitute a proper subset of the **indexed languages**, but they are still capable of handling **cross-serial dependencies**. TAGs were developed by Aravind Joshi and his colleagues, beginning with Joshi *et al.* (1975); convenient introductions are Joshi (1985, 1987).

tree-adjoining language *n.* (**TAL**) A language defined by a **tree-adjoining grammar**.

tree-adjunction *n.* The distinctive type of **adjunction** which is employed in **tree-adjoining grammars**.

tree diagram See **tree**.

tree-pruning /'pruːnɪŋ/ *n.* In classical TG, a convention by which any node in a tree which, as a result of the operation of transformations, came to dominate no material at all was automatically deleted from the tree. The convention was rendered redundant with the acceptance of the **Structure-Preservation Constraint** and the introduction of **traces**. Ross (1966).

tree structure See **tree**.

trial /'traɪəl/ *adj.* A distinct **number** category expressing exactly three entities. Very few languages have such a form, and clear examples are hard to find; the 'trial' traditionally imputed to Fijian, for instance, has turned out to be a **paucal**. However, the Austronesian language Larike has recently been found to have a true trial (Laidig and Laidig 1990).

triangle notation /'traɪæŋgl̩ nəʊˌteɪʃn̩/ *n.* A notational device used to simplify tree structures by omitting the details of some branch of the tree whose internal structure is not at issue. The suppressed subtree is represented merely by a triangle with a node label at the top and the lexical items at the bottom. See the example on p. 288.

trickling /'trɪklɪŋ/ See **percolation**.

trigger /'trɪgə/ *n.* Any element in a sentence which makes some requirement elsewhere in the sentence. For example, a subject NP which requires agreement in the verb is said to 'trigger' agreement in the verb, or to act as an agreement 'trigger', the verb being the agreement 'target'. Similarly, a verb or a preposition in a case-marking language may trigger a particular case form on its object NP.

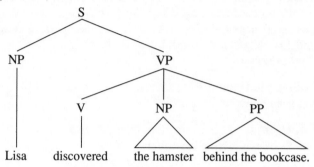

tuple /'tjuːpl̩/ See **n-tuple**.

Turing machine /'tjʊərɪŋ məˌʃiːn/ *n*. The most powerful type of **automaton**. Turing machines can be constructed which are capable of carrying out any kind of computation which can be performed on finite strings at all. See Partee *et al.* (1990) for a brief introduction. Turing machines were conceived by the British mathematician Alan Turing in the 1930s. See also **universal Turing machine**.

TVP See **transitive verb phrase**.

type 0 grammar /taɪp 'əʊ/ See **unrestricted grammar**. Chomsky (1959).

type 1 grammar /wʌn/ See **context-sensitive grammar**. Chomsky (1959).

type 2 grammar /tuː/ See **context-free grammar**. Chomsky (1959).

type 3 grammar /θriː/ See **regular grammar**. Chomsky (1959).

NOTE on the above: in some of his other early publications, Chomsky used a different numbering system from that given here, which is the one that has gained general acceptance.

typology /taɪˈpɒlədʒi/ *n*. The classification of languages in terms of their structural features. Morphologically based typologies were introduced very early in the nineteenth century, the most famous being the **isolating/agglutinating/inflecting** typology of Wilhelm von Humboldt. See Horne (1966) for a brief history of morphological typology. Syntactically based typologies date only from the 1960s, the pioneering work being that of Joseph Greenberg (1963) on **basic**

word order typology; since then, very many syntactic typologies have been proposed, involving such classes as **non-configurational**, **reference-dominated** and **topic-prominent** languages. See Croft (1990) for a summary. *Adj.* **typological** /taɪpə'lɒdʒɪkl̩/.

U

UCFG See **unordered context-free grammar**.

UCG See **Unification Categorial Grammar**.

UG /juː 'dʒiː/ 1. See **universal grammar**. 2. See **unification grammar**.

ultimate constituent /'ʌltɪmət/ *n.* Any element, normally a word or a morpheme, which is a constituent of some category and which cannot itself be broken down into smaller constituents.

Umlaut /'ʊmlaʊt/ *n.* A type of inflection by vowel change in the root, as in *tooth/teeth* and *mouse/mice*. Umlaut differs from **Ablaut** only in its historical source, and both terms are usually only used by linguists who are aware of the historical facts.

unaccusative /ʌnə'kjuːzətɪv/ *n.* or *adj.* Denoting an intransitive verb or predicate, or a construction involving one of these, whose subject NP is not an agent or (sometimes) not an actor, or, in some conceptions, whose surface subject is an underlying (direct) object. Typical unaccusatives are *die, melt, explode, fall down, exist, vanish, be small, be red* and many aspectual verbs. Unaccusative predicates exhibit distinctive grammatical behaviour in some languages, for example by taking postverbal subjects when other intransitives take preverbal subjects. Unaccusatives receive a distinctive grammatical analysis in certain theories of grammar, notably RG and GB. See Grimshaw (1987). Cf. **unergative**. Geoff Pullum (unpublished work); Perlmutter (1978). NOTE: recently the term 'ergative', popularized by Keyser and Roeper (1984), has been widely used for those unaccusatives which can be used both transitively and intransitively, particularly in GB; see the remarks under **ergative** (sense 5).

Unaccusative Hypothesis /haɪ'pɒθəsɪs/ *n.* The proposal that **unaccusative** verbs and predicates have an underlying direct object but no underlying subject. This analysis is accepted in certain derivational theories of grammar, notably RG and many versions of GB. The first explicit published proposal of this hypothesis was that of Perlmutter (1978), but the idea had earlier been put forward by

Paul Postal and, less explicitly, by others; see Pullum (1988) for a historical summary.

unbounded /ʌn'baʊndɪd/ *adj*. Denoting any phenomenon involving two elements which may be arbitrarily far apart. Cf. **local**.

unbounded dependency *n*. (also **long-distance dependency**) Any **dependency** (sense 1) the two ends of which may be separated by any arbitrary distance. The most familiar example in English is **WH-questions**, but **clefting**, **topicalization** and **relative clauses** may also involve unbounded dependencies. The existence of unbounded dependencies constitutes a major headache for syntactic analysis, and all sorts of special machinery have been postulated to deal with them. Classical TG made liberal use of the theoretically problematic **unbounded movement rules**. Both GB and GPSG reanalyse unbounded dependencies as consisting of chains of **local dependencies**, GB by using **traces** and GPSG by using its **slash** feature. LFG does something similar by using arcs in f-structures.

undergoer /ʌndə'gəʊə/ *n*. In RRG, a superordinate **semantic role** typically assumed by the lower-ranking (on a certain hierarchy) of two argument NPs in a clause. Cf. **actor**.

underlying /ʌndə'laɪɪŋ/ *adj*. Denoting any abstract representation which differs appreciably from the surface form it is posited as representing. Many (not all) linguists would argue that *won't*, for instance, is a realization of an underlying *will not*, or that *conjugable* realizes an underlying *conjugate* plus *-able*. Theories of grammar differ greatly in the extent to which they are willing to countenance underlying representations. Derivational theories of grammar like TG and GB often postulate highly abstract underlying representations of syntactic structure: for example, *Lisa seems to be happy* is often assumed to realize an underlying structure along the lines of *Tense seem [Lisa (to) be happy]*. The term 'underlying form' was first used by Bloomfield (1933:218), though Bloomfield's use was slightly different from the modern use.

underspecification /ˌʌndəspesɪfɪ'keɪʃn/ *n*. An analysis in which some feature value whose overt presence is required on the surface is left underlyingly unspecified and must therefore be provided by a default mechanism. *V*. **underspecify** /ʌndə'spesɪfaɪ/.

unergative /ˌʌn'ɜːgətɪv/ *n*. or *adj*. Denoting an intransitive verb or predicate whose subject is an agent NP or (sometimes) an actor NP. Typical unergatives are *run*, *jump*, *sing*, *dance*, *reside* and, less obviously, *receive*, *sleep* and *dream*. In English, unergatives often permit (pseudo-)passivization: *The fence was jumped over by the horse*; *This bed was slept in by George Washington*. Other intransitives (**unaccusatives**) do not permit passivization: **Mexico was vanished in by Ambrose Bierce*; **This bed was died in by George Washington*. Unergatives receive a distinctive grammatical analysis in certain theories of grammar, notably RG. Cf. **unaccusative**. Geoff Pullum (unpublished work); Perlmutter and Postal (1984).

ungrammatical /ʌngrəˈmætɪkl̩/ (also **deviant** (sense 1)) See **ill-formed**.

unification /ˌjuːnɪfɪˈkeɪʃn̩/ *n*. In various theories of grammar making use of explicit and well-developed systems of syntactic features, a formal procedure for combining two categories into one. Two categories can unify as long as they do not contain conflicting information; the resulting category contains all the information in each of the two initial categories. The concept of unification was introduced by Kay (1979); it has given rise to a whole family of grammatical frameworks collectively known as **unification grammars**, among which LFG, GPSG and HPSG are particularly prominent. In these frameworks unification plays a crucial role in passing information around nodes in trees so as to handle such phenomena as agreement.

Unification Categorial Grammar *n*. (UCG) An elaborated version of **Categorial Grammar** in which categories may be further specified by features and may contain variables which are instantiated by **unification** with other categories. Each expression in UCG belongs to a syntactic category and has a phonological form and a semantic representation.

unification grammar *n*. (UG) A generic label for any grammatical framework in which **unification** plays a prominent part. See Shieber (1986) for an introduction to unification grammars.

uniformity /juːnɪˈfɔːmɪti/ *n*. (also **uniform bar-level hypothesis**) In the X-bar system, the requirement that every maximal projection should carry the same number of bars. Implicit in early discussions of the X-bar system, uniformity was explicitly advocated by Jackendoff (1977), who proposed three bars for maximal projections. Uniformity is widely accepted, and at present there is something of a consensus in favour of two bars on maximal projections, though several linguists have argued for one bar, others have proposed larger numbers than three, and a few have rejected uniformity entirely. See Kornai and Pullum (1990) for discussion and references.

unisinistrality /ˌjuːnɪsɪnɪsˈtrælɪti/ *n.* The property of a **rewrite rule** which has exactly one category to the left of the arrow, identified by Manaster-Ramer and Kac (1990) as the central notion underlying most conceptions of the notion (**context-free) phrase structure rule**.

universal /ˌjuːnɪˈvɜːsl̩/ *n.* Any object or property which is posited as being present in the grammars of all languages, or at least as being 'available' to those grammars, even if not actually realized in some. Universals are sometimes divided into **formal universals**, having to do with the form a grammar can take, and **substantive universals**, having to do with the objects which can be present in a grammar; see examples under those entries. See also **absolute universal**, **relative universal**.

Universal Base Hypothesis /haɪˈpɒθəsɪs/ *n.* 1. In TG, the conjecture that the phrase structure rules of the **base** (sense 4) might be identical in the grammars of all languages, first suggested (rather inexplicitly) by Chomsky (1965:117). 2. Sometimes, by extension, any proposal that the principal structure-building rules might be the same in the grammars of all languages.

universal grammar *n.* (UG) Those grammatical properties which hold for the grammars of all existing and possible natural languages, which define the notion 'possible grammar'. The elucidation of the properties of universal grammar is one of the chief goals of syntactic theory.

universal Turing machine *n.* A particular **Turing machine** which is capable of emulating the behaviour of any other Turing machine. See Partee *et al.* (1990) for discussion.

unmarked form /ʌnˈmɑːktˌfɔːm/ *n.* That one of two or more competing forms which is in some sense the 'simplest' or 'most basic'. For examples and discussion, see under **marked form**.

unordered context-free grammar /ʌnˈɔːdəd/ *n.* (UCFG) A type of context-free grammar consisting only of **immediate dominance rules**, with no statements of linear precedence. A UCFG generates **wild trees**. Barton *et al.* (1987).

***un*passive** /ʌnˈpæsɪv/ *n.* or *adj.* An English construction in which the prefix *un-* is attached to the passive participle of a transitive verb, which may be accompanied by an agent phrase, as in *His arrival was unnoticed by the crowd*. *Un*passives present difficulties of analysis, since they have no corresponding active: **The crowd unnoticed his arrival*. They represent a clear case of morphosyntactic mismatch, since *unnoticed* is a morphological unit, while the syntactic structure required appears to be *un-[noticed by the crowd]*.

unproductive /ˌʌnprəˈdʌktɪv/ *adj.* Denoting an affix or a pattern which occurs in certain cases of word formation in a language but which cannot be extended to new instances of word formation. An English example is the suffix *-ship*, which occurs in such words as *kingship* and *friendship* but which cannot be extended to new instances. It is possible for an unproductive pattern to become productive; an example is the suffix *-wise*, which was until recently entirely confined to a handful of words like *clockwise*, *otherwise* and *lengthwise*, but which has now become productive: *moneywise*, *productionwise*, *healthwise* and so on.

unrestricted grammar /ʌnrɪˈstrɪktɪd/ *n.* (also **type 0 grammar**) A type of formal grammar employing the **rewrite rule** formalism in which any arbitrary string may be rewritten as any other arbitrary string, the only limitation being that there must be at least one non-null category on the left of the rule. The class of unrestricted grammars is the most powerful class of grammars which can be defined, and such grammars can weakly generate any system which can be generated at all. Unrestricted grammars are therefore equivalent to **Turing machines**, and are generally regarded as being vastly too powerful to be of any linguistic interest. See also **Peters–Ritchie results**. Chomsky (1959).

unspecified object deletion /ʌnˈspesɪfaɪd/ *n.* The phenomenon in which an intrinsically transitive verb appears in an apparently intransitive construction with no overt direct object, but the subject is still interpreted as the agent and some unspecified entity is understood as the direct object. Examples include *Lisa is eating*, *I've been painting for years*, *He drinks too much* and *He will kill again*. In English, only certain transitive verbs can be so used: **We were discussing*; **I often imagine*. See **absolute transitive** and cf. **mediopassive**.

untensed /ʌnˈtenst/ *adj.* A synonym for **non-finite**, one often preferred by generative grammarians.

up arrow /ˈʌp ærəʊ/ *n.* In LFG, the symbol ↑ , attached to a node in a tree to mark functional information passed up to the f-structure of the node's mother. See the examples under **functional schema**.

utterance /ˈʌtərəns/ *n.* A particular piece of speech produced by a particular individual on a particular occasion. The American structuralists regarded utterances as constituting the primary data for linguistic investigation; generative grammarians, in contrast, frequently attach little importance to utterances, regarding them as crude reflections at best of an underlying linguistic reality and preferring to focus their attention on introspections. See Labov (1975) for a critical discussion of the theoretical status of utterances.

V

V See **verb**.

valency /'veɪlənsi/ *n.* 1. The number of arguments for which a particular verb subcategorizes: *rain* is avalent (no arguments), *die* is monovalent (one argument), *describe* is divalent (two arguments) and *give* is trivalent (three arguments). 2. More generally, the subcategorization requirements of any lexical item. Tesnière (1959), from chemistry.

value /'væljuː/ See **feature value**.

variable /'vɛəriəbl̩/ *n.* 1. An algebraic symbol which may assume any one of a specified range of values. For example, in the X-bar system, the variable X is often used to represent the range of lexical categories which can be projected into phrasal categories, including at least Noun, Verb, Adjective and Preposition, and possibly other lexical categories. Similarly, the notation V^n, where the superscript n is a variable, may be used to represent any projection of the category Verb, with n typically ranging over the values 0, 1 and 2. 2. In GB, another name for a **WH-trace**.

vastness theorem See **NL vastness theorem**.

V-bar /viː'bɑː/ *n.* In the X-bar system, the one-bar projection of the lexical category Verb. Analyses differ as to whether this category should be recognized at all and also as to what, if it is recognized, it should correspond to. Early versions of the X-bar system usually identified V-bar with the category VP, with V-double-bar identified as S; however, a number of phenomena (fronting, deletion, etc.) strongly suggest that VP must be a maximal projection, and hence most current analyses simply deny the existence of the one-bar projection. Recent versions of GB recognize a distinction between V-bar and VP; the distinction, however, is not strongly motivated, and it appears that the label 'VP' is assigned somewhat arbitrarily to the highest V-bar in a tree. See Haegeman (1991) for discussion. Cf. **verb phrase**.

verb /vɜːb/ *n*. (**V**) One of the most important **lexical categories**, and one which is seemingly universal. The class of verbs in every language is both large and **open**. Grammatically speaking, verbs are most obviously distinguished by the fact that each verb typically requires the presence in its sentence of a specified set of NP **arguments**, each of which typically represents some particular **semantic role** and each of which may be required to appear in some particular grammatical form (particular case marking, particular preposition, etc.). In a very high proportion of languages, though not in all, verbs serve as the locus of marking for tense, and often also for aspect, mood and agreement in person and number with subjects and sometimes other argument NPs. Semantically, verbs most typically express actions, events and states of affairs: *eat*, *die*, *know*, *collapse*.

verbal noun /ˈvɜːbl̩/ *n*. Any form of a verb which can serve as the head of a noun phrase in a **nominalization**, particularly a **gerund**.

verb-complement clause *n*. A **complement clause** which serves as a complement to a verb, as in the examples *Lisa wants* [*to buy a BMW*] and *Lisa enjoys* [*watching rugby*].

verb-final /ˈfaɪnl̩/ *adj*. 1. Denoting a clause in which the verb occurs at the end. 2. Denoting a language in which this is the normal pattern, such as an **SOV language**.

verb-initial *adj*. 1. Denoting a clause in which the verb occurs at the beginning. 2. Denoting a language in which this is the normal pattern, such as a **VSO language**.

verb-medial *adj*. 1. Denoting a clause in which the verb occurs neither initially nor finally. 2. Denoting a language in which this is the normal pattern, such as an **SVO language**.

verb phrase *n*. (**VP**) 1. The syntactic category consisting of a verb and its complements and also, in most analyses, its adjuncts; this category most typically functions as a predicate. The category VP behaves like a maximal projection in several respects and accordingly, within the X-bar system, it is usually regarded as the maximal projection V″ of the lexical category Verb, though in some early versions of the X-bar system, VP was identified as the one-bar projection V′, V″ being identified with S. Virtually all analyses agree that, in a simple example such as *Lisa bought this skirt in Paris*, the sequence *bought this skirt in Paris* is a VP. There is less agreement, however, about constructions involving verb-complement VPs. In the example *Lisa has finished her essay*, the sequence *finished her essay* is regarded by all as a VP, but the longer sequence *has finished her essay* is treated differently in different frameworks. Many approaches, including GPSG, regard this as a larger VP with the structure [$_{VP}$V VP]. TG and the earlier versions of GB, however, did not even regard this sequence as a constituent, preferring instead to analyse the whole sentence as having the structure [$_S$NP AUX VP], with the auxiliary *has* located under the AUX node. Recent versions of GB, in contrast, treat *has finished her essay* as a constituent, but not as a VP; instead, it is regarded as I-bar, the one-bar projection of INFL, with the internal structure [$_{I'}$INFL VP] and *has* located under INFL. There is considerable controversy as to whether the category VP is universally present in languages, or even in configurational languages; in particular, languages with the basic word orders VSO and OSV are sometimes regarded as lacking the category. Cf. **V-bar**, **sentence** (sense 2), and see also **phantom category**. 2. In traditional grammar, a label often applied to a sequence of auxiliary and main verbs, such as *may have been writing* in *She may have been writing letters*. No contemporary theory of grammar recognizes such a sequence as constituting a constituent.

Verb Phrase Deletion See **VP deletion**.

verb-second phenomenon /vɜːb 'sekənd fə,nɒmɪnən/ *n.* (also **V2 phenomenon**) The phenomenon occurring in certain languages by which the finite verb must be the second element in the sentence. German is a well-known example: the German sentence *Er hat gestern mit meiner Frau getanzt* 'He danced with my wife yesterday', literally 'he has yesterday with my wife danced', can be recast as *Gestern hat er mit meiner Frau getanzt* or *Mit meiner Frau hat er gestern getanzt*, but any ordering that puts the finite verb in other than second position is ill-formed: **Gestern er hat mit meiner Frau getanzt*.

verb serialization /,sɪəriəlaɪ'zeɪʃn̩/ See **serial verb construction**.

verification system /verɪfɪ'keɪʃn̩/ See **evidential**.

version /'vɜːʒn̩/ *n.* An *ad hoc* label applied to various inflectional distinctions in the verbal morphologies of various languages. The term is most often used in connection with Georgian, in which it denotes certain inflectional distinctions of valency distinct from transitivity, but it is also applied, for example, to the distinctive affirmative and negative verb forms of Aleut. The term has no general linguistic significance.

vertical bar /ˌvɜːtɪkl̩ 'bɑː/ *n.* An **abbreviatory convention** serving to collapse two or more phrase structure rules or immediate dominance rules which rewrite the same category. For example, the schema C → | BCF | CG | BH | I serves to abbreviate the four rules C → BCF, C → CG, C → BH and C → I.

Visser's Generalization /'vɪsəz/ *n.* The observation that an object NP with a following complement can always and only be passivized if that complement relates to the object. For example, *We persuaded Lisa to go* and *We regarded Janet as incompetent* can be passivized to *Lisa was persuaded to go* and *Janet was regarded as incompetent*, while *We promised Lisa to go* and *Janet struck us as incompetent* cannot be passivized to **Lisa was promised to go* and **We were struck by Janet as incompetent*. Observation: Visser (1963–73, III:2.2118); name: Joan Bresnan (unpublished work, 1976); Bresnan (1982b).

vocative /'vɒkətɪv/ *n.* or *adj.* 1. A noun phrase used for direct address, such as *Lisa* in *Would you give me a hand, Lisa?* 2. A morphologically distinctive case form occurring in some languages and typically serving this function, such as Latin *amice*, vocative of *amicus* 'friend'.

voice /vɔɪs/ *n.* The grammatical category expressing the relationship between, on the one hand, the **participant roles** of the NP arguments of a verb and, on the other hand, the **grammatical relations** borne by those same NPs. In European languages, the most familiar voice contrast is that between **active** and **passive** constructions. In an active construction, such as *Lisa wrote this paper*, the grammatical subject typically expresses an agent, and the direct object typically expresses a patient. In the corresponding passive, as in *This paper was written by Lisa*, the subject is typically a patient and an oblique object, if present, expresses an agent. Other categories of voice exist in some languages, such as **middle, reflexive, causative** and **adjutative**, to name a few. See also **diathesis**, and see Shibatani (1988) for some discussion.

volitive /'vɒlɪtɪv/ *n.* or *adj.* The **mood** category which expresses a wish, sometimes subdivided into **desiderative** and **optative**. NOTE: the term 'boulomaic' is also found, but is rejected by Palmer (1986) as etymologically ill-formed.

VOS language /viː əʊ 'es/ *n.* A language whose basic word order is Verb–Object–Subject, such as Malagasy (Austronesian) or Terena (Arawakan). VOS languages are rare, the known examples all occurring in Mexico and Central America, in Amazonia or in the Austronesian family.

vowel alternation /'vaʊəl ɔːltə,neɪʃn̩/ See **Ablaut**.

VP See **verb phrase**.

VP deletion /viː 'piː/ *n.* (also **VP anaphora**) The phenomenon in which the second of two identical VPs occurring in a sentence can be suppressed. This phenomenon is usual in English. Thus, for example, the second clause in *Fenella won't have been writing letters, but Lisa will have been writing letters* would normally be reduced to one of . . . *but Lisa will have been* e, . . . *but Lisa will have* e or . . . *but Lisa will* e, the different possibilities reflecting the suppression of different VPs.

VP preposing *n.* The construction, occurring in certain circumstances in English, in which a verb phrase precedes the rest of its clause, as in *She had to pass that exam, and [pass it] she did.*

VSO language /viː es 'əʊ/ *n.* A language in which the normal order of elements in a sentence is Verb–Subject–Object, such as Welsh. VSO languages universally tend to exhibit certain typological characteristics, such as prepositions, absence of case systems and right-branching structures in which modifiers follow their heads, as first pointed out by Greenberg (1963).

W

Wackernagel's Law /'vɑːkəˌnɑːgl̩z ˌlɔː/ *n*. The statement that clitics tend universally to occupy the second position in a sentence, where 'second position' can mean either 'after the first word' or 'after the first phrase'. This tendency is illustrated by the following examples from Serbo-Croatian, in which *mi* and *je* are clitics:

Taj-mi-je   pesnik napisao knjigu.
that-me-Past poet   wrote   book
'That poet wrote me a book.'

Taj pesnik-mi-je napisao knjigu.
that poet-me-Past wrote   book
'That poet wrote me a book.'

Wackernagel (1892).

Wackernagel's position *n*. The second position in a sentence, in which clitics tend universally to occur.

***wanna*-contraction** /'wɒnə/ *n*. The phenomenon, observable in most North American varieties of English, by which the sequence *want to* (and other similar sequences) can be contracted if, and only if, there is no **gap** present between *want* and *to*. For example, *I want to do it* can be contracted to *I wanna do it*; *Lisa is the woman I want to see* e can be contracted to *Lisa is the woman I wanna see*; but *Lisa is the woman I want* e *to get the job* cannot be contracted to **Lisa is the woman I wanna get the job*. Such data have often been interpreted as providing direct evidence for the existence of gaps in syntactic structures; their significance was first pointed out by Lakoff (1970).

weak conditions of adequacy See under **adequacy**.

weak crossover /ˌwiːk/ *n*. The usual label for a set of **crossover phenomena** involving the coindexing with empty categories of NPs inside genitives, as in **Who$_i$ does his$_i$ mother love e$_i$?* This appears to be ill-formed, though perhaps less strongly so than cases of **strong crossover**, but the coindexing of *his* with the empty category is not prohibited by any of the principles of GB's Binding Theory. The **Leftness Condition** has been proposed to deal with cases of this sort.

weak equivalence /ɪˈkwɪvələns/ *n.* (also **string equivalence**) The relation which holds between two formal grammars which have the same **weak generative capacity**, i.e., which generate exactly the same set of strings. Cf. **strong equivalence**.

weak generative capacity *n.* Of a particular formal grammar or class of formal grammars, the set of sentences which it can generate when these are regarded merely as linear strings of elements, with no consideration of any structures which may be assigned; cf. **strong generative capacity**. Weak generative capacity might appear to be of limited linguistic interest, but, unlike strong generative capacity, it has proved to be mathematically tractable, and a number of interesting results have been proved which are certainly of linguistic interest. See the **Peters–Ritchie results**, **cross-serial dependencies**, **Ziff's law**, and see also the **Chomsky Hierarchy**.

Weak Lexicalist Hypothesis *n.* The view that inflectional and derivational morphology are fundamentally different, in that derivational morphology is handled in the lexicon, while inflectional morphology is treated in the syntax. Cf. **Strong Lexicalist Hypothesis**.

weak verb *n.* In certain languages, notably the Germanic languages (including English), a verb which inflects by affixation, rather than by internal vowel change: *love, loved, loved*; *smile, smiled, smiled*. Cf. **strong verb**.

weather *it* /weðər ˈɪt/ *n.* The dummy *it* that occurs as the subject of weather verbs, as in *It's raining*, when this is distinguished from other occurrences of dummy *it*, such as that occurring in extraposed structures.

weather verb *n.* A verb expressing a meteorological phenomenon, such as *rain, snow, drizzle* or *freeze*. Weather verbs, and weather expressions generally, universally tend to exhibit unusual syntactic properties; in English, for example, weather verbs require a non-referential dummy subject *it*, as in *It's raining*; they permit no other subjects at all, and are otherwise devoid of subcategorization requirements.

well-formed /wel ˈfɔːmd/ *adj.* (also **grammatical**) Denoting a structure, particularly a sentence, which is consistent with all the requirements of the grammar of a particular language. A well-formed sentence is not necessarily regarded as acceptable by native speakers; processing difficulties arising from length or complexity, or pragmatic implausibility, may induce a speaker to reject a proposed sentence which is incontrovertibly well-formed. As an example, consider the sentence *Flounder flounder badger badger flounder.* In any reasonable view of English syntax, this is well-formed, but speakers presented with it often reject it because the processing difficulties it presents are so formidable that they cannot understand it. (Cf. the identically formed sentence *Games children play include marbles*, which presents no such processing difficulties.)

WG See **Word Grammar**.

WH-cleft /ˌdʌbljʊ ˈeɪtʃ/ See **pseudo-cleft sentence**.

WH-dependency *n.* A type of **dependency** involving a **WH-item** and a corresponding gap, as illustrated by the example *Who$_i$ did you say Lisa was talking to* e$_i$? WH-dependencies in English and many other languages represent the outstanding examples of **unbounded dependencies**.

WH-Fronting See **WH-Movement**.

whimperative /wɪmˈperətɪv/ *n.* An utterance which has the form of a question but the force of a request or a command: *Could you open the door?*; *Would you sit down, please?*; *Can you hand me the pliers?* Sadock (1970).

WH-Island Constraint *n.* An **island constraint** which states that no dependency may reach inside an embedded WH-question, as illustrated by the example **Who did Lisa tell you when she had seen* e? Ross (1967).

WH-item /ˈaɪtm̩/ *n.* A lexical item which serves intrinsically to ask a question, such as *who, what, when, where, why* or *how* in English, or an equivalent item in another language. Such items have distinctive grammatical properties in many languages. NOTE: the name derives from the incidental fact that most of the English ones begin with the orthographic sequence *wh-*.

WH-Movement *n.* 1. (also **WH-Fronting, WH-Preposing, WH-Raising**) The phenomenon by which a **WH-item** appears in sentence-initial or clause-initial position, rather than in the 'logical' position typical of non-WH-items of the same category. Examples include *What did you say?*, *Who was Lisa talking to last night?*, *Did she tell you what she wanted?* and *The day when I met Lisa was a memorable one*. 2. In various derivational theories of grammar, the putative grammatical process by which a WH-item is moved from its underlying position to its surface position; in GB, this is regarded as a particular instance of **Alpha Movement**.

WH-question *n*. A question involving a **WH-item**, such as *What are you doing?* Cf. **yes–no question**.

WH-trace *n*. (also **variable**) In GB, the **empty category** which is left behind when a WH-item is moved and which is coindexed with the moved item, as illustrated by the derivation from *Lisa was talking to who?* of *Who$_i$ was Lisa talking to* e$_i$? See also **Binding Theory** and **A-bar binding**.

wild tree /waɪld/ *n*. A three-dimensional type of tree structure resembling a mobile, sometimes suggested as appropriate for free-word-order languages; constituent structure is assigned in a conventional manner within the tree, but there is no linear ordering of elements. Linearization is produced by some kind of additional machinery. One novel proposal is that the tree should cast a 'shadow' onto a flat surface, with different orientations of the tree producing different linear orders, corresponding to the different word orders possible in such a language; such a tree is called a 'Boas–Moulton mobile' by Nash (1980). While possibly appealing, the idea is very difficult to formalize in a useful way, and the suggestion has not been seriously taken up so far. Nash (1980).

word /wɜːd/ *n*. 1. A **lexical item**; a single item belonging to some **lexical category**, having an identifiable meaning or grammatical function and typically a fairly consistent phonological shape, though possibly exhibiting a certain amount of **inflectional** variation reflecting its grammatical environment in particular sentences. In this sense of the term 'word', such forms as *go*, *goes*, *went*, *going* and *gone* are all forms of a single word (lexical item) *go*. 2. A **word form**; a particular morphosyntactic form of a lexical item occurring in a particular grammatical environment. In this sense of the term 'word', the forms *go*, *goes*, *went*, *going* and *gone* are all different words; in fact, they are usually regarded as representing more than five word forms, since the *go* of *I go to Rome on Tuesday* and the *go* of *I want to go to Rome* are regarded as syntactically distinct in spite of their identical form, and much the same is true of *going* and *gone*, which also each represent two syntactically distinct forms. NOTE: it is essential to distinguish these two quite distinct senses of the term 'word'. Observe also that, outside grammar, the term 'word' is used in yet other senses, as in 'phonological word' and 'orthographic word'. 3. In formal language theory, a string that is a member of a language; a **sentence**.

Word-and-Paradigm *adj.* **(WP)** Denoting an approach to grammatical characterization which relies largely on the division of lexical items into inflectional classes and the presentation of **paradigms** (complete sets of inflected forms) for all classes. The WP approach is strongly characteristic of traditional descriptions of Latin and Ancient Greek, two highly inflecting languages which lend themselves to this sort of presentation, and is still used today by grammarians of a traditional persuasion, but it finds no more than incidental use within the mainstream of linguistics. Hockett (1954).

word class /klɑːs/ See **lexical category**.

word form /fɔːm/ *n.* (also **morphosyntactic word**) A particular morphosyntactic form of a lexical item occurring in certain grammatical environments. For example, singular *book* and plural *books* are two different word forms representing the single lexical item *book* in different grammatical circumstances; the same is true of *this* and *these* and of *eat*, *eats*, *ate*, *eating* and *eaten* (at least; in fact the *eat* of *I eat too much* and the *eat* of *I don't want to eat this* are usually regarded as distinct word forms, since they occur in quite different grammatical circumstances, and similarly for the *eaten* of *I have eaten the cake* and the *eaten* of *The cake has been eaten*). The complete set of word forms which can represent a single lexical item constitutes the **paradigm** of that lexical item; an example would be the full conjugation of a Spanish verb or the full declension of a Russian noun.

word formation /fɔːˈmeɪʃn̩/ *n.* A collective term for the set of processes by which lexical items are derived from, or related to, other lexical items. In English and in many other languages, the principal devices for forming words are **compounding** and **derivation** (sense 1), though other devices exist. The study of word formation is often referred to as **derivational morphology**; this is in general quite distinct from **inflectional morphology**. In most languages, word-formation processes constitute the most striking examples of **partially productive** processes. In the 1960s, there were attempts to integrate word formation into syntax, but these attempts were not very successful, and most current frameworks handle word formation by **lexical rules** contained within the **lexicon**, though some approaches postulate a distinct component of the grammar to deal with word formation.

word-formation rule *n*. In some approaches to word formation, a rule which is posited within that component of the grammar dealing with word formation and which serves to identify a (typically partially productive) process involved in the formation of certain words. A simple example is the following rule for the use of the English agent suffix *-er*, as in *writer*, *singer*, *rider*:

$$[[X]_V\#er]]_N \text{ 'one who Xs habitually, professionally . . .'}$$

Word-formation rules were first proposed by Halle (1973); they have been particularly developed by Aronoff (1976) and Scalise (1984).

Word Grammar *n*. (WG) A theory of grammar developed by Richard Hudson in the 1980s. WG is a version of **dependency grammar**: grammatical information is almost entirely contained in the lexical entries for particular lexical items, and syntax is seen as consisting primarily of rules for combining words. The central syntactic relation is that of **dependency** (sense 2) between words; constituent structure is not recognized except in the special case of coordinate structures. Statements about words and their properties form a complex network of propositions, and there is little emphasis upon the conventional division between different grammatical components. The framework is presented in Hudson (1984, 1990), which are the most accessible introductions.

word order /'ɔːdə/ *n*. 1. The linear sequence in which words occur in a constituent or in a sentence. 2. By extension, and very frequently, the order in which phrases occur in a sentence. See also **basic word order**, **free word order**.

WP See **Word-and-Paradigm**.

wrap /ræp/ *n*. A cover term for the operations of **right wrap** and **left wrap**.

W-star language /'dʌbljʊ stɑː/ *n*. (also **W* language**, **word-star language**) A synonym for **non-configurational language**; the term derives from the suggestion that such a language has as its only phrase structure rule the regular expression S → W*, where W represents the category 'word', most other syntactic machinery being located in lexical entries. Hale (1981).

X

XADJUNCT In LFG, the usual abbreviation for open adjunct (see under **open function**).

X-bar system /ˌeksˈbɑː/ *n.* (also **X-bar theory**) A system designed to formalize the traditional notion 'head of a construction' and to constrain the range of possible phrase structure rules. The heart of the system is the recognition that syntactic categories are **projected** from lexical items which are their lexical heads, so that the category Noun Phrase, for example, is analysed as differing from the category Noun primarily in respect of the value assigned to a feature conventionally called [BAR]: Noun is [NOUN] [BAR 0], while NP is [NOUN] [BAR 2] (variously abbreviated as $\overline{\overline{N}}$, N″ or N^2) in most current versions of the system), though some earlier proposals suggested [NOUN] [BAR 3]). The system obliges us to regard syntactic categories as **complex symbols**. Most versions of the system incorporate some kind of requirement that a category should have a head, a requirement which, in principle at least, greatly reduces the number of phrase structure rules which can be written. The X-bar system was first suggested, in a somewhat in-explicit form, by Zellig Harris (1951); it was revived by Noam Chomsky (1970), and developed by Joseph Emonds (1976) and more particularly by Ray Jackendoff (1977). Almost all contemporary theories of grammar incorporate some version of the system; that associated with GPSG, as presented in Gazdar *et al.* (1985), is particularly well articulated. A critical review of X-bar practice is given in Kornai and Pullum (1990); these authors identify six properties which are commonly associated with the X-bar system: **lexicality**, **succession**, **uniformity**, **maximality**, **centrality** and **optionality**.

XCOMP In LFG, the usual abbreviation for open complement (see under **open function**).

Y

yes–no question /ˌjes ˈnəʊ/ *n.* A question which expects one of the answers *yes* or *no*, such as *Are you coming?*; a **polar question**.

Yiddish fronting /ˈjɪdɪʃ/ *n.* A semi-jocular label applied to instances of the fronting of focused elements which are typical of the Yiddish-influenced English of the New York City area but which sound odd to most other speakers of English. Examples are *My brother-in-law he wants to be* and *A German car I should buy?*

Z

zero See **null element**.

zero anaphora /ˈzɪərəʊ/ *n*. The use of a **null element** as an **anaphor** (sense 1), as in *Lisa came in and* e *sat down*.

zero-bar category *n*. In the X-bar system, any category whose representation involves a bar value of zero; a **lexical category**.

zero-derivation *n*. (also **conversion**) A type of word formation in which a word is shifted from one lexical category to another without the use of any affixes: for example, the derivation of the verbs *access*, *network* and *napalm* from the corresponding nouns, of the verbs *goofproof* and *brown* from the corresponding adjectives and of the nouns *wash* and *delay* from the corresponding verbs.

zero determiner *n*. A determiner which, in some analyses, is postulated as being present in NPs containing no overt determiner, such as *spaghetti*, *Spanish wine* and *Lisa*. Such a determiner is assumed to be an actual lexical item which happens to have no phonetic content. This analysis has the advantage of greatly simplifying the syntactic representation of such noun phrases by making them identical in form to other NPs containing overt determiners.

zeugma /ˈzjuːgmə/ *n*. 1. A construction in which a word or phrase which is required to be construed with two other items can in fact only be correctly construed with one of them: *Have you ever wanted to learn French but didn't know how to go about it?* Cf. **anacoluthon**. 2. (also **syllepsis**) A coordinate structure in which each conjunct bears a semantically or grammatically different relation to the rest of the sentence, the result ranging from the comical to the ill-formed: *He took his hat and his leave*; *He watched the battle with interest and a telescope*; **Hiram picked up his rifle and off a British officer*.

Ziff's Law /ˈzɪfs ˌlɔː/ *n*. The observation that any arbitrary string can be interpreted as a proper name. This observation has potentially serious consequences for the investigation of **weak generative capacity**: such a string as *of admiration delaying after sees whistled* *never the go* would not normally be regarded as a string of English, but what is to stop us from interpreting it as a well-formed string of the form NP *sees* NP, with two rather strange proper names as the NPs? Ziff (1960); Manaster-Ramer (1988).

References

Abbreviations

BLS n	*Proceedings of the nth Annual Meeting of the Berkeley Linguistics Society*. Berkeley: University of California.
CLS n	*Papers from the nth Regional Meeting of the Chicago Linguistic Society*. Chicago: University of Chicago.
Comp. Ling.	*Computational Linguistics*
FL	*Foundations of Language*
IJAL	*International Journal of American Linguistics*
JL	*Journal of Linguistics*
LA	*Linguistic Analysis*
Lg.	*Language*
LI	*Linguistic Inquiry*
L & P	*Linguistics and Philosophy*
NELS n	*Proceedings of the nth Annual Meeting of the North Eastern Linguistic Society*
NLLT	*Natural Language and Linguistic Theory*
SL	*Studies in Language*

Aho, Alfred V. (1968) 'Indexed grammars – an extension of context-free grammars', *Journal of the Association for Computing Machinery* 15: 647–71.

Aissen, Judith (1977) 'The interaction of clause reduction and causative clause union in Spanish', *NELS* 7, Cambridge, MA: MIT Press. Revised version published as Judith Aissen and David Perlmutter, 'Clause reduction in Spanish', in David Perlmutter (ed.), *Studies in Relational Grammar 1*, Chicago: University of Chicago Press, 1983, pp. 360–403.

—— (1987) *Tzotzil Clause Structure*, Dordrecht: D. Reidel.

Aissen, Judith and David Perlmutter (1983) 'Clause reduction in Spanish', in David Perlmutter (ed.), *Studies in Relational Grammar 1*, Chicago: University of Chicago Press, pp. 360–403.

Ajdukiewicz, Kasimierz (1935) 'Die syntaktische Konnexität', *Studia Philosophica* 1: 1–27. Translated as 'Syntactic connexion' in Storrs

McCall (ed.), *Polish Logic 1920–1939*, Oxford: Oxford University Press, 1967.

Anderson, John M. (1971) *The Grammar of Case: towards a Localistic Theory*, Cambridge: Cambridge University Press.

Anderson, Henning (1989) 'Markedness theory – the first 150 years', in Olga M. Tomić (ed.), *Markedness in Synchrony and Diachrony*, Berlin: Mouton de Gruyter, pp. 1–46.

Anderson, Stephen A. (1985) 'Inflectional morphology', in Timothy Shopen (ed.), *Language Typology and Syntactic Description*, Vol. 3, Cambridge: Cambridge University Press, pp. 150–201.

Anderson, Stephen A. and Edward L. Keenan (1985) 'Deixis', in Timothy Shopen (ed.), *Language Typology and Syntactic Description*, Vol. 3, Cambridge: Cambridge University Press, pp. 259–308.

Andrews, Avery D. (1988) 'Lexical structure', in Frederick J. Newmeyer (ed.), *Linguistics: the Cambridge Survey*, Vol. I: *Linguistic Theory: Foundations*, Cambridge: Cambridge University Press, pp. 60–88.

Aoun, Joseph and Dominique Sportiche (1982) 'On the formal theory of government', *Linguistic Review* 2: 211–36.

Aronoff, Mark (1976) *Word Formation in Generative Grammar*, Cambridge, MA: MIT Press.

Austin, J. L. (1962) *How To Do Things with Words*, Oxford: Clarendon Press.

Bach, Emmon (1970) 'Problominalization', *LI* 1: 121–2.

—— (1974) *Syntactic Theory*, New York: Holt, Rinehart, Winston.

—— (1979) 'Control in Montague grammar', *LI* 10: 515–31.

Bach, Emmon and William Marsh (1987) 'An elementary proof of the Peters–Ritchie theorem', in Walter J. Savitch, Emmon Bach, William Marsh and Gila Safran-Naveh (eds), *The Formal Complexity of Natural Language*, Dordrecht: D. Reidel, pp. 41–55.

Bar-Hillel, Yehoshua (1953) 'A quasi-arithmetical notation of syntactic description'. *Lg.* 19: 47–58. Reprinted in Yehoshua Bar-Hillel, *Language and Information*, Reading, MA: Addison-Wesley, 1964, pp. 61–74.

—— (1964) *Language and Information*, Reading, MA: Addison-Wesley.

Bar-Hillel, Yehoshua, M. Perles and E. Shamir (1961) 'On formal properties of simple phrase structure grammars', *Zeitschrift für Phonetik, Sprachwissenschaft und Kommunikationsforschung* 14: 143–72. Reprinted in R. D. Luce, R. R. Bush and E. Galanter (eds), *Readings in Mathematical Psychology*, New York: John Wiley, 1965, pp. 75–104.

Barker, Chris and Geoffrey K. Pullum (1990) 'A theory of command relations', *L & P* 13: 1–34.

Barlow, Michael and Charles A. Ferguson (eds) (1988) *Agreement in Natural Language: Approaches, Theories, Descriptions*, Stanford, CA: CSLI.

Barton, G. E., R. C. Berwick and E. S. Ristad (1987) *Computational Complexity and Natural Language*, Cambridge, MA: MIT Press.

Baudoin de Courtenay, J. (1895) *Versuch einer Theorie der phonetischen Alternationen*, Strasbourg.

Bauer, Laurie (1983) *English Word-formation*, Cambridge: Cambridge University Press.

Berwick, Robert C. (1984) 'Strong generative capacity, weak generative capacity, and modern linguistic theories', *Comp. Ling.* 10: 189–202.

—— (1987) 'Computational complexity, mathematical linguistics, and linguistic theory', in Alexis Manaster-Ramer (ed.), *Mathematics of Language*, Amsterdam: John Benjamins, pp. 1–17.

Blake, Barry J. (1990) *Relational Grammar*, London: Routledge.

Blansitt, Edward L. (1984) 'Dechticaetiative and dative', in F. Plank (ed.), *Objects: towards a Theory of Grammatical Relations*, New York: Academic Press, pp. 127–50.

Bloomfield, Leonard (1917) *Tagalog Texts with Grammatical Analysis*, University of Illinois Studies in Language and Literature, Vol. 3, nos 2–4.

—— (1933) *Language*, New York: Holt, Rinehart, Winston.

Bolinger, Dwight (1977) *Meaning and Form*, London: Longman.

Bréal, Michel (1911) *Essai de semantique*, Paris: Hachette.

Bresnan, Joan W. (1976) 'On the form and functioning of transformations', *LI* 7: 3–40.

—— (1978) 'A realistic transformational grammar', in M. Halle, J. Bresnan and G. A. Miller (eds), *Linguistic Theory and Psychological Reality*, Cambridge, MA: MIT Press, pp. 1–59.

—— (1980) 'Polyadicity: Part I of a theory of lexical rules and representations', in T. Hoekstra, H. van der Hulst and M. Moortgat (eds), *Lexical Grammar*, Dordrecht: Foris, pp. 97–121.

—— (ed.) (1982a) *The Mental Representation of Grammatical Relations*, Cambridge, MA: MIT Press.

—— (1982b) 'Control and complementation', in J. Bresnan (ed.), *The Mental Representation of Grammatical Relations*, Cambridge, MA: MIT Press, pp. 292–390.

Bresnan, Joan W., Ronald M. Kaplan, Stanley Peters and Annie Zaenen (1982) 'Cross-serial dependencies in Dutch', *LI* 13: 613–35. Reprinted in Walter J. Savitch, Emmon Bach, William Marsh and Gila Safran-Naveh (eds), *The Formal Complexity of Natural Language*, Dordrecht: D. Reidel, pp. 286–319.

Burzio, Luigi (1981) 'Intransitive verbs and Italian auxiliaries', unpublished Ph.D. thesis, MIT.

—— (1986) *Italian Syntax: a Government–Binding Approach*, Dordrecht: D. Reidel.

Butler, Chris (1985) *Systemic Linguistics: Theory and Applications*, London: Batsford.

Bybee, Joan (1985) 'Diagrammatic iconicity in stem–inflection relations', in John Haiman (ed.), *Iconicity in Syntax*, Amsterdam: John Benjamins, pp. 11–48.

Cattell, Ray (1984) *Syntax and Semantics*, Vol. 17: *Composite Predicates in English*, New York: Academic Press.

Chafe, Wallace L. (1967) *Seneca Morphology and Dictionary* (Smithsonian Contributions to Anthropology, Vol. V), Washington, DC: Smithsonian Press.

—— (1970) *Meaning and the Structure of Language*, Chicago: University of Chicago Press.

Chapman, Nigel P. (1987) *LR Parsing: Theory and Practice*, Cambridge: Cambridge University Press.

Chomsky, Noam (1956) 'Three models for the description of language', *IRE Transactions on Information Theory*, Vol. IT-2, pp. 113–24. Reprinted in R. D. Luce, R. R. Bush and E. Galanter (eds), *Readings in Mathematical Psychology*, New York: John Wiley, 1965, pp. 105–24.

—— (1957) *Syntactic Structures*, The Hague: Mouton.

—— (1959) 'On certain formal properties of grammars', *Information and Control* 2: 137–67. Reprinted in R. D. Luce, R. R. Bush and E. Galanter (eds), *Readings in Mathematical Psychology*, New York: John Wiley, 1965, pp. 125–55.

—— (1961) 'Some methodological remarks on generative grammar', *Word* 17: 219–39.

—— (1964) *Current Issues in Linguistic Theory*, The Hague: Mouton.

—— (1965) *Aspects of the Theory of Syntax*, Cambridge, MA: MIT Press.

—— (1968) *Language and Mind*, New York: Harcourt Brace Jovanovich.

—— (1970) 'Remarks on nominalization', in R. A. Jacobs and P. S. Rosenbaum (eds), *Readings in English Transformational*

Grammar, Waltham, MA: Ginn, pp. 184–221. Reprinted in Noam Chomsky, *Studies on Semantics in Generative Grammar*, The Hague: Mouton, 1976, pp. 11–61.

—— (1971) 'Deep structure, surface structure and semantic interpretation', in R. Jakobson and S. Kawamoto (eds), *Studies in General and Oriental Linguistics Presented to Shiro Hattori on the Occasion of his Sixtieth Birthday*, Tokyo: TEC. Reprinted in Noam Chomsky, *Studies on Semantics in Generative Grammar*, The Hague: Mouton, 1976, pp. 62–119.

—— (1973) 'Conditions on transformations', in S. R. Anderson and P. Kiparsky (eds), *A Festschrift for Morris Halle*, New York: Holt, Rinehart, Winston, pp. 232–86. Reprinted in Noam Chomsky, *Essays on Form and Interpretation*, New York: North-Holland, pp. 81–160.

—— (1975a) [written 1955] *The Logical Structure of Linguistic Theory*, New York and London: Plenum Press.

—— (1975b) *Reflections on Language*, London: Fontana/Collins.

—— (1976) *Studies on Semantics in Generative Grammar*, The Hague: Mouton.

—— (1977a) 'On WH-movement', in P. W. Culicover, T. Wasow and A. Akmajian (eds), *Formal Syntax*, New York: Academic Press, pp. 71–132.

—— (1977b) *Essays on Form and Interpretation*, New York: North-Holland.

—— (1980) 'On binding', *LI* 11: 1–46. Reprinted in F. Heny (ed.), *Binding and Filtering*, London: Croom Helm, 1981, pp. 47–103.

—— (1981) *Lectures on Government and Binding*, Dordrecht: Foris.

—— (1986) *Barriers*, Cambridge, MA: MIT Press.

Chomsky, Noam and Howard Lasnik (1977) 'Filters and control', *LI* 8: 425–504.

Chung, Sandra (1976) 'An object-creating rule in Bahasa Indonesia', *LI* 7: 41–87.

Clark, Stephen W. (1863) *A Practical Grammar*, New York.

Comrie, Bernard (1975) 'The antiergative: Finland's answer to Basque', *CLS* 11: 112–21.

—— (1976) *Aspect*, Cambridge: Cambridge University Press.

—— (1978) 'Ergativity', in W. P. Lehmann (ed.), *Syntactic Typology*, Austin, TX: University of Texas Press, pp. 329–94.

—— (1981) *The Languages of the Soviet Union*, Cambridge: Cambridge University Press.

—— (1985a) *Tense*, Cambridge: Cambridge University Press.

—— (1985b) 'Causative verb formation and other verb-deriving morphology', in Timothy Shopen (ed.), *Language Typology and Syntactic Description*, Vol. 3, Cambridge: Cambridge University Press, pp. 309–48.

—— (1989) 'Some general properties of reference-tracking systems', in D. Arnold, M. Atkinson, J. Durand, C. Grover and L. Sadler (eds), *Essays on Grammatical Theory and Universal Grammar*, Oxford: Clarendon, pp. 37–51.

Comrie, Bernard and Sandra A. Thompson (1985) 'Lexical nominalization', in Timothy Shopen (ed.), *Language Typology and Syntactic Description*, Vol. 3, Cambridge: Cambridge University Press, pp. 349–98.

Cook, Walter A. (1969) *Introduction to Tagmemic Analysis*, London and New York: Holt, Rinehart, Winston.

Cooper, Robin (1980) 'Montague's syntax', in Edith A. Moravcsik and Jessica R. Wirth (eds), *Syntax and Semantics*, Vol. 13: *Current Approaches to Syntax*, New York: Academic Press, pp. 19–44.

Corbett, Greville (1991) *Gender*, Cambridge: Cambridge University Press.

Croft, William (1990) *Typology and Universals*, Cambridge: Cambridge University Press.

Culy, Christopher (1985) 'The complexity of the vocabulary of Bambara', *L & P* 8: 345–51. Reprinted in Walter J. Savitch, Emmon Bach, William Marsh and Gila Safran-Naveh (eds), *The Formal Complexity of Natural Language*, Dordrecht: D. Reidel, 1987, pp. 349–57.

Dahl, Östen (1985) *Tense and Aspect Systems*, Oxford: Blackwell.

Derbyshire, Desmond C. (1961) 'Hixkaryana (Carib) syntax structure', *IJAL* 27: 125–42; 226–36.

—— (1979) *Hixkaryana* (Lingua Descriptive Studies 1), Amsterdam: North-Holland.

Derbyshire, Desmond C. and Geoffrey K. Pullum (1981) 'Object-initial languages', *IJAL* 47: 192–214.

—— (1986) *Handbook of Amazonian Languages*, Vol. 1, Berlin: Mouton de Gruyter.

Dik, Simon C. (1978) *Functional Grammar*, Amsterdam: North-Holland.

—— (1980) 'Seventeen sentences: basic principles and application of Functional Grammar', in Edith A. Moravcsik and Jessica R. Wirth (eds), *Syntax and Semantics*, Vol. 13: *Current Approaches to Syntax*, New York: Academic Press, pp. 45–75.

Dirr, Adolf (1912) 'Rutulskij jazyk' ['The Rutul language'], *Sbornik Materialov dlya Opisaniya y Plemen Kavkaza* (Tbilisi) 42,3: 1–204.

Dixon, Robert M. W. (1972) *The Dyirbal Language of North Queensland*, Cambridge: Cambridge University Press.
— (ed.) (1976) *Grammatical Categories in Australian Languages*, Canberra: AIAS.
— (1977a) 'Where have all the adjectives gone?', *SL* 1: 19–80. Reprinted in R. M. W. Dixon, *Where Have All the Adjectives Gone? and Other Essays on Semantics and Syntax*, Berlin: Mouton, 1982, pp. 1–62.
— (1977b) *A Grammar of Yidiɲ*, Cambridge: Cambridge University Press.
— (1979) 'Ergativity'. *Lg.* 55: 59–138.
— (1980) *The Languages of Australia*, Cambridge: Cambridge University Press.
— (1986) 'Noun classes and noun classification in typological perspective', in C. G. Craig (ed.), *Noun Classes and Categorization*, Amsterdam: John Benjamins, pp. 105–12.
Downing, Bruce T. (1974) 'Correlative relative clauses in universal grammar', *Minnesota Working Papers in Linguistics*, no. 2, pp. 1–17.
Dowty, David (1979) *Word Meaning and Montague Grammar*, Dordrecht: D. Reidel.
Dowty, David, Lauri Karttunen and Arnold M. Zwicky (eds) (1985) *Natural Language Parsing*, Cambridge: Cambridge University Press.
Dressler, Wolfgang U. (1985) 'On the predictiveness of Natural Morphology', *JL* 21: 321–37.
Dryer, Matthew (1986) 'Primary objects, secondary objects and antidative', *Lg.* 62: 808–45.
Earley, Jay (1970) 'An efficient context-free parsing algorithm'. *Communications of the Association for Computing Machinery* 14: 453–60. Reprinted in Barbara J. Grosz, Karen S. Jones and Bonnie L. Webber (eds) *Readings in Natural Language Processing*, Los Altos, CA: Morgan Kaufmann, 1986, pp. 25–33.
Eckman, Fred R., Moravcsik, Edith A. and Wirth, Jessica R. (eds) (1986) *Markedness*, New York: Plenum Press.
Emonds, Joseph (1970) *Root and Structure-Preserving Transformations*, Bloomington, IN: Indiana University Linguistics Club.
— (1976) *A Transformational Approach to English Syntax: Root, Structure-Preserving, and Local Transformations*, New York: Academic Press.
Engdahl, Elisabet (1983) 'Parasitic gaps', *L & P* 6: 5–34.
Espinal, M. Teresa (1991) 'The representation of disjunct constitu-

ents', *Lg.* 67: 726–62.

Faltz, Leonard M. (1978) 'On indirect objects in universal syntax', *CLS* 14: 76–87.

Fillmore, Charles J. (1963) 'The position of embedding transformations in a grammar', *Word* 19: 208–31.

—— (1968) 'The case for case', in E. Bach and R. T. Harms (eds), *Universals in Linguistic Theory*, New York: North-Holland, pp. 1–88.

—— (1977) 'The case for case reopened', in P. Cole and J. M. Sadock (eds), *Syntax and Semantics*, Vol. 8: *Grammatical Relations*, New York: Academic Press, pp. 59–81.

Firth, J. R. (1951) *Papers in Linguistics, 1934–1951*, London: Oxford University Press.

Fodor, Jerry A. (1983) *The Modularity of Mind*, Cambridge, MA: MIT Press.

Fodor, Jerry A. and Jerrold J. Katz (eds) (1964) *The Structure of Language: Readings in the Philosophy of Language*, Englewood Cliffs, NJ: Prentice-Hall.

Foley, William A. (1980) 'Toward a universal typology of the noun phrase', *SL* 4: 171–99.

—— (1986) *The Papuan Languages of New Guinea*, Cambridge: Cambridge University Press.

Foley, William A. and Robert D. Van Valin (1984) *Functional Syntax and Universal Grammar*, Cambridge: Cambridge University Press.

Fowler, H. W. (1965) *A Dictionary of Modern English Usage*, Oxford: Oxford University Press.

Fowler, H. W. and F. G. Fowler (1906) *The King's English*, Oxford: Clarendon Press.

Fries, Charles C. (1952) *The Structure of English: an Introduction to the Construction of English Sentences*, New York: Harcourt, Brace.

Gammon, E. R. (1963) 'On representing syntactic structure', *Lg.* 39: 369–97.

Garey, H. B. (1957) 'Verbal aspect in French', *Lg.* 33: 91–110.

Gazdar, Gerald (1982) 'Phrase structure grammar', in Pauline Jacobson and Geoffrey K. Pullum (eds), *The Nature of Syntactic Representation*, Dordrecht: D. Reidel, pp. 131–86. Reprinted in J. Kulas, J. H. Fetzer and T. L. Rankin (eds), *Philosophy, Language and Artificial Intelligence*, Dordrecht: Kluwer, 1988, pp. 163–218.

—— (1985) *Applicability of Indexed Grammars to Natural Languages* (Report no. CSLI-85-34), Stanford, CA: CSLI.

Gazdar, Gerald, Ewan Klein, Geoffrey K. Pullum and Ivan A. Sag

(1985) *Generalized Phrase Structure Grammar*, Oxford: Blackwell.

Gazdar, Gerald and Geoffrey K. Pullum (1981) 'Subcategorization, constituent order and the notion "head" ', in M. Moortgat, H. van der Hulst and T. Hoekstra (eds), *The Scope of Lexical Rules*, Dordrecht: Foris, pp. 107–23.

—— (1985) 'Computationally relevant properties of natural languages and their grammars', *New Generation Computing* 3: 273–306. Reprinted in Walter J. Savitch, Emmon Bach, William Marsh and Gila Safran-Naveh (eds), *The Formal Complexity of Natural Language*, Dordrecht: D. Reidel, 1987, pp. 387–437.

Gazdar, Gerald, Geoffrey K. Pullum, Robert Carpenter, Ewan Klein, Thomas E. Hukari and Robert D. Levine (1988) 'Category structures', *Comp. Ling.* 14: 1–19.

Gazdar, Gerald and Ivan A. Sag (1981) 'Passive and reflexives in phrase structure grammar', in J. Groenendijk, T. Janssen and M. Stokhof (eds), *Formal Methods in the Study of Language*, Amsterdam: Mathematical Centre Tracts, pp. 131–52.

Givón, Talmy (1980) 'The binding hierarchy and the typology of complements', *SL* 4: 333–77.

Gleitman, Lila R. (1965) 'Coordinating conjunctions in English', *Lg.* 41: 260–93.

Gotteri, Nigel (1984) 'The evasive neuter in Polish', in F. E. Knowles and J. I. Press (eds), *Papers in Slavonic Linguistics*, Vol. II, Birmingham: University of Aston, pp. 1–8.

Grady, Michael (1965) 'The medio-passive voice in modern English', *Word* 21: 270–2.

Greenberg, Joseph H. (1963) 'Some universals of grammar with particular reference to the order of meaningful elements', in Joseph H. Greenberg (ed.), *Universals of Grammar*, Cambridge, MA: MIT Press (2nd edn 1966), pp. 73–113.

Grimm, Jakob (1819) *Deutsche Grammatik*,

Grimshaw, Jane (1987) 'Unaccusatives – an overview', *NELS* 17, 1: Amherst, MA: GLSA, University of Massachusetts, pp. 244–58.

Grinder, John T. (1970) 'Super Equi-NP Deletion', *CLS* 6: 297–317.

Grinder, John T. and Paul M. Postal (1971) 'Missing antecedents', *LI* 2: 269–312.

Grosz, Barbara J., Karen S. Jones and Bonnie L. Webber (eds) (1986) *Readings in Natural Language Processing*, Los Altos, CA: Morgan Kaufmann.

Gruber, Jeffrey (1965) 'Studies in lexical relations', unpublished Ph.D. thesis, MIT.

—— (1967) *Functions of the Lexicon in Formal Descriptive Grammars*

(TM/3770/000/00), Santa Monica, CA: System Development Corporation.

Haegeman, Liliane (1991) *Introduction to Government and Binding Theory*, Oxford: Blackwell.

Hagège, Claude (1974) 'Les pronoms logophoriques', *Bulletin de la Société de Linguistique de Paris* 69: 307–61.

—— (1976) 'Relative clause center-embedding and comprehensibility', *LI* 7: 198–201.

Haiman, John (ed.) (1985) *Iconicity in Syntax*, Amsterdam: John Benjamins.

Hale, Kenneth (1976) 'The adjoined relative clause in Australia', in Robert M. W. Dixon (ed.), *Grammatical Categories in Australian Languages*, Canberra: AIAS, pp. 78–105.

—— (1981) *On the Position of Walbiri in a Typology of the Base*, Bloomington, IN: Indiana University Linguistics Club.

Halle, Morris (1973) 'Prolegomena to a theory of word-formation', *LI* 4: 3–16.

Halle, Morris, Joan W. Bresnan and George A. Miller (eds) (1978) *Linguistic Theory and Psychological Reality*, Cambridge, MA: MIT Press.

Halliday, Michael A. K. (1961) 'Categories of the theory of grammar', *Word* 17: 241–92.

—— (1967) 'Notes on transitivity and theme in English', *JL* 3: 37–81; 199–244; (1968) *JL* 4: 179–215.

—— (1976) 'Types of process', in G. R. Kress (ed.), *Halliday: System and Function in Language*, London: Oxford University Press, pp. 159–73.

Halvorsen, Per-Kristian and William A. Ladusaw (1979) 'Montague's "Universal Grammar": an introduction for the linguist', *L & P* 3: 185–223.

Harel, David (1987) *Algorithmics: the Spirit of Computing*, Wokingham: Addison-Wesley.

Harman, Gilbert (1963) 'Generative grammars without transformation rules: a defense of phrase structure', *Lg.* 39: 597–616.

Harris, Zellig S. (1951) *Methods in Structural Linguistics*, Chicago: University of Chicago Press.

—— (1957) 'Co-occurrence and transformation in linguistic structure', *Lg.* 33: 283–340. Reprinted in H. Hiz (ed.), *Papers in Syntax*, Dordrecht: D. Reidel, 1981, pp. 143–210.

Hawkins, John A. (1983) *Word Order Universals*, New York: Academic Press.

Heath, Jeffrey (1975) 'Some functional relationships in grammar',

Lg. 51: 89–104.

—— (1986) 'Syntactic and lexical aspects of nonconfigurationality in Nunggubuyu (Australia)', *NLLT* 4: 375–408.

Heny, Frank (1979) Review of Chomsky, *The Logical Structure of Linguistic Theory*, *Synthèse* 40: 317–52.

Hill, Archibald A. (1958) *Introduction to Linguistic Structures*, New York: Harcourt Brace Jovanovich.

Hockett, Charles F. (1947) 'Problems of morphemic analysis', *Lg.* 23: 321–43. Reprinted in Martin Joos (ed.), *Readings in Linguistics*, Vol. I, Chicago: University of Chicago Press, 1957, pp. 229–42.

—— (1954) 'Two models of grammatical description', *Word* 10: 210–33.

—— (1961) 'Grammar for the hearer', in R. Jakobson (ed.), *Proceedings of Symposia in Applied Mathematics*, Vol. XII: *Structure of Language and its Mathematical Aspects*, Providence, RI: American Mathematical Society, pp. 220–36.

Hopper, Paul J. and Sandra A. Thompson (1980) 'Transitivity in grammar and discourse', *Lg.* 56: 251–99.

Horn, Laurence R. (1989) *A Natural History of Negation*, Chicago: University of Chicago Press.

Horne, Kibbey M. (1966) *Language Typology: Nineteenth and Twentieth Century Views*, Washington, DC: Georgetown University Press.

Horrocks, Geoffrey (1987) *Generative Grammar*, London: Longman.

Householder, Fred W. (1973) 'On arguments from asterisks', *FL* 10: 365–76.

Huck, Geoffrey J. and Almerindo E. Ojeda (eds) (1987) *Syntax and Semantics* Vol. 20: *Discontinuous Constituency*, New York: Academic Press.

Huddleston, Rodney D. (1972) 'The development of a non-process model in American structural linguistics', *Lingua* 30: 333–84.

—— (1976) 'Some theoretical issues in the description of the English verb', *Lingua* 40: 331–83.

Hudson, Richard A. (1976) *Arguments for a Non-Transformational Grammar*, Chicago: University of Chicago Press.

—— (1984) *Word Grammar*, Oxford: Blackwell.

—— (1990) *English Word Grammar*, Oxford: Blackwell.

Huybregts, M. A. C. (1984) 'The weak inadequacy of context-free phrase structure grammars', in G. de Haan, M. Trommelen and W. Zonneveld (eds), *Van Periferie naar Kern*, Dordrecht: Foris.

Jackendoff, Ray S. (1972) *Semantic Interpretation in Generative Grammar*, Cambridge, MA: MIT Press.

—— (1977) *X̄ Syntax: a Study of Phrase Structure*, Cambridge, MA: MIT Press.

Jacobsen, William H. (1967) 'Switch-reference in Hokan-Coahuiltecan', in D. Hymes and W. Bittle (eds), *Studies in Southwestern Ethnolinguistics*, The Hague: Mouton, pp. 238–63.

—— (1979) 'Why does Washo lack a passive?', in F. Plank (ed.), *Ergativity: towards a Theory of Grammatical Relations*, London: Academic Press, pp. 117–43.

Jacobson, Pauline and Geoffrey K. Pullum (eds) (1982) *The Nature of Syntactic Representation*, Dordrecht: D. Reidel.

Jakobson, Roman (1971) 'Shifters, verbal categories, and the Russian verb', in R. Jakobson, *Selected Writings*, Vol. 2, The Hague: Mouton, pp. 130–47.

Jespersen, Otto (1924) *The Philosophy of Grammar*, London: Allen & Unwin.

—— (1933) *Essentials of English Grammar*, London: Allen & Unwin.

—— (1937) *Analytic Syntax*, London: Allen & Unwin.

—— (1961) (originally 1909–49) *A Modern English Grammar on Historical Principles*, London: Allen & Unwin.

Johnson, David E. and Paul M. Postal (1980) *Arc Pair Grammar*, Princeton, NJ: Princeton University Press.

Jones, Linda K. (1980) 'A synopsis of Tagmemics', in Edith A. Moravcsik and Jessica R. Wirth (eds), *Syntax and Semantics*, Vol. 13: *Current Approaches to Syntax*, New York: Academic Press, pp. 77–96.

Joos, Martin (ed.) (1957) *Readings in Linguistics*, Vol. I, Chicago: University of Chicago Press.

Joshi, Aravind K. (1983) 'Some formal results about Tree Adjunct Grammars', *Proceedings of the Twenty-first Annual Meeting of the Association for Computational Linguistics*, Morristown, NJ: Association for Computational Linguistics.

—— (1985) 'Tree adjoining grammars: How much context-sensitivity is required to provide reasonable structural descriptions?' in David Dowty, Lauri Karttunen and Arnold M. Zwicky (eds), *Natural Language Parsing*, Cambridge: Cambridge University Press, pp. 206–50.

—— (1987) 'An introduction to tree adjoining grammars', in Alexis Manaster-Ramer (ed.), *Mathematics of Language*, Amsterdam: John Benjamins, pp. 87–114.

Joshi, Aravind K., L. Levy and M. Takahashi (1975) 'Tree adjunct grammars', *Journal of the Computer and System Sciences* 10: 136–63.

Kac, Michael B. (1975) *Corepresentation of Grammatical Structure*, London: Croom Helm.

—— (1980) 'Corepresentational Grammar', in Edith A. Moravcsik and Jessica R. Wirth (eds), *Syntax and Semantics*, Vol. 13: *Current Approaches to Syntax*, New York: Academic Press, pp. 97–116.

Kac, Michael B., Alexis Manaster-Ramer and William C. Rounds (1987) 'Simultaneous-distributive coordination and context-freeness', *Comp. Ling.* 13: 25–30.

Kaplan, Ronald M. and Joan W. Bresnan (1982) 'Lexical-functional grammar: a formal system for grammatical representation', in Joan W. Bresnan (ed.), *The Mental Representation of Grammatical Relations*, Cambridge, MA: MIT Press, pp. 173–281.

Katz, Jerrold J. and Jerry A. Fodor (1963) 'The structure of a semantic theory', *Lg.* 39: 170–210. Reprinted in Jerry A. Fodor and Jerrold J. Katz (eds), *The Structure of Language: Readings in the Philosophy of Language*, Englewood Cliffs, NJ: Prentice-Hall, 1964, pp. 479–518.

Katz, Jerrold J. and Paul M. Postal (1964) *An Integrated Theory of Linguistic Descriptions*, Cambridge, MA: MIT Press.

Kay, Martin (1979) 'Functional grammar', *BLS* 5: 142–58.

—— (1985) 'Parsing in Functional Unification Grammar', in David Dowty, Lauri Karttunen and Arnold M. Zwicky (eds), *Natural Language Parsing*, Cambridge: Cambridge University Press, pp. 251–78. Reprinted in Barbara J. Grosz, Karen S. Jones and Bonnie L. Webber (eds), *Readings in Natural Language Processing*, Los Altos, CA: Morgan Kaufmann, 1986, pp. 125–38.

—— (1984) 'Functional Unification Grammar: a formalism for machine translation', in *Proceedings of the Tenth International Conference on Computational Linguistics: Coling 84*, Menlo Park, CA: Association for Computational Linguistics, pp. 75–8.

Keenan, Edward L. (1974) 'The functional principle: generalizing the notion of "subject of" ', *CLS* 10: 298–309. Reprinted in Edward L. Keenan, *Universal Grammar: Fifteen Essays*, London: Croom Helm, 1987, pp. 361–74.

—— (1976a) 'Towards a universal definition of "subject" ', in Charles N. Li (ed.), *Subject and Topic*, New York: Academic Press, pp. 247–302. Reprinted in Edward L. Keenan, *Universal Grammar: Fifteen Essays*, London: Croom Helm, 1987, pp. 89–120.

—— (1976b) 'Remarkable subjects in Malagasy', in Charles N. Li (ed.), *Subject and Topic*, New York: Academic Press, pp. 303–33.

—— (1985a) 'Passive in the world's languages', in Timothy Shopen (ed.), *Language Typology and Syntactic Description*, Vol. 1, Cambridge: Cambridge University Press, pp. 243–81.

—— (1985b) 'Relative clauses', in Timothy Shopen (ed.), *Language Typology and Syntactic Description*, Vol. 2, Cambridge: Cambridge University Press, pp. 141–70.

—— (1987) *Universal Grammar: Fifteen Essays*, London: Croom Helm.

Keenan, Edward L. and Bernard Comrie (1977) 'Noun phrase accessibility and universal grammar', *LI* 8: 63–99. Reprinted in Edward L. Keenan *Universal Grammar: Fifteen Essays*, London: Croom Helm, 1987, pp. 1–45.

Keyser, Samuel J. and Thomas Roeper (1984) 'On the middle and ergative constructions in English', *LI* 15: 381–416.

Kisseberth, Charles W. and Mohammad Imam Abasheikh (1977) 'The object relationship in Chi-Mwi:ni, a Bantu language', in P. Cole and J. M. Sadock (eds), *Syntax and Semantics*, Vol. 8: *Grammatical Relations*, New York: Academic Press, pp. 179–218.

Kleene, S. C. (1956) 'Representation of events in nerve nets and finite automata', *Automata Studies*, Princeton, NJ: Princeton University Press, pp. 3–42.

Klima, Edward S. (1964) 'Negation in English', in Jerry A. Fodor and Jerrold J. Katz (eds), *The Structure of Language: Readings in the Philosophy of Language*, Englewood Cliffs, NJ: Prentice-Hall, pp. 246–323.

Koopman, Hilda and Dominique Sportiche (1982) 'Variables and the bijection principle', *The Linguistic Review* 2: 139–60.

Kornai, András and Geoffrey K. Pullum (1990) 'The X-bar theory of phrase structure', *Lg.* 66: 24–50.

Kulas, J., J. H. Fetzer and T. L. Rankin (eds) (1988) *Philosophy, Language and Artificial Intelligence*, Dordrecht: Kluwer.

Kuryłowicz, Jerzy (1946) 'Ergativnost′ i stadial′nost′ v jazyke', *Izvestija Akademii Nauk Sojuza SSR. Fak. Lit. i Jaz.* 5: 387–93. Reprinted in *Esquisses linguistiques*, Polska Akademii Nauk, Komitet Jezykoznawstwa, Prace jezykonawcze 19. Wroklaw and Kraków: PAN, 1960, pp. 95–103. English translation by P. Culicover: 'Ergativeness and the stadial theory of linguistic development', in *The Study of Man* 2: 1–21, University of California, Irvine, 1973.

Labov, William (1975) *What Is a Linguistic Fact?* Lisse: Peter de Ridder Press.

Ladusaw, William A. (1988) 'A proposed distinction between *levels* and *strata*', in The Linguistic Society of Korea (eds), *Linguistics in the Morning Calm: Selected Papers from SICOL-1986*, Seoul: Hanshin, pp. 37–51.

Laidig, Wyn D. and Carol J. Laidig (1990) 'Larike pronouns: duals and trials in a central Moluccan language', *Oceanic Linguistics* 29: 87–109.

Lakoff, George (1970) 'Global rules', *Lg.* 46: 627–39.

—— (1973) 'Fuzzy grammar and the performance/competence terminology game', *CLS* 9: 271–91.

—— (1976) [written 1963] 'Toward generative semantics', in James D. McCawley (ed.), *Syntax and Semantics*, Vol. 7: *Notes from the Linguistic Underground*, New York: Academic Press, pp. 43–61.

—— (1977) 'Linguistic Gestalts', *CLS* 13: 236–87.

Lamb, Sidney M. (1966) *Outline of Stratificational Grammar*, Washington, DC: Georgetown University Press.

Langacker, Ronald W. (1969) 'On pronominalization and the chain of command', in D. A. Reibel and S. A. Schane (eds), *Modern Studies in English*, Englewood Cliffs, NJ: Prentice-Hall, pp. 160–86.

—— (1987) *Foundations of Cognitive Grammar*, Vol. I: *Theoretical Prerequisites*, Stanford, CA: Stanford University Press.

—— (1988) 'An overview of cognitive grammar', in B. Rudzka-Ostyn (ed.), *Topics in Cognitive Linguistics*, Amsterdam: John Benjamins, pp. 3–48.

—— (1991) *Foundations of Cognitive Grammar*, Vol. II: *Descriptive Applications*, Stanford, CA: Stanford University Press.

Langendoen, D. Terence and Paul M. Postal (1984) *The Vastness of Natural Languages*, Oxford: Blackwell.

Lasnik, Howard (1976) 'Remarks on coreference', *LA* 2: 1–22.

Lepschy, Giulio C. (1982) *A Survey of Structural Linguistics*, 2nd edn, London: André Deutsch.

Leśniewski, S. (1929) 'Grundzüge eines neuen Systems der Grundlagen der Mathematik', *Fundamenta Mathematicae* 14: 1–81.

Levin, Beth and Malka Rappaport (1986) 'The formation of adjectival passives', *LI* 17: 623–61.

Lewis, G. L. (1967) *Turkish Grammar*, Oxford: Clarendon Press.

Li, Charles N. (ed.) (1976) *Subject and Topic*, New York: Academic Press.

Li, Charles N. and Sandra A. Thompson (1976) 'Subject and topic: a new typology of language', in Charles N. Li (ed.), *Subject and Topic*, New York: Academic Press, pp. 457–89.

Lieber, Rochelle (1980) 'The organization of the lexicon', unpublished Ph.D. thesis, MIT.

—— (1982) 'Allomorphy', *LA* 10: 27–52.

Lockwood, David G. (1972) *Introduction to Stratificational Linguistics*, New York: Harcourt Brace Jovanovich.

Luce, R. D., R. R. Bush and E. Galanter (eds) (1965) *Readings in Mathematical Psychology*, New York: John Wiley.

Lyons, John (1968) *Introduction to Theoretical Linguistics*, Cambridge: Cambridge University Press.

McCawley, James D. (1968) 'Concerning the base component of a transformational grammar', *FL* 4: 243–69.

—— (1971) 'Tense and time in English', in C. J. Fillmore and D. T. Langendoen (eds), *Studies in Linguistic Semantics*, New York: Holt, Rinehart, Winston, pp. 96–113.

—— (ed.) (1976) *Syntax and Semantics*, Vol. 7: *Notes from the Linguistic Underground*, New York: Academic Press.

—— (1982) 'Parentheticals and discontinuous constituent structure', *LI* 13: 91–106.

—— (1988) *The Syntactic Phenomena of English*, 2 vols, Chicago: University of Chicago Press.

McCloskey, James (1988) 'Syntactic theory', in Frederick J. Newmeyer (ed.), *Linguistics: the Cambridge Survey*, Vol. I: *Linguistic Theory: Foundations*, Cambridge: Cambridge University Press, pp. 18–59.

Manaster-Ramer, Alexis (ed.) (1987a) *Mathematics of Language*, Amsterdam: John Benjamins.

—— (1987b) 'Dutch as a formal language', *L & P* 10: 221–46.

—— (1988) Review of Savitch *et al. The Formal Complexity of Natural Language* (1987) *Comp. Ling.* 14: 98–103.

Manaster-Ramer, Alexis and Michael B. Kac (1990) 'The concept of phrase structure', *L & P* 13: 325–62.

Marcus, Mitchell P. (1980) *A Theory of Syntactic Recognition for Natural Language*, Cambridge, MA: MIT Press.

Matthews, Peter H. (1972) *Inflectional Morphology*, Cambridge: Cambridge University Press.

—— (1974) *Morphology*, Cambridge: Cambridge University Press (2nd edn 1991).

—— (1981) *Syntax*, Cambridge: Cambridge University Press.

May, Robert (1985) *Logical Form: Its Structure and Derivation*, Cambridge, MA: MIT Press.

Mel'čuk, Igor A. (1988) *Dependency Syntax: Theory and Practice*, Albany, NY: SUNY Press.

Merlan, Francesca (1985) 'Split intransitivity: functional oppositions in intransitive inflection', in Johanna Nichols and Anthony C. Woodbury (eds), *Grammar Inside and Outside the Clause*, Cambridge: Cambridge University Press, pp. 324–62.

Montague, Richard (1970) 'English as a formal language', in B. Visentini *et al.* (eds), *Linguaggi nella società e nella tecnica*, Milan: Edizioni di Communità, pp. 189–224. Reprinted in R. H. Thomason (ed.) (1974), *Formal Philosophy: Selected Papers of Richard Montague*, New Haven: Yale University Press, pp. 188–221.

Moravcsik, Edith A. and Jessica R. Wirth (eds) (1980) *Syntax and Semantics*, Vol. 13: *Current Approaches to Syntax*, New York: Academic Press.

Morley, G. D. (1985) *An Introduction to Systemic Grammar*, London: Macmillan.

Müller, Max (1880) *Lectures on the Science of Language*, 2 vols, 6th edn, London: Longmans, Green.

Muysken, P. (1982) 'Parametrizing the notion "head" ', *Journal of Linguistic Research* 2: 57–75.

Nash, D. (1980) 'Topics in Warlpiri grammar', unpublished Ph.D. thesis, MIT.

Newmeyer, Frederick J. (1986) *Linguistic Theory in America*, 2nd edn, New York: Academic Press.

—— (ed.) (1988) *Linguistics: the Cambridge Survey*, Vol. I: *Linguistic Theory: Foundations*, Cambridge: Cambridge University Press.

Nichols, Johanna (1986) 'Head-marking and dependent-marking grammar', *Lg.* 62: 56–119.

Nichols, Johanna and Anthony C. Woodbury (eds) (1985), *Grammar Inside and Outside the Clause*, Cambridge: Cambridge University Press.

Nida, Eugene A. (1946) *Morphology: the Descriptive Analysis of Words*, Ann Arbor: University of Michigan Press.

—— (1948) 'A system for the identification of morphemes', *Lg.* 24: 414–41.

—— (1960) *A Synopsis of English Syntax*, The Hague: Mouton.

Noonan, Michael (1985) 'Complementation', in Timothy Shopen (ed.), *Language Typology and Linguistic Description*, Vol. 2, Cambridge: Cambridge University Press, pp. 42–140.

Oehrle, Richard T., Emmon Bach and Deirdre Wheeler (eds) (1988) *Categorial Grammars and Natural Language Structures*, Dordrecht: D. Reidel.

Olson, Michael L. (1981) 'Barai clause junctures: toward a functional theory of inter-clause relations', unpublished Ph.D. thesis,

Australian National University.

Oosten, Jeanne van (1977) 'Subjects and agenthood in English', *CLS* 13: 459–71.

Palmer, Frank R. (1986) *Mood and Modality*, Cambridge: Cambridge University Press.

— (1987) *The English Verb*, 2nd edn, London: Longman.

Partee, Barbara H., Alice ter Meulen and Robert E. Wall (1990) *Mathematical Methods in Linguistics*, Dordrecht: Kluwer.

Patten, Terry and Graeme Ritchie (1987) 'A formal model of Systemic Grammar', in G. Kempen (ed.), *Natural Language Generation: Recent Advances in AI, Psychology and Linguistics*, Amsterdam: Kluwer, pp. 279–99.

Payne, John R. (1985a) 'Negation', in Timothy Shopen (ed.), *Language Typology and Syntactic Description*, Vol. 1, Cambridge: Cambridge University Press, pp. 197–242.

— (1985b) 'Complex phrases and complex sentences', in Timothy Shopen (ed.), *Language Typology and Linguistic Description*, Vol. 2, Cambridge: Cambridge University Press, pp. 3–41.

Perceval, W. Keith (1976) 'On the historical source of immediate constituent analysis', in James D. McCawley (ed.), *Syntax and Semantics*, Vol. 7: *Notes from the Linguistic Underground*, New York: Academic Press, pp. 229–42.

Pereira, Fernando C. N. and David H. D. Warren (1980) 'Definite Clause Grammars for language analysis: a survey of the formalism and a comparison with Augmented Transition Networks', *Artificial Intelligence* 13: 231–78. Reprinted in Barbara J. Grosz, Karen S. Jones and Bonnie L. Webber (eds), *Readings in Natural Language Processing*, Los Altos, CA: Morgan Kaufmann, 1986, pp. 101–24.

Perlmutter, David M. (1971) *Deep and Surface Structure Constraints in Syntax*, New York: Holt, Rinehart, Winston.

— (1978) 'Impersonal passives and the unaccusative hypothesis', *BLS* 4: 157–89.

— (1980) 'Relational Grammar', in Edith A. Moravcsik and Jessica R. Wirth (eds), *Syntax and Semantics*, Vol. 13: *Current Approaches to Syntax*, New York: Academic Press, pp. 195–229.

— (1983a) 'Personal versus impersonal constructions', *NLLT* 1:141–200.

— (ed.) (1983b) *Studies in Relational Grammar*, Vol. 1, Chicago: University of Chicago Press.

— (1984) 'The inadequacy of some monostratal theories of passive', in David M. Perlmutter and C. Rosen (eds), *Studies in Relational Grammar*, Vol. 2, Chicago: University of Chicago Press, pp. 3–37.

Perlmutter, David M. and Paul M. Postal (1984) 'The 1–advancement exclusiveness law', in David M. Perlmutter and C. Rosen
(eds), *Studies in Relational Grammar*, Vol. 2, Chicago: University
of Chicago Press, pp. 81–125.

Perlmutter, David M. and C. Rosen (eds) (1984) *Studies in Relational
Grammar 2*, Chicago: University of Chicago Press.

Perrault, C. Raymond (1984) 'On the mathematical properties of
linguistic theories', *Comp. Ling.* 10: 165–76. Reprinted in Barbara
J. Grosz, Karen S. Jones and Bonnie L. Webber (eds), *Readings in
Natural Language Processing*, Los Altos, CA: Morgan Kaufmann,
1986, pp. 5–16.

Peters, P. Stanley and Robert W. Ritchie (1971) 'On restricting the
base component of transformational grammars', *Information and
Control* 18: 483–501.

Peters, P. Stanley and Robert W. Ritchie (1973) 'On the generative
power of transformational grammars', *Information Sciences* 6: 49–
83.

Pollard, Carl J. (1984) *Generalized Phrase Structure Grammars,
Head Grammars, and Natural Languages*, unpublished Ph.D.
thesis, Stanford University.

Pollard, Carl J. and Ivan A. Sag (1987) *Information-Based Syntax
and Semantics. Vol. 1: Fundamentals*, Stanford, CA: CSLI.

Pollock, Jean-Yves (1989) 'Verb movement, universal grammar, and
the structure of IP', *LI* 20: 365–424.

Postal, Paul M. (1964a) 'Limitations of phrase structure grammars',
in Jerry A. Fodor and Jerrold J. Katz (eds), *The Structure of
Language: Readings in the Philosophy of Language*, Englewood
Cliffs, NJ: Prentice-Hall, 1964, pp. 137–51.

—— (1964b) *Constituent Structure: A Study of Contemporary Models
of Syntactic Description*, *IJAL* 30: 1 (Part II). 2nd edn 1967,
Bloomington, IN: Indiana University Press.

—— (1969) 'Anaphoric islands', *CLS* 5: 205–39.

—— (1971) *Cross-Over Phenomena*, New York: Holt, Rinehart,
Winston.

—— (1982) 'Some arc pair grammar descriptions', in Pauline
Jacobson and Geoffrey K. Pullum (eds), *The Nature of Syntactic
Representation*, Dordrecht: D. Reidel, pp. 341–425.

Pullum, Geoffrey K. (1981) 'Languages with object before subject: a
comment and a catalogue', *Linguistics* 19: 147–55.

—— (1982) 'Free word order and phrase structure rules', *NELS* 12:
209–20.

—— (1983) 'How many possible human languages are there?', *LI* 14:

447–67.

—— (1984a) 'Syntactic and semantic parsability', in *Proceedings of the Tenth International Conference on Computational Linguistics: Coling 84*, Menlo Park, CA: Association for Computational Linguistics, pp. 112–22.

—— (1984b) 'On two recent attempts to show that English is not a CFL', *Comp. Ling.* 10: 182–6.

—— (1986a) 'Footloose and context-free', *NLLT* 4: 409–14. Reprinted in Geoffrey K. Pullum, *The Great Eskimo Vocabulary Hoax and other Irreverent Essays on the Study of Language*, Chicago: University of Chicago Press, 1991, pp. 131–8.

—— (1986b) 'On the relations of IDC-command and government', *West Coast Conference on Formal Linguistics* 5: 192–206.

—— (1987) 'Nobody goes around at LSA meetings offering odds', *NLLT* 5: 303–9. Reprinted in Geoffrey K. Pullum, *The Great Eskimo Vocabulary Hoax and Other Irreverent Essays on the Study of Language*, Chicago: University of Chicago Press, 1991, pp. 139–46.

—— (1988) 'Citation etiquette beyond Thunderdome', *NLLT* 6: 579–88. Reprinted in Geoffrey K. Pullum, *The Great Eskimo Vocabulary Hoax and Other Irreverent Essays on the Study of Language*, Chicago: University of Chicago Press, 1991, pp. 147–58.

—— (1989) 'Formal linguistics meets the Boojum', *NLLT* 7: 137–43. Reprinted in Geoffrey K. Pullum, *The Great Eskimo Vocabulary Hoax and Other Irreverent Essays on the Study of Language*, Chicago: University of Chicago Press, 1991, pp. 47–55.

—— (1991) *The Great Eskimo Vocabulary Hoax and Other Irreverent Essays on the Study of Language*, Chicago: University of Chicago Press.

Pullum, Geoffrey K. and Gerald Gazdar (1982) 'Natural languages and context-free languages', *L & P* 4: 471–504. Reprinted in Walter J. Savitch, Emmon Bach, William Marsh and Gila Safran-Naveh (eds), *The Formal Complexity of Natural Language*, Dordrecht: D. Reidel, pp. 138–82.

Pullum, Geoffrey K. and Deirdre Wilson (1977) 'Autonomous syntax and the analysis of auxiliaries', *Lg.* 53: 741–88.

Quang Phuc Dong [pseudonym of James D. McCawley] (1971) 'English sentences without overt grammatical subject', in A. M. Zwicky, P. H. Salus, R. I. Binnick and A. L. Vanek (eds), *Studies Out in Left Field: Defamatory Essays Presented to James D. McCawley*, Edmonton and Champaign: Linguistic Research, Inc., pp. 3–10.

Quirk, Randolph, Sidney Greenbaum, Geoffrey Leech and Jan Svartvik (1972) *A Grammar of Contemporary English*, Harlow, Essex: Longman.

Quirk, Randolph, Sidney Greenbaum, Geoffrey Leech and Jan Svartvik (1985) *A Comprehensive Grammar of the English Language*, Harlow, Essex: Longman.

Radford, Andrew (1988) *Transformational Grammar: a First Course*, Cambridge: Cambridge University Press.

Reed, Alonzo and Brainerd Kellogg (1877) *Higher Lessons in English*, New York.

Reich, Peter A. (1969) 'The finiteness of natural language', *Lg.* 45: 831–43. Reprinted in F. W. Householder (ed.), *Syntactic Theory 1: Structuralist*, Harmondsworth, Middlesex: Penguin, 1972, pp. 258–72.

Reinhart, Tanya (1974) 'Syntax and coreference', *NELS* 5: 92–105.

Rosenbaum, Peter S. (1967) *The Grammar of English Predicate Complement Constructions*, Cambridge, MA: MIT Press.

Rosenschein, S. J. and Stuart M. Shieber (1982) 'Translating English into logical form', in *Proceedings of the Twentieth Annual Meeting of the Association for Computational Linguistics*, Toronto: University of Toronto, pp. 1–8.

Ross, John Robert (1966) 'A proposed rule of tree-pruning', *Mathematical Linguistics and Automatic Translation Report No. NSF-17 to the National Science Foundation*, Harvard University Computation Laboratory.

—— (1967) 'Constraints on variables in syntax', Ph.D. thesis, MIT. Published as *Infinite Syntax!*, Norwood, NJ: Ablex, 1986.

—— (1969) 'Guess who', *CLS* 5: 252–86.

—— (1970) 'Gapping and the order of constituents', in M. Bierwisch and K. Heidolph (eds), *Progress in Linguistics*, The Hague: Mouton, pp. 249–59.

—— (1972a) 'Double-ing', *LI* 3: 61–86.

—— (1972b) 'The category squish: endstation Hauptwort', *CLS* 8: 316–28.

—— (1973a) 'Slifting', in M. Gross, M. Halle and M. P. Schutzenberger (eds), *The Formal Analysis of Natural Languages*, The Hague: Mouton, pp. 133–69.

—— (1973b) 'The Penthouse Principle and the order of constituents', in C. Corum, T. C. Smith-Stark and A. Weiser (eds), *You Take the High Node and I'll Take the Low Node: Papers from the Comparative Syntax Festival*, Chicago: Chicago Linguistic Society, pp. 397–422.

Sadock, Jerrold M. (1970) 'Whimperatives', in J. M. Sadock and A. L. Vanek (eds), *Studies Presented to Robert E. Lees by his Students*, Edmonton: Linguistic Research, pp. 223–39.

—— (1971) 'Queclaratives', *CLS* 7: 223–31.

—— (1985) 'Autolexical syntax: a theory of noun incorporation and similar phenomena', *NLLT* 3: 379–440.

—— (1991) *Autolexical Syntax*, Chicago: University of Chicago Press.

Sampson, Geoffrey (1975) 'The single mother condition', *JL* 11: 1–11.

Sanders, Gerald A. (1972) *Equational Grammar*, The Hague: Mouton.

—— (1974) 'On the notions "optional" and "obligatory" in linguistics', *Minnesota Working Papers in Linguistics and Philosophy of Language* 2: 145–86.

—— (1980) 'Equational rules and rule functions in syntax', in Edith A. Moravcsik and Jessica R. Wirth (eds), *Syntax and Semantics*, Vol. 13: *Current Approaches to Syntax*, New York: Academic Press, pp. 231–66.

Sapir, Edward (1917) Review of 'Het passieve karakter van het verbum transitivum of van het verbum actionis in talen van Noord-Amerika', by C. C. Uhlenbeck, *IJAL* 1: 82–6.

—— (1921) *Language*, New York: Harcourt Brace.

Šaumjan, Sebastian K. (1977) *Applicational Grammar: a Semantic Theory of Natural Language*, Chicago: University of Chicago Press.

Saussure, Ferdinand de (1916) *Cours de linguistique générale*, ed. C. Bally, A. Sechehaye and A. Riedlinger. Lausanne: Payot. English translation by W. Baskin, *Course in General Linguistics*. New York: McGraw-Hill, 1966.

Savitch, Walter J., Emmon Bach, William Marsh and Gila Safran-Naveh (eds) (1987) *The Formal Complexity of Natural Language*, Dordrecht: D. Reidel.

Scalise, Sergio (1984) *Generative Morphology*, Dordrecht: Foris.

Schachter, Paul (1976) 'The subject in Philippine languages: topic, actor, actor–topic, or none of the above?', in Charles N. Li (ed.), *Subject and Topic*, New York: Academic Press, pp. 491–518.

—— (1980) 'Daughter-Dependency Grammar', in Edith A. Moravcsik and Jessica R. Wirth (eds), *Syntax and Semantics*, Vol. 13: *Current Approaches to Syntax*, New York: Academic Press, pp. 267–99.

—— (1981) 'Lovely to look at', *LA* 8: 431–48.

—— (1985) 'Parts-of-speech systems', in Timothy Shopen (ed.),

Language Typology and Syntactic Description, Vol. 1, Cambridge: Cambridge University Press, pp. 3–61.

Schlegel, August Wilhelm von (1818) *Observations sur la langue et la littérature provençales*, Paris: Librairie grecque–latine–allemande.

Sebba, Mark (1987) *The Syntax of Serial Verbs*, Amsterdam: John Benjamins.

Seely, Jonathan (1977) 'An ergative historiography', *Historiographica Linguistica* 4: 191–206.

Sells, Peter (1985) *Lectures on Contemporary Syntactic Theories*, Stanford, CA: CSLI.

Shibatani, Masayoshi (ed.) (1976) *Syntax and Semantics*, Vol. 6: *The Grammar of Causative Constructions*, New York: Academic Press.

—— (ed.) (1988) *Passive and Voice*, Amsterdam: John Benjamins.

Shieber, Stuart M. (1985) 'Evidence against the context-freeness of natural language', *L & P* 8: 333–43. Reprinted in Walter J. Savitch, Emmon Bach, William Marsh and Gila Safran-Naveh (eds), *The Formal Complexity of Natural Language*, Dordrecht: D. Reidel, 1987, pp. 320–34. Also reprinted in J. Kulas, J. H. Fetzer and T. L. Rankin (eds) *Philosophy, Language and Artificial Intelligence*, Dordrecht: Kluwer, 1988, pp. 79–92.

—— (1986) *An Introduction to Unification-Based Approaches to Grammar*, Stanford, CA: CSLI.

Shieber, Stuart M., Hans Uszkoreit, F. C. N. Pereira, J. J. Robinson and M. Tyson (1983) 'The formalism and implementation of PATR-II', in *Research on Interactive Acquisition and Use of Knowledge*, Menlo Park, CA: Artificial Intelligence Center, SRI International.

Shopen, Timothy (ed.) (1985) *Language Typology and Syntactic Description*, 3 vols, Cambridge: Cambridge University Press.

Siewierska, Anna (1984) *The Passive: a Comparative Linguistic Analysis*, London: Croom Helm.

—— (1991) *Functional Grammar*, London: Routledge.

Silverstein, Michael (1976) 'Hierarchy of features and ergativity', in Robert M. W. Dixon (ed.), *Grammatical Categories in Australian Languages*, Canberra: AIAS, pp. 112–71.

Spencer, Andrew (1991) *Morphological Theory*, Oxford: Blackwell.

Stark, Bruce R. (1972) 'The Bloomfieldian model', *Lingua* 30: 385–421.

Starosta, Stanley (1988) *The Case for Lexicase: an Outline of Lexicase Grammatical Theory*, London and New York: Pinter.

Stowell, Timothy A. (1981) 'Origins of phrase structure', unpublished Ph.D. thesis, MIT.

Sullivan, William J. (1980) 'Syntax and linguistic semantics in stratificational theory', in Edith A. Moravcsik and Jessica R. Wirth (eds), *Syntax and Semantics*, Vol. 13: *Current Approaches to Syntax*, New York: Academic Press, pp. 301–27.

Sweet, Henry (1898) *A New English Grammar, Logical and Historical*, Part 2: *Syntax*, Oxford: Clarendon Press.

Taraldsen, Knut Tarald (1980) 'The theoretical interpretation of a class of 'marked' extractions', in *Proceedings of the Third GLOW Conference. Annali della Scuola Normale Superiore di Pisa*.

Tesnière, Lucien (1959) *Eléments de syntaxe structurale*, Paris: Klincksieck.

Thompson, Sandra A. and Robert E. Longacre (1985) 'Adverbial clauses', in Timothy Shopen (ed.), *Language Typology and Syntactic Description*, Vol. 2, Cambridge: Cambridge University Press, pp. 171–234.

Tomić, Olga M. (ed.) (1989) *Markedness in Synchrony and Diachrony*, Berlin: Mouton de Gruyter.

Trask, R. L. (1991) *A Textbook of Syntax* (Cognitive Science Research Report, no. 204), Brighton: University of Sussex.

Van Valin, Robert D. (1985) 'Case marking and the structure of the Lakhota clause', in Johanna Nichols and Anthony C. Woodbury (eds), *Grammar Inside and Outside the Clause*, Cambridge: Cambridge University Press, pp. 363–413.

—— (1991) 'A synopsis of Role and Reference Grammar', in R. D. Van Valin (ed.), *Advances in Role and Reference Grammar*, Amsterdam: John Benjamins.

Van Valin, Robert D. and William A. Foley (1980) 'Role and reference grammar', in Edith A. Moravcsik and Jessica R. Wirth (eds), *Syntax and Semantics*, Vol. 13: *Current Approaches to Syntax*, New York: Academic Press, pp. 329–52.

Vendler, Zeno (1967) *Philosophy in Linguistics*, Ithaca: Cornell University Press.

Visser, F. Th. (1963–73) *An Historical Syntax of the English Language*, 4 vols, Leiden: E. J. Brill.

Wackernagel, Jakob (1892) 'Über ein Gesetz der indogermanischen Wortstellung', *Indogermanische Forschungen* 1: 333–436.

Wells, Rulon S. (1947) 'Immediate constituents', *Lg.* 23: 81–117. Reprinted in Martin Joos (ed.), *Readings in Linguistics*, Vol. I, Chicago: University of Chicago Press, 1957, pp. 186–207.

Welmers, William E. (1973) *African Language Structures*, Berkeley: University of California Press.

Whorf, Benjamin Lee (1956) *Language, Thought and Reality:*

Selected Writings of Benjamin Lee Whorf, ed. J. B. Carroll. Cambridge, MA: MIT Press.

Wijngaarden, A. van (1969) 'Report on the algorithmic language ALGOL68', *Numerische Mathematik* 14: 79–218.

Williams, Edwin S. (1975) 'Small clauses in English', in J. Kimball (ed.), *Syntax and Semantics*, Vol. 4, New York: Academic Press, pp. 249–73.

—— (1978) 'Across-the-board rule application', *LI* 9: 31–43.

—— (1981) 'On the notions "lexically related" and "head of a word" ', *LI* 12: 245–74.

Woods, W. A. (1970) 'Transition network grammars for natural language analysis', *Communications of the Association for Computing Machinery* 13: 591–606. Reprinted in Barbara J. Grosz, Karen S. Jones and Bonnie L. Webber (eds), *Readings in Natural Language Processing*, Los Altos, CA: Morgan Kaufmann, 1986, pp. 71–87.

Wundt, Wilhelm (1900) *Völkerpsychologie: eine Untersuchung der Entwicklungsgesetze von Sprache. Mythus und Sitte*, Vol. II: *Die Sprache, Zweiter Teil*, Leipzig: W. Engelmann.

Yngve, Victor H. (1960) 'A model and an hypothesis for language structure', *Proceedings of the American Philosophical Society* 104: 444–6.

Young, R. and W. Morgan (1980) *The Navajo Language*, Albuquerque: University of New Mexico Press.

Ziff, P. (1960) *Semantic Analysis*, Ithaca, NY: Cornell University Press.

Ziv, Yael and Gloria Sheintuch (1979) 'Indirect objects – reconsidered', *CLS* 15: 390–403.

Zwicky, Arnold M. (1985) 'Heads', *JL* 12: 245–74.

—— (1987) 'Constructions in monostratal syntax', *CLS* 23: 389–401.

Zwicky, Arnold M. and Jerrold M. Sadock (1975) 'Ambiguity tests and how to fail them', in J. P. Kimball (ed.), *Syntax and Semantics*, Vol. 4, New York: Academic Press, pp. 1–36.